Hannah Arendt and the Uses of History

HANNAH ARENDT AND THE USES OF HISTORY

Imperialism, Nation, Race, and Genocide

Edited By

Richard H. King and Dan Stone

Berghahn Books

New York • Oxford

First published in 2007 by

Berghahn Books

www.berghahnbooks.com

©2007, 2008 Richard H. King & Dan Stone
First paperback edition published in 2008

Library of Congress Cataloging-in-Publication Data

Hannah Arendt and the uses of history: imperialism, nation, race, and genocide / edited by Richard King and Dan Stone.
    p. cm.
Includes bibliographical references.
ISBN 978-1-84545-361-9 (hardback: alk. paper) -- 978-1-84545-589-7 (paperback: alk. paper)
1. Arendt, Hannah, 1906-1975. Origins of totalitarianism. 2. Totalitarianism. 3. Racism. 4. Imperialism. 5. Political violence. I. King, Richard H. II. Stone, Dan, 1971-

JC480.A743H36 2004
320.53--dc22

2007024366

British Library Cataloguing in Publication Data
A catalogue record for this book is available from the British Library

Printed on acid-free paper
ISBN 978-1-84545-361-9 hardback
ISBN 978-1-84545-589-7 paperback

CONTENTS

for our wives,
Charlotte and Hilary

ACKNOWLEDGEMENTS

Another version of chapter 10 (Andre Duarte, "Biopolitics and the Problem of Violence") appears in Garrath Williams, ed., *Hannah Arendt: Critical Assessment of Leading Political Philosophers* (Routledge, 2007).

Parts of the Conclusion (Richard H. King, "Arendt between Past and Future") are taken from Wilfred M. McClay, ed., *Figures in the Carpet: Finding the Human Person in the American Past* (William B. Eerdmans Publishing Co., 2006).

INTRODUCTION

Richard H. King and Dan Stone

One hundred years after her birth, Hannah Arendt (1906–1975) scarcely needs the usual sort of introduction, since her work has become so well known of late. Much of it has at least. The point of this collection is to foreground aspects of her work, especially drawn from *The Origins of Totalitarianism* (1951), which bear on imperialism, slavery, race, and genocide but have been neglected in the general revival of interest in Arendt.

There are several ways to characterize the new perspective on Arendt that we are trying to develop. First, we want to shift attention away from Arendt the political philosopher and towards Arendt the historical thinker. Seen in this light, she used the momentous historical events of her time to think through the nature of history, the philosophical and anthropological implications of violence, the emergence of modern imperialism and colonial domination, the relationship of racism and genocide to the European nation-state, and even of evil as an historical phenomenon. This also means that the focus of her work and the focus on her work moves to the historical interaction between Europe and the non-European world, particularly Africa. Thus, for instance, we are less interested in rehearsing the question as to whether Arendt was correct (historically or politically) to characterize both Nazi Germany and Stalin's Soviet Union as totalitarian regimes and more concerned to explore the importance of the mutual interaction of Europe—and not just Germany—with the colonized parts of the globe.[1] Moreover, as Richard Shorten's essay in this collection suggests, Arendt's introduction of imperialism into the equation made the question of comparability between Nazi Germany and the Soviet Union much more complicated than it had been earlier. Finally, several of the essays reflect on the degree to which the disturbing history of Europe's relationship with the non-European world forces us to reexamine both Arendt's thought and its relationship to other thinkers, some already commonly linked to her (Montesquieu, Tocqueville, and Heidegger) and some not (Levinas, Foucault, and Agamben).

Another way to understand our intentions for this volume is to note the various disciplines and approaches represented here. Above all, we consider our volume a contribution to "Arendt Studies," since it is her work that provides our focus and our point of departure. Yet, several of the essays here, for example Tony Barta's on Darwin and Marx, could certainly be read as straightforward contributions to European intellectual history or the history of ideas. Still others straddle the line between intellectual history and political, cultural, and social history (European and African, past and contemporary). Arendt's influence on interdisciplinary fields such as African Studies and Postcolonial Studies is (surprisingly) important and is discussed in the essays by Robert Bernasconi, Kathryn Gines, and Christopher Lee. Indeed, *Origins* has recently been described as one of the "constitutive books of postcolonial studies," while the editors of a canonical collection devoted to the intellectual origins of postcolonial theory recognized Arendt's importance for that newly emerging field of study nearly two decades ago.[2] Finally, Genocide Studies also takes Arendt's *Origins* as seminal, particularly for its focus on the premonitory historical role that European imperialism played in genocide on European soil and the value that Arendt's book still possesses, as Dan Stone makes clear in his contribution, for understanding the burden of our time, as well as hers.

Our hope is that this volume of essays will help stimulate the vital work of uncovering the "contributions" that European imperialism made to the horrifically costly civil war that decimated Europe between 1914 and 1945, and which permanently distorted the lives of non-European peoples to this day. Since the original motive for putting together this collection was to expose—and investigate—the "subterranean stream" that linked imperialism in Asia and Africa with the emergence of genocidal, totalitarian regimes in Europe, we want to spend most of this Introduction discussing the history, critique, and future viability of what has become known as Arendt's "boomerang" thesis.

The Boomerang Thesis

The Origins of Totalitarianism was among the first works to claim that European theories of racial and cultural superiority and their totalitarian consequences were in part created by economic expansion into, and exploitation of, much of Asia and Africa, as well as the establishment of white settler colonies around the globe. Indeed, the expansionist impulse of the nineteenth century, Arendt suggested, outstripped the economic motivations that originally gave rise to it. This European experience in the colonies, which was fed by and bred a psychology of domination, had far-reaching effects back in Europe. Racist theories and non-democratic political assumptions (rule by decree and enforcement by bureaucracy) and particular practices (forced population transfers, protogenocidal massacres, and a profound heedlessness about human life) fed back into European (and Western hemispheric) political and intellectual cultures. For instance, colonial powers tested the early use of aerial bombardment upon subject populations in their colonies, while Hitler was a great admirer of the British Empire, and Nazi Germany formulated its racial laws of 1935 using the example of the South in the United States. The result was a strengthening of authoritarian modes of political rule, along with something approaching an addiction to racial thinking and augmentation of racist ideologies in Europe, particularly after the early 1880s. Moreover, the ideology of imperial grandeur and/or mission helped mask class and ideological fissures in various European societies.[3]

As a way of characterizing the dynamic link between empire and European heartland, Arendt suggested the phrase "boomerang effect(s)."[4] Near the end of chapter 7 of *Origins*, she writes that the boomerang effect of the imperial experience created a situation in which "the stage seemed to be set for all possible horrors. Lying under anybody's nose were many of the elements which gathered together could create a totalitarian government on the basis of racism."[5] Specifically, she makes some (underdeveloped) claims about the German version of the boomerang effect: "African colonial possessions became the most fertile soil for the flowering of what later was to become the Nazi elite."[6] Overall, then, Arendt contended that imperialism and colonialism played a crucial role in creating the conditions of possibility for totalitarianism in Europe.

Yet three qualifications need to be stated at the outset by way of forestalling misunderstandings of Arendt's claims in this area. First, "Imperialism," as she designated part II of *Origins*, was by no means the only "element" that contributed to the rise of totalitarianism in Germany and the Soviet Union. In fact, she rejected the notion that there was any single cause of totalitarianism; rather, a variety of forces and factors "crystallized" into the phenomenon itself. In addition, to identify elements of the future totalitarian systems as already present in the colonial setting—e.g. forced population transfers or planned massacres, even genocide— was not to claim that the colonial political and social order, say, in German Southwest Africa (or anywhere else) was already totalitarian in nature. Second, Arendt always insisted that the totalitarian temptation had been a European, and not just a German, phenomenon. Thus her "boomerang" thesis suggests that the effects of racial imperialism were felt throughout European thought and culture, politics and society, and not just in Germany. It is important to note as well that she also took into account an ideology of "continental imperialism," which had particular impact in Central Europe and Russia where the influence of overseas European imperialism was scarcely felt.[7] Third, although her insight about the boomerang effect was a brilliantly provocative one, it was, as Tony Barta's essay in this volume suggests, seriously underdeveloped in *Origins* and elsewhere in her work. In retrospect, it is best considered, we would suggest, as a research hypothesis rather than a fully proven historical claim.

Remarkably, no other postwar white European analyst of totalitarianism or fascism besides Arendt incorporated the European imperial experience into his or her analysis of totalitarianism. Aside from France where, as Ned Curthoys's essay makes clear, an important debate took place among European intellectuals such as Jean-Paul Sartre and Albert Camus, along with intellectuals from North Africa such as Albert Memmi and Martinique's Frantz Fanon about colonialism in general and the Algerian War in particular, intellectuals on the left were surprisingly reticent about the causes or effects of the colonial experience and its racial and ethnic dimensions after World War II. In retrospect, one could be forgiven for thinking that the second age of imperialism and colonialism (culminating in the late nineteenth century) and then totalitarianism were, as Robert J. C. Young notes, "a unique aberration, a dark perversion of western rationalism or a particular effect of German culture"[8] rather than a direct outgrowth of factors and forces at work all across Europe.

Specifically, no debate about colonialism such as raged among French intellectuals in the 1950s seems to have dominated public discourse in Great Britain, Belgium, or Holland, not to mention Germany, after World War II. Certainly, anticolonialism scarcely figured in the considerations of white American intellectuals: indeed, white conservative intellectuals voiced more opposition to decolonization in Africa than liberal or left-wing intellectuals voiced their active support for desegregation in the South or for independent governments in Africa and Asia. But, as Robert Bernasconi emphasizes in his contribution to this volume, black diasporic intellectuals such as America's W. E. B. Du Bois and Martinique's Aimé Césaire assumed that the links between colonialism and fascism, colonial racism in Black Africa and racism in metropolitan Europe and the United States were all too obvious. Overall, for such intellectuals, as for many French intellectuals on the left, fascism was "European colonialism brought home."[9]

Though Arendt's position was close to that of the francophone intellectuals, it did not exactly duplicate theirs. First, she thought that European racism and anti-Semitism were the result of a specific concatenation of historical factors rather than an inevitable outcome of European racism, capitalism, or imperialism. According to her overly optimistic understanding of the Western tradition, totalitarianism, including genocide, was foreign to the thinking of its canonical thinkers and texts. In this sense it was a "subterranean stream," an aberration or a break from mainstream Western thought, a position she later partially retracted when she realized the totalitarian potential of Marxism, which *was* a product of mainstream Western thought. But, as already mentioned, she certainly agreed that totalitarianism and racism/anti-Semitism was a European rather than just a German phenomena.

Yet, it is strange that the "boomerang" thesis has been relatively neglected in the critical literature dealing with Arendt until the last decade or so. When it was mentioned, it was only in passing and then quickly dismissed as unproved or an exaggeration or both. Besides that, *Origins* was increasingly neglected after the 1960s. For many historians and political scientists, especially those on the left, *Origins* came to seem an outdated Cold War tract, although not without its own brilliance. They thus failed to appreciate the way it transcended both a rightist-conservative explanation via totalitarianism, or a leftist-progressive-"third-world-ist" explanation via fascism, of Nazi-inspired genocide. Very few managed to mention Arendt without the reader having the sense that they were cursing under their breath. At best, they damned with faint praise: her work, however brilliant, was overwrought and historically misjudged. To be sure, the controversy surrounding Arendt's *Eichmann in Jerusalem* (1963) put her in the spotlight. For a time, historians of what was increasingly called "the Holocaust" took her indictment of Jewish leadership in Poland and Eastern Europe as a starting point, though hardly ever as the final word, for how the Final Solution had been planned and implemented. But in general the Imperialism section of *Origins* simply did not figure very prominently in the criticism of Arendt as it began emerging in the 1970s, in the histories of Nazi Germany, or of colonialism itself.

Interestingly, early studies in the 1950s of the Nazi occupation of Eastern Europe used imperialism as an explanatory framework, and much of it is still cited regularly by scholars who work on the topic. Indeed, Germany's *Drang nach Osten* was, and is, frequently compared to, say, the expansion of settlers across the North American continent.[10] But most of this work was written without reference to Arendt at all. If even historians who wrote on the subject of German imperialism and its relation to Nazism—as was the case with Woodruff D. Smith later on[11]—could do so without reference to Arendt, it is hardly surprising that there is very little to be said about the reception of her ideas on imperialism in general by historians from the 1950s to the end of the Cold War. (The major exception is the book *The Rulers of German Africa* by L.H. Gann and Peter Duignan, which linked Arendt's thesis to the work of the German historian of South West Africa, Helmut Bley, and we will return to it shortly.) Still, the historiographical situation was no different from what one finds in other disciplines in this regard.[12] By and large, while political scientists objected to Arendt's thesis concerning the connections between imperialism and totalitarianism, historians tended to dismiss it without much further ado.

By the time of her death in 1975, Hannah Arendt was not seen as the historical analyst of totalitarianism at all, but as a normative theorist of politics, action, and participatory freedom, of the public-private (in Arendt's terms, the political-social) question, and of the problem of political judgment. These crucial issues for political philosophy were raised in particular in her works *The Human Condition* (1958) and to a lesser degree *On Revolution* (1963). To be sure *On Revolution* had a strong historical dimension and addressed, among other things, the contrasting historical and political meanings of the American and French Revolutions. Still, most political theorists and historians of political thought tended to slight *On Revolution* as providing only a (shaky) historical exemplification of Arendt's political ideas. Most historians of America paid little attention to the book, even though its central concern with participatory freedom dovetailed quite neatly with, even anticipated, the rediscovery of republicanism in the historiography of early American political thought in the 1960s and 1970s.[13] At best, there were two Arendts—one, the historically oriented theorist of political culture in the tradition of Montesquieu, Burke, and Tocqueville, as Steven Douglas Maloney discusses here, and, second, the pure political theorist/ phenomenologist of political speech and action. Symptomatically, historian Stephen J. Whitfield was to assert in *Into the Dark* (1980) that after *The Origins of Totalitarianism*, Arendt's work was marked by a "loss of interest in modern tyranny so decisive that genuine disjunctions emerged, contradictions that could not easily be reconciled." Arendt the historical thinker now took a back seat to Arendt the political theorist.[14]

In retrospect, however, the neglect of the historical dimension in Arendt's work (and indeed of her life) was bound to end, The publication of Elisabeth Young-Bruehl's biography of Arendt in 1982 called attention to her personal relationship with Martin Heidegger, which in turn raised important questions about their philosophical connection, as well about the philosophical relationship with her other mentor, Karl Jaspers. Thus Arendt's personal life and her intellectual-philosophical sources gradually emerged as objects of scholarly inquiry in the 1990s. For the first time, she seemed to acquire an actual personal and intellectual history, whereas before she had been defined by her post-War prominence among New York intellectuals or was seen as a quite creative, if idiosyncratic, political philosopher, perhaps best located, for want of any other labels, in the tradition of civic humanism/republicanism.

Even more important was Margaret Canovan's archive-based study of Arendt in 1992, which revealed just how important *Origins* had been for the entire body of her thought. With this, Canovan cast considerable doubt on the idea that there were two Arendts. Though in her first book on Arendt in 1974, Canovan had written that, "It is as a thinker rather than as an historian that Hannah Arendt has a claim to fame,"[15] her later study portrayed a more historically sensitive Arendt by asserting that "her theory of action, like the rest of her political thought, is rooted in her response to totalitarianism and is not an exercise in nostalgia for the Greek polis."[16] Thus, not only were there no longer two Arendts, she was now a modernist thinker rather than the antimodernist champion of the "tyranny of Greece over Germany."[17]

Thirdly, the post-1960s emergence of issues of race, ethnicity, nationality, and gender, along with the collapse of the Soviet Empire in Eastern Europe and the reemergence of civil society there, also focused attention on new aspects of Arendt's thought. Since 1990 volumes have appeared exploring the implications of her thought for feminism and women's studies and for the American civil rights movement, along with biographical profiles linking her with Simone Weil and Rosa Luxemburg, not to mention several volumes of her correspondence with a variety of figures including her husband Heinrich Blücher, novelist and essayist, Mary McCarthy, and, of course, Heidegger. Moreover, the emergence of Postcolonial Studies has meant that the implications of Arendt's work for the former Third World have been (re)discovered. Paul Gilroy's *Between Camps* (2000) and *After Empire* (2004) refer to her boomerang thesis several times, while the essays of Kathryn

Gines and Christopher Lee in this volume make clear her influence on academic work in African Studies. Thus we now have a more worldly and more widely relevant Arendt than would have been thought possible earlier.

Overall, Arendt studies are now in the midst of an "historical turn" that we hope this volume will further encourage. With respect to the Holocaust, one scholar writes, perhaps over optimistically, that, "Historians now seem to agree that German colonial practice, including the colonial wars in Africa and the increased organizing of German society by racial categories, prefigured National Socialism in complex ways."[18] For instance, Helmut W. Smith has detected a future-oriented, racially inflected conservatism and liberalism in the *Reichstag* debates over South West Africa, while Elisa von Joeden-Forgey's essay in this collection analyzes the public debate in Germany about the anthropological and political status of the indigenous peoples of Germany's African colonies, and Isabel Hull has also analyzed the German military's role in the genocide against the Herero and Nama in Southwest Africa.[19] Closely focussed studies such as these give the Arendt thesis a much needed specificity and confirm what she only gestured toward. Indeed, the wave of interest in German colonial history, especially as written by cultural and literary historians, can reasonably be seen as a direct result of the return to fashion of Arendt's ideas as set out in her "big book."

A more interesting question concerns when and if historians of the British Empire will begin to confront the Arendtian claim that the effects of the British Empire, too, helped pave the way for continental European fascism and subtly, but seriously, affected British politics and culture. As Robert Bernasconi reminds us in his essay in this volume, Arendt treated British colonialism rather gently in *Origins*, despite the fact that she ascribes some of the most blatant imperial ideological fantasies to men such as Cecil Rhodes who were instrumental in its establishment and maintenance. Recent studies of the dark side of the British Empire, especially in Kenya, do not seem to have registered either with the scholarly or wider cultural *Zeitgeist* in the same way as have studies of German colonialism.[20] Some historians still contend that Arendt merely claimed that Nazism was prefigured in colonialism and fail to notice the long sections in *Origins* on race-thinking, where she emphasizes the interplay between the intellectual baggage that was taken to the colonies and the ways it was transformed under the experience of imperialism.

Still, her influence is beginning to seep in. For instance, the title of Enzo Traverso's *The Origins of Nazi Violence* (2003) certainly reveals an Arendtian inspiration. Traverso makes good on the allusion to Arendt by providing a causal background to European fascism in extra-European imperialism, and thus targets interpretations of fascism (such as Sternhell's and Mosse's) that are entirely Europe-focused.[21] Besides the specific thesis of books such as Traverso's, her claims have proven as relevant to understanding genocides in non-European contexts as they have in explaining the Holocaust or the Gulag. A recent issue of the journal *Patterns of Prejudice* devoted to "colonial genocide" drew its inspiration from Arendt's ideas, and essays explored genocide in Haiti and Australia, as well as in the context of German South West Africa and the Third Reich.[22] In his articles, "The birth of the *Ostland* out of the spirit of colonialism" and "Colonialism and the Holocaust," Jürgen Zimmerer, one of the leading historians of the Herero genocide in German Southwest Africa, convincingly shows that there are continuities of ideology and practice between the German-perpetrated genocide of the Hereros in 1904–1905 in what is now Namibia and the Holocaust. Similarly, A. Dirk Moses argues in several important articles that, on many levels, there are meaningful comparisons to be drawn between the Holocaust and the earlier genocide of Australian Aborigines. In other words, the current thrust of comparative genocide scholarship is to show that "Holocaust" is not a separate category from "genocide" but that the Holocaust was an extreme variant of genocide, while the concept of totalitarianism largely disappears as a concern. There are, this scholarship indicates, many aspects of the Holocaust that are akin to earlier colonial genocides or genocidal massacres; indeed it is unlikely that the Holocaust could have taken place without the precedent of colonial massacres.

In this work, the ghost of Arendt hovers quite clearly in the background, though never entirely easily. Arendt herself wrote of the Nazi crimes that the "moral point of this matter is never reached by calling what happened by the name of 'genocide' or by counting the many millions of victims: exterminations of whole peoples had happened before in antiquity, as well as in modern colonization."[23] The result is to complicate today's appeal to her as the inspiration for the theoretical framework that links colonial genocide and the Holocaust, although naturally it neither invalidates it nor automatically leads one to call into question the connection between colonialism and Nazism.

It is important to note, therefore, that scholars of genocide do not simply turn the earlier criticisms of Arendt on their heads. Rather than uncritically advocating the notion that colonial genocide holds the key to understanding the Holocaust, they are careful to note where the similarities end. Thus Zimmerer writes:

> With its central concepts of "race" and "space," the Nazi policy of expansion and annihilation stood firmly in the tradition of European colonialism, a tradition also recognizable in the Nazi genocides. Yet, it would be wrong to see the Third Reich's murderous policies in the East merely as a copy of the conquests of the Americas, Australia, or Southern Africa; they constituted instead an extremely radicalized variant. Particularly with regard to its readiness to wipe out whole peoples, European colonialism stood at the beginning of a development of particular notions of space and race that found its culmination in the "hunger plan" of 1941, the genocidal massacres in the context of combating partisans, and the utilization of gas for organized suffocation.[24]

Furthermore, it is noteworthy that much contemporary genocide scholarship focuses on the Holocaust as its point of comparison. For it was the Holocaust—though not yet known by that name—that drove Arendt to undertake her research, much in the same vein as that of Raphaël Lemkin, the 'father' of the UN Genocide Convention (1948), whose work was largely inspired by the experience of the Jews during World War II.[25] After several decades of intensive research on the Holocaust in isolation, the wheel has now turned full circle, and a broader framework—one initially formulated by Arendt—is now being proposed and implemented.

The Boomerang Thesis and its Critics

How does Arendt's boomerang thesis look after over half a century? As already indicated in the previous section, extended discussions of the boomerang thesis have been surprisingly few, despite the fact that Arendt devoted just over 200 pages to "Imperialism" (Part II) in *Origins*. Perhaps because it is the most historically detailed section of the book, it has not caught the fancy of political theorists. Yet, the person who has devoted perhaps most attention to it has been an historian of political thought, Margaret Canovan, whose extended engagement with the Arendt thesis came in her first book on Arendt in 1974. There she noted that the Imperialism section contains "some of the most brilliant and at the same time some of the most questionable of her ideas"[26] and thus hints at the reason why many analysts of Arendt have shied away from confronting the boomerang thesis. [27]

One of the most extensive and searching examinations of the Arendt thesis in regards to Germany came from L. H. Gann and Peter Duignan in their *The Rulers of German Africa, 1884–1914* (1977). Although they began by admitting that "Arendt's interpretation has some merit,"[28] they spent most of their time disabusing readers of any such notion. Colonialism, they contended, was relatively short-lived and had little influence on German politics or thought. There had been a variety of ideologies and justifications for colonialism at play in Germany from the late nineteenth century on; but neither the ideology of National Socialism nor Hitler himself was particularly concerned with overseas colonialism. In particular, *Der Führer* was much more concerned with conquering and resettling the lands to the east of the Fatherland, especially in the Soviet Union. Expansionist though Nazi ideology may have been, its motive force was a *Drang nach Osten*, not *nach Süden*. Nor did the colonial experience or the structure of society in German colonies particularly mirror the fascist model of an organic society. Generally, Gann and Duignan also insisted that "World War I not the colonial experience"[29] was crucial for the development of a totalitarian Germany. Finally, German behavior as colonialists was no worse than that of the Australians in Tasmania, the Americans toward the Native Americans, or the Hausa toward the Ibo in Nigeria; yet in none of those countries did a totalitarian movement develop. Gann and Duignan concluded with a moralistic flourish by charging that "to confuse" Nazi totalitarianism with "colonial rule—German or non-German"—is to "subtly excuse the evil of Nazi tyranny."[30]

After the 1960s, numerous symposia and collections of essays on Arendt's work appeared, especially important being those published by *Social Research*, the inhouse journal of the New School for Social Research in New York, and *Salmagundi*.[31]

But of greatest interest was the emergence in the 1980s of a new type of criticism directed at Arendt's work on imperialism in Africa. Shiraz Dossa's landmark 1980 essay, "Human Status and Politics: Hannah Arendt on the Holocaust," shifted the focus from the effects of the imperial experience on European political cultures to Arendt's own perspective on sub-Saharan Africans as reflected in the language with which she described the indigenous populations. According to Dossa, there was an "ethnocentric strain" in her characterizations of Africans that echoed rather than distanced itself from the mentality of the white Europeans who conquered central and southern Africa. Arendt, according to Dossa, presents the African as a "natural man" and thus "the 'inhumanity' of blacks is self-evident."[32] But his powerful indictment of Arendt's Eurocentrism was challenged by George Kateb's penetrating two pages "On Racism in Africa" in his 1983 study of Arendt. According to Kateb, Arendt had dared risk a "reconstruction of experience"[33] of the Boers in Africa and her methodological "generosity"[34] had only made it seem as though she shared the racial attitudes she imputed to the Boers. Kateb also suggested, somewhat cryptically, that Arendt's discussion of the "pathologies of racism and imperialism" actually "contains more than it needs," as though she had deployed too many types of explanation for what happened in Europe.[35] Thus, though Dossa and Kateb differed on just how to characterize Arendt's rhetoric of description, they obviously agreed that Arendt's own racial views added a problematic element to the whole debate about the boomerang thesis.

The 1990s finally saw the boomerang thesis and Arendt's own attitudes toward Africans discussed with increasing frequency in the Arendt literature itself. In his 1994 essay "Is Totalitarianism a New Phenomenon?," John Stanley suggested that the Zulu chieftain, Shaka, whom Arendt had briefly mentioned in *Origins*, came close to meeting the criteria she set for a totalitarian leader, despite her claim that totalitarianism was a distinctly modern phenomenon. Stanley notes that the Zulu king had murdered thousands, maybe millions, and exerted his sway with a totalistic fervor. In fact, Dossa had already questioned Arendt's characterization of totalitarianism as an exclusively modern phenomenon when he pointed out that genocide was, by her own admission, frequently found in the ancient world.[36] In 1995, Anne Norton joined Dossa as one of Arendt's sternest critics. In a wide ranging essay that linked Arendt's hostile attitude toward Black militancy in the 1960s with her writing about Africa, Norton echoed Dossa's hostile reaction to Arendt's "voicing" of Boer racial views as though they were her own and charged that she "left the African silent."[37] By way of generally agreeing with Dossa and Norton, Hannah F. Pitkin noted in her 1998 study of Arendt that she "simply shares the European prejudice against so-called primitive cultures as somehow less cultured or more natural—in a pejorative sense—than the European."[38] Though the note was a way of generally agreeing with Dossa and Norton, ironically it illuminated the point to which Arendt had herself called attention during World War II—the threat to the concept of human equality that would arise when Europeans came into contact with non-European cultures.[39]

In perhaps the most philosophically wide-ranging book on Arendt in the 1990s, Seyla Benhabib devoted several pages to Arendt's thesis about the origins of European racism in Africa and the way it constituted a "threat to the limits of

European identity and civilization."[40] But she took Norton to task for imposing a particular version of American race relations on an African situation totally alien to it, while demanding that Arendt bring the same attitude to bear on both. But Benhabib returned to the boomerang thesis by suggesting that Arendt had failed to "translate the insight into a causal or genetic account."[41] Since then, the problematic matter of Arendt's racial attitudes has been explored in numerous studies, including ones by the authors of this Introduction and several contributors to this volume, especially Kathryn Gines and Robert Bernasconi.[42]

Still, the community of Arendt scholars remained divided on the issue. In the 2002 issue of *Social Research* devoted to *Origins* on the occasion of its fiftieth anniversary, Jerome Kohn, the editor of several volumes of Arendt's essays and Director of the Arendt Center at the New School for Social Research, devoted several pages to the influence of Joseph Conrad on Arendt's conception of Africa. The essay very importantly noted, against the standard misreadings by political theorists and historians, that Arendt was "not saying that racism or any other element of totalitarianism *caused* the regimes of Hitler or Stalin, but rather that those hidden elements, which include anti-Semitism, ... crystallized in the movements from which those regimes arose."[43] Yet, just preceding that valuable clarification, Kohn writes that Conrad's Kurtz was the "real 'heart of darkness,' rather than the *uncivilized* [my italics] but not inhuman darkness of Africa."[44] With this "uncivilized but not inhuman darkness," Kohn's characterization of sub-Saharan Africans was no less problematic than Arendt's. As far as any reader could tell, neither Arendt nor Kohn had studied the history or anthropology (not to mention the art history) of sub-Saharan Africa in order to arrive at the view that the Africans encountered by Europeans in central or southern Africa were "uncivilized"—whatever that might mean.

From Debate to Research Program

It is not our intention to settle the debate over Arendt's boomerang thesis or her racial attitudes once and for all, but to allow contemporary scholars from various fields to expand on Arendt's thesis specifically and, more generally, to explore the relevance of her work for an understanding of the history of our time. Still, it might be helpful to summarize the main criticisms of Arendt on this issue and offer the briefest of responses. For this we will refer most often to Margaret Canovan's analysis of the boomerang thesis in her 1974 study of Arendt, since among Arendt scholars, she confronted it earlier and more systematically than anyone else.

The first issue has to do with the importance of imperialism and colonialism in the emergence of totalitarianism and mass murder in Nazi Germany and the Soviet Union. According to Canovan, the "quasi-causal link between imperialism and Nazism is plausibly made through Pan-Germanism"; but it is much more difficult to link Pan-Slavism and Stalinism.[45] She goes on to point out that the history of state bureaucracy, the use of secret police, and the proliferation of ethnic and racial prejudice in, say, the Russian and the Austro-Hungarian empires scarcely needed reenforcement by the European experience in Africa and Asia.[46] This was another way of saying in specific terms what George Kateb later suggested: perhaps Arendt did not need Africa to explain European totalitarianism and thus had violated the historian's version of Ockham's razor. Defenders of the boomerang thesis might make a concession (and distinction) here to the effect that German expansion into Central and Eastern Europe, along with expansionist impulses of other nationalist movements in the interwar years, did not need the African experience to explain "continental imperialism" in their part of Europe, but the boomerang thesis still had importance for Western Europe, especially Belgium and the Netherlands, along with Germany, Britain, and France.

A similar argument might be made about the importance of color-coded racism in the spread of ethnic animosity and above all of anti-Semitism in Europe. It is not clear to what degree and in what ways that anti-Semitism was given a genocidal impetus by the experience of Germans—or Europeans—in Africa. It would be surprising if one type of prejudice did not reenforce the other. On the other hand, anti-Semitism and color-coded racism do not generally have the same aetiology, dynamic, or goals historically, particularly when the experience of the United States is factored in. Historically, for instance, Arthur de Gobineau, one of the founders of European racism, was in close touch with the so-called "American School" of ethnology in mid-nineteenth century America where the object of intellectual address was color-based racism.[47] Still, in Western Europe, endemic religious and social anti-Semitism, under the force of secularization, was relatively easily racialized, though there was nothing inevitable about the transformation. In *Origins* Arendt stresses the differences between religious and biological anti-Semitism but is of little help in deciding the degree to which racism from the colonies joined, or remained separate from, European anti-Semitism of whatever sort.

Second, along with others, Canovan suggested that Arendt's claim about the destructive effects of racism and bureaucracy on the various European nation-states was misdirected: "But what national states," asks Canovan," were in fact destroyed by imperialism?"[48] Put more specifically, why and how were the two largest colonial powers—Britain and France—able to preserve their democratic institutions and political cultures at home during the imperial era and afterwards, if imperialism had such a disastrous boomerang effect? Conversely, neither Italy nor Germany, the two most prominent fascist powers, was a major player in the "scramble for Africa," though both had participated in it to a degree.

In certain ways, this is one of the strongest criticisms of the Arendt thesis. Yet there is also something about it that suggests a narrowness, a certain tone-deafness to the arguments about the corrupting effects of colonialism and imperialism on supposedly democratic European and American regimes. Even after World War II, the Algerian War actually brought down the Fourth Republic and civil liberties in Britain were significantly curtailed by the post–1972 "troubles" in Northern Ireland. One could also argue that the fact that Britain and France did not develop large fascist movements, much less totalitarian governments, actually underlines Arendt's point about the lack of historical inevitability to the emergence of totalitarianism or genocide. Those who press this argument seem to reason that, because totalitarian or genocidal movements did not develop in Britain and France but did in Germany, the colonial experience, racist ideologies, and techniques of imperial rule were of little significance in shaping any of these political cultures. But this "everywhere or nowhere"/"everything or nothing" argument is a fallacious one. On this issue, Arendt is the better conventional historian, since she persistently argued against inevitability and for the particularity of causal sequences according to the particular context.

There are other aspects of the Arendt thesis in relation to the liberal democracies that need further exploration. A more general understanding of the boomerang thesis would also dictate further interest in the effects of colonialism and imperialism on the intellectual, literary, and cultural traditions of the colonizing countries. In this volume, Robert Eaglestone explores the way German children's stories reflected the German experience in Southwest Africa, and certainly Britain has a strong tradition of fiction dealing with the colonial experience, a point that Edward Said made most extensively in his *Culture and Imperialism*, whose focus was "the role of culture in the modern imperial experience."[49] Certainly a major strand of the literature of the United States from Frederick Douglass and Herman Melville through Mark Twain and W.E. B. Du Bois to William Faulkner, and including Ralph Ellison, Toni Morrison, and much of modern writing coming out of Latin America have explored the pervasive impact of the history of slavery and racism on national consciousness. Indeed, in these areas, literary scholars and students of postcolonialism are far ahead of the historians and political scientists. Overall, it only stands to reason that if the colonial experience has been such a strong explicit and implicit influence on European thought and culture, it must have also had similarly pervasive effects on its political culture and institutions, along with the structure and essence of academic disciplines.

The relative claims of the human sciences and literature are also reflected in a closely related line of criticism of Arendt. Canovan, Dossa, Benhabib and others also criticize Arendt for having failed to provide satisfactory evidence to underpin plausible or creative arguments; instead, she relied on intuitions and hunches. For instance, Arendt's discussion of the morally vertiginous European confrontation with Africa seems to have been largely shaped by Conrad's fictional vision in *Heart of Darkness*. Indeed, her research notes include the cryptic sentence: "Conrad's Kurtz inspite [sic] of being a fiction [sic] has become a reality in the Nazi character."[50] Of course, Arendt's hunches and intuitions should be developed or rejected based on further investigation. Her strongest defenders can hardly deny that her boomerang thesis is underdeveloped, but this is just the point of having historians—to follow up on other people's intuitions.

Canovan also raised a shrewd, epistemological point when she referred to Arendt's deep ambivalence, or lack of clarity, about what she was trying to do in *The Origins of Totalitarianism*: "the last thing she wished to do was to produce a chain of causes that would seem to show that totalitarianism was inevitable."[51] It would have been convenient for us had she committed herself to some form of causal explanation recognizable to professional historians (in the Anglo-American tradition). The problem is that she tended to identify causal language, including that of historians, with the language of the natural sciences implying determinism and inevitability. As a result the nature of her claim about the relationship between imperialism and totalitarianism never quite came into focus. At times, she seems to be arguing for a certain evidentiary underdetermination: no one thing, or series of things, could adequately explain the emergence of totalitarianism in Europe. Yet, Gann and Duignan and others go to the other extreme and sound as though Arendt must have intended a tight, one-to-one, causal connection between the African experience and the European result, and then criticize her for not producing it.

Finally, the criticisms of Arendt's own rhetoric of description and moral standpoint vis-à-vis the people of sub-Saharan Africa seem to us justified by and large. But though this issue has come to dominate the discussion whenever Arendt's boomerang thesis is raised, it is important not to see them as inextricably yoked together. One can accept the broad claims of the boomerang thesis and still call attention to the dubious nature of Arendt's language of description. Put more abstractly, the question might be raised as to whether her ethnocentric cultural anthropology discredits her philosophical anthropology, that is, her account of the human condition of plurality and political being in the world. Did her emphasis upon human plurality and difference too easily give way to a tendency to reify cultural pluralism and differences? The essays by Eaglestone and Stone in this volume explore the issue of how to relate a cultural understanding and philosophical understanding of human "being." How much did her shock at the way the camp inmates had been shorn of culture and thus had *become* scarcely human feed back into her depiction of Africans as hardly possessing the rudimentary forms and institutions of human culture? Finally, we need to ask whether Arendt was exceptional in her views about African culture or whether those views were shared by some, even most, of her contemporaries. In other words, we need much more work on the context which shaped Arendt's views on race and culture.

Overall, then, we assume in this volume that Arendt's work in the areas of the nation, race, genocide, slavery, and imperialism focuses on three separate, though obviously related, matters. The first concerns the destructive effects of imperialism and colonialism on the established liberal political-legal institutions and normative political values of European nation-states, which eventually led to the rise of totalitarian regimes in Germany and the Soviet Union. There is still much work to be done, but we think the essays collected here are valuable in their own right and will stimulate further work. The contributions of Marcel Stoetzler and Vlasta Jalušič, for example, make clear the contemporary relevance of the nation/state dichotomy, whether in nineteenth century France or late-twentieth-century Yugoslavia. Second, her thesis suggested, rather than convincingly demonstrated, that the experience of imperial rule and the construction of racism in the colonies played a part in creating the conditions for the emergence of a totalitarian regime in Germany and thus paved the way for the Holocaust. Much important historical work has been, and is being done, on the specific case of Germany. By and large, her suggestions and intuitions are in the process of being confirmed. Third, and more subtly, Arendt's thesis suggested that the emergence of imperial-colonial Europe in the latter part of the nineteenth century must have profoundly affected European intellectual and cultural traditions, its self-image and identity, and its intellectual traditions in short, medium, and long range terms. Notions of racial and cultural superiority not only were widespread within Europe up to World War II but have been also since then. No one "gets over" colonialism and imperialism easily, if at all, whether they be the colonizers or the colonized. Indeed, the ease with which victims become executioners is testimony to this fact. For this reason, we want to emphasize Arendt's relevance for understanding the history and politics of our time as well as of the past, and for the non-European as well as the European world. There is a line running through the phenomena that Arendt perceived and began to bring to light. In this book, we seek to make it plainly visible.

Notes

1. See, for instance, Anson Rabinbach, "Moments of Totalitarianism," *History and Theory* 45, no. 2 (2006): 72–100. However valuable his essay is otherwise, Rabinbach nowhere mentions Arendt's "boomerang" thesis and in fact only mentions Arendt once in his review essay.

2. Pascal Grosse, "From Colonialism to National Socialism to Postcolonialism: Hannah Arendt's *The Origins of Totalitarianism,*" *Postcolonial Studies* 9, no. 1 (2006): 35–52; Patrick Williams and Laura Chrisman, "Colonial Discourse and Post-Colonial Theory: An Introduction," in *Colonial Discourse and Post-Colonial Theory,* ed. Patrick Williams and Laura Chrisman (Hemel Hempstead, 1993), 7.

3. See Ira Katznelson, *Desolation and Enlightenment: Political Knowledge after Total War, Totalitarianism, and the Holocaust* (New York, 2003), 19; Dan Stone, "Britannia Waives the Rules: British Imperialism and Holocaust Memory," in *History, Memory and Mass Atrocity: Essays on the Holocaust and Genocide* (London, 2006), 174–195; Stefan Kuehl, *The Nazi Connection: Eugenics, American Racism and German National Socialism* (New York, 1994); Giuseppe Finaldi, "European Empire and the Making of the Modern World: Recent Books and Old Arguments," *Contemporary European History* 14, no. 2 (2005): 248–50.

4. Hannah Arendt, *The Origins of Totalitarianism,* 2nd ed. (Cleveland, 1958), 206, 223.

5. Ibid., 221.

6. Ibid., 206.

7. Ibid., chapter 8.

8. Robert Young, *White Mythologies: Writing History and the West* (New York and London, 1990), 125.

9. Ibid., 8. See also Richard H. King, *Race, Culture and the Intellectuals, 1945–1970* (Baltimore, and Washington, D.C., 2004).

10. Indeed, the work of Robert Lewis Koehl and Alexander Dallin is remarkably valuable even after half a century. See Robert Lewis Koehl, "A Prelude to Hitler's Greater Germany," *American Historical Review* 59, no. 1 (1953): 43–65; idem. "Colonialism Inside Germany: 1886–1918," *Journal of Modern History* 25, no. 3 (1953): 255–272; idem., *RKFDV: German Resettlement and Population*

Policy 1939–1945: A History of the Reich Commission for the Strengthening of Germandom (Cambridge, 1957); Alexander Dallin, *German Rule in Russia, 1941–1945* (London, 1957).

11. His standard work, *The Ideological Origins of Nazi Imperialism* (New York, 1986), is written without reference to Arendt.

12. For a rare, brief discussion, see Hugh Ridley, "Colonial Society and European Totalitarianism," *Journal of European Studies* 3, no. 2 (1973): 147–159. For a book that has an Arendtian feel to it, since it links colonial genocide to the Holocaust, but only mentions her in the foreword, see Sven Lindqvist, *"Exterminate All the Brutes"* (London, 1997).

13. In his landmark study of the tradition of civic humanism, *The Machiavellian Moment* (Princeton, 1973), J. G. A. Pocock acknowledged Arendt's influence (516, 550).

14. Stephen J. Whitfield, *Into the Dark: Hannah Arendt and Totalitarianism* (Philadelphia, PA., 1980), 134. More recently, David Scott has compared C. L. R. James's *The Black Jacobins* (1938) with Arendt's *On Revolution*, but also criticized Arendt for having "forgotten" the other eighteenth century New World revolution, the Haitian revolution. See David Scott, *Conscripts of Modernity: The Tragedy of Colonial Enlightenment* (Durham and London, 2004), 217–8.

15. Margaret Canovan, *The Political Thought of Hannah Arendt* (New York, 1974), 50.

16. Margaret Canovan, *Hannah Arendt: A Reinterpretation of Her Political Thought* (Cambridge, UK, 1992), 2.

17. Elizabeth Butler, *The Tyranny of Greece over Germany* (Boston, 1958[1935]). Butler's seldom read book now desperately needs bringing up to date and amending to include German-Jewish culture and thought. For a recent effort to do something like that, see Suzanne L. Marchand, *Down from Olympus: Archaeology and Philhellenism in Germany, 1750–1970* (Princeton, 1996).

18. Uta G. Poiger, "Imperialism and Empire in Twentieth-Century Germany," *History & Memory* 17, nos. 1 and 2 (2005): 122.

19. See Helmut Walser Smith, "The Talk of Genocide, the Rhetoric of Miscegenation: Notes on Debates in the German Reichstag Concerning Southwest Africa, 1904–14," in *The Imperialist Imagination: German Colonialism and Its Legacy*, ed. Sara Friedrichsmeyer, Sara Lennox, and Susanne Zantop(Ann Arbor, 1998), 107–23; and also Isabel V. Hull, "Military Culture and the Production of 'Final Solutions' in the Colonies: The Example of Wilhelminian Germany," in *The Specter of Genocide: Mass Murder in Historical Perspective*, ed. Robert Gellately and Ben Kiernan (New York, 2003), 141–62.

20. See, for instance, Caroline Elkins, *Britain's Gulag: The Brutal End of Empire in Kenya* (London, 2005) and David Anderson, *Histories of the Hanged: The Dirty War in Kenya and the End of Empire* (London, 2005). See also Stone, "Britannia Waives the Rules," 174–195.

21. Enzo Traverso, *The Origins of Nazi Violence* (New York, 2003); Ze'ev Sternhell, *The Birth of Fascist Ideology: From Cultural Rebellion to Political Revolution* (Princeton, 1995); George L. Mosse, *The Fascist Revolution: Toward a General Theory of Fascism* (New York, 1999).

22. *Patterns of Prejudice* 39, no. 2 (2005). Also published in book form as A. Dirk Moses and Dan Stone, eds., *Colonialism and Genocide* (London and New York, 2007).

23. Hannah Arendt, "Personal Responsibility under Dictatorship," in *Responsibility and Judgment*, ed. Jerome Kohn (New York, 2003), 42.

24. A. Dirk Moses, "An Antipodean Genocide? The Origins of the Genocidal Moment in the Colonization of Australia," *Journal of Genocide Research* 2, no. 1 (2000): 89–106; "Coming to Terms with Genocidal Pasts in Comparative Perspective: Germany and Australia," *Aboriginal History* 25 (2001): 91–115; "The Holocaust and Genocide," in *The Historiography of the Holocaust*, ed. Dan Stone (Basingstoke and New York, 2004), 533–55; "Genocide and Settler Society in Australian History," in *Genocide and Settler Society: Frontier Violence and Stolen Indigenous Children in Australian History*, ed. A. Dirk Moses (New York, 2004), 3–48; Jürgen Zimmerer, "Colonialism and the Holocaust: Towards an Archaeology of Genocide," in *Genocide and Settler Society*, ed. Moses, 67.

25. Dan Stone, "Raphael Lemkin on the Holocaust," *Journal of Genocide Research* 7, no. 4 (2005): 539–550. See also Dan Stone, ed., *The Historiography of Genocide* (Basingstoke and New York, forthcoming 2008) for detailed discussions.

26. Canovan, *The Political Thought of Hannah Arendt*, 30.
27. Strangely, Stephen J. Whitfield's *Into the Dark*, perhaps the most historically informed and intricate of the full-length studies of Arendt, and one of the most acute in its criticism, hardly mentioned imperialism, Africa, or racism (as opposed to anti-Semitism).
28. L. H. Gann and Peter Duignan, *The Rulers of German Africa, 1884–1914* (Stanford,1977), 226.
29. Ibid., 237.
30. Ibid., 238.
31. The contributors to Melvyn Hill's 1979 collection of essays, compiled from a conference on Arendt in Toronto, were largely silent on the importance of Africa or racism in the context of imperialism's role in the emergence of totalitarianism, except for a brief mention by Bernard Crick in his essay on *Origins*. A 1989 collection of essays on Arendt compiled by Australia-based scholars devoted a bit of attention to racism and imperialism but not a lot, even though the collection included a section on "Feminism" and also one on "Jewish Identity and conscience." See Melvyn A. Hill, ed., *Hannah Arendt: The Recovery of the Public World* (New York, 1979) and Gisela T. Kaplan and Clive S. Kessler, eds., *Hannah Arendt: Thinking, Judging, Freedom* (Sidney, 1989).
32. Shiraz Dossa, "Human Status and Politics: Hannah Arendt on the Holocaust," *Canadian Journal of Political Science* 13, 2 (1980): 320–1.
33. George Kateb, *Hannah Arendt: Politics, Conscience, Evil* (Oxford, 1983), 61–3.
34. Ibid., 57.
35. Ibid., 52, 56.
36. John Stanley, "Is Totalitarianism a New Phenomenon?," in *Hannah Arendt: Critical Essays*, ed. Lewis P. Hinchman and Sandra K. Hinchman (Albany, 1994), 1–40; Dossa, "Human Status," 317.
37. Anne Norton, "Heart of Darkness: Africa and African Americans in the Writings of Hannah Arendt," in *Feminist Interpretations of Hannah Arendt*, ed. Bonnie Honig (University Park, 1995), 253.
38. Hannah F. Pitkin, *The Attack of the Blob: Hannah Arendt's Concept of the Social* (Chicago, 1993), 293, note 16,.
39. See Hannah Arendt, "Organized Guilt and Universal Responsibility"(1945), in *Essays in Understanding, 1930–1954* (New York, 1994), 131.
40. Seyla Benhabib, *The Reluctant Modernism of Hannah Arendt* (Thousand Oaks, 1999), 83.
41. Ibid., 86.
42. Dan Stone, "Ontology or Bureaucracy? Hannah Arendt's Early Interpretations of The Holocaust," in *History, Memory and Mass Atrocity: Essays on the Holocaust and Genocide* (London, 2006), 53–69; King, *Race, Culture and the Intellectuals*, 115–9.
43. Jerome Kohn, "Arendt's Concept and Description of Totalitarianism," *Social Research* 69, no. 2 (2002): 626.
44. Ibid., 626.
45. Canovan, *The Political Thought of Hannah Arendt*, 38.
46. Ibid., 44.
47. See James W. Ceaser, *Reconstructing America: The Symbol of America in Modern Thought* (New Haven, 1997) for an account of Gobineau's links both with Alexis de Tocqueville and American racial theorists of the mid-nineteenth century.
48. Ibid., 42.
49. Edward W. Said, *Culture and Imperialism* (London, 1993), 3.
50. Letter to Mary Underwood, Arendt Papers, Library of Congress, Container 16, 4.
51. Canovan, *The Political Thought of Hannah Arendt*, 44.

Part I

IMPERIALISM AND COLONIALISM

Chapter 1

RACE POWER, FREEDOM, AND THE DEMOCRACY OF TERROR IN GERMAN RACIALIST THOUGHT

Elisa von Joeden-Forgey

When Chancellor Bismarck suddenly undertook a policy of overseas expansion in 1884, Germany was almost wholly unprepared for the legal and ideological stresses of colonial domination. Since it was determined from the outset that overseas polities would not be brought into the German federation as member states, the German constitution provided no model for the incorporation of colonial territories and German citizenship law was equally useless for defining the status of Germany's new subjects. Dominant thinking among officials and the public was very much influenced by the traditions of the old Prussian territorial state, where expansion was generally coupled with inclusion, irrespective of national or ethnic affiliations. So, for example, Prussia counted Danish and Polish speakers as its citizens and defined belonging in terms of loyalty and obedience to the monarchy. This tradition of legal assimilation informed the approach of many officials and members of the public towards Germany's colonies and especially towards the people living there, leading to confusion and contradiction among legal scholars, state offices, colonial bureaucrats, the press, and ordinary Germans.

When one examines official documents relating to the early years of colonial rule, the absence of any clear language of race difference is striking. Officials and the public tended to define difference according to assumed cultural distances and what Gerrit Gong has called the "standard of civilization."[1] Although these modes of demarcating difference drew from the often racialized stereotypes and bigotries about the world beyond the borders of Europe that had gained currency in the nineteenth century, they still allowed for border crossings, for cultural and civilizational naturalization.[2] So, for example, we find early metropolitan officials referring to new subjects as *Schutzgenosse* (fellow protected persons), a term drawn from consular law that had historically referred only to other Europeans.[3] The state initially gave high status Africans from the colonies an audience with the Crown Prince and quite positively supported the naturalization of an African in Hamburg who planned to marry the daughter of a local police official.[4] The German press had the maddening habit, at least from the point of view of the state, of referring to colonial subjects as *Reichsangehörige* (citizens) and *Landesleute* (fellow countrymen).[5]

Despite the pronounced cosmopolitanism of the Germany that undertook its overseas project, racism emerged within two decades as the dominant language of colonial governance. The state passed travel bans in the late 1890s and early 1900s to limit the flow of people and information between colony and metropole precisely because such border crossing was undermining an emerging racialist argument in favor of colonial domination. Citizenship applications from colonial subjects show that naturalizations were becoming more fraught with racist anxiety. Mixed marriages became the almost unanimous subject of scorn within the middle classes. In public discussions, colonial subjects were frequently described as radically *alterior*—as existing in a separate dimension and, increasingly as time went on, outside of the boundaries of humanity. Among colonial scholars, colonial racism became so taken-for-granted that in 1909 a professor of National Economy at Hamburg's Colonial Institute could elevate race to a psychological explanation for colonization itself: "Is the presence of a racially foreign underclass not also one of the psychological bases for colonization? What attracts the colonizer and satisfies him? Certainly the freedom to be a master [*Herr*] and to belong to the upper caste. Who of us, who has lived with peoples of a foreign race, does not know this feeling? Or the feeling of discomfort when one sees a white man working together with colored peoples to produce an ordinary handicraft?"[6] In this lecture, given upon his assumption of the position of the chairman of the Institute's Professors Council, Karl Rathgen promoted the creation overseas of an aristocratic form of racialized governance, where whites would form an eternal ruling strata over "colored peoples." Given that Rathgen's racialized view of the colonial project was rather routine by this time, the question becomes how we can begin to account for this radical shift in perspective between the 1880s and World War I, and what, if any, long-term consequences such a shift might have had.

Racializing Expansion

The dramatic shift in the official and intellectual conception of colonial subjects in the metropole can be linked to the trauma of colonial realities. Between the early 1890s and 1906 Germany was beset by constant colonial scandals, thoroughly exploited by the anti-colonial Progressive and Social Democratic Parties and avidly presented to the public by the press. Such scandals raised the glaring contradiction between the values and norms of metropolitan German society and the day-to-day brutalities of colonial rule, which were in direct opposition to the traditions of *Kultur* and the *Rechtsstaat.* It may seem natural, then, that Germans would turn to race theory to smooth out the rough edges of empire. Historical studies of racism have shown the usefulness of racist ideology to democratic or liberal systems, which are engaged in violent exploitation, since racism posits unbridgeable and inalterable differences between human groups and purports to ground these differences within natural hierarchies. Thus racism served to legitimate the Atlantic slave trade, New World slavery, the massive land expropriation, and the near total annihilation of indigenous polities within settler colonies like the United States and the British Dominions—all based on the premise that certain groups had certain natural fates based on their racial essence. Two recent comparative treatments of the history of racism, by the historian George Fredrickson and the political scientist Anthony Marx, have both argued strongly for the state-based nature of the production of racism in the modern world.[7] In Marx's words, "states made race."[8]

But the German story of the history of racism shows a much less cynical and predictable development of race language in political thought and praxis. This statist interpretation of the origin of public race consciousness is apt in the German case only after a certain point in time. The German state turned to the language and logic of race-thinking after a decade and a half of colonial experience. Initially the state only generated the legal categories, and thus the political realities, that were to offer formal race-thinking an entrée into respectable political culture. Once race-thinking was given entrée, once, that is, the political system offered it a potential role, race-thinking took on a "powerful negative force of its own," to quote from Kwame Anthony Appiah.[9] The direction of this negative force was unpredictable, and its unleashing quite unintentional. What the German state experience with overseas imperialism shows us is that the production of racialist systems is too complex to be reduced to conscious actions on the part of state officials, and as a consequence, racialist systems are profoundly insidious and can be established incrementally through the uncoordinated synergy of individual actions and historical events.

In Germany, the history of official and pragmatic race-thinking began with a category. When the German state set out to establish a legal apparatus for colonial domination, its key concern was to give the *Kaiser* a free hand.[10] Officials had to find a way, then, to include colonial subjects within the boundaries of German state power (sovereignty) while excluding them from any institutions that would limit that power. Furthermore, wary of state involvement in overseas rule, Bismarck was also set upon the private funding of colonization and hence had to ensure the ability of private companies to pursue their economic objectives. Officials and parliament both assumed that African and other colonized polities were too culturally different to warrant inclusion in the federation of states that made up the German empire. Given these realities, the state chose to leave for some later date the positive definition of the legal status of colonial subjects vis-à-vis the power of the state. Since their main aim was simple exclusion from limiting institutions, they defined this status negatively instead: colonial subjects, referred to in law as

Eingeborene ("native"), while subsumed beneath the sovereign power of the state, did not fall under the jurisdiction of regular civil or criminal law. The "law" that was to apply to them was left up to the praxis of the men sent to rule over them. The law for *Eingeborenen*, then, was little more than caprice, and *Eingeborene* became a category for the limitless expansion of state power.

The consequence of this negative definition was rampant atrocity. Bismarck himself complained of a *furor regiminalis* that appeared to beset Prussian bureaucrats sent to the tropics, many of whom treated *Eingeborenen* in ways antithetical to established traditions of Prussian state-subject relations.[11] By the 1890s, newspapers were laced with lurid stories of official misconduct, including rapes, massacres, summary executions, trophy beheading, and the rampant use of flogging. Flogging was so widespread in fact that the colony of *Kamerun* in West Central Africa was popularly known as "the twenty-five country," referring to the number of lashes regularly given.[12] By including *Eingeborenen* within the reach of the sovereign state and its monopoly of violence while simultaneously excluding them from any protective institutions or traditions, the German state had effectively, but unintentionally, created a potentially genocidal category of person—someone who existed wholly outside the community of moral obligation, without moral boundaries, whose very murder technically would not be illegal.

Because of its radical potential, the moral emptiness of the category of *Eingeborene* could support even a rational state policy of genocide. Franz Giesebrecht, editor of the reformist collection of essays entitled *The Treatment of Natives in the German Colonies* (1898), commented that:

> Admittedly, life is often more brutal than the man, and when in the struggle of the races [*Rassenkampf*] the extermination of the population of an entire continent is postulated, that is certainly a standpoint of monstrous cruelty, a standpoint that we hold to be false and therefore that must be fought with all our energy, but that we must recognize as an historically and philosophically legitimate [one]. In contrast, we refuse all brutality that is committed by one colonizer against individual *Eingeborene*.[13]

For Giesebrecht and other reformers, it was not a conscious policy of annihilation that had to be refused categorically as illegitimate, but rather the arbitrary action of the individual bureaucrat against individual *Eingeborenen*. He was willing to grant a conceptual legitimacy to genocide as a state policy, both in the past (historically) and more generally (philosophically), thereby allowing genocide into the space of reasonable policy discourse.[14] A conscious policy of annihilation happened, of course, between 1904 and 1907, when up to eighty percent of the Herero peoples in South West Africa were murdered as a consequence of the war pursued by the general sent there to put down the Herero insurrection.[15]

The emerging racialist definition of colonial subjects only began to crop up in legal explanations of the term *Eingeborene* after the turn of the century. This coincided with the shift in the political language of colonialism away from Germany's cosmopolitan traditions and towards the racialized reformism typified by many of the contributions to Giesebrecht's volume. The law student Emil Peters, for example, concluded in his 1906 dissertation that "under the category Eingeborene we should understand the colored persons of a colony, so long as they have not naturalized as German citizens or as members of a state recognized by international law, or so long as they are not granted an exemption by the Governor empowered by the Chancellor."[16] A few years later the Governor of South West Africa, Theodor Seitz, wrote to the State Secretary of the Colonial Office that he believed that legal status in the colonies should be based not on formal citizenship status (that is, naturalizations), but "alone on belonging to the 'Eingeborenen.'" Referring to Germany's cosmopolitan traditions, he remarked, "it may be that in Germany no difference is made between black and white, but not, however, in the colonies."[17] When explicitly racialized, *Eingeborene* lost its political and legal meaning and came to identify a biological essence.

The radical alterity of the term *Eingeborene* was eventually worked into images of and prescriptions for colonial domination. In fact, the package of ideas that finally came to dominate political language about colonial questions was based in the juridical-anthropological notion of a separate sphere of governance called *Eingeborenenrecht*. *Eingeborenenrecht* was a concept that denoted the "customary law" of the *Eingeborenen*. Colonial reformers, many of them from the National Liberal Party, fleshed out the concept in the 1890s in response to the numerous colonial scandals that were attracting unwanted international attention and domestic outcry. *Eingeborenenrecht*, though it provided the fiction of governance according to local forms, never was meant to prevail over the decrees of colonial bureaucrats, colonial governors, or the Colonial Department in Berlin. Nor was it intended to limit the discretion of Germany's men on the spot, or to curtail the often lethal use of flogging and imprisonment in chains. In fact, most descriptions of *Eingeborenenrecht* incorporated these official German decrees into the definition of "native [customary] law."[18] Nonetheless, it was widely publicized as a humanitarian gesture, and predictably became an official part of the state's colonial public relations campaign during the so-called "Hottentott Elections" of 1906 and 1907, when the central state launched a concerted (and successful) effort to get pro-colonial delegates elected to the majority of seats in the German parliament.[19] Nowhere in the empire was formalized rule through *Eingeborenenrecht* ever seriously attempted. In many ways, *Eingeborenenrecht* was a term of collective delusion, which functioned to shield national identity from colonial contradictions and realities. This was especially the case once the state began in the early 20th century to limit the flow of potential opponents to and from the colonies, including lawyers, journalists, and colonial subjects themselves. The effect was to limit the information available to parliamentarians and the public.

The language of color-coded racism only gradually and unintentionally entered public and official discourse. Most colonial bureaucrats, colonial settlers, and some scholars were of course committed to a racialist understanding of colonization. They were constant sources of explicit race discourse, and often put pressure on Berlin to give proper attention to race questions.[20] But by and large, race began to govern public discussion of colonial political questions as a way to account for the enormous violation of public values and ethics that colonization symbolized. The ideas of *Eingeborene* and *Eingeborenenrecht* offered a new paradigm through which people could assess the colonial situation, one that accounted for atrocity within the rubric of humanitarianism. An implicit form of race-thinking about colonial questions spread as a result.

The kind of racism that gained widespread support through this mechanism had been thoroughly adapted to the respectable language of politics, incorporating very little of the crass racist terminology associated with colonial bureaucrats and settlers, or, for that matter, with the radical racist fringe elements within anti-Semitic movements and the Pan German League. The humanitarian advocacy of *Eingeborenenrecht* hid the routine abuse that characterized the treatment of *Eingeborene* by casting it as customary and racially appropriate. The routinization and broad acceptance of atrocity, especially the liberal use of flogging for minor infractions of petty laws, created an image of the *Eingeborene* as a kind of being that existed outside of normal life. By generating an impression of a radically alterior moral type, colonial spaces of violence gradually normalized such treatment within a modern world that prided itself on humanism and the principle of equality before the law.

The racialized, anthropological category of *Eingeborene* offered colonial enthusiasts as well as nationalists of a racist bent a vision of a new kind of governance, racially defined, in which there were people who were inside German sovereign borders but outside of the moral community. And it offered this new vision not in the abstract but in the real world of Germany overseas. This made a difference to the impact of the term. People who were thinking about the world in racialized ways often looked to the colonies for guidance and examples. It is therefore of serious consequence that the Pan Germans looked very much to the model of Germany's settler colonies, especially South West Africa, when imagining the exclusion of "race aliens" at home.

Race Power and the Democracy of Terror

One particular aspect of colonial governance that became a stock issue among race-thinkers in Germany was the "problem" of "race-mixing." The concept of degeneracy was spread in Germany as elsewhere by the rising popularity of Social Darwinism, eugenics, and, especially, the writings of Comte Joseph Arthur de Gobineau, who first suggested in the early 1850s that race-mixing was the source of all civilizational decline. But colonial questions raised the stakes considerably. No longer was "race-mixing" abstract. It was a fact—and not only in the colonies. The press, the parliament, and colonial agencies were full of stories of colonial subjects in Germany, mostly Africans, and their love affairs with white German women. The question of "mixed marriages" became a serious matter of debate during the deliberations about the 1913 citizenship law.[21]

"Mixed marriages" were not, however, the only realm of contact between citizens and colonial subjects about which the state was seriously concerned. Colonization raised the stakes of contact between whites and the *Eingeborene* in general by the mere fact that contact in any form tended to generate colonial criticism, if not outcry, since it allowed stories of exploitation to reach public view and challenged the state's allegation of vast civilizational differences between citizen and subject. Racialist rationales for measures to address the "problem" of mixing—whether geographic, social, economic, symbolic, or biological—allowed officials to side step the very pragmatic and political reasons for such measures. In other words, it was much easier to argue that mixing was scientifically harmful to whites and *Eingeborene* alike than to risk calling attention to the state's colonial crimes by grounding travel bans and other policies in *Realpolitik* considerations.

Where mixing was unavoidable in "colonial spaces," like settler regions of South West Africa and East Africa or the language institutes in Germany which employed African language assistants, strict hierarchies were to be maintained over every detail of daily life. Karl Rathgen, for example, believed that the entire future of German colonization rested on the question of whether Germans would be able to set up an effectively racialized aristocracy. His colleague Carl Meinhof, professor of linguistics and director of the Seminar for Colonial Languages, emphasized the need to maintain strict boundaries between students and African language assistants.[22] Both of these men also linked these hierarchies to their understanding of the nature of freedom. For Rathgen, freedom was the "freedom to be master and to belong to the upper caste." For Meinhof, the existence of colonies was itself proof that Germans were a free people, and colonies were important as places that could liberate the mind, leading to a greater understanding of the self and the world.[23]

The emphasis on total control over all forms of "mixing," the spacialization of difference, and the linkage between colonization and race (or *volk*) freedom was hardly their invention, and they certainly were not alone in propounding them. The noted woman of letters Frieda von Bülow imagined that the colonizing experience created stronger and freer men.[24] These ideas can be found, in various forms, in the writings of nineteenth century racialists, of extremist nationalists, and especially of anti-Semites.[25] As a response to the political pressures of the colonial project, however, colonial enthusiasts and extreme nationalists more generally brought these ideas together to constitute an ideal-type mode of governance based on a "race power" complex that linked true cosmic power—true freedom—to the ritual exercise of race terror.

The idea of freedom that emerged out of colonialism was, as we know in the case of the settler community in South West Africa, both populist with respect to whites and racist with respect to colonial subjects. This is a common feature of all institutionalized systems of white supremacy. In the case of German colonization, the colonial "race power" complex is of particular interest, because up to 1914 white supremacy was a dominant feature only of its overseas territories. It existed in the metropole only in small pockets, where aspects of colonial race power were operative in less comprehensive and violent ways. Since German colonial reformers were using colonial settler demands for greater autonomy ("self-administration") to press for greater democratization at home, the ideas of popular sovereignty that emerged in the colonies is of considerable importance. One of the features of German colonization most frequently remarked upon by travelers to the colonies was the ubiquitous nature of whips. State Secretary Bernhard Dernburg noted in 1908 that in German East Africa, most white men—officials and private persons—would not go out without one.[26] To the dismay of many metropolitan officials, the central state had relinquished part of its monopoly of violence to citizens in its overseas territories, with few effective limitations.[27] The privilege to flog had become a kind of birthright for colonial Germans, an exercise of citizenship. Sovereignty—freedom—was thereby becoming associated with the brutalization of the bodies of racial others. The idea of popular governance that emerged in the colonies was therefore a democracy of terror, in which a racial underclass was a necessary component of a people's exercise and expression of real power.

Although the German colonies did not begin as racial states, the contradictions of colonization made them into places where people could fantasize about all sorts of new race possibilities. Members of the Pan German League saw colonial possibilities as practical and useful for German expansion eastwards. Drawing on the violent nineteenth-century current of racialist anti-Semitism, they began as early as 1905 to think about governance within Central Europe in quasi-colonial terms, with Jews and other "non-Germanic peoples" taking the place of colonial subjects as *Eingeborenen*. In applying this potentially genocidal category of person to minority groups in the metropole and to majority populations in adjacent states, these racialist anti-Semites were proposing the creation of legalized spaces of brutality as a central principle of governance in general. As had been the case in the German colony of South West Africa, where an estimated eighty percent of the Herero population was annihilated by German military forces between 1904 and 1907, these legalized spaces of brutality could include, under proper circumstances, a policy of genocide. When we treat the violence of Germany's colonial project as an insignificant side show to domestic affairs, we fail to appreciate that the boundaries between colony and metropole that we may draw as historians after the fact were not always operative at the time.

Advocates of political racialism exalted race to the single analytical category through which world politics should be viewed. They believed that colonial governance should have taught the German state three principal things: that "mixing" was a threat to national well being, that race difference was a radical phenomena involving completely opposing cosmic spaces, and that humanity (humanitarianism) must be exercised in conformity with racism's scientific laws. These lessons were all part of the new concept of power that had emerged out of Germany's debate about its own imperial role. Pan German racialists developed an understanding of power that required the existence of alien and alterior races that would be governed through total separation and control. Although they all professed faith in a triumphant future for the German race, a future in which lower races would either have disappeared or have been adequately pacified, the visions of power they described suggest that it was the domination of these lower races that acted as proof that they—and their "Germany"—were powerful. This form of governance—modeled on the image of colonial governance—was for them the only way of demonstrating Germany's cosmic superiority.

This concept of power became increasingly popular in the radical right, and, based on the new possibilities that had been forged in the colonies, they described this new form of governance in the language of violent colonial domination and extended it to Europe itself. Thus, in works like Josef Reimer's *Ein Pangermanisches Deutschland* (1905), Klaus Wagner's *Krieg* (1906), and Pan-German League leader Heinrich Class's *If I Were the Emperor* (1912), we find colonial-inspired scenarios applied to Eastern expansion, whereby "nonassimilable" peoples (such as Jews and Slavs) were to be excluded from the Germanic community, governed by specific laws, and subjected to statecraft not "limited" by "humanity."[28] In some cases, nonassimilable peoples were to die out within a few generations, in others they were to be permanently relocated to reservations outside of Europe.

Marcia Klotz has recently argued that, by 1914, nineteenth-century European expansion had encouraged a widespread image of the world as a "racialized globe."[29] This is certainly true of the nationalist German intelligentsia, especially nationalists like Heinrich von Treitschke, who, in Leon Poliakov's words, "considered the white race the aristocracy of the human species whose mission was to divide and rule the planet."[30] As Poliakov points out, Treitschke believed a state's level of power to be defined by the volume of global territory it controlled. In this way, European overseas colonization in general led people to understand the exercise of power internationally as a matter of race power, that is, the territorial rule of a specific subset of whites over nonwhites. Colonization also influenced German thought on power in more direct ways that stemmed from Germany's specific experience with colonial governance. After the turn of the century, when racialized arguments about colonial governance were becoming common and influential, we see the publication of pan-Germanist and *völkish* tracts where authors gave race a central and irreducible place in their thinking on global politics, domestic agendas, and world history.

The authors of pan-German racist tracts credited nineteenth-century racialists like Comte Arthur de Gobineau, Houston Stewart Chamberlain, Ludwig Woltmann, and Woltmann's journal, the *Politisch-anthropologische Revue* (founded in 1902), as their direct intellectual precursors. In addition to these acknowledged influences, their writings imply a deep engagement with the immediate—and broadly publicized—colonial debates of the early century. Reimer, Wagner, and Class, for example, each took anxieties common to debates about colonial governance and applied them to politics in general. So, at the same moment when colonial reformers were beginning to gain ground in their attempt to reframe the political spaces of Germany's overseas empire in racial terms, pan-Germanists began to racialize politics in general as a matter of incommensurable alterior spaces. They were convinced that the major threat facing the "Germanic race" (for Reimer the *Germanen*, for Wagner the *Germanoiden*) was the threat of bastardization. Their political thought grew from this pan-European colonial *idée fixe*, the centerpiece of Gobineau's *Essai sur l'inegalité des races humaines*, which had been popularized in Germany with the founding of the Gobineau Society in 1894. Wagner summed up the modern imperial experience thus: "Everywhere where different and distant races [*verschiedene, fernstehende Rassen*] live close together there arises a culture-annihilating mixing. . . . He who reads the history of civilizations and looks at the larger connections, he who is not blind to the history of the day, he can see the meaning of race everywhere, for the history of the world is the history of the development of human races."[31] Bastardization was a threat not only—and not even primarily—in colonies like South West Africa, but in and around Germany itself, because of the conspiracy of various historical trends: liberalism, which allowed for the naturalization of "*Agermanen*" (non-Germanic peoples); Prussian expansion, which had incorporated non-Germanic peoples without adequately separating them from the German population; Jewish emancipation, which had given a "foreign race" a strong foothold in the heart of the German empire; and political movements like pacifism (themselves symptoms of racial degeneration), which were serving to weaken the German race and leave it open to foreign invasion.

The German racialists of the early twentieth century were looking back over the history of the German people, racially defined, from the vantage point of an imperial nation whose overseas colonies were appearing to prove the value of race theory. For them, Germany was, like South West Africa, facing a constant threat of cultural, spiritual, and biological pollution from alien races, which would, if not properly addressed, lead to the demise of the Germanic race in favor of more self-conscious races. They extended the vociferous arguments of colonial administrators and settlers to the metropole: non-Germans belonging to the German state should not be able to share in the rights of "proper" race citizens. Because of this, they believed that the first task of all domestic and foreign politics must be the promotion of strict racial separation. Without it, the Germanic race would go the way of ancient Rome, where, as Reimer put it, "from the powerful Roman people, who created order in the world, a world of bastards arose, a 'chaos of peoples' [*Völkerchaos*], incapable of sustaining itself, itself an atrocity that fled into the cloisters and still exists indigestible in our midst."[32]

The problem they saw was precisely that world power—the sole true form of power-required expansion—and expansion itself had only led to the "accumulation of different races."[33] Rome's own bastardization was a direct consequence of its imperial policies, which Reimer saw as the result of the "contradiction between its expansive force and the political boundaries of empire, [which led] the real Roman-Greek blood to be overgrown with Asian and African [blood]."[34] In other words, the original body politic could not withstand expansion in the context of Rome's universalist political goals. Germany was committing the same crime in South West Africa, where "the German colonial administration unashamedly imposes their bastards in southern Africa on us as Germans." For him this was "indeed the greatest universalist nonsense ever achieved."[35] Most pan-Germans after the turn of the century no longer believed overseas expansion to be a politically feasible solution to the need for more territory; they saw the overseas colonies as a small part of a much more important continental program of expansion. They therefore saw the threat of imperial "accumulation" in the Prussian east, in France, in Southern Europe, and in Germany proper—in other words, everywhere where remnants of "Aryan" blood were fighting it out with alien elements. The entire world had been infected by "accumulation." For the Germanic race to survive, it would have to undo the damage of ill-conceived universalism. The stakes were very high. As Reimer noted, the stakes concerned the definition of humanity and the relationship between its composite groups:

> In such times of the accumulation of different races the question of the relationship between general humanity to its parts and of the latter to one another always becomes a burning one: that was already the case in Rome, where they opted for universalism (the mixing of everyone with everyone else on the basis of animalistic equality).[36]

The pan-German solution to the ills of nineteenth-century imperial *Völkerchaos* involved a race-conscious form of imperialism, that is, the creation of a Germanic *Stammesreich* (tribal empire) that would stretch, depending on the author, from Poland to France, to Scandinavia, Great Britain, the United States, South America, and Southern Africa.[37]

The creation of a *Stammesreich* would require a redefinition of the concept of humanity because of the level of violence and coercion it would involve. Turn-of-the-century pan-German racialists emphasized the newness of their ideas and recognized that their ideas could only take root in places where the nineteenth-century idea of humanity had been compromised.[38] In seeking to redefine the concept they drew right from the logic of the colonial reformers: a German understanding of humanitarianism vis-à-vis foreign races would need to be expanded to account for the radical racial alterity of occupied (colonial) subjects and the demands they placed on state officials. In Reimer's mind, a false empathy for all humanity needed to be tempered by the objective facts of natural history. The struggle for existence [*Kampf ums Dasein*] that existed between the various races made false humanity, in the long run, a great source of suffering, for lesser and unworthy elements would be allowed to be brought into the world. He was convinced that if the Germanic race were victorious there could be "no doubt about the exalted future of all humanity."[39] Morality, humanity, and progress were reworked by the pan-Germanists to be a matter of ensuring cultural and racial purity, and they believed a Germanic *Stammesreich* was historically destined to do this. Germany's future was defined by race-power goals. A Germanic victory would be good for all humanity because Germany had the greatest creative and nurturing power [*positiven Schaffen*] of all the world's peoples:

> Today the earth is closed to us; no barbarian peoples can break suddenly into our culture as God's scourge and destroy [*vernichten*] it, but likewise no fountain of youth stands at our disposal apart from our own youthful energy. The history of our times is only one day in the countless centuries that the world has before it. We must therefore do justice to the recognition of our value to the things of this world and false humanity would be a criminal act for all future human beings, for millions upon millions of our children and our children's children.

If the Germanic race refused to recognize its world-historical responsibility and engaged instead in a debilitating false humanity that embraced all peoples as equals, "race aliens" [*Rassenfremde*] would be able to "smuggle" themselves into the German body politic by virtue of the political openness fostered by false ideas of humanity. It was precisely the ultimate form of race aliens, the "bastards" of the Roman Empire, who introduced the bastard-idea of universal humanity into the world. Universalism and everything the pan-Germans associated with it—international institutions, cosmopolitan citizenship laws, legalized labor migration, concepts of political rights—were believed to be the antithesis of a race-consciousness based in science; in Wagner's words, "the *volk*-adverse and therefore nature-adverse and therefore also culture-adverse consciousness of common humanity of a raceless world bourgeoisie has brought forth the idea of world unity [*Erdeneinheit*] and the striving for a world community [*Erdenbundbestrebungen*] and the plans for an international court of the eternal friends of peace."[40] Reimer argued that Germany had inherited the universalist idea from Rome, and that explained why German leaders up to Reimer's time had not shown the requisite empathy for the Germanic race, but rather allowed the race to be weakened by the political equality of lesser and dangerous peoples, such as the "Jews, Slavs and Negroes."

In the Edenic age of pure races, Reimer mused romantically, a moral feeling of empathy [*Mitleid*]—humanity—had existed in individuals with respect to their *Stamm.* "Pure race was originally patient towards those who believed differently [*Andersgläubige*]," he wrote, "but, since they did not find any shared feeling or internal harmony in them, they also remained alien and closed towards them in respect to this limited humanity."[41] In other words, they were hardened and distanced from the sufferings of persons from other races, as good colonial administrators were supposed to be in cases of flogging and other such colonial "necessities." Reimer hoped that this "true" understanding of humanity might awaken German youth to the new possibilities, the new necessities, which were facing them. First, the German state had to expand. This was of course the core element of the pan-German agenda. The expansion would serve the purpose of refreshing Germanic blood (by opening up new spaces for settlement and inbreeding) and of strengthening the Germanic race through war, a key element in the survival of the fittest schema. Second, a strict separation of the races had to take place in the occupied territories as well as at home. Persons with Germanic blood would be taken into what Reimer calls the *civitas Germanica* and given equal rights. The so-called *Agermanen*, people with alien blood, would be treated according to whether they "stood in the way" of German development or not. If they did not, "they would be allowed to continue developing according to the prescriptions of their nature."[42] If they were determined to stand in the way, both Reimer and Wagner proposed the creation of a commission of anthropologists, animal breeders, artists, and medical doctors who would work on "race-hygienic, aesthetic selections" of the subject populations. This they found to be more humane than the old imperial policies, where subject populations were "annihilated," "hunted," or "indiscriminately mixed-up."[43] In Germany proper, *Agermanen* would be excluded from the *civitas Germanica* and given limited citizenship [*Staatsbürgerschaft*]. They would be granted the rights necessary to personal freedom, especially in economic matters *(commercium)*, but excluded from marriage privileges *(connubium)*. They would be forbidden to have any children, and the state would ensure this through all measures available. In the occupied territories, *Agermanen* would be expropriated and forced to move so that they would not threaten by proximity new German settlers. Wagner imagined that they could be placed in stringently controlled reservations. Wagner and Reimer also imagined that nonassimilable peoples would be deported to non-Western territories—Eastern Russia, Asia, Northern and Sub-Saharan Africa. So that expropriated peoples would not become dangerous proletarian elements, Reimer cynically suggested that they be given life insurance, accident insurance, old age insurance, and other such amenities by the state until they all died out.

The main target of German racists was of course "the Jews," a group which they defined as the "anti-race" of sorts—in Roger Chickering's words, "the race that not only survived, but thrived in race-mixing, the very process that negated the integrity of blood and culture in other races."[44] Colonial race thinking provided some racialist anti-Semites a set of pragmatic proposals, a toolbox of approaches to the domination of alien races, as well as a set of lessons learned in the chaotic first years of Germany's overseas expansion. So, as we have seen, racialist anti-Semites after the turn of the century were preoccupied with separating the *Agermanen* out of Germanic society both legally and spatially as well as with finding ways to argue that such proposals were humanitarian. The absolute necessity that colonized persons be seen as completely separate from metropolitan humanity and the ideas that sprang from this necessity offered racialist thinkers in Germany a set of concepts that were easily translated to continental concerns.

It was, therefore, the process of becoming an overseas empire—the grimy, day-to-day challenges this posed at home and abroad—that facilitated the transplantation of race-thinking to state officials and, less intensively, to ordinary Germans. This transplantation was gradual, unequally dispersed, and often unintentional. It occurred as a consequence of the trauma colonization caused to long-cherished traditions of German *Kultur* and the German *Rechsstaat*. Perhaps the most important players in the racialization of German overseas colonization were the colonial reformers—committed colonial enthusiasts, many of them National Liberal Party members, who were appalled by the rampant colonial atrocities that became public knowledge in the 1890s. Their particular concerns were tied to Germany's new membership in the community of world powers—colonial reformers feared that Germany's poor treatment of its new colonial subjects, and the poor management of colonial administrators, would undermine internationally Germany's claims to being an orderly and civilized empire (a fear that became reality after World War I, when the Allied Powers argued against Germany's colonial claims by pointing to its record of atrocity). But they were also laboring to find ways to reduce colonial abuses, if only in their own minds (and in the press). They seem to have believed that *Eingeborenenrecht* was indeed a humanitarian effort, which saved German virtue even if it never became the effective determinant of facts on the ground. Thus race thinking became grounded in respectable discourse almost entirely through the seemingly non-racialist efforts at humanitarian reform.

While many liberals saw *Eingeborenenrecht* as a way to save the German soul, radical nationalists found in it a whole new set of potentials that supported their Gobineau Society racism and racialist anti-Semitism. When scholars and political activists began to think about colonial statecraft as a mode of governing alien races, the models they created cast colonies as places without limit. Colonies were used as a space of institutional innovation, where violence could be imagined to serve scientific purposes. Their mere existence transformed political language, such that colonial scholars could casually refer to forced labor and genocide as if these things were part of the sanitary operation of a normal political process. By 1910, when the myth of colonial reform had gained the upper-hand in Germany's parliament, the middle classes could easily choose either to ignore the crass frontier bravado of many colonial administrators or to embrace it as an ultimate kind of liberation, a democracy (or aristocracy) of terror. Therefore, "race power," a system of rule that involved both crass realities and humanitarian delusions, could be presented in the violent language of flogging and in the more poetic language of German nationalism.

When Hannah Arendt wrote her famous and groundbreaking work *Imperialism*, book two of her three-volume *Origins of Totalitarianism*, she was addressing this radical potential of colonialism to create new political ideas, categories, and possibilities. It is perhaps not surprising that she was German, since in Germany the stories of resident Africans and the abuses they brought to public attention had become an integral part of anti-colonial political culture. This was so much the case that Arendt referred to the 1905 protest letter sent to the German parliament by Duala notables that had become a cause célèbre among parliamentarians and journalists critical of the colonial adventure and concerned about the erosion of the concept of common humanity.[45] This might help explain her unique sensitivity to the humiliation and trauma that colonialism was for democratic, liberal, and plural polities—and the radical political effects that this trauma could have on the language of rule.

Although Hannah Arendt has been criticized frequently for including imperialism in her analysis of the roots of National Socialism and Soviet Communism, her insights into the effects of colonialism on metropolitan political culture remain unrivalled.[46] By focusing on the "concept of unlimited expansion" that characterized late nineteenth-century imperialism, she was able to capture the mentalities of those persons for whom power and violence appeared to be "the conscious aim of the body politic or the ultimate goal of . . . definite policy."[47] She rightly tied this "concept of unlimited expansion" with the potential "destruction of all living communities, those of the conquered peoples as well as of the people at home," a process that she referred to as the "boomerang effect of imperialism on the homeland," which she saw operating within the pan-movements.[48] Although she focused on the British colonial experience, it is safe to assume that much of her insight came from Germany's experience. The colonial "race power" complex, as I have called it, did indeed infect metropolitan political culture—colonial enthusiasts and scholars saw it as the basis of policy and scholarship, and radical racist anti-Semites saw it as the basis for worldwide expansion and rule. The color-coded racism of the project of *Eingeborenenrecht* effectively racialized the understanding of governance with regard to Africans within respectable society, which helps us explain the virulent postwar campaign, among all political parties except the USPD (*Unabhängige Sozialdemokratische Partei Deutschlands*), against the French use of colonial soldiers in their occupation of the Rhineland. By then German society had become thoroughly imbued with colonial-era anxieties about race-mixing and racio-spatial propriety. Though racialist anti-Semitism was never the dominant political tendency in Wilhelmine Germany, the small coterie that advocated it, and the ideas they garnered from Germany's colonial experience, were to have unforeseeable consequences for Germany's postwar history. Colonialism did not cause Nazism, as Arendt herself recognized,[49] but it can help explain the nature of some of the racial anxieties within the NSDAP program and why Weimar Germany appeared so complacent about it.

Notes

1. For critical studies of the standard of civilization see Gerrit Gong, *The Standard of Civilization in International Society* (Oxford, 1984) and Antony Anghie, "Finding the Peripheries: Sovereignty and Colonialism in Nineteenth Century Colonial Law," *Harvard International Law Journal* (Winter 1999).

2. Many scholars have recently remarked upon the relatively cosmopolitan nature of German arts and sciences prior to the late nineteenth century and the important shift towards essentialist and race-based thinking that occurred around the turn of the century. Woodruff D. Smith, *Politics and the Sciences of Culture in Germany, 1840–1920* (New York/Oxford, 1991); Russell A. Berman, *Enlightenment or Empire: Colonial Discourse in German Culture* (Lincoln/London, 1998); Andrew Zimmerman, *Anthropology and Antihumanism in Imperial Germany* (Chicago/London, 2001); H. Glenn Penny, *Objects of Culture: Ethnology and Ethnographic Museums in Imperial Germany* (Chapel Hill/London, 2002); Pascal Grosse, "Turning Native? Anthropology, German Colonialism, and the Paradoxes of the 'Acclimatization Question,' 1885–1914," in *Wordly Provincialism: German Anthropology in the Age of Empire*, ed. H. Glenn Penny and Matti Bunzl (Ann Arbor, 2003), 179–197.

3. See the story of John Dickson in Elisa von Joeden-Forgey, "Nobody's People: Colonial Subjects, Race Power and the German State, 1884–1945" (Ph.D. diss., University of Pennsylvania, 2004), 157–60.

4. See the stories of Prince Samson Dido and Mandenga Diek, both from Douala, Cameroon, in Joeden-Forgey, "Nobody's People," 62–66, 213–16.

5. For examples of the use of these two integrationist terms, see Joeden-Forgey, "Nobody's People," 174, 309.

6. K. Rathgen, "Die Besiedlung der deutschen Kolonien," *Rede gehalten von dem Vorsitzenden des Professorenrat. Hamburgisches Kolonialinstitut Bericht über das zweite Studienjahr 1909/1910* (Hamburg, 1910), 20.

7. George M. Fredrickson, *Racism: A Short History* (Princeton, 2002); Anthony W. Marx, *Making Race and Nation: A Comparison of the United States, South Africa and Brazil* (Cambridge, 1998).
8. Marx, *Making Race and Nation*, 2.
9. Kwame Anthony Appiah, "'Racism': A History of Hatred," *The Affirmative Action and Diversity Project: A Web Page for Research* (2002), http://aad.english.ucsb.edu/docs/appiah.html
10. For an extended discussion of early construction of colonial subjecthood, see Joeden-Forgey, "Colonial Legal Identities: From Territorium Nullius to Populi Nullius" in "Nobody's People," 134–184.
11. Jake Spidle, "The German Colonial Civil Service: Organization, Selection and Training" (Ph.D. diss., Stanford University, 1972), 7.
12. Helmuth Stoecker, "The German empire in Africa before 1914: General Questions," in *German Imperialism in Africa*, ed. Helmuth Stoecker (London, 1986), 206. This number of lashes was enough to kill a person, especially if the whip being used cut deeply into the flesh and damaged the internal organs. F. F. Müller, *Kolonien unter der Peitsche* (Berlin, 1962), 99.
13. Franz Giesebrecht, *Die Behandlung der Eingeborenen in den deutschen Kolonien* (Berlin, 1898), 183.
14. It is important to note that Giesebrecht included an essay advocating genocide in his collection. See the contribution by Major Boshart in *Die Behandlung der Eingeborenen*, 39–45.
15. Helmut Bley, *Namibia under German Rule* (Hamburg, 1996); Gesine Krüger, *Kriegsbewältigung und Geschichtsbewußtsein* (Göttingen, 1999); Jan-Bart Gewald, *Herero Heroes: A Socio-Political History of the Herero of Namibia, 1890–1923* (Oxford, 1999); John Bridgman and Leslie J. Worley, "Genocide of the Hereros," in *Century of Genocide: Eyewitness Accounts and Critical Views*, ed. Samuel Totten, William S. Parsons, and Israel W. Charny (New York/London, 1997).
16. Emil Peters, "Der Begriffs sowie die staats- und völkerrechtliche Stellung der Eingeborenen in den deutschen Schutzgebieten nach dem deutschem Kolonialrecht" (Ph.D. diss., 1906), 14–15.
17. BA-Berlin R1001 Bd. 5418, 291–293. Quoted from Harald Sippel, "Die Klassifizierung 'des Afrikaners' und 'des Europäers' im Rahmen der dualen kolonialen Rechtsordnung am Beispeil von Deutsch-Südwestafrika," in *Transformationen der europäischen Expansion vom 16. bis zum 20. Jahrhundert*, ed. Andreas Eckert and Jürgen Müller (Rehburg-Loccum, 1997), 163–64.
18. For example, see the definition in the *German Colonial Lexicon*, which was published after World War I but largely completed and laid out beforehand. *Deutsches Kolonial-Lexicon*, ed. Heinrich Schnee (1920; Wiesbaden, 1996), 507–508.
19. The importance of the colonial reform movement to the gradual normalization of colonial race politics in metropolitan political discourse is examined in Pascal Grosse, *Kolonialismus, Eugenik und bürgerliche Gesellschaft in Deutschland, 1850–1918* (Frankfurt, 2001).
20. Elisa von Joeden-Forgey, ed., *Mpundu Akwa: The Case of the Prince from Cameroon* (Hamburg, 2002), esp. 121–123.
21. Lora Wildenthal, "Race, Gender and Citizenship in the German Colonial Empire," in *Tensions of Empire: Colonial Cultures in a Bourgeois World*, ed. Frederick Cooper and Ann Laura Stoler (Berkeley/Los Angeles, 1997).
22. Sara Pugach, "Afrikanistik and Colonial Knowledge: Carl Meinhof, the Missionary Impulse, and African Language and Culture Studies in Germany, 1887–1919" (Ph.D. diss., University of Chicago, 2001), 260.
23. Carl Meinhof, "Deutsche Erziehung," *Deutsche Vorträge Hamburgischer Professoren 9* (Hamburg, 1914), 4; Carl Meinhof, "Deutschland und die preußische Geist," *Vorträge gehalten im Hamburger Volksheim Nr. 16* (1915), 12.
24. Lora Wildenthal, "The Feminine Radical Nationalism of Frieda von Bülow," in *German Women for Empire, 1884–1945* (Durham, 2001), 54–78.
25. Leon Poliakov, *The History of Anti-Semitism*, vol. III (Philadelphia, 1968), esp. chapter 11; William I. Brustein, *Roots of Hate: Antisemitism in Europe before the Holocaust* (Cambridge, 2003), esp. chapter 3.

26. Trutz von Trotha, "'One for the Kaiser': Beobachtungen zur politischen Soziologie der Prügelstrafe am Beispiel des 'Schutzgebietes Togo,'" in *Studien zur Geschichte des deutschen Kolonialismus in Afrika*, ed. Peter Heine and Ulrich van der Heyden (Pfaffenweiler, 1995), 533.
27. Although the central state tried a few legal reforms, flogging continued, and even appears to have grown substantially after 1910. Müller, *Kolonien unter der Peitsche*.
28. For a discussion of these works and their links to National Socialist ideology, see Leon Poliakov, *The Aryan Myth: A History of Racist and Nationalistic Ideas in Europe* (1971; New York, 1996), 301–304.
29. Marcia Klotz, "Global Visions: From the Colonial to the National Socialist World," *The European Studies Journal* 16, no. 2 (1999): 37–68.
30. Poliakov, *The Aryan Myth*, 301.
31. Klaus Wagner, *Krieg: eine politisch-entwickelungsgeschichtliche Untersuchung* (Jena, 1906), 60–61.
32. Josef Ludwig Reimer, *Ein pangermanisches Deutschland. Versuch über die Konzequenzen der gegenwärtigen wissenschaftlichen Rassenbetrachtung für unsere politischen und religiösen Probleme* (Berlin/Leipzig, 1905), 22–23.
33. Ibid., 13.
34. Ibid., 124.
35. Ibid., 130 (footnote).
36. Ibid., 13.
37. See Reimer, "Das größere Deutschland als germanisches Stammesreich," in Ibid.
38. Ibid., 261.
39. Ibid., 268.
40. Wagner, *Krieg*, 67–68.
41. Reimer, *Ein pangermanisches Deutschland*, 255.
42. Ibid., 130.
43. Ibid., 139.
44. Roger Chickering, *We Men Who Feel Most German: A Cultural Study of the Pan-German League, 1886–1914* (Boston, 1984), 239.
45. Hannah Arendt, *Imperialism: Part Two of the Origins of Totalitarianism* (San Diego/New York, 1968), 14.
46. Most criticisms of Arendt's *Imperialism* have been expressed in short or unpublished comments. For one of the more detailed treatments, see L. H. Gann and Peter Duignan, "End of Empire," in *Rulers of German Africa* (Stanford, 1977), 216–238.
47. Arendt, *Imperialism*, 17.
48. Ibid., 17, 35.
49. Margaret Canovan, "Arendt's Theory of Totalitarianism: A Reassessment," in *The Cambridge Companion to Hannah Arendt*, ed. Dana Villa (Cambridge, 2000), 25–43.

Chapter 2

RACE THINKING AND RACISM IN HANNAH ARENDT'S *THE ORIGINS OF TOTALITARIANISM*

Kathryn T. Gines

In Part Two of *The Burden of Our Time* (1951), published as *The Origins of Totalitarianism* in America and then reissued with additional prefaces in 1958 and 1966, Hannah Arendt utilizes her usual method of distinction making by differentiating colonialism and imperialism along with race-thinking and racism.[1] In what follows I examine how these sets of distinctions are interrelated and how they influence Arendt's analysis of Africans and African Americans in the contexts of imperialism and slavery. As I outline (and when necessary summarize) Arendt's analysis, I make the following arguments: (1) The systematic oppression that occurred during the "colonial" era in the Americas had very "imperialist" undertones and that the groundwork for race thinking and racism was laid long before what Arendt considers to be the age of imperialism—between 1884 and 1914; (2) Her suggestion that racism is a byproduct of imperialism undermines the relationship between racism (not just race-thinking) and slavery in Europe and the Americas during and after the colonial era; (3) Despite the fact that Arendt seeks to take a position against racism, there are still traces of racism in her own analysis. This is marked by her frequent use of the term "savage" as well as the way that she naturalizes Africans, asserting that they are pure nature and suggesting that they are somehow not capable of culture and the formation of (or participation in) that which is political.[2]

Colonialism and Imperialism

In *Origins* Arendt asserts that the difference between colonialism and imperialism has been neglected, along with distinctions between Commonwealth and Empire, plantations and possessions, and colonies and dependencies.[3] Some of the differences between colonialism or colonial trade and imperialism that Arendt emphasizes include the following: when she speaks of colonialism, she has in mind the European colonization of America and Australia, and when she speaks of imperialism, she has in mind the expansion of European countries into Africa and Asia, and the racism, exploitation, and violence that was entailed therein. For Arendt, *colonialism* involved more of an extension of the laws and ideals of the mother country into the colonial territory, while *imperialism* often denied the extension of these laws, denied efforts at assimilating the foreign country, and focused on economic expansion for the mother country at the expense of the conquered country through racist ideologies and through violence. She dates the period of imperialism from 1884 to 1914 (between the "scramble for Africa" and the Pan-movements), and argues that the political ideals of *imperialism* have "expansion as a permanent and supreme aim of politics."[4]

According to Arendt, imperialism grew out of colonialism and, with the help of Cecil Rhodes, took expansion for the sake of expansion as its focal point no earlier than 1884. She emphasizes the fact that although imperialism may have grown out of colonialism, imperialism represents something that is radically different and new in the history of political thought and action.[5] But I want to make the case that, even if we acknowledge that imperialism is quite possibly a new concept, the relationship between colonialism and imperialism still needs to be underscored. When we consider the genocide of Native Americans in the Americas and of Aboriginals in Australia, along with the enslavement and mass murder of Africans (in Africa, through the Middle Passage, and in the Americas), it is evident that colonialism shares many violent and expansionist characteristics with imperialism. While imperialism may differ from colonialism in its timing, some of its motivations, and its role as a precursor to totalitarianism, it is also the case that, like imperialism, colonialism in the Americas and Australia employed similar violent, religious, and even racist tactics for the purpose of economic expansion.

Arendt seems to overlook this aspect of colonialism when she denies that these continents had a precolonial history or culture. She states that, "Colonization took place in America and Australia, the two continents that, without a culture and a history of their own, had fallen into the hands of Europeans."[6] However, later (in *Origins*, but not in *The Burden of Our Time*) Arendt acknowledges the violent and oppressive circumstances surrounding colonization saying, "through centuries the extermination of native peoples went hand and hand with colonization in the Americas, Australia and Africa."[7] Arendt does recognize (even if she does not stress) the similarities between the motivations and oppressive methodologies of colonialism in the Americas and Australia and the later phenomenon of imperialism in Africa and Asia. But her analysis leads her to connect racism to imperialism rather than identify the seeds of racism that were already planted during colonialism.

Arendt does not draw the connection between race-thinking and racism already at work both in precolonial slavery and during colonialism. This relationship is explored by Colin Palmer in "Rethinking American Slavery." Palmer asserts:

[B]y the fifteenth century, the Spaniards, Portuguese, and probably other Europeans had already assumed a posture of superiority over black Africans, based on cultural or phenotypical (racial) differences . . . some scholars are now suggesting that by the end of the European Middle Ages the terms *slavery* and *race* were becoming interchangeable and negative 'racial' characteristics began to be applied to Africans in intellectual and public discourse.[8]

This takes place long before race-thinking and racism were used as tools for imperialism and totalitarianism. While Arendt suggests (and some contemporary race theorists and historians would agree) that there was not a cohesive theory of race before and during the colonial era, I am arguing that the genocide, oppression, and aggression characteristic of this era still operated along the lines of categories that we now classify as racial.[9]

Arendt bypasses the development of race-thinking and racism in the colonial context, and instead attributes racism to imperialism. For her, the period of imperialism was a "preparatory stage for the coming catastrophes" of totalitarianism.[10] Arendt's assessment here is motivated by her concern with the rise of imperialism as a precursor to the rise of totalitarianism. According to Dana Villa, she thought that "Nazi and Soviet totalitarianism were not aberrations born of peculiarly dysfunctional national characters or political histories; rather, they were phenomena made possible by a particular constellation of events and tendencies within modern European history and culture."[11] These events and tendencies included the expansionist model of imperialism as well as the evolution and spread of racism, particularly by those in the West. In a sense, the origins of imperialism are overlapping with the origins of totalitarianism.

Operating in the background of this analysis is Arendt's attempt to elucidate Nazism and the Holocaust. Like the political theorist and Nēgritude poet Aimé Césaire (*Discourse on Colonialism*, 1955), Arendt identifies the relationship between the bourgeoisie, racism, and imperialism on the one hand, and anti-Semitism and the attempted obliteration of the Jewish people on the other. According to Césaire (who uses the term colonialism rather than imperialism) European/Western civilization has caused two problems that it cannot solve: the problem of the proletariat and the colonial problem.[12] Césaire explains that the bourgeoisie is awakened to a boomerang effect of its actions, namely Nazism. His analysis is worth quoting at length here:

> The gestapos are busy, the prisons filled up, the torturers at work . . . People are surprised, they become indignant. They say: 'how strange! But never mind—its Nazism, it will pass!' And they wait and they hope; and they hide the truth from themselves . . . that it is Nazism, yes, but that before they were its victims, they were its accomplices; that they tolerated that Nazism before it was inflicted on them, that they absolved it, shut their eyes to it, legitimized it, because, until then, it had been applied only to non-European peoples; that they have cultivated that Nazism, that they are responsible for it, and that before engulfing the whole edifice of Western, Christian civilization in its reddened waters, it oozes, seeps, and trickles from every crack.[13]

Here Césaire is asserting that the colonial system created by Europeans and targeting "non-European peoples" eventually ushered in Nazism against European peoples. He is also claiming that Europeans, particularly the bourgeoisie, are the accomplices of both colonialism and Nazism. Throughout *Discourse on Colonialism,* Césaire criticizes colonialism along the lines of race and economics. He offers an explicitly racial and socialist critique.

While Arendt also offers a racial and an economic analysis, these analyses have been criticized by Gale Presbey in an essay titled "Critique of Boers or Africans?" Although Arendt is explicitly critical of imperialism for bringing economics into the political realm and making expansion a national agenda, Presbey problematizes what Arendt *neglects* to criticize about imperialism (and even forms of slavery that resulted from imperialism), particularly in the actions of the Boers and the British. Presbey charges: "[Arendt] does not say that what the Boers and the British did was wrong because: (1) they practiced slavery; (2) they engaged in unfair discriminatory labor practices; (3) they appropriated for themselves all of the land, which they acquired through the use of force; (4) they committed massacres and conducted cruel and unusual punishments."[14] Presbey questions the basis of Arendt's analysis and suggests that if the Boers had relied on slave labor in order to engage in political activity (in the ancient Greek sense), then "Arendt might have praise for them."[15] Presbey may be exaggerating here by suggesting that Arendt would have praised the Boers for political activity, nevertheless she raises an important point. Rather than criticizing the methods (or means) of exploitation, Arendt criticizes the ends of the exploitation.

This is not only true in Arendt's critique of the Boers and the British, but also of the French brand of imperialism. For example, she asserts that if France's methods and motives for imperialism had been along the same lines as those of Rome, the "events that followed" (i.e. the events of mass exploitation and oppression) would have been "more humanly tolerable."[16] Here Arendt is prioritizing the political over economics, which for her is social rather than political.[17] If imperialism had aimed at empire building, allowing the conquering nation to spread its form of government and politics abroad, the oppression required to do so perhaps would have been more acceptable. But since imperialism was largely an economic and expansionist venture, the oppressive means used to achieve these economic ends were not as tolerable to Arendt.

Perhaps it should not be surprising that Arendt presents a paradigm that prioritizes the political over economics (i.e., the social), given the way she later builds on this model in *The Human Condition* (1958) and *On Revolution* (1963). In both of these works Arendt argues that the concept of the political (which is marked by a distinction between public and private space) has been distorted by what she describes as the rise of the social (which includes attempts to bring issues of economics, poverty, and racial oppression into the public realm). We see the earlier stages of this framework throughout *The Origins of Totalitarianism* where we must not only pay attention to her account of expansion and imperialism but also her examination of race and imperialism.

Race-Thinking and Racism

In "Race-Thinking Before Racism" Arendt claims that it was not race-thinking, but the new era of imperialism that gave rise to racism. She distinguishes between *race-thinking*, such as pseudo-scientific and anthropological studies about racial hierarchies and origins, and *racism*, which she describes as the ideology eventually used as a justification for the national political agendas of imperialism.[18] Furthermore, whereas race-thinking is largely a matter of free opinion, racism is more ideological because it permeates public opinion and leads people to abandon concrete facts for racist principles. For Arendt, ideologies are "systems based upon a single opinion that proved strong enough to attract and persuade a majority of people and broad enough to lead them through the various situations of an average modern life."[19] Ideologies differ from opinions in that an ideology claims to have the key insight or knowledge to history, to all the world's problems, or to universal laws. According to Arendt, the ideology of race "interprets history as a natural fight of races."[20]

While Arendt sees race-thinking as a political tool, she tends to emphasize its political aspects in France and Germany more than in Britain or the United States. For example, in the case of France, Arendt traces the "germs" of "the nation destroying and humanity-annihilating power of racism" to the Comte de Boulainvilliers, whom she describes as a nobleman of France. According to her, during the eighteenth century Boulainvilliers' theory of two distinct peoples of France was used to "counteract the new national idea."[21] She adds that at the outbreak of the French Revolution these thoughts about race were used for political purposes.[22] For Arendt these ideas about race are forms of race-thinking, not racism.

Arendt juxtaposes the race-thinking in France which was used as "a weapon for civil war and splitting a nation" with that in Germany which she asserts was useful in uniting Germans against domination from foreign elements.[23] Race-thinking in Germany became a rallying point for the joining together of various German states. Consequently, Arendt explains, in Germany it is hard to distinguish "mere nationalism and clear-cut racism" because "[h]armless national sentiments expressed themselves in *what we know today* to be racial terms."[24] Arendt claims that German racism and imperialism did not fully develop until after 1870 and contends that Nazism is not the same as German nationalism.[25]

As a transition from French and German race-thinking to English race-thinking, Arendt uses Arthur de Gobineau whom she claims "invented racism almost by accident."[26] Gobineau is well known for his influential and racist work *The Inequality of Human Races* (1853–1855). Arendt's summation of Gobineau's thesis is that "the fall of civilization is due to a degeneration of race and the decay of race is due to a mixture of blood. This implies that in every mixture the lower race is always dominant."[27] She also says in passing that Gobineau tried to get a larger audience in the United States by siding with slavery.[28] However, before taking up the issue of slavery and race in America, let us first address the issue of English race-thinking.

In England, Arendt argues, the seeds of race-thinking were developed during the French Revolution. But she also claims that the English and German versions of race-thinking had more similarities to one another than to the French version insofar as both England and Germany tended to reject the invented ideals of *Liberté–Égalité–Fraternité* and the "Rights of Man."[29] One idea that did appeal to the English was Edmund Burke's concept of inheritance, which the English connected to liberty and nationalism.[30] Arendt draws a correlation between the more historical concepts of inheritance and the more modern concept of eugenics.[31]

Arendt is clear that one of the major problems faced by Continentals, the British, and others who claimed to include all people in the concept of humanity was the fact that they had to contend with the differences between Europeans and non-European "others" whom they treated as subhuman, as animals, or as property. She explains that, although Christianity had founded a notion of unity and equality of all human beings coming from the same lineage all the way back to Adam and Eve, this notion was challenged as soon as Europeans encountered tribes who lacked reason, passion, and culture. She asserts that the crucial question became:

> whether the Christian tenet of the unity and equality of all men, based upon common descent from one original set of parents, would be kept in the hearts of men who were faced with tribes which, as far as we know, never had found by themselves any adequate expression of human reason or human passion in either cultural deeds or popular customs, and which had developed human institutions only to a low level.[32]

Arendt appears to be speaking in her own voice here and she uses the pronoun "we" rather than "they" suggesting that she may agree with claims that tribes (specifically African tribes) did not adequately express human reason, passion, culture, or customs. What is at work behind Arendt's claims here? In order to respond to that question, we have to return to the distinction that she makes between race-thinking and racism and consider how these concepts operate in her own perceptions about "others."

Recall that Arendt describes race-thinking as a matter of opinion that often uses pseudo-science and anthropology to support claims to racial hierarchies. Racism on the other hand is ideological, abandons facts for racist principles, and interprets history as a fight of the races.[33] She claims that racism is not so much a byproduct of race-thinking, as it is a byproduct of imperialism. And since imperialism needed justification, racism would have been invented even in the absence of race-thinking. She correctly identifies racism as a tool used by Europeans to justify exploitation and oppression in the form of imperialism. However, her analysis is also problematic because it discounts the possibility that race-thinking (in utilizing science, anthropology, or any other such tools to support claims about racial hierarchies, which are in turn used to justify or excuse racial oppression based on those hierarchies) is already racist, even if it has not yet been developed into a fully accepted ideology. Furthermore, Arendt's analysis of race-thinking and racism in relation to imperialism does not take into account the fact that this very possibility was the reality of racialized institutions of slavery long before race became the excuse for imperialism.

Another difference Arendt highlights between race-thinking and racism is how each relates to nationalism and to principles of equality. For her, not only is racism not equivalent to nationalism, racism actually undermines nationalism. While I would not argue that racism is the same as nationalism, because it is certainly not the case that all nationalisms are racist, it is also true that racism and nationalism are not as mutually exclusive as Arendt suggests. She states:

> From the very beginning, racism deliberately cut across all national boundaries, whether defined by geographical, linguistic, traditional, or any other standards, and denied national-political standards as such. Historically speaking, racists have a worse re-cord of patriotism than the representatives of all other international ideologies to-gether, and they were the only ones who consistently denied the great principle upon which national organizations are built, the principle of equality and solidarity of all peoples guaranteed by the idea of mankind.[34]

It is suggested here that since racism cuts across national boundaries, is somehow unpatriotic, and rejects principles of equality, a person or a nation may *not* be racist if that person or nation accepts the principle of equality, which Arendt describes as the central pillar of genuine nationhood. For example, she identifies Nazism as a form of racism and yet denies that Nazism is a form of German nationalism. Arendt seems to overlook cases where a person or nation accepts the principle of equality in theory, but intentionally and systematically rejects this principle in practice. Or we might consider cases where a person or nation accepts the prin-ciple of equality among certain groups (or races) of people, but rejects notions of equality and solidarity of all peoples. These points are not intended to prompt an abstract thought experiment; rather, they direct us to situations in which this line of thinking is deeply engrained in a country's history from its inception. One example that I will now examine is the preservation of a racial system of slavery alongside the foundation of freedom and justice as fundamental principles in the United States. Later I will also take up the example of the racist Afrikaner nation-alism of the Boers.

Slavery and Race in the United States

Arendt discusses American slavery in several of her works, including *Origins* and the later chapter "The Social Question" from *On Revolution*. For example, in her account of the American Revolution, Arendt prioritizes the American Revolution over the French Revolution because "The problem they [America] posed was not social but political, it concerned not the order of society but the form of govern-ment."[35] However, she quickly notes that "the absence of the social question from the American scene was, after all, quite deceptive" and that "abject and degrading misery was present everywhere in the form of slavery and Negro labor."[36] Here, Arendt highlights slavery not as a racial institution of labor exploitation, but as a "social question." This theme also carries over into her analysis of segregation in education in "Reflections on Little Rock" where she reduces racism to discrimina-tion and describes it as a social, or at times a private, issue but not a political one.

However, in *On Revolution* Arendt does recognize that slavery is "the primordial crime on which the fabric of American society rested."[37] She also states that Thomas Jefferson and the founding fathers knew that the institution of slavery was incompatible with the founding of freedom. Arendt describes their acceptance of these conditions as indifference to the slaves. But we know that Thomas Jefferson in particular was not indifferent to those who were enslaved insofar as he owned slaves.[38] In his autobiography, Jefferson attempts to redeem himself and explains that he had included an antislavery clause (directed at the king of England) in the Declaration of Independence. He states, "The clause too, reprobating the enslaving the inhabitants of Africa, was struck out in complaisance to South Carolina and Georgia, who had never attempted to restrain the importation of slaves, and who on the contrary still wished to continue it."[39] Jefferson presents himself as taking a stand against slavery (although he did own slaves) and he reveals how determined slaveholders were to preserve institutional slavery.

The United States is a country that claimed to adhere to the principles of equality of all men and yet simultaneously and intentionally enslaved a significant portion of the population. And for this reason Frederick Douglass in "What to the Slave is the Fourth of July?" declares:

> I am not included within the pale of this glorious anniversary! Your high independence only reveals the immeasurable distance between us. The blessings in which you, this day, rejoice, are not enjoyed in common. The rich inheritance of justice, liberty, prosperity and independence, bequeathed by your fathers, is shared by you, not by me. The sunlight that brought life and healing to you, has brought stripes and death to me. This forth [of] July is *yours*, not *mine. You* may rejoice, *I* must mourn.[40]

Douglass is giving testimony to the hypocrisy of the United States from its very foundation. It is and has always been a nation that believed in equality for a select group at the expense of oppressing several less favored groups. This is a country where racism and nationalism have gone hand in hand.

In *The Burden of Our Time* Arendt understands that:

> Slavery's fundamental offense against human rights was not that it took liberty away (which can happen in many other situations), but that it excluded a certain category of people even from the possibility of fighting for freedom—a fight possible under tyranny, and even under the desperate conditions of modern terror (but not under any conditions of concentration camp life). Slavery's crime against humanity did not begin when one people defeated and enslaved its enemies (though of course this was bad enough), but when slavery became an institution in which some men were "born" free and others slave, when it was forgotten that it was man who had deprived his fellowmen of freedom, and when the sanction for the crime was attributed to nature.[41]

Here she identifies several harms caused by the institution of slavery. It took away liberty; it prevented those who were enslaved from the possibility of fighting for freedom; and it allowed some men to be born slaves and others to be born free—a determination attributed to nature. And finally, slavery was a crime instituted by man against his fellow man, not against subhumans or animals.

Having just mentioned Aristotle in this section, it is possible that Arendt has in mind the issue of slavery in general, or perhaps even ancient forms of slavery. However, when we look at the specific case of slavery in the United States, we find a system in which *black* people were born slaves and *white* people were born free. This omission is significant because in an earlier section of *Origins*, Arendt asserts that although slavery was "established on a strict racial basis, [it] did not make the slave-holding peoples race-conscious before the nineteenth century. Throughout the eighteenth century, American slave-holders themselves considered it a temporary institution and wanted to abolish it gradually."[42] But the opposite is true. America's commitment to slavery and slaveholders was demonstrated in the editing of the Declaration of Independence in the late eighteenth century. Jefferson rebukes the king of Great Britain, but the phrase "Determined to keep open a market where MEN could be bought and sold" was removed because it also represented an indictment of American slavery.[43]

It also seems contradictory for Arendt to claim that slavery was both an institution established on a *racial* basis and that slaveholders were not conscious of race. While some may argue that it would be anachronistic to apply the phrase "race-consciousness" to slaveholders before the nineteenth century, it is still the case that slaveholders had to be aware of some concept of race, or at least the values of "black" versus "white" skin, to determine which race would consist of the slaveholders and the free and which would consist of the slaves and the unfree. And even if they were not race-conscious, in the sense of being conscious of their own whiteness, racism alongside economic motivations were certainly at the heart of slavery long before the era of imperialism as described by Arendt.

The racialized institution of slavery, which determined that white people would be born free and black people would be born slaves, is something that developed over time with the passing of specific laws that set broad precedents. In *Slavery in the Making of America*, historians James and Lois Horton explain that in "the early colonial period, American concepts about race, slavery and standards for race relations were still being formulated and were not as fixed as they would become in the eighteenth century. Still, by the mid-seventeenth century it was becoming clear that Africans and white servants received different treatment."[44] For example, in 1640 three servants (two white and one black) ran away from a plantation in Virginia. Once captured, the two white servants were punished with two more years added to their time of servitude. But the black servant, named John Punch, was sentenced to a lifetime of slavery.[45] Edmund Morgan asserts in *American Slavery, American Freedom* that "whether or not race was a necessary ingredient of slavery, it *was* an ingredient. If slavery might have come to Virginia without racism, it did not. The only slaves in Virginia belonged to races alien from the English. And the new social order that Virginians created after they changed to slave labor was determined as much by race as by slavery."[46]

Over time it became evident that the system of indentured service was disadvantageous to those who exploited the labor because once the servants were freed, they posed a threat to their former masters. Gradually landowners turned to the establishment of a racialized slave system. According to the Hortons, "By the 1660s the Chesapeake colonies began establishing the legal foundation for racial distinctions that created the formal structure for eighteenth century racial slavery."[47] In 1662 it became law in Virginia that children would take on the status of their mother, ensuring multigenerational resources of slave labor.[48] In 1691 South Carolina presented the "first comprehensive slave code . . . [which] defined 'all Negros, Mulattoes, and Indians' sold into or intended for sale . . . as slaves."[49] By 1705 Massachusetts law prohibited interracial relationships, and the severity of punishments were issued based according to race and gender.[50] Overall, the history of slavery, including the laws that transformed it into a racialized institution, reveals patterns of law making that have been used as early as the seventeenth century to oppress and exploit people along what we know as racial lines. The example of the United States demonstrates that a country claiming to believe in principles of equality in word can still fail to adhere to those principles in deed.

The Boers and South Africa

Having examined the relationship between slavery and race in the United States, let us now turn our attention to the section in *Origins* entitled "Race and Bureaucracy" where Arendt focuses on the Boers in South Africa as a representative model of the evils of imperialism. The problem of the Boers in South Africa is another example of nationalism founded in racism. In "Prelude to a Disaster: An Analysis of the Racial Policies of Boer and British Settlers in Africa Before 1910," Okon Edet Uya describes several characteristics of the Boers' Afrikaner nationalism. First, the Boers were violently oppressive towards the native population of South Africa. Second, the Boers were antagonistic toward the British. And third, the Boers came to see South Africa as their own fatherland. Citing Floris Van Jaarsveld, Uya argues that the Boers became unified in South Africa before the nineteenth century by both anti-African and anti-British sentiments. The former sentiment was fed by a sense of racial superiority buttressed by claims that the Boers were God's chosen people and that racial discrimination was the will of God. The latter sentiment was an expression of their disdain for the principle of equality that the British came to represent (in theory, if not in practice) and a response to the meddling of the British government in South Africa. Uya explains that the conflict between the Boers and the British can be interpreted as a competition for control over South Africa.

Ironically, the coherence of the Boers under the banner of Afrikaner nationalism was stimulated more by the conflicts with the British than by their racist attitudes of superiority over the indigenous South Africans. And although these conflicts may suggest otherwise, the mindset of the Boers and the British toward Africans were not that distinct from one another. As Uya states, "the actions of the British settlers in Natal tend to show that, where fundamental issues were concerned, the attitude of the British settlers toward Africans was not very different from that of the Boers."[51] But this background is not the focal point of Arendt's analysis, which is both insightful and problematic. Arendt's analysis is insightful because she seems to be able to get into the minds of the oppressors. But this also proves problematic, because she is somehow unable to take a step back and separate herself from their racist characterizations and constructions of Africans. Arendt has been critiqued on this basis by Gail Presbey and Norma Mouruzzi.

Gail Presbey challenges Arendt's historical claims about imperialism and the population demographics in South Africa along with her criticisms (or the lack thereof) of the British and the Boers' agenda in South Africa. Presbey notes that although some of Arendt's most severe criticisms of capitalism are contained in her analysis of imperialism in *Origins*, this criticism is less effective when Arendt seemingly excuses the actions of European expansionists, accusing them of absent-mindedness rather than intentional harm. According to Presbey, "This suggestion that the British were not 'conscious' of what they were doing, although not intended to absolve them from responsibility for the consequences of their actions, can sound very much like apologetics."[52]

The idea that Arendt's analysis sometimes seems to blame the "victims" rather than the offenders for detestable events in history is not new. Her general representation of Jews in *Origins* as well as in her report on the Eichmann trial has also been criticized along these lines. For example, Seyla Benhabib explains in "Arendt's *Eichmann in Jerusalem*" that this report by Arendt, in comparison to all her other writings, has resulted in "by far the most acrimonious and tangled controversy, which has since cast a long shadow on her eventful but otherwise respectable and illustrious career."[53] But Presbey explains that, unlike the literature that has been written critiquing Arendt's position on Eichmann, "where many intellectuals were outraged over her suggestion that Eichmann did not intend evil but was merely *thoughtless*, there has been little or no outrage in the intellectual community over Arendt's repeated suggestions that the British did not intend evil when they expanded their empire but were merely being thoughtless."[54]

While Presbey may be right about the lack of "outrage" expressed over Arendt's suggestion that the British did not intend evil toward the people of Africa, I think that Presbey misunderstands how Arendt uses the notion of thoughtlessness. The case can be made that for Arendt, thoughtlessness may be worse—or at least more disturbing—than intentional harm. For Arendt, who is thinking within the framework of moral or ethical philosophy, thought or the act of thinking is related to judgment or the act of judging. When Arendt accuses Eichmann of thoughtlessness, she is criticizing his claim that he was merely doing his job well and his failure to judge his actions as wrong. Following this line of thinking, one might argue that for Arendt, the British and the Boers were responsible for a similar failure to judge their actions in South Africa as wrong. And although Arendt clearly judges the violent actions of the Boers and the British as wrong, she is disturbingly sympathetic to their reactions to what she perceives to be savagery in the "Dark Continent" of Africa.

Dark Hearts and Dark Continents

As critical of racism as Arendt is throughout *Origins*, she seems nonetheless convinced that racism is a fathomable response by Europeans toward Africans who (in her estimation) lacked civilization, reason, culture, history, and political institutions. Race became "the emergency explanation of human beings whom no European or civilized man could understand and whose humanity so frightened and humiliated the immigrants that they no longer cared to belong to the same human species."[55] In this passage Arendt acknowledges Africans as human beings, while suggesting that they were frightening and uncivilized. Arendt describes European xenophobia at the sight of Africans, or their unwarranted fear and contempt for those who became defined as different and "other," as the impetus for raced societies and perhaps also for racial oppression.

It is remarkable that Arendt points out the fallacy of race-thinking and the lack of foundation for racial stereotypes and yet incorporates this thinking into her own description and characterization of Africans. For example, she constantly refers to Africans as savages, backward, and lacking in history and culture. Arendt integrates these stereotypes into her own investigation of the actions of the Boers in South Africa. For example, in her description of the Boers' practice of slavery Arendt states:

> First of all, slavery, though it domesticated a certain part of the savage population, never got hold of all of them, so the Boers were never able to forget their first horrible fright before a species of men whom human pride and the sense of human dignity could not allow them to accept as fellow-men. This fright of something like oneself that still under no circumstances ought to be like oneself remained at the basis of slavery and became the basis for a race society.[56]

Rather than making a commentary about slavery and race society in general, Arendt is focusing specifically on slavery (though she claims that slavery "is a very inadequate word to describe what actually happened"[57]) and the race society established by the Boers in South Africa. The case could be made that in the latter part of this quote Arendt is not giving her own description, but rather thinking from the perspective of the Boers. However, the first part of the quote seems to represent her position and not the Boers' and it remains problematic that Arendt describes slavery as a means to "domesticate" what *she* calls the "savage population."[58]

Arendt goes on to say that "The great horror which had seized European men at their first confrontation with native life was stimulated by precisely this touch of inhumanity among other human beings who apparently were as much a part of nature as wild animals."[59] She makes it clear that the separation between the "savages" and the rest of humanity is not an issue of skin color, but one of behavior. She explains, "What made them [Africans] different from other human beings was not at all the color of their skin but the fact that they behaved like a part of nature, that they treated it as their undisputed master, that they had not created a human world, a human reality."[60] This is Arendt's personal description of Africans, not just an adaptation of a European perspective. And yet, even if Arendt is describing the perspective of European imperialists towards Africans and not her own, it is problematic that she presents this view uncritically (or in Presbey's words, almost as an apologetic).

Some have suggested that Arendt's account is troublesome because she is providing a narrative that is not representative of her perspective. For example, Dana Villa argues that Arendt is simply taking us into the minds of the racist Europeans and their initial encounter with the people of Africa.[61] But others, like Norma Moruzzi, are more critical, describing Arendt's analysis as Eurocentric and classically Orientalist. Writes Moruzzi, "[T]the description Arendt gives of it [this encounter], while repudiating brutal excess, is structured by her empathic participation in a descriptive discourse that is fundamentally Eurocentric and emotionally charged."[62] Both Moruzzi and Presbey assert that part of the problem is Arendt's use of Joseph Conrad's novel *Heart of Darkness* (which Arendt describes as "the most illuminating work on actual race experience in Africa"[63]) as a representation of the Boers' attitudes in particular and of African behavior in general. Arendt uncritically accepts Conrad's depiction of Africa as a savage world with creatures who "were as incomprehensible as the inmates of a madhouse."[64] *Heart of Darkness* is a thoroughly racist text, even if it also functions to expose and possibly condemn imperialism. Conrad's *Heart of Darkness*, like Arendt's *Origins*, (re)presents the ravaging effects of imperialism, yet without satisfactory reprimand or reproach.[65] The fact that Arendt accepts and embraces this racist image of Africa undermines her efforts to position herself against racism.

I am not attempting to dismiss Arendt's thought altogether and label her as a racist. Arendt is a valuable resource for philosophers, political theorists, and others who do not have all of the answers, but who also understand the importance of asking the tough questions. In *Origins*, Arendt thinks through difficult questions and attempts to make sense of difficult times and circumstances. In most cases, her line of inquiry is extremely helpful and productive. Her ability to trace totalitarianism back to the violent system of imperialism is quite insightful. But there are also some major blind spots in her analysis, particularly when it comes to the issue of anti-Black or anti-African racism.

Arendt's association of racism with imperialism ignores the problems of racism that were already a part of race-thinking during the colonial era, including the creation of racial hierarchies in relationship to the transatlantic slave trade and the resulting establishment of racial systems of slavery. Thus, it would have been more accurate for Arendt to note that not just imperialism, but long before imperialism, the racialized institution of slavery gave rise to racism in both Europe and the Americas. I would go further to say that the historical fact of the exploitation of people on the basis of "race" through the transatlantic slave trade, along with the institution of slavery, made it possible to attempt to conceptualize and then to justify imperialism with racism in the late nineteenth century.

Furthermore, the fact that Arendt does not see the compatibility of racism with nationalism leads her to overlook ways in which the birth of a nation (i.e., the United States) and the establishment of nationalism (i.e., Afrikaner nationalism), in these instances, were both firmly rooted in racism. Finally, Arendt's attempt to criticize the race-thinking and the racism used to justify imperialism is weakened by her inability to distance herself from a very racist (even essentialist) characterization of African people. In this essay I hope to have exposed some of these blind spots in an effort to stimulate more questions about race as an idea, an identity, and even as a problem.

Notes

1. I mention the earlier and later editions of this text because there are differences between them to which I will call attention.
2. Arendt does acknowledge that Africans, in particular the (former) slaves of South Africa, were "well on their way to becoming workers, a normal part of human civilization" at the time she was writing *Origins*. This may suggest that by becoming workers these South Africans become humanized rather than naturalized. See Hannah Arendt, *Origins* (New York, 1966), 195.
3. Arendt, *Origins* (1966), 131.
4. Ibid., 125.
5. Ibid., 125.
6. Ibid., 186.
7. Ibid., 440. This quotation is not contained in the section on "Totalitarianism and Power" in *The Burden of Our Time*, but is added to *Origins*.
8. Colin Palmer, "Rethinking American Slavery," in *The African Diaspora*, ed. Alusine Jalloh and Stephen E. Maizlish (College Station, 1996): 75. I cite Palmer here because he identifies European attitudes of superiority towards Africans as early as the fifteenth century. He also cites several sources on the issue of Iberian attitudes towards Africans including: A.J.R. Russell-Wood, "Iberian Expansion and the Issue of Black Slavery: Changing Portuguese Attitudes, 1440–1770," *American Historical Review* 85, no. 1 (1978): 16-42; and David Eltis, "Europeans and the Rise and Fall of African Slavery in the Americas: An Interpretation," *American Historical Review* 98. no. 1 (1993): 1399–1423.
9. I am not dismissing contemporary race theorists and historians who situate biological race-thinking in the eighteenth century; rather, I want to interrogate theoretical frameworks that minimize questions of "difference" (religious, cultural, or racial) and yet are used to describe categories and events that have come to shape our understanding of slavery and genocide during the colonial era.
10. Arendt, *Origins* (1966), 123.
11. Dana Villa, ed., *The Cambridge Companion to Hannah Arendt* (Cambridge, 2000): 3.
12. Aimé Césaire, *Discourse on Colonialism*, trans. Joan Pinkham, (New York, 2000): 31. This was originally published as *Discours sur le colonialisme* (Paris, 1950).

13. Ibid., 36.
14. Gail Presbey, "Critique of Boers or Africans," in *Postcolonial African Philosophy: A Critical Reader*, ed. Emmanuel Chukwudi Eze (Oxford,1997): 167.
15. Ibid., 168.
16. Arendt, *Origins* (1966), 132.
17. For a more exhaustive analysis of economics and the political in Arendt's work, see Robert Bernasconi's "The Double Face of the Political and the Social: Hannah Arendt and America's Racial Divisions," *Research in Phenomenology* 26, (1996): 3–24.
18. Arendt, *Origins* (1966), 160.
19. Ibid., 159.
20. Ibid.
21. Ibid., 163.
22. Ibid.
23. Ibid., 165.
24. Ibid. My Emphasis.
25. Ibid.
26. Ibid., 172. It is significant that Arendt seems to credit Gobineau with the invention of racism, particularly since his essays were published between 1853 and 1855, about thirty years before what Arendt describes as the age of imperialism.
27. Ibid., 172-173.
28. Arendt may have been unaware that Gobineau's popularity in the United States probably resulted more from his translators than from Gobineau himself. Robert Bernasconi explains in *The Idea of Race* that the first two essays of *The Inequality of Human Races* were published in 1853, and three years later it was translated into English by Josiah Nott and Henry Hotz. Bernasconi asserts, "The result was a seriously doctored text." See Robert Bernasconi and Tommy Lott, eds., *The Idea of Race* (Indianapolis, 2000): 45.
29. Arendt, *Origins* (1966), 175.
30. Ibid., 176.
31. Ibid.
32. Ibid., 177.
33. Early on in *Origins* (1966), Arendt describes ideologies (of racism) as "systems based upon a single opinion that proved strong enough to attract and persuade a majority of people and broad enough to lead them through the various situations of a modern life" (159). She expands on her analysis of ideologies in relationship to totalitarianism later in *Origins* when she asserts that ideologies have three totalitarian elements: (1) ideology has a tendency to explain not what is, but what becomes; (2) ideology becomes independent of all experience from which it cannot learn anything new; (3) since the ideologies have no power to transform reality, they achieve this emancipation of thought from experience through certain methods of demonstration (470-471). When facts that contradict ideologies are presented, the facts are rejected while the ideas behind the ideologies are embraced.
34. Ibid., 161.
35. Arendt, *On Revolution* (London,1963): 68.
36. Ibid., 70.
37. Ibid., 71.
38. It has also been alleged that Jefferson fathered children by Sally Hemmings, an enslaved woman that he owned. For example, in *Slavery in the Making of America*, Horton states, "he was almost certainly the father of his own slaves born to Sally Hemmings, also a Jefferson slave." James Horton and Lois Horton, *Slavery in the Making of America* (Oxford, 2005): 56.
39. Thomas Jefferson, *Writings* (New York, 1984): 18. For a closer analysis of Jefferson's writings on race, see K. Anthony Appiah and Amy Gutmann, *Color Conscious* (Princeton, 1996): 42–52.
40. Frederick Douglass, *The Frederick Douglass Papers*. Series I, Vol. 2, 1847–54, ed. John W. Blassingame (New Haven, 1982): 368.

41. Arendt, *The Burden of Our Time* (London, 1951): 294. I quote from the first edition here because Arendt revises this part of the text later in *Origins*. The revised version of the passage is on page 297 of *Origins* where there is no longer a reference to concentration camps or to modern terror. Arendt also added several additional paragraphs to the second edition to clarify her assertion and defend it against critics.

42. Arendt, *Origins* (1966): 177.

43. Thomas Jefferson, *Writings*, 22.

44. James Horton and Lois Horton, *Slavery*, 29.

45. Ibid., 29; Also see Darlene Hine, William Hine, and Stanley Harrold, *The African American Odyssey*, 3rd ed. (Upper Saddle River, 2003): 57.

46. Edmund Morgan, *American Slavery, American Freedom* (New York, 1975): 315.

47. James Horton and Lois Horton, *Slavery*, 18.

48. Ibid., 30.

49. Ibid., 32.

50. Ibid., 30.

51. Okon Edet Uya, "Prelude to Disaster: An Analysis of the Racial Policies of Boer and British Settlers in Africa before 1910," in *Africa and the Afro American Experience*, ed. Loraine Williams (Washington, D.C., 1977): 114.

52. Presbey, "Critique of Boers or Africans," 172.

53. Seyla Benhabib, "Arendt's *Eichmann in Jerusalem*," in *The Cambridge Companion to Hannah Arendt*, ed. Dana Villa (Cambridge, 2000): 65. Benhabib and others argue that this controversy results in large part from a misinterpretation of Arendt's work. Some examples include: Bernard Bergen, *The Banality of Evil: Hannah Arendt and "The Final Solution"* (New York, 1998); Richard Bernstein, "From Radical Evil to the Banality of Evil: From Superfluousness to Thoughtlessness," in *Hannah Arendt and the Jewish Question* (Cambridge, MA, 1996): 137–53; and Dana Villa, "Conscience, the Banality of Evil, and the Idea of a Representative Perpetrator," in *Politics, Philosophy Terror: Essays on the Thought of Hannah Arendt* (Princeton, 1999): 39–60.

54. Presbey, "Critique of Boers or Africans," 173.

55. Arendt, *Origins*, 185.

56. Ibid., 192.

57. Ibid.

58. The argument that slavery domesticates or civilizes an animalistic slave population has frequently been used to defend and justify slavery in the United States as well as the imperialist projects in Africa, Asia, and other parts of the globe. Violent oppression of entire populations has been justified by claims that the oppressors were spreading civilization, Christianity, or (more recently) democracy and freedom.

59. Arendt, *Origins* (1966), 194.

60. Ibid., 192.

61. Villa, ed., *The Cambridge Companion to Hannah Arendt*, 4.

62. Norma Claire Moruzzi, *Speaking Through the Mask: Hannah Arendt and the Politics of Social Identity* (Ithaca, 2001): 97.

63. Arendt, *Origins* (1966), 185.

64. Ibid., 190. Arendt is quoting here from Joseph Conrad's *Heart of Darkness*.

65. Conrad's *Heart of Darkness* is often debated among scholars. In an address titled "An Image of Africa," Chinua Achebe asserts that Conrad is a racist and that *Heart of Darkness* represents white racist attitudes towards Africa that have become such a normal way of thinking that they frequently go unnoticed. See Chinua Achebe, "An Image of Africa," in *The Massachusetts Review* 18, no.4 (1977): 788. Peter E. Firchow defends *Heart of Darkness* in *Envisioning Africa: Racism and Imperialism in Conrad's Heart of Darkness* (Lexington, 2000).

Chapter 3

WHEN THE REAL CRIME BEGAN

Hannah Arendt's *The Origins of Totalitarianism* and
the Dignity of the Western Philosophical Tradition

Robert Bernasconi

After the end of the Second World War a number of Black philosophers attacked the tendency of most European and North American observers to isolate the Nazi genocide from the history of the West. In the view of these Black philosophers, Nazism had been prepared for by the crimes of colonialism and imperialism. They also argued that many of the canonical figures of the Western philosophical tradition were implicated in these same crimes, for example, by investing in, supporting, or remaining silent about, the Atlantic slave trade or, later, imperialism. Furthermore, they claimed that the failure of philosophers and others subsequently to address this history contributed to the climate that made the Holocaust possible. Later, particularly in the 1960s, there were White historians who similarly sought to place the crimes of National Socialism within the context of Western intellectual history; one might think, for example, of Léon Poliakov's *The Aryan Myth* or George L. Mosse's *The Crisis of German Ideology*.[1] However, in the immediate aftermath of the Second World War the dominant tendency among White intellectuals was to construct an intellectual genealogy that could serve as an exercise in containment: a few thinkers and styles of thought would be sacrificed as tainted for the purpose of exonerating others. Lukacs' *The Destruction of Reason* can be read as an exercise of this kind.[2] In what follows I will consider the extent to which Hannah Arendt's *The Origins of Totalitarianism* took up this same task of trying to determine what National Socialism revealed about "the West."

It has to be remembered that "the West" is a construction that has in intellectual circles for some time served the purpose of minimizing the extent to which the rest of the world contributed to its formation. Because, since the Enlightenment, the West has come to see itself as virtually the exclusive source and harbinger of the great humanitarian values, the existence of National Socialism at its heart called this whole self-image into question. Arendt's *Origins* addresses this question, but before reading it in this light, I should say a little more about the critique of the West on the part of certain Black philosophers, as they pose the question most forcefully.[3]

When, in 1950, Aimé Césaire questioned whether Western civilization was worthy of the name, he specifically highlighted the role that colonization had played in reducing it to barbarism. He maintained that colonization had worked to decivilize the colonizers and that the encouragement of racial pride had led Europe to savagery.[4] He argued

> that no one colonizes innocently, that no one colonizes with impunity either; that a nation which colonizes, that a civilization which justifies colonization—and therefore force—is already a sick civilization, a civilization that is normally diseased, that irresistibly, progressing from one consequence to another, one denial to another, calls for its Hitler, I mean its punishment.[5]

According to Césaire, what was unacceptable to Whites was that Hitler had applied Europe's colonialist procedures against Whites. Europe's moral indifference to the suffering of the colonized had come back to haunt them. Césaire proposed a clinical study to show that the humanistic, Christian, bourgeois European of the twentieth century has a Hitler inside of him.[6] Frantz Fanon developed this perspective in *Black Skin, White Masks* in 1952 when he argued that Whites, by focusing on the racism of a few select individuals, had found a way of ignoring the fact that Europe had a racist structure.[7] Nazism had revealed "a colonial system in the very heart of Europe."[8] When Fanon claimed that some of the most qualified representatives of European civilization were responsible for colonial racism,[9] the argument was directed against the upper level administrators in the so-called mother country, but the same issue can be raised against its most celebrated thinkers, like Kant, on whom I shall focus later. I highlight Kant, not because I believe that he should be considered the decisive figure in accounts of the prehistory of totalitarianism, but because he is widely considered as the personification of the dignity of the Western philosophical tradition, and, as I shall show, that is what is at stake in *Origins*.

However, Césaire and Fanon were not the first to launch this critique. Already in 1947, W. E. B. Du Bois asserted:

> There was no Nazi atrocity—concentration camps, wholesale maiming and murder, defilement of women or ghastly blasphemy of childhood—which the Christian civilization of Europe had not long been practicing against colored folk in all parts of the world in the name of and for the defense of a Superior Race born to rule the world.[10]

In the same year C. L. R. James insisted that the West had something to answer for, something that compromised its self-image as the primary agent of historical progress. He wrote with reference to Nazi Germany and Stalinist Russia that,

"Only a shallow empiricism can fail to see that such monstrous societies are not the product of a national peculiarity (the German character) or a system of government ('communism') but are part and parcel of our civilization."[11]

Although James regarded Arendt's *Origins* as weak in its understanding of the economic basis of society, he regarded it as "incomparably the best that has appeared in the post-war world" on account of "her knowledge and insight into the totalitarian monsters *and their relation to modern society.*"[12] The phrase italicized by James himself seems to suggest that he saw Arendt as one of the few European philosophers willing to address the connection between imperialism and National Socialism. In any event, whether or not this is the precise reason for James's admiration for Arendt's book, it makes an appropriate point of entry for re-examining her treatment of their relation and for posing the question: is twentieth-century totalitarianism an anomaly, or does it tell us something decisive about the Western philosophical tradition?

Arendt's *Origins* is an indispensable study on the implications of the Nazi crimes for our understanding of the Western philosophical tradition, but it is nevertheless flawed. Her starting point is that with totalitarianism "[t]he subterranean stream of Western history has finally come to the surface and usurped the dignity of our tradition."[13] She was even more direct in a letter to Karl Jaspers: "I have a suspicion that philosophy is not completely innocent in this business. Not of course in the sense that Hitler had anything to do with Plato. (I have after all not taken such trouble to disentangle the elements of totalitarian forms of governments in order to purify of all such suspicion the Western tradition from Plato to Nietzsche inclusive)."[14] However, one should not imagine that Arendt thought that one could separate what was good from what was bad in the Western philosophical tradition in the way an analytical philosopher might do it, that is to say, by renouncing ideas no longer welcome on the grounds that there is no necessary connection between these ideas and the ideas one wants to retain. Arendt renounced this procedure in the Preface to the First Edition: "we can no longer afford to take that which was good in the past and simply call it our heritage, to discard the bad and simply think of it as a dead load which by itself time will bury in oblivion."[15]

Nevertheless, Arendt's acknowledgment that a "subterranean stream of Western history" has "usurped the dignity of our tradition" seems to suggest that she still hopes that, by acknowledging the subterranean stream, she can restore something of the proper dignity of the tradition. The obvious question then becomes: how deep does this subterranean stream run? If, as the Black philosophers I cited at the beginning of the essay suggested, the cruelty of National Socialism was prepared for by the cruelties of imperialism, then, given the widespread enthusiasm for imperialism among most European countries and also the United States of America, it is hard to argue persuasively that what was revealed in National Socialism does not tell us something important about the West that Westerners had not previously recognized as clearly as they should have done.[16]

Arendt certainly saw a strong connection between imperialism and totalitarianism, but although she presented evidence for that connection, she never stated unambiguously how she understood it. This has presented difficulties for even some of her best commentators when they come to restate her thesis.[17] The difficulties extend even to the second title of the book *Origins* as she herself conceded. She did not attempt to supply an answer to the question of totalitarianism's origins: she intended to provide only "a historical account of the elements which crystallized into totalitarianism."[18] That is to say, she did not set out to write a history of totalitarianism, but to identify certain important elements. Is the image she is suggesting one of chemical elements that are controllable in isolation but dangerous in combination? Or is she, for example, saying that these were weapons available to the Nazis that were not so threatening in other hands? In any event, even though it is possible to list the elements identified by Arendt—anti-Semitism, decay of the nation state, racism, expansion for expansion's sake, and the alliance between capital and mob—the process of crystallization is left unclear.[19] Furthermore, her decision late in the day to incorporate Stalinism into her analysis, alongside National Socialism, undoubtedly caused further confusion because she made nothing like the same effort to examine its historical basis.

The fact of the matter is that, even though Arendt explicitly raises the question of the Western tradition's involvement in totalitarianism, both publicly in the Preface and privately in her 1951 letter to Jaspers, she never directly addresses the question in the book. Perhaps the enormity of the stakes made it hard for her to do so. Arendt insists on the novelty of totalitarianism,[20] but she does not want to separate it totally from imperialism and other related movements of the late nineteenth century, such as racism. However, that means that she also isolates these movements of the late nineteenth century from what precedes them: imperialism is distinguished from colonialism, anti-Semitism from Jew hatred, and racism from race thinking.[21] There is an epochal account of history but no theory of epochality. However, the presentation reveals a strategy. In the light of the book's overall project, it becomes apparent that a main function of the section on imperialism is to act as a kind of buffer that separates the bulk of Western history from the Holocaust. This strategy is evident, for example, in Arendt's attempt to show that racism arose only in the late nineteenth century, and that it was distinct from the race-thinking that preceded it, even though the former had sufficient superficial similarities with the latter for its novelty and its destructiveness to be virtually invisible to contemporaries: "without this appearance of national respectability or the seeming sanction of tradition, [the new doctrine of racism] might have disclosed its utter incompatibility with all Western political and moral standards of the past."[22]

Another example of Arendt's strategy at work, this time in separating imperialism from what followed in the shape of totalitarianism, is on display when, having highlighted expansion for expansion's sake and power for power's sake as characteristic of imperialism, she insists that the totalitarian form of governments has "very little to do . . . with the game of power for power's sake."[23] Moreover, imperialism, like the tradition itself, was, in her view, an ambiguous phenomenon in which the good and bad are strangely intertwined: it is in that spirit that she declares that without imperialism and its passion for expansion "the world might never have become one,"[24] which she assumes to be a value.

At the heart of Arendt's treatment of imperialism is her identification of expansion as its central political idea. She also highlights the inherent insanity of the project insofar as the project of indefinite expansion ultimately contradicts the human condition and the limitations of the globe precisely as a globe.[25] This helps to explain why she puts such weight on Cecil Rhodes's desire to annex the planets, even if it meant distorting the evidence available to her. "'Expansion is everything,' said Cecil Rhodes, and fell into despair, for every night he saw overhead 'these stars . . . these vast worlds which we can never reach. I would annex the planets if I could.'"[26] Sarah Gertrude Mullin, whom Arendt cites as her source for this comment, had found the passage about the stars in W. T. Stead's memoir, but she dismisses the idea that Rhodes said any such thing.[27] Arendt gives no explanation why she overrules Mullin's judgment, particularly as she does not appear to have consulted Stead's text. Worse still, neither Mullin, nor Stead, attribute to Rhodes the phrase: "Expansion is everything."[28]

To be sure, there is no doubting Rhodes's enthusiasm for the idea of expansion. Arendt is not wrong to attribute the idea to Rhodes, even if she apparently has no basis for attributing the specific phrase to him. She is also right to present it as a core idea of imperialism. However, the formulation is intriguing because it is a direct play on a familiar expression within late nineteenth century England, "race is everything." Benjamin Disraeli, in 1847, had Sidonia, a character in his novel, *Tancred*, say "All is race; there is no other truth."[29] Disraeli repeated the formulation in a number of contexts over the next few years including his biography of Lord George Bentinck. Arendt appropriately pays a great deal of attention in her discussion of imperialism to Disraeli, but even though she repeatedly cites *Lord George Bentinck* she never quotes the statement found there that "All is race."[30] Nevertheless, there is a certain displacement at work in the use of the phrase. An expression that was current throughout the second half of the nineteenth century was "Race is everything." Robert Knox had repeated it some five times in *The Races of Men*.[31] Furthermore the phrase was repeated with specific reference to Disraeli and the Jews by no less a figure than Houston Stewart Chamberlain in 1899 in another book Arendt cited, *Foundations of the Nineteenth Century*.[32] Because some scholars still turn to her discussion of race, the complaint that Arendt minimized the role of race, and often misunderstood that role when she did address it, may seem an implausible one, and yet this is precisely what I will argue here. Familiarity with the sources Arendt employed shows this, as does her neglect of the widespread idea "race is everything" in favor of the significant, but perhaps less fundamental notion, "expansion is everything."

Arendt's attempt to separate what she regards as problematic from the mainstream of Western thought is nowhere more in evidence than in her argument that, although race-thinking had its roots in Germany in the eighteenth century, it was only at the end of the nineteenth century that it was accorded "dignity and importance . . . as though it had been one of the major spiritual contributions of the Western world."[33] At this point Arendt cites Eric Voegelin's *Rasse und Staat* as her source. She praises this book as "the best historical account of race-thinking in the pattern of a 'history of ideas.'"[34] However, when one consults Voegelin's *The History of the Race Idea From Ray to Carus*, which much better fits that description and which is also included in Arendt's bibliography, one gets a very different impression of the development of the notion than one finds in Arendt. Voegelin clearly states that, "Kant offered the first systematic justification for the use of the word *race* in connection with the description of man."[35] When Voegelin wrote this in 1933, it would not have been news. Before the Second World War, Kant's role in the development and spread of the idea of race was widely known. It was only after the war that the veil of silence fell on this aspect of Kant's thought. To be sure, Voegelin focuses only on Kant's idea of race and not his racism, but one wonders why Arendt, when she was in the course of investigating the question of the elements that crystallized into totalitarianism, did not follow this trail, unless she had already decided on her conclusion.

It seems that, like many philosophers since, Arendt was determined to protect Kant's reputation, instead of asking if some of the best representatives of the Western philosophical tradition were not responsible for the spread of racism. Kant's opposition to race-mixing, which extended to praising attempts to outlaw it, is a remote forerunner of the ideas that established the structures of apartheid and segregation.[36] Kant was not the first to oppose race-mixing, but he was the first to develop a specific idea of race that focused specifically on race-mixing. More precisely, he was the first to argue that the possibility of fruitful sexual unions between two different types, where the skin color of the offspring was midway between that of the two parents, defined those types as races.[37] If one also takes into consideration Kant's failure to condemn chattel slavery, in spite of the fact that it was one of the leading moral issues of the day, then one cannot look to Kant for evidence of the dignity of the Western tradition.

Furthermore, Arendt, like many post-Holocaust historians, neglects the fact that important nineteenth century thinkers, like Ernst Haeckel and Houston Stewart Chamberlain, were aware of how Kant prepared the way for them.[38] Arendt references both of them and highlights Ernst Haeckel's proposal that mercy-killing would save both families and states from wasting their money on the incurable.[39] To be sure, ever since Arthur Lovejoy's essay in the *Popular Science Monthly* for January 1911, there has been no excuse for not recognizing the gulf separating Kant from Darwin that seems to have been largely invisible to many Germans on their first acquaintance with Darwinism in the late nineteenth century.[40] However, there is also no denying Kant's role in preparing the way for a eugenics based on ideas of racial purity. For example, Fritz Lenz concludes his 1923 study of intellectual inheritance by citing "the Nordic thinker" Kant's statement in the *Anthropology* that "the inborn character is formed by the mingling of the blood in man, and the acquired and artificial character is only the outcome thereof." In subsequent editions Lenz adds a plea for eugenics at this point.[41]

Arendt might also be criticized for devoting little more than three pages to Social Darwinism.[42] Arguably this movement provided the indispensable background to many of the genocides of the twentieth century, and not just the Holocaust. But what makes her relative neglect of Social Darwinism so significant is that this was a widespread movement that dominated the intellectual climate of the Western world and had a deep impact not only on the theorists of imperialism, but also on its practitioners. It therefore belies Arendt's attempt to downplay any purported claims about the "immanent logic" of ideas creating thereby "an abyss" between, on the one hand, "the men of brilliant and facile conceptions" and, on the other, "men of brutal deeds and active bestiality."[43] Her point is that no intellectual explanation can bridge that abyss.[44] However, Rhodes, whose speeches reveal that his positions on race are anything but extreme compared with those of his contemporaries,[45] adopted a form of Social Darwinism that employed the doctrine of perfection as a basis from which to advocate the elimination of the unfit.[46] An even more important example is Carl Peters, whom Arendt sees as a wild murderer and a possible model for Conrad's Kurtz,[47] but who was also a philosopher by training, strongly influenced by Darwinism.[48] It was not just the few who bridged the abyss. Arendt herself quotes one of her sources as acknowledging the role of Darwinism in the formation of South Africa.[49] But that understates it. A culture insensitive to genocide had been created.[50]

I have made the point that Arendt does not state her thesis clearly, but the fact of the matter is that as soon as one abandons the notion that the only legitimate connections between ideas are analytic connections, a notion useless to the historian because analytic connections do not go much further than allowing us to see a relation between unmarried men and bachelors, one has moved into a world of speculation. It is a strength of Arendt's approach that, when she is not guided by her longing to save the Western tradition, she finds ways of showing connections, where others only see oppositions. (In another intellectual climate one might call these connections dialectical.) One too readily thinks of the Enlightenment as opposed to racism without thinking of how they might be connected. Arendt herself at one point acknowledges the intimacy of the idea of humanity with racism: "Ever since the European peoples made practical attempts to include all the peoples of the earth in their conception of humanity, they have been irritated by the great physical differences between themselves and the peoples they found on other continents."[51] Nothing more is said and for the most part Arendt continues with her strategy of considering the conception of humanity as the authentic Western idea and racism as anomalous. However, at least here there is a willingness on her part to look for a reason that the idea of cosmopolitanism and the scientific idea of race arose at the same time and often in the same thinkers.

Arendt claims that the term "race" "has a precise meaning only when and where peoples are confronted with such tribes of which they have no historical records and which do not know any history of their own."[52] This clear revival of Hegel's description of Africa as outside history only serves to underline the philosophical heritage of this idea and its philosophical currency prior to the period she describes as the period of racism. To be sure, as Arendt points out, there is a gulf separating Hegel's philosophy of history from the philosophies of history of Gobineau, Disraeli, and Spengler,[53] but Arendt's claim is that Hegel was "never interested in the rise and fall of cultures as such or in any law which would explain the death of nations."[54] However, the fact is that race is a decisive category for Hegel's philosophy of history; he has many important things to say about the decline of civilizations, and above all he justifies the loss of peoples.[55] This should have been important to Arendt, who rightly acknowledges the significance of the idea that peoples might be sacrificed to the "supposedly superhuman laws of history."[56] One of the authors she cites as evidence of this view is the pseudonymous author, Al. Carthill, who wrote: "One must always feel sorry for those persons who are crushed by the triumphal car of progress."[57] However, nobody did more to introduce these laws into the philosophy of history than Hegel, who adopted Schiller's phrase that "world history is the world tribunal" with precisely this intent. The decisive difference between Hegel and an author like Carthill is that Hegel expressed no sorrow. It should be more widely known that Hegel issued the shocking judgment: "No people ever suffered wrong; what it suffered, it had merited."[58]

According to Arendt, "race" is "the emergency explanation of human beings no European or civilized man could understand and whose humanity so frightened and humiliated the immigrants that they no longer cared to belong to the same human species."[59] As stated, the idea is not only false but dangerously so, because in her hands this becomes a way of naturalizing the feelings of the colonizers toward the indigenous populations they encountered. Arendt arrives at that version of events based on an examination of late nineteenth century accounts of the hostility between Blacks and Whites, accounts such as Joseph Conrad's *The Heart of Darkness*. However, the historical record seems to show something very different from the version offered by Arendt, which draws more from Voltaire's speculation "how great must have been the surprise of the first Negro and the first white man who met"[60] than from actual historical records. She fails to acknowledge that most often the initial responses of the Europeans to these other races were less hostile than they later became, and that it was the propaganda of the pro-slavery lobby that helped to create the image she seeks to explain as natural.[61]

However, Arendt is not satisfied with finding the "basis" for racism in South Africa, she also explicitly identifies the "excuse" for it. She finds that excuse in "a horrifying experience of something alien beyond imagination or comprehension."[62] She is referring to the Boers and "their first horrible fright before a species of men whom human being and the sense of human dignity could not allow them to accept as fellow-men."[63] She explains that because "the black men stubbornly insisted on retaining their human features," the Boers could not use this horrifying experience to declare these aliens not to be human beings. On this basis she describes as "logical and unavoidable" their decision to consider themselves as "more than human" because they "wanted to deny radically all common bonds with savages."[64] Nevertheless, she does not ask if this idea of the "more than human" was already latent in the Western idea of the "more human" that was integral to humanism as an educational ideal.[65] One might wonder why Arendt is not satisfied with exposing "the excuse" for this form of racism, but insists on finding that "excuse" logical and unavoidable. It is tempting to think that her use of the word "excuse" as a slip of the pen. However, within eleven pages and in the very same chapter the word reappears: "there could be no excuse and no humanly comprehensible reason for treating Indians and Chinese as though they were not human beings. In a certain sense, it is only here that the real crime began, because here everyone ought to have known what he was doing."[66] These sentences sound even worse in context that they do in isolation because she issues a succession of similar remarks that suggest that crimes against those who are judged to be most different from us are more intelligible and more excusable than those against people who are judged to be less different.

To be sure, Arendt's aim was not to excuse anti-Black racism, but to highlight what she judged to be new about the racism directed against Indians and the Chinese, so as to understand better what was new about the anti-Semitism that led to the Holocaust. However, by judging crimes committed by Whites against Blacks to be excusable and intelligible, whereas similar crimes that they committed against some other races were not, and to leave it at that, Arendt failed to challenge at its root the racial hierarchy that was being propounded by those she was seeking to expose. Her failure to do so was no doubt a consequence of her commitment to offer a phenomenological description of this particular form of anti-Black racism, but her willingness to take this case on in its own terms contrasted with her approach to the racisms that Whites directed against other groups, about which she was much less critical.

Arendt's inability to be scandalized by the way Europeans treated Africans as opposed to, for example, the Chinese, is confirmed by a footnote to a discussion of the German response to the Boxer insurrection in China, in which she cites one authority who estimated that the native population of the Congo was reduced under Leopold II's direction from 20 or even 40 million to 8,500,000 during the period 1890 to 1911.[67] One cannot help wondering how many more Africans Leopold II needed to kill to break her impression that these years were marked by moderation. Arendt is not simply engaged in presenting a phenomenology of racist sentiments, she is trying to explain the inexplicable, or, more precisely, to offer some account of how this crime came about so as to highlight what to her was inexplicable.[68] That is why she approached the anti-Black racism that took place in Africa in the way that she did. The title of the first chapter of *Origins* is: "Antisemitism as an outrage to Common Sense."[69] In a way that is truly extraordinary Arendt seems to be at pains to show that the same was not true of anti-Black racism.[70]

In this chapter I have not answered the question of the extent to which imperialism prepared for National Socialism. My concern here has been to argue that the evidence Arendt employs is inadequate for her purposes and that her use of the evidence available to her betrays a bias that throws the argument into doubt. Perhaps the worst example of the latter lies in her treatment of Charles Dilke's *Greater Britain*. Arendt cites E. H. Damce's claim that imperialism began with this book.[71] That is why it is all the more remarkable to find her including Dilke in a group whom she describes as never having been seriously concerned with "discrimination against other peoples as lower races, if only for the reason that the countries they were talking about, Canada and Australia, were almost empty and had no serious population problem."[72] However, Dilke in fact makes some extraordinary claims in the book that Arendt cites that contradict this characterization. It is hard to imagine how Arendt could not have been struck by the way that Dilke celebrates the Saxon's genius for what since 1944 we call "genocide."

> The Saxon is the only extirpating race on earth. Up to the commencement of the now inevitable destruction of the Red Indians of Central North America, of the Maories, and of the Australian by the English colonist, no numerous race had been blotted out by an invader.[73]

Dilke was well aware that North America and Australia had been populated and that the process of emptying them had been a violent one. It is extraordinary that Arendt not only missed this aspect of Dilke's promotion of Britain's "paternal despotism,"[74] but that she also underestimated the role of these genocides in preparing the way to the Holocaust. Similarly, when Arendt refers to a time before Nazism tried to turn man into a beast,[75] she seems to forget that this was a common expression in late nineteenth century and early twentieth century debates on race, even giving rise in 1900 to Charles Carroll's book *The Negro A Beast*.

I have focused here on Arendt's insistence on separating the Western philosophical tradition from the Nazi horrors. I have not challenged her claim about the novelty of totalitarianism as a form of government,[76] but concentrated instead on her account of the relation of imperialism to what took place in Europe under the National Socialists. I grant that Arendt saw more clearly than most Europeans the way in which imperialism was a forerunner of totalitarianism. Yet, Arendt's use of the ideas of imperialism and race in an effort to understand National Socialism had already been anticipated by Franz Neumann in *Behemoth*, a book first published in 1942. Neumann had recognized Germany's expansion as the central issue, but he also understood that issue through the lens of race. For this reason he subsumed National Socialism under the label of "a racial proletarian imperialism."[77] Admittedly, Neumann had relatively little to say about race, under the circumstances, but the fact that Arendt had initially adopted the phrase "race-imperialism" to describe what she only later called totalitarianism indicates that her approach is less novel than some readers today imagine.[78] Nevertheless, even if Arendt is relatively enlightened for a European, she simply does not show sufficient sensitivity to the suffering of Blacks and that, more than any arguments or historical details, seems to account for the very different assessments given by her, on the one hand, and by Du Bois, Césaire, and Fanon, on the other. To confirm this one can point to the very first paragraph of the section on Imperialism. Arendt begins by acknowledging that the fundamental aspects of the period of imperialism "appear so close to totalitarian phenomena of the twentieth century that it may be justifiable to consider the whole period a preparatory stage for coming catastrophes."[79] However, in the next sentence Arendt refers to "the quiet" of the imperial period and then acknowledges "a certain nostalgia . . . for an age . . . when even horrors were still marked by a certain moderation and controlled by respectability, and therefore could be related to the general appearance of sanity."[80] Every acknowledgement of the crimes of imperialism seems to be qualified by the sentiment that this was not where the real crimes began.

Arendt writes that race thinking gave to the new doctrine of racism "a certain tradition [that] served to hide the destructive forces of the new doctrine which, without this appearance of national respectability or the seeming sanction of tradition, might have disclosed its utter incompatibility with all Western political and moral standards of the past, even before it was allowed to destroy the comity of European nations."[81] But this argument presupposes that race thinking can be isolated as anomalous. Because Kant is central to that tradition, along with Locke, Hume, and Hegel, to mention only a few, this judgment is impossible to sustain. In this way the argument is fundamentally flawed. Her claim that racism—even extreme forms of racism—are utterly incompatible with "*all* Western political and moral standards of the past" is pure ideology as Arendt herself understands the term: an explanatory idea about history that is presented as a conclusion but which actually functions as a premise.[82]

Notes

1. Léon Poliakov, *The Aryan Myth* (New York, 1996) and George L. Mosse, *The Crisis of German Ideology* (New York, 1964).
2. Georg Lukacs, *The Destruction of Reason*, trans. Peter Palmer (Atlantic Highlands, 1981). One should also refer to the writings of Theodor Adorno, although he showed very little interest in the history of colonialism and imperialism, which is my focus here.
3. Richard H. King has already located Arendt's The *Origins of Totalitarianism* in this same context, and I believe that it is important to repeat it, expand on it, and reflect on it further. I trust that my understanding of Arendt's book is significantly different from his to warrant returning to the same issues. *Race, Culture, and the Intellectuals 1940–1970* (Baltimore and Washington, D.C, 2004).
4. Aimé Césaire, *Discours sur le colonialisme* (Paris, 1950), 14; trans. Joan Pinkham, *Discourse on Colonialism* (New York, 1972), 13.
5. Césaire, *Discours*, 16–17; trans. *Discourse*, 18.
6. Césaire, *Discours*, 12–13; trans. *Discourse*, 14.
7. Frantz Fanon, *Peau noire, masques blancs* (Paris, 1952), 72; trans. Charles Lam Markmann, *Black Skin, White Masks* (New York, 1967), 92.
8. *Peau noire*, 40; trans. *Black Skin*, 33.
9. *Peau noire*, 72; trans. *Black Skin*, 90.
10. W. E. B. DuBois, *The World and Africa* (New York, 1947), 23.
11. C. L. R. James, "Dialectical Materialism and the Fate of Humanity," *Spheres of Existence* (London, 1980), 70.
12. C. L. R. James, "Books to Read," *Modern Politics* (Detroit, 1973), 157.
13. Hannah Arendt, *The Origins of Totalitarianism* (San Diego, 1976), ix.

14. Hannah Arendt to Karl Jaspers, 4 March 1951, *Briefwechsel 1926–1969*, ed. Lotte Köhler and Hans Saner (Munich, 1985), 203. I have corrected the translation by Robert and Rita Kimber, *Correspondence 1926–1969* (New York, 1992), 166. I have not addressed Nietzsche in this essay, but it should be noted that his reputation has been enhanced since Arendt wrote her study, and philosophers have for the most part been remarkably unconcerned with the question of the impact of his works on National Socialism. The rejected idea that there is a suggestion between Plato and Hitler might be a reference to Karl Popper's *The Open Society and Its Enemies*, which was first published in 1945. It should also be mentioned that in an earlier version of the argument Arendt cited Karl Jaspers himself as showing that Nietzsche was not the spiritual father of the "master-race" in his *Nietzsche* (1938). See her "Race-Thinking Before Racism," *Review of Politics* 6, no. 1 (1946): 41.

15. Arendt, *Origins*, ix.

16. Recently Sankar Muthu has argued that certain prominent Enlightenment thinkers were against imperialism. There is some basis for this claim, although it can be argued—and Arendt would—that imperialism arose only a century later and that they were opposing a very different process. However, Muthu's book on occasion abandons all pretense of scholarship and becomes pure ideology. For example, the suggestion in the course of two sentences that Kant did not believe in the preeminence of Whites and that Christoph Girtenner's (sic) *Über das Kantische Prinzip für die Naturgeschichte* is largely confined to nonhuman species shows a surprising ignorance of sources the author claims to have read. Sankar Muthu, *Enlightenment Against Empire* (Princeton, 2005), 184.

17. See the valuable discussion by Seyla Benhabib, *The Reluctant Modernism of Hannah Arendt* (Thousand Oaks, 1996), 62–75.

18. Hannah Arendt, *Essays in Understanding 1930–1954* (New York, 1993), 403.

19. Margaret Canovan provides this list of elements from one of Arendt's manuscripts. See *Hannah Arendt* (Cambridge, U.K., 1992), 28–29.

20. Arendt, *Origins*, 460.

21. Arendt's distinction between race-thinking and racism has been given a new lease on life because of the parallel periodization in Michel Foucault's *Society Must Be Defended* (New York, 2003), 258. For that reason it should be noted that the term "race-thinking" is far too neutral a formulation, as is particularly clear when one contrasts it with the parallel term "Jew-hatred."

22. Arendt, *Origins*, 184.

23. Ibid., 407.

24. Ibid., viii.

25. Ibid., 124 and 144.

26. Ibid., 124.

27. Sarah Gertrude Mullin, *Rhodes* (London, 1933), 138. See already Hannah Arendt, "Imperialism, Nationalism, Chauvinism," *Review of Politics* 7, no. 4 (1945): 44.

28. W. T. Stead, *The Last Will and Testament of Cecil John Rhodes* (London, 1902), 190.

29. Benjamin Disraeli, *Tancred: or, The New Crusade* (London, 1850), 303.

30. Benjamin Disraeli, *Lord George Bentinck* (London, 1852), 331.

31. Robert Knox, *The Races of Men* (London, 1850), v, 2, 6, 8, and 131.

32. Houston Stewart Chamberlain, *Die Grundlagen des neunzehnten Jahrhunderts*, vol.1 (Munich, 1899), 274n; trans. John Lees, *Foundations of the Nineteenth Century*, vol. 1 (London, 1913), 271n. Arendt cites the translation, not the original, where Disraeli is misquoted as saying, "Race is everything."

33. Arendt, *Origins*, 158.

34. Ibid., 158n.

35. Eric Voegelin, *The History of the Race Idea from Ray to Carus* (Baton Rouge, 1998), 75. I have summarized the arguments for this claim in "Who Invented the Concept of Race?" in *Race*, ed. Robert Bernasconi (Oxford, 2001), 11-36.

36. See, for example, Immanuel Kant, *Anthropologie im pragmatischer Hinsicht*, Akademie Textausgabe (Berlin, 1968), vii, 320; trans. Victor Lyle Dowdell, *Anthropology from a Pragmatic Standpoint* (Car-

bondale, 1996), 236. See also Robert Bernasconi, "Kant as an Unfamiliar Source of Racism," in *Philosophers on Race*, ed. Julie K. Ward and Tommy L. Lott (Oxford, 2002), 145–166. I explore the distance between Kant's conception and later ideas in "General Introduction," *Race, Hybridity, and Miscegenation*, vol. I (Bristol, 2005), vii–xi. Arendt was well aware of the importance of ideas of race-mixing for framing the debate about what imperialism could accomplish. At *Origins*, 143 she cites Al. Carthill, *The Lost Dominion* (Edinburgh and London, 1924), 209. The full passage is even more remarkable than Arendt's brief quotation indicates.

37. Immanuel Kant, "Von den verschiedenen Racen der Menschen," in *Werke*, Akademie Textausgabe, vol. 2, 429–430; trans. Jon Mark Mikkelsen, "Of the Different Human Races," in *The Idea of Race*, ed. Robert Bernasconi and Tommy Lott (Indianapolis, 2000), 8–9.

38. See Robert Bernasconi, "Why Do the Happy Inhabitants of Tahiti Bother to Exist at All?" in *Genocide and Human Rights*, ed. John K. Roth (New York, 2005), 144–45

39. See Ernst Haeckel, *Die Lebenswunder* (Stuttgart, 1904), 135; trans. Joseph McCabe, *The Wonders of Life* (New York, 1905), 119. Cited in Arendt, *Origins*, 179. As an indication of what one might make of Haeckel on this issue, see Daniel Gosman, *The Scientific Origins of National Socialism* (London, 1971), 82–105.

40. Arthur O. Lovejoy, "Kant and Evolution," *Popular Science Monthly* 78 (January 1911), 36–51. Reprinted in *Forerunners of Darwin*, ed. Bentley Glass, et al. (Baltimore, 1959), 173–206.

41. Erwin Baur, Eugen Fischer, and Fritz Lenz, *Menschliche Erblichkeitslehre und Rassenhygiene* (Munich, 1923), 433. The passage in the 1927 edition from the same publishers is found on page 583; trans. Eden and Cedar Paul, *Human Heredity* (London, 1931), 699.

42. Arendt, *Origins*, 178–79, 463.

43. Ibid., 183.

44. Canovan highlights that issue in *Hannah Arendt*, 36–37. This same sense of an abyss in theory that is bridged in practice reappears at *Origins*, 153.

45. Vindex, *Cecil Rhodes. His Political Life and Speeches* (London, 1900), 371–390.

46. W. T. Stead, *Last Will and Testament*, 95.

47. Arendt, *Origins*, 185, 189.

48. Arne Perras, *Carl Peters and German Imperialism 1856–1918* (Oxford, 2004), 25–30.

49. C. W. de Kiewiet, *A History of South Africa* (Oxford, 1941), 181. Quoted in *Origins*, 195.

50. Bernasconi, "Why do the Happy Inhabitants of Tahiti Bother to Exist at All?" 139–148.

51. Arendt, *Origins*, 176.

52. Ibid., 192.

53. Ibid., 171.

54. Ibid.,171.

55. Robert Bernasconi, "With What Must the Philosophy of World History Begin?" *Nineteenth Century Contexts* 22, no. 2 (2000): 178–201.

56. Arendt, *Origins*, 143.

57. Al. Carthill, *Lost Dominion* (Edinburgh, 1924): 209. Cited by Arendt in *Origins*, 143.

58. G. W. F. Hegel, *Vorlesungen über Naturrecht und Staatswissenschaft* (Hamburg, 1983), 257; trans. J. Michael Stewart and Peter C. Hodgson, *Lectures on Natural Right and Political Science* (Berkeley, 1995), 307. It should be emphasized that this text was not published in Arendt's lifetime, but the general attitude is already clear from the *Philosophy of Right.*

59. Arendt, *Origins*, 185.

60. Quoted by Arendt in *Origins*, 176.

61. There seems to be no escaping the fact that Arendt's discussion of Africa is not based on the same level of research that is on display in the first part of the book. She relies heavily in the chapter "Race and Bureaucracy" in C. W. de Kiewiet's *A History of South Africa* and Selwyn James's journalistic account in *South of the Congo.*

62. Arendt, *Origins*, 195.

63. Ibid., 192.

64. Ibid., 195.

65. The original sense of *humanitas* in Varro and Cicero was as an equivalent of *paideia* or education. This meant not only that not all human beings share equally in *humanitas*, but that some have more *humanitas* than others, and some are *maximi humanissimi*, more highly humanized. Aulus Gellius, *The Attic Nights*, 2, Book 13, xvii,; trans. John C. Rolfe (London, 1948), 456–457.

66. Arendt, *Origins*, 206.

67. Arendt, *Origins*, 185.

68. George Kateb was among the first to highlight these pages as "upsetting to an unusual degree," but his description of her approach as one of "empathetic imagination" has in my view been rightly criticized by Gail Presbey and, particularly, by Anne Norton as offering some kind of justification of the horror expressed by the imperialists. I find Seyla Benhabib's reversion to Kateb's position unpersuasive. It is noteworthy that in her attack on Norton she does not address the main issues. George Kateb, *Hannah Arendt: Politics, Conscience, Evil* (Totowa, 1984), 60–63; Gail Presbey, "Critic of Boers or Africans: Arendt's Treatment of South Africa in *The Origins of Totalitarianism*," in *Postcolonial African Philosophy*, ed. Emmanuel Chukwudi Eze (Oxford, 1997), 172; Anne Norton, "Heart of Darkness: Africa and African Americans in the Writings of Hannah Arendt," in *Feminist Interpretations of Hannah Arendt*, ed. Bonnie Honig (University Park, PA, 1995), 252–256; and Benhabib, *Reluctant Modernism*, 83–86. See also King, *Race, Culture, and the Intellectuals*, 115–118.

69. Arendt, *Origins*, 3.

70. Arendt's focus on South Africa in *Origins* is entirely laudable because she is clearly attentive to events in South Africa that took place when she was writing (*Origins*, 195n), but one is puzzled at her blindness to the history and continuing reality of the United States. That blindness continued through the Civil Rights Era and is revealed in her response to the events at Little Rock and her account of slavery in the American Revolution in *On Revolution*. See Robert Bernasconi, "The Double Face of the Political and the Social: Hannah Arendt and America's Racial Divisions," *Research in Phenomenology* 26 (1996): 3–24.

71. Arendt, *Origins*, 181n.

72. Ibid., 182.

73. Charles Wentworth Dilke, *Greater Britain: A Reward of Travel in English-speaking Countries during 1866 and 1867*, I (London, 1869), 308–309.

74. Ibid., vii.

75. Arendt, *Origins*, 179.

76. Ibid., 461.

77. Franz Neumann, *Behemoth: The Structure and Practice of National Socialism 1933–1944* (New York, 1942), 187.

78. Elisabeth Young-Bruehl, *Hannah Arendt: For Love of the World* (New Haven, 1982), 203.

79. Arendt, *Origins*, 123.

80. Ibid., 123.

81. Ibid., 184.

82. Ibid., 469.

Chapter 4

RACE AND BUREAUCRACY REVISITED
Hannah Arendt's Recent Reemergence in African Studies

Christopher J. Lee

In October 1904, an extermination order was issued by General Lothar von Trotha in the sparsely colonized territory of German Southwest Africa (contemporary Namibia). As a consequence of an anti-colonial uprising that had broken out in early January of that year, members of the Herero community were to be shot on sight, with those escaping direct execution to be driven into the Omaheke Desert where they would be left to die from exposure. This policy did not exclude women or children. In short, this order sought in explicit terms to eliminate the Herero people and thus end a conflict that had persisted in various forms since Germany first declared its imperial intentions over the region in 1884. The brutality of this policy was underscored by the fact that it was issued *after* the Herero had been defeated militarily in the Battle of the Waterberg. An estimated 60,000–70,000 Herero people, out of a total of approximately 80,000, were eventually killed. Many died from starvation in the Omaheke after being separated from their cattle and sources of water. The level of German oppression was such that it sparked a second anti-colonial revolt by the Nama with parallel results. By 1908, roughly half of the Nama community had died as well.[1]

These episodes of violence during the first decades of Africa's modern colonization would not be as widely noted or even necessarily remarkable were it not for the implementation of similar genocidal policies by the Nazi government in Central and Eastern Europe approximately four decades later. Indeed, violence was a ubiquitous aspect of colonization throughout the continent, witnessed in conflicts ranging from the Battle of Blood River in South Africa (1838), the Battle of Adowa in Ethiopia (1896), the First Chimurenga in Southern Rhodesia (1896–7), and the Maji Maji Rebellion in Tanganyika (1905–6), in addition to undocumented incidents of everyday violence against African colonial subjects. When the momentum of decolonization took hold during the post-Second World War period, violence again emerged as a predominant theme, most vividly in the Mau Mau Revolt of late colonial Kenya (1952–60) and the Algerian Revolution (1954–62), with intellectuals such as Frantz Fanon arguing forcefully for general recognition of this intrinsic aspect of colonialism. Still, the events in German Southwest Africa have acquired particular notoriety for their explicit genocidal nature. Not until 1994 and the genocide in Rwanda would the expression reappear.[2]

Following Hannah Arendt's lead regarding the role of imperialism in setting the stage for the rise of European totalitarianism, the genocidal policies against the Herero and Nama have since been identified as significant precursors to the perspectives and attitudes that produced the Holocaust. However, unlike this later tragedy, colonial officials expended little effort before, during, and after to conceal their orchestrated nature. Consequently these events make transparent the types of conditions and rationales that enable the very possibility of genocidal behavior on the part of states and individuals alike. As Arendt perceived, the institutions and ideologies of imperialism were key elements for rethinking local genocidal violence as well as the colonial roots of European totalitarianism, thus suggesting the circular impact of ideas and practices between metropole and colony. Overall, these interactive elements of ideology and institutional behavior constituted a broad spectrum for examining state violence over and above individual spectacles of genocide, and they have accordingly demanded wide examination by scholars.[3]

With these general observations in mind, this essay is concerned with the unexamined impact Hannah Arendt has had on scholarship in African studies—particularly on debates over modern bureaucratic state formation and the relationship of such developments to the origins of colonial and post-colonial violence—as reflected by recent work in the field.[4] This essay specifically draws from Chapter Seven of *The Origins of Totalitarianism* (1951) entitled "Race and Bureaucracy" and its importance as a template for rethinking the aforementioned issues and, more generally, the nature of state power in Africa. Particular attention is directed to her discussion of the dialogue between racial ideologies and bureaucratic institutions as a central aspect of rule, in addition to her broader argument that colonies provided "fertile soil" for the growth of ideas that informed later policies of genocide in Europe. As a whole, the trajectory of Arendt's career was such that Africa and its history did not fundamentally shape her philosophical outlook. Her work has similarly faced widespread neglect among scholars of Africa. Nevertheless, her groundbreaking exploration of the connections between race and modern state power and her provocative attempt to place colonial states and sovereign nation-state forms of government within a single framework remain remarkable, prefiguring contemporary discussions on the continuities and breaks—in the realms of economy, culture, and political institutions—between Europe and its overseas possessions during the period of modern imperialism. This essay therefore explores the main facets of this emergent legacy to argue for her under-recognized place and significance within the intellectual history of post-colonial studies generally.[5]

"Race and Bureaucracy" in Retrospect:
Arendt and the Politics of Imperial State Formation in Africa

Though often linked with Arendt's ideas on the connections between imperialism and totalitarianism, it is important to note at the outset that the events of German Southwest Africa are unmentioned in her three-part study. German Southeast Africa—contemporary Tanzania—is discussed in passing, particularly through the case of Carl Peters, a late nineteenth century explorer, entrepreneur, and colonial administrator. For Arendt, Peters illustrates the sense of disconnect and antagonism felt at times between the German government and colonial administrators, and his example highlights Germany's presence on a spectrum of colonial violence that included the "extermination of Hottentot tribes" in South Africa and the "decimation of the peaceful Congo population" in central Africa through the labor policies of King Leopold of Belgium.[6] Recognizing colonial violence as commonplace, she underscores the ramifications of such events, writing at one point, in an oft-cited passage, that "African colonial possessions became the most fertile soil for the flowering of what later was to become the Nazi elite." In Africa, Europeans "had seen with their own eyes how peoples could be converted into races and how, simply by taking the initiative in this process, one might push one's own people into the position of the master race."[7] Even so, what is initially striking about her work is its disengagement from these widely-discussed examples of genocide that have so often been associated with Germany's colonial experience in Africa and her understanding of the preconditions for the rise of totalitarian state power.

This initial observation and correction point to the compelling and frustrating aspects of *Origins*. On the one hand, her general attempt at locating the rise of "totalitarianism"—a new form of absolute state power embodied in the Nazi and Stalin regimes—within an expansive global geography inclusive of colonial Africa has been highly suggestive. It prefigured contemporary research that has sought to readdress the mutually constitutive relationship between Europe and its colonies and marks the originality of her perspective. On the other hand, her empirical gaps and causal imprecision—the latter largely informed by a philosophical aversion to any form of historical determinism—has complicated, for historians at least, her exact point of view on the connections between anti-Semitism, imperialism, and state forms such as totalitarianism, even if it is agreed that direct connections may be tenuous. Indeed, it is important to emphasize, for example, that British imperialism, not German, was her primary focus.

Causality as such has therefore been a much-discussed and debated aspect of Arendt's work. Such issues do not necessarily undermine the import of her study, however. Even if contemporary critics find fault with her in retrospect for these lacunae, what has been of value is her delineation of the conditions for such historical trends, rather than a narrowly conceived explanation of events themselves. This section is concerned with these conditions. Two were central.[8]

In the beginning of "Race and Bureaucracy," Arendt puts forth the argument that two fundamental innovations were cultivated during the rise of modern imperialism: the first was "race as a principle of the body politic"; the second was "bureaucracy as a principle of foreign domination."[9] She locates the development of these two aspects—ideological and institutional, respectively—to experiences in Africa during the nineteenth century, the former principle to South Africa and the latter to Algeria and Egypt.[10] Arendt elaborates the origins of these two characteristics as reflective of separate conditions—"they were discovered and developed independently"—with racism in the settler colony of South Africa being oriented around white fear, "the barely conscious reaction to tribes of whose humanity European man was ashamed and frightened."[11] Bureaucratic state measures, on the other hand, were the result of more benevolent motives—if nonetheless still imbued with power—intended for colonial subjects who were perceived by European administrators as "hopelessly their inferiors and at the same time in need of their special protection."[12] Such "exaggerated sense of responsibility" was, in her perspective, an effect of the British Empire being acquired in a "fit of absent-mindedness." A more thoroughgoing rationale was subsequently needed to supplant this sense of surreptitious rule, to transform "the accident" of imperialism into "a kind of willed act."[13]

Race and bureaucracy consequently formed twin poles of a tense relationship between humanitarian principle and transparent racial difference and oppression that characterized overseas imperialism. Their coexistence possessed a complex irony that was not lost on Arendt: "Race, in other words, was an escape into an irresponsibility where nothing human could any longer exist, and bureaucracy was the result of a responsibility that no man can bear for his fellowman and no people for another people."[14] The irreconcilable tensions of humane and inhumane impulses implicit between the two were mitigated in the abstract by differences in location. "Race societies" with their glaring forms of discrimination occurred in settler colonies like South Africa, whereas benevolent bureaucracies developed in nonsettler contexts such as Egypt. In practice, the distinctions between the two were frequently blurred, with issues of race and bureaucracy cohabiting the same territory. Whether a colonial state was more oppressive or more "benevolent" was a matter of degree, not a static institutional condition or hermetic racial outlook. Indeed, as Arendt suggests, these two contrasting perspectives of race and bureaucracy, despite their ostensible moral distance, appeared as mutually reinforcing. In its effort to provide and "civilize," colonial bureaucracy itself gave institutional form to ideological notions of racial difference.

With these two elements as a backdrop, Arendt's analysis advances further questions regarding the necessary conditions for producing such aspects of governance and what exactly to call the state established. In her view, the marriage between race and bureaucracy overseas created a "hybrid form of government," an expression borrowed from Lord Cromer, the well-known British Consul General of Egypt from 1883 to 1907. This descriptive expression captured the peculiar state form that imperialism inaugurated, specifically the double-sided nature of local rule: its combination of contingent and absolute power—of "despotism and arbitrariness"— that reflected neither popular will nor the interests of the metropole entirely.[15]

This unique, semiautonomous situation—which, in her words, depicted "a way of life without precedent in the south, a government without precedent in the north"— was further constituted and enabled by two unelected functionaries within the system, the bureaucrat and the secret agent.[16] As a whole, identifying this state form is crucial to her general argument, moving her depiction of imperialism as "expansion for expansion's sake" away from individuals such as Cecil Rhodes to broader sets of institutional conditions and processes encompassing this ethos.[17] Such conditions were often complemented and further informed by the interests of European settler communities. It is thus important to understand the placement of these principles within a more wide-ranging analysis throughout her text regarding the provisional alliance of variegated social forces that possessed the potential for ushering in autocratic, and ultimately totalitarian, forms of rule.

Arendt uses different expressions—the masses, the mob, and the elite—to capture and define these multiple forces and their contingent role in crystallizing social movements inclined toward exclusionary political forms as circumstances dictated. Her understanding of the rise of totalitarianism is linked particularly to the role of "the mob." Such states were in effect the instruments of this social category. The mob as historical phenomenon is consequently a thread that runs throughout her text and forms a key aspect of the continuum between imperial and totalitarian states. In the first part of her study, "Anti-Semitism," Arendt defines the mob as "primarily a group in which the residue of all classes are represented," although it is important not to confuse "the mob for the people."[18] If "the people" in principle sought political representation through majority rule, the mob comprised an aberration from this aim. Accordingly it held a sense of being excluded from political representation and thus sought power through alternative means.[19] Such political behavior—at once marginal and yet reflective of ideas held across social groups—represented a breakdown of the basic principles and practices of the European nation-state and was summarily manifested in the rise of such figures as Hitler and Stalin.[20]

In the context of imperialism, the mob as social formation gains a renewed form of currency as a category that reconciled competing tensions between the interests of capital and members of the work force who became "superfluous" to the growth of modern industrial economies in the West.[21] In Arendt's interpretation, imperial expansion and the establishment of settler colonies overseas provided a vent for this "human debris" similar to surplus capital, thus helping to assuage temporarily the sets of contradictions and potential class antagonisms inherent between the two in the metropole. This situation correspondingly created provisional, mob-like alliances between elite and proletarian interests in local colonial settings. If perceived as counterintuitive from a class standpoint, such cohesion was achieved nevertheless through notions of racial difference. For Arendt, this state of affairs transpired most clearly in South Africa with the ascendance of the white community providing "the great lesson . . . that through sheer violence an underprivileged group could create a class lower than itself . . . and that foreign or backward peoples offered the best opportunities for such tactics."[22] Such political behavior oriented around race, incipient nationalism, and mob behavior combined to defer class conflict—that in principle would have crossed racial lines—and create a "race society" in its place. The idea of "race as a principle of the body politic" would later manifest itself in Europe.

Overall this interpretation contributes crucially to her attempt to move beyond earlier Marxist perspectives on imperialism that argued for economic determinism and the seeds of an international proletarian solidarity embedded therein. Indeed, Arendt questions Marxist approaches for their misguided interpretation of imperial behavior and their misplaced faith in the libratory potential of an international proletariat. As she writes:

> In Marxist terms the new phenomenon of an alliance between mob and capital seemed so unnatural, so obviously in conflict with the doctrine of class struggle, that the actual dangers of the imperialist attempt—to divide mankind into master races and slave races, into higher and lower breeds, into colored peoples and white men, all of which were attempts to unify the people on the basis of the mob—were completely overlooked. Even the breakdown of international solidarity at the outbreak of the First World War did not disturb the complacency of the socialists and their faith in the proletariat as such.[23]

The result of such oversight was a conceptual failure to recognize the importance of the "race factor" in underwriting the endurance of imperialism and that "only a few elderly gentlemen in high finance still believed in the inalienable rights of the profit rate."[24] The political consequences of such misinterpretation were, by extension, even greater.

From the perspective of area studies scholarship, Arendt's recognition of and argument for these institutional and ideological elements of imperialism set her study apart from earlier and more widely cited critiques of empire, namely economic interpretations in the vein of J. A. Hobson and V. I. Lenin.[25] Her alternative view possesses a lasting, separate value for scholars seeking to address the local institutional dynamics of imperialism. Though the expansion of foreign capital is nonetheless integral to the historical portrait she provides, it is her two-part conceptualization of imperial rule and the social criteria in its establishment that have suggested new sets of research questions, especially among scholars seeking to work within and beyond imperialism as a framework of analysis. The next section addresses this issue of applicability and the ways scholars of Africa have reimplemented and revised her ideas in the contexts of apartheid South Africa and the Rwandan genocide of 1994.[26]

"Race and Bureaucracy" Revised: Apartheid South Africa, the 1994 Rwanda Genocide, and the Reemergence of Arendt in African Studies

As discussed earlier, Arendt's work on imperialism has been relatively neglected by scholars of Africa. This predicament can be attributed primarily to disciplinary reasons. Since the foundation of the postcolonial study of Africa in the early 1960s, scholarship has tended to emphasize African perspectives and agency vis-à-vis larger processes of historical change, a turn reflective of changes in academic method and the political interests of newly independent African nation-states alike. The three-part outcome of this initial agenda has been a prevailing emphasis on African history during the precolonial period, a critical concern for the legacies of colonialism in Africa, and a concurrent realignment of imperial history as a part of European history. In sum, approaches such as Arendt's that conjoined metropole and colony into a single framework were marginalized in favor of recovering more "authentic" African histories against Eurocentric accounts that had existed previously. Although South Africa's historiography is more complex in origin and in many ways distinct from the rest of the continent's, this general agenda gained predominance there as well. Since the early 1970s, many South African scholars have embraced the perspectives and methods of the then-new social histories being written in Great Britain and elsewhere, with the intention of capturing the unwritten lives of black peasants, workers, women, and other marginalized communities.[27]

This approach of history from below began to shift, however, during the 1980s as scholars began to question more directly the origins and rationales of the apartheid system. Radical historians sensed that conventional forms of Marxist analysis had reached their limit. This shift was additionally a reflection of political changes then occurring. If social histories written by such scholars as Shula Marks, Colin Bundy, and Charles van Onselen during the 1970s and early 1980s were in keeping with a politics of resistance that had emerged during that period, this new body of scholarship arose during the late 1980s when the apartheid system appeared to be finally collapsing, a result of widespread activism as well as internal contradictions that were increasingly unsustainable and difficult to reform.[28] The most fundamental among these tensions was an economy highly dependent on black labor within a system of state governance that sought extreme levels of legal, social, and geographic separation on the basis of race. Social divisions were established most succinctly in the series of "ethnic homelands" that were created beginning in the early 1950s. By the 1970s, the "race society" that Arendt described two decades earlier had achieved a startling level of fruition. The subsequent breakdown of the system from internal pressures as well as a global anti-apartheid movement forced questions as to how such a system had been rationalized—ideologically and bureaucratically—for so long. It is in this context that the study of race and bureaucracy has reentered the mainstream of South Africa's historiography, with Arendt's ideas reappearing, if tentatively, within these debates.[29]

Though Chapter Seven of *Origins* focuses primarily on the turn of the twentieth century, it is important to recognize the remarkable prescience of Arendt's ideas vis-à-vis mid century developments in South Africa. The apartheid period began formally in 1948 with the victory of the National Party (NP) in parliament elections held that year. Given the British-style parliamentary system then in place, a majority win by the conservative, Afrikaner-based NP enabled it to take over the executive and legislative branches at once. This election result had been unexpected in so far that the NP had supported the racial ideologies and discriminatory policies of Nazi Germany since the 1930s. The NP's election defeat by the pro-Allies United Party in 1943, combined with the subsequent Allied victory, suggested that the NP and its socially conservative platform were increasingly marginalized in the early postwar period. Social liberalism appeared to be the global path of the post-World War II moment, particularly given the shift to decolonization in Asia and Africa that took hold soon after the war's end. However, rapid transformations during the war—specifically black migration to cities and a consequent growth in labor unions and political activism—played a key role in South Africa's conservative turn. These changes converged with preexisting racist sentiments and acts of segregation to usher in a new period of racial oppression countervalent to developments elsewhere on the continent. Persisting for almost half a century, apartheid ended formally in 1994 with the country's first fully democratic presidential election.[30]

Given its complex origins and prolonged duration, apartheid has provoked a number of debates among historians and other social scientists. Within this wide-ranging discussion, key questions have centered on the continuities and differences between segregation (1910–1948) and apartheid (1948–1994) periods. A primary issue has been whether "apartheid"—an Afrikaans neologism meaning "apartness"—constituted a fundamental break from segregation-era policies and practices. A related question has been to what extent apartheid was preconceived as part of a "grand plan" or represented instead the product of debate and compromise over time among government officials. Though different in approach, these two questions have often been linked since the debate over origins has in turn informed discussion regarding the continuities and contrasts between both periods.

One illustration of these concerns can be pointed to in the realm of law. Among the key legislative acts implemented during the early apartheid period were the Prohibition of Mixed-Marriages Act (1949), the Immorality Act (1950), Population Registration Act (1950), the Group Areas Act (1950), and the Bantu Education Act (1953). In many cases these laws were reflective of earlier legislation during the segregation period, the most significant being the 1911 Mines and Works Act (enforcing segregation in employment), the 1913 Natives Land Act (enforcing rural segregation), the 1923 Native Urban Areas Act (enforcing urban segregation), and the 1936 Representation of Natives Act (removing the remaining black voters from voting registries and ending the possibility of electing black members to parliament). The comparative similarities between both sets of law have consequently generated discussion as to the exact qualitative differences between both periods.[31]

Such comparative discussion has also initiated reconsideration of the South African state and the factor of institutional change and continuity between both periods. The work of sociologist Ivan Evans has been a key intervention in this regard. In *Bureaucracy and Race* (1997), Evans traces the institutional transformations of the Department of Native Affairs (DNA) from the interwar period up to

1960, thus covering the transition from segregation to apartheid. In a fine-grained analysis that seeks to avoid a static portrait of either system, Evans uses the DNA as a lens for examining the ways in which state bureaucracy became an increasingly common and invasive presence in the lives of black South Africans during the apartheid period. As the first sentence of his study puts it: "Black South Africans are depressingly familiar with the phenomenon of *administration.*"[32] Evans is ultimately a proponent of the differences between the two eras, and he takes a long view to make this point, with his institutional focus on the DNA placing the start of his history during the first decade of the century. Covering the same historical ground as Arendt, Evans points to the creation of the South African Native Affairs Commission in 1903 as a key moment in the formulation of policy on the "native" question following the South African War (1899–1902). This commission summarily recommended a general approach of racial segregation for the Union of South Africa, a self-governing member of the British Commonwealth founded in 1910. However, although legislation was enacted along this line in the decades that followed, it was not until the apartheid period that, in Evans's view, the DNA achieved a level of independence and power such that it appeared as a "state within a state." Black South Africans were effectively placed outside the laws and representation of the national government. He attributes much of this transformation and accrual of power to H. F. Verwoerd, who was Minister of Native Affairs from 1950 to 1958.

Unlike related studies by Deborah Posel and Adam Ashforth, Evans approaches the question of change in the South African state not from ideological or discursive perspectives, but by engaging with the interactive role that bureaucrats had between racial ideologies and realizing policy on an everyday level.[33] In this sense, his work is more reflective of Arendt's earlier conceptualizations. He argues for better recognition of an "internal architecture" of states, possessing a "specific configuration" that is crucial in determining the conduct of day-to-day operations as well as overall success in executing policies.[34] Evans is careful to itemize the features of the apartheid state, including the role and growth of native administrative law and the hierarchy and autonomy of bureaucrats. These aspects in turn underscore Evans's thesis that the apartheid state was semi-autonomous, neither reducible to class interests nor—given a basic operating premise of political and fiscal need—entirely free from political debate either. Nevertheless, the DNA achieved a remarkable level of independence during the apartheid period in the following ways: first, by limiting dissent among state managers and creating homogeneity of opinion within its ranks; second, through an ability to generate its own fiscal scheme by placing much of the financial burden on African communities through taxation; and third, by placing importance on "scientific" studies that enabled the DNA to improve its functioning capacity to execute policies over time. These aspects differentiated the apartheid-era DNA qualitatively from its earlier incarnation during the segregation era.[35]

Juxtaposing Evans with Arendt not only underlines the higher level of detail in his study, but also the comparative insight such detail can provide when one is considering the historical transformations of the South African state over half a century. Arendt of course could not have imagined fully what apartheid would be like in 1951 when *Origins* first appeared. Even so, Evans's study shows that the relationship between race and bureaucracy soon reached its most transparently oppressive form in the 1950s, thus illustrating the prescience, if thinner substantiation, of her basic ideas. Earlier policies and action of the DNA were ambivalent and weak by comparison. Evans himself comments little on Arendt's ideas directly even though his book's title refers to Arendt's chapter. He invokes her phrase "the banality of evil" to describe the behavior of the South African state, although he suggests that applying this idea to the South African case may be "inappropriate, perhaps even tasteless."[36] The South African state sought to manage and exploit black South Africans as a form of cheap labor; genocide as such was never an intention. Still, Evans concedes that the expression captures the bureaucratic nature of racial oppression in South Africa and the fundamental involvement of civilian administrators in this capacity.[37]

If Evans has sought to revise and expand Arendt's ideas about governance in South Africa, Mahmood Mamdani, a political scientist, has gone further to place her ideas within a wider African context, if not an imperial one *per se*. Indeed, if Evans and Mamdani share a general point of revision, it is their greater sense of historical accuracy and focus as contrasted with Arendt's more sweeping interpretations. Nonetheless, Mamdani has revisited her ideas to inform his analyses of the apartheid system and the Rwandan genocide of 1994 with an ambition reflective of hers. In his wide-ranging 1996 study *Citizen and Subject: Contemporary Africa and the Legacy of Late Colonialism*, Mamdani proposes a new paradigm for rethinking the connections between colonial state forms and postcolonial problems of governance in Africa. Similar to Evans, Mamdani's text reflects a particular historical moment just after the end of apartheid when scholars were beginning to take stock of the period and discuss its broader meaning and implications for understanding state power in Africa. Seeking to integrate South Africa's experience into academic concerns and discussions occurring elsewhere on the continent, Mamdani's primary goals are three-fold: to undermine South Africa's perceived "exceptionalism" vis-à-vis the rest of Africa; to explain the reasons for contemporary autocratic politics and ethnic violence in postcolonial Africa; and to offer a framework of analysis that is situated in and defined by conditions on the continent and thus avoid what he terms "history by analogy," whereby Africa is measured by Western norms.[38]

Collecting these three aims into a cohesive whole, Mamdani relies upon a model of indirect rule, the British form of governance that took hold in colonies throughout Africa between World Wars I and II. First conceived in British Natal during the late nineteenth century, this system, which employed local chiefs as colonial administrators, was conceptually elaborated by Lord Frederick Lugard, a British high commissioner, in his treatise *The Dual Mandate in British Tropical Africa* (1922).[39] The characteristic use of local authorities and legal systems to promulgate colonial policy defined this system, invoking the notion of partnership encompassed in the expression "dual mandate," as well as the sense of implicit colonial power suggested by "indirect rule." As Lugard himself wrote, "If continuity and decentralization are . . . the first and most important conditions in maintaining an effective administration, cooperation is the keynote of success in its application—continuous cooperation between every link in the chain . . . above all, between the provincial staff and the native rulers."[40] In his assessment, Mamdani variously refers to this system as both a "bifurcated state" and, more strongly, "decentralized despotism." Both expressions reflect the intrinsic sensibilities of Arendt's notion of a "hybrid form of government" with its aspects of "despotism and arbitrariness" as discussed earlier. Like Arendt, Mamdani portrays this "Janus-faced" state form as the historical outcome of Europe's encounter with Africa, a system of governance that had "two forms of power under a single hegemonic authority" with a principle of "differentiation to check the concentration of power," while also allowing "fusion to ensure a unitary authority."[41] In sum, Mamdani, parallel to Arendt, argues for a unique state form introduced by imperialism that encompassed both contingent and absolute power.

Where Mamdani ventures forth to revise Arendt's model is in the realm of race and its relationship to colonial state bureaucracies. In an effort to complicate South African exceptionalism, he proposes that apartheid was not unique, but in fact, a "generic form" of colonial governance by arguing that political control in South Africa and elsewhere in Africa centered on two options: ruling by race versus ruling by "tribe" or ethnicity.[42] The latter option proved to be more favorable since it appeared more "natural and traditional," while in the same stroke dividing black political majorities that characterized all colonies.[43] The upshot of this approach was the employment of "native" policies that used a political language invoking the self-governing capacity of various ethnic groups to conceal, if in the end unsuccessfully, broader racial social orders that were being constructed. Mamdani points to the 1927 Native Administration Act that reinstitutionalized customary authorities and incorporated them into the state bureaucracy as South Africa's key moment in this ubiquitous process of ethnic division employed for larger aims of racial segregation. This ethnic approach would be elaborated further during the apartheid period with the establishment of "ethnic homelands" for black South Africans. If cultural relativism provided a rationale for such divisions, activists nevertheless recognized and struggled against the transparent racial subtext of such policies throughout the twentieth century. Urban areas in particular evinced racial division with great clarity, where laws such as the 1923 Native Urban Areas Act during the segregation era and the 1950 Group Areas Act during the apartheid period made notions of a "race society" inescapable. Mamdani's intervention on the political interaction between race, ethnicity, and bureaucracy is consequently an important one, revising Arendt's understanding to include the collaborative role of local African authorities, customary law, and ethnic identity generally in the creation of colonial social orders.

This interpretive approach achieves particular analytic power when applied to the Rwandan genocide of 1994. Mamdani's study of this event, *When Victims Become Killers: Colonialism, Nativism, and the Genocide in Rwanda* (2001), builds upon the ideas of his previous book to argue that the legacy of colonialism in Rwanda has fundamentally informed genocidal violence between Hutus and Tutsis since political independence in 1962. Mamdani extends his binary of citizen and subject—that in his previous book reflected the two kinds of status under indirect rule—to argue for a distinction between "settlers" and "natives," a variation with an emphasis on indigeneity. In the context of Rwanda, Belgian policies crystallized this dynamic during the first three decades of the twentieth century, assigning Tutsis as racially superior and nonindigenous. In conflicts up to 1994, this status, according to Mamdani, translated into situations whereby "native" Hutus sought to exterminate "settler" Tutsis. Tutsis, who had occupied positions of power under colonial rule, found themselves resented and perceived as an "alien" presence in the postcolonial period.[44]

This nonindigenous status, if initially the product of a colonial political imagination, became a reality for many. As a consequence of violence as early as 1959, tens of thousands of Tutsis were forced into exile to neighboring countries such as Burundi, Uganda, and Tanzania over the next three decades. The 1994 genocide erupted during a period of civil war that started in 1990, when the Tutsi-led Rwanda Patriotic Front (RPF) invaded Rwanda with the intent of replacing the government and escaping the political pressures of exile in Uganda. By April 1994 when a number of contingent circumstances had converged—including the assassination of moderate Rwandan President Juvénal Habyarimana and the appearance that the RPF would soon take control of the country—genocidal action was taken by Hutus against armed and unarmed Tutsis under a motto of Hutu Power. An estimated 500,000 to 1,000,000 Tutsis were killed over the course of approximately one hundred days, with reciprocal violence by Tutsis against Hutus occurring in parallel. Despite such atrocities, the RPF gained political control in July to end the genocide with an estimated two million Hutu refugees fleeing to Tanzania and the eastern part of the Democratic Republic of Congo to avoid violent retribution. Overall, as in his previous book, Mamdani underscores the categorical legacies of colonial policy that in turn crystallized political identities, which eventually came into conflict during the postcolonial period.[45]

Given the direct element of genocide in Rwanda, Mamdani's engagement with Arendt is more explicit in *When Victims Become Killers*, though not without some critique. He lauds Arendt for her early insight that "genocide had a history and, more specifically, that modern genocide was nurtured in the colonies."[46] Furthermore, with his repeated concern to make the Rwandan genocide "thinkable," he supports her assertion that "genocide had to be linked to race ideology and bureaucratic efficiency if it was to be brought within the realm of comprehension."[47] Indeed, unlike conventional views that have posed the 1994 genocide as ethnic in orientation, Mamdani maintains that Hutu and Tutsi identities—which were defined in part by notions of the Hamitic myth—must be understood as *racial* in character. The main outcome of this argument, reflective of Arendt's "race society" thinking, is that it identifies a common ground between the Holocaust, the Herero genocide, and the Rwandan genocide. It points to why the latter two events must be perceived as qualitatively similar to the Holocaust against critics who might think otherwise. As Mamdani writes:

> there is a link that connects the genocide of the Herero and the Nazi Holocaust to the Rwandan genocide. That link is *race branding*, whereby it became possible not only to set a group apart as an enemy, but also to exterminate it with an easy conscience.[48]

By extension, he argues further for the resulting distinction between levels of violence and their corresponding relation to ethnic and racial identities: "ethnic violence can result in massacres, but not genocide. Massacres are about transgressions, excess; genocide questions the very legitimacy of a presence as alien."[49]

It is this issue of alien status that also forms a basis of departure from Arendt and captures a key aspect of Mamdani's contribution to genocide studies. Drawing from Frantz Fanon, Mamdani differs with the perspective he attributes to Arendt regarding the "relatively uncomplicated relationship between settlers' genocide in the colonies and the Nazi Holocaust at home." He argues instead that settler violence toward natives, as with the Herero, is the exact opposite of what occurred in Europe. "When Nazis set out to annihilate Jews," he writes, "it is far more likely that they thought of themselves as natives, and Jews as settlers."[50] This novel interpretation is congruent with his argument on Rwanda. As mentioned before, Hutus, in his view, saw themselves as "natives" seeking to eradicate "settler" Tutsis, the situation in Rwanda in 1994 thus being an example of "a natives' genocide," not settler genocide, and an unexpected fulfillment of Frantz Fanon's notion of "violence to end violence."[51] For Fanon, the humanity of the colonized could only be proven by responding to colonial violence through anticolonial violence. In Mamdani's account, this dialectic took a disastrous turn in Rwanda during the postcolonial period with Tutsis facing the brunt of "native" resentment and retribution due to their elevated status during the colonial period. Overall, this settler/native dynamic suggests that the Holocaust and the Rwandan genocide must be interpreted as approximating each other, more so than the Holocaust and the Herero genocide or, more provocatively, the Herero and Rwandan genocides.

This distinction of "native genocide" in contrast to more the widely cited case of "settler genocide" is Mamdani's main contribution to discussions of genocidal violence. It has also underpinned the complexity of finding justice since 1994. Mamdani himself has argued that essentially two forms of justice coexist. First, there is a Tutsi-oriented "victor's justice"—whereby Tutsi identity and status would be preserved at the risk of reproducing tense relations between Hutu and Tutsi communities in the future. Second, there is a mutually held "survivor's justice"—whereby political reform would recognize past violence directed at both communities and the need to find justice for each.[52] Though neither option is transparent to undertake, the latter option offers the better possibility of avoiding future conflict. Such questions of justice for Rwanda relate to parallel questions pertaining to post-apartheid South Africa. As Mamdani argues, differences are present between the countries in so far that Rwanda had many perpetrators of violence but few "beneficiaries"(Mamdani's term), whereas in South Africa there were few perpetrators but many beneficiaries. Such conditions underscore the complex, multiple legacies created by ruling principles of race and bureaucracy and the ensuing difficulties in deciding upon formulas for achieving reconciliation at political and societal levels.[53]

The question of justice points similarly to the prescience and dilemma that Arendt's argument about "mob" behavior has presented, specifically the predicament of identifying such trends in advance and thereby avoiding such abuses of state power in the future. Furthermore, finding justice in the aftermath of such behavior seems elusive. Though balanced by intellectual and political convictions, *Origins* is vague about resolving these issues, a problem again rooted in her ambivalence toward causality. A number of scholars have described the contingent racial alliances of white workers, politicians, and intellectuals in South Africa during the first half of the twentieth century in the lead up to apartheid, though without embracing a "mob" notion as such.[54] This absence appears to be an outcome of Arendt's marginalized influence generally, though it is also perhaps a reflection of distaste for Arendt's dated language of analysis. "Race" and "bureaucracy" are far more neutral in tone. Mamdani points to the role of the Hutu and Tutsi middle classes in Rwanda's violence—"Power struggles in the bipolar world of Hutu and Tutsi are marked by a truism: not only are members of the middle class the main beneficiaries of every victory, they are also the core victims in every defeat." But he declines to employ "the mob" as an expression to capture their political behavior, or that of any other political grouping.[55] If the use of this term to understand Nazi Germany and Stalin's Soviet regime was acceptable at one time, it appears less appealing and useful now, especially in contexts that are continuing to seek a kind of justice that avoids political branding and its potential consequences for the future.[56]

Conclusion

To conclude, this chapter has sought to locate the contemporary influence of Hannah Arendt's thought in African studies. Once marginalized and still tentative, her ideas remain a resource and indeed have anticipated aspects of what has recently been called the "new imperial history."[57] The crucial point of Arendt's general argument on imperialism that contrasts with previous interpretations centers on her observations regarding the social forces at work beyond the strict interests of capital, in particular racial difference and its institutional validation within state bureaucracies. As she has written, "profit motives are not holy and can be overruled . . . societies can function according to principles other than economic, and . . . such circumstances may favor those who under conditions of rationalized production and the capitalist system would belong to the underprivileged."[58] The "race society" that developed in South Africa is a significant illustration of this alternative perspective on imperialism and its contingent outcomes. It demonstrates that the interaction of racial ideologies and the threat of violence could secure the ruling power of an otherwise underprivileged and vulnerable community, in this case a white minority over a black majority. Such ideological and institutional conditions fostered the establishment of similar hybrid forms of government elsewhere, states that represented diverse, provisional interests that nevertheless became despotic. By identifying these patterns of state behavior, Arendt's ideas have proven still valuable and enduring.

However, perhaps the most provocative aspect of *Origins* for scholars of imperialism remains her expansive framework. Its suggestion of the connections and genealogies between metropole and colony has opened a realm of research that remains to be fully explored. Indeed, recent scholarship has seen a rethinking of the role of imperialism in the twentieth century by viewing colonies as "laboratories of modernity," an argument that reminds one of Arendt's comment about African colonial possessions being "fertile soil" for ideas later manifested in Europe.[59] The idea that colonies could impact Europe and not simply the opposite, as so often assumed, has contrasted with many mainstream notions of imperialism and world history, from Hobson to Wallerstein.[60]

At the same time, it is important to recognize Arendt's own resistance to causal explanations as discussed earlier, and it should be reemphasized that totalitarianism is not a necessary, logical outcome of anti-Semitism and imperialism. Her elusiveness on causality and the connections, fragile at times, between these realms of historical experience remain limitations within her work. Given the title, structure, and historical discussion of *Origins*, it can be difficult to accept her distinctions between "origins" and "causes" and the difference between historical causality and, in her words, "a historical account of the elements which crystallized into totalitarianism."[61] Though her emphasis on a historical period's "unique distinction and its eternal meaning" is understood and appreciated, the necessary mutual exclusivity implied between causes and historical novelty loses meaning in an empirically dense, chronologically structured study such as hers. Furthermore, her aversion to causes leaves unanswered complex moral questions as to how to address totalitarian political behavior of the past and possibly preempt it in the future.

Moving beyond such debate, scholars have gone on to illuminate the research possibilities presented by the causal linkages intimated by her work, if unintended by Arendt herself.[62] Such work has demonstrated in addition a shared position between her critique of Western modernity with its potential for "radical evil" and those by intellectuals found outside of Europe such as Aimé Césaire, Frantz Fanon, and others.[63] Revisiting Arendt's work and comparing her ideas with these contemporary and later critics provide yet another approach to rethinking the mutually constitutive interrelationships between the former colonial world and Europe. Furthermore, interweaving these intellectual histories that are currently out of dialogue evinces the potential for illuminating a common ground of experience—greater and richer than previously imagined—for discerning meanings of the humane and the inhumane during the twentieth century, in time for the twenty-first.

Notes

1. For discussion of these events, see Horst Drechsler, *"Let Us Die Fighting": The Struggle of the Herero and the Nama against German Imperialism, 1884–1915* (London, 1980); Tilman Dedering, "The German-Herero War of 1904: Revisionism of Genocide or Imaginary Historiography?" *Journal of Southern African Studies* 19, no. 1 (1993): 80–88; Jan-Bart Gewald, *Herero Heroes: A Socio-Political History of the Herero of Namibia, 1890–1923* (Oxford, 1999); Mahmood Mamdani, *When Victims Become Killers: Colonialism, Nativism, and the Genocide in Rwanda* (Princeton, 2001), 11.

2. For Fanon's perspective on violence, see Frantz Fanon, *The Wretched of the Earth* (New York, 1966). For comparable episodes of extreme violence, beyond the 1994 Rwanda Genocide which will be discussed later, see, for example, Adam Hochschild, *King Leopold's Ghost: A Story of Greed, Terror, and Heroism in Colonial Africa* (New York, 1998); Michael R. Mahoney, "The Zulu Kingdom as Genocidal and Post-Genocidal Society, c.1810 to the Present," *Journal of Genocide Research* 5, no. 2 (2003): 251–268; Caroline Elkins, *Imperial Reckoning: The Untold Story of Britain's Gulag in Kenya* (Boston, 2005).

3. For studies exploring the connections between colonialism and the policies of Nazi Germany, see, for example, Sven Lindqvist, *Exterminate All the Brutes*, trans. Joan Tate (New York, 1996); Jürgen Zimmerer, "Colonialism and the Holocaust," in *Genocide and Settler Society: Frontier Violence and Stolen Indigenous Children in Australian History*, ed. A. Dirk Moses (New York, 2004); Isabel V. Hull, "Military Culture and the Production of 'Final Solutions' in the Colonies," in *The Specter of Genocide*, ed. Robert Gellately and Ben Kiernan (Cambridge, MA, 2003); Benjamin Madley, "From Africa to Auschwitz: How German South West Africa Incubated Ideas and Methods Adopted and Developed by the Nazis in Eastern Europe," *European History Quarterly* 35, no. 3 (2005): 430.

4. Even though countries such as Egypt and Algeria are mentioned in this essay, "African studies" in this context refers to sub-Saharan Africa. In addition, it should be mentioned here that though "colonialism" and "imperialism" are often thought of as interchangeable, they do possess different uses and meanings based on scale and perspective. "Imperialism" typically refers to the global interactions of power between specific nation-states and overseas territory. This can take economic, political, and cultural forms; it can also be considered formal and informal. "Colonialism" is typically considered smaller in scale, referring to foreign domination within a particular region, often a future nation-state. Their invocation here reflects these respective meanings.

5. For recent work that has placed metropole and colony similarly into a single frame, see Edward Said, *Culture and Imperialism* (New York, 1993); Frederick Cooper and Ann Laura Stoler, eds., *Tensions of Empire: Colonial Cultures in a Bourgeois World* (Berkeley, 1997); Catherine Hall, ed., *Cultures of Empire: Colonizers in Britain and the Empire in the Nineteenth and Twentieth Centuries* (New York, 2000); Antoinette Burton, ed., *After the Imperial Turn: Thinking With and Through the Nation* (Durham, 2003); Kathleen Wilson, ed., *A New Imperial History: Culture, Identity and Modernity in Britain and the Empire, 1660–1840* (Cambridge, U.K., 2004). Arendt was not the only intellectual to point out the connections between colonialism and fascism at the time. Figures such as Ralph Bunche, George Padmore, C. L. R. James, and W. E. B. Du Bois recognized these comparisons as well. For one example, see Aimé Césaire, *Discourse on Colonialism* (New York, 2000). Paul Gilroy has compared the perspectives of Césaire and Arendt in *Against Race: Imagining Political Culture Beyond the Color Line* (Cambridge, MA, 2001), 61, 66, 76, 85.

6. Hannah Arendt, *The Origins of Totalitarianism*, new ed. (London, 1968), 134, 185.

7. Ibid., 206.

8. Various scholars have examined her reluctance to offer "causes" for totalitarianism. This position can be attributed largely to her philosophical outlook informed by German phenomenology and a concomitant critical distance from the historical determinism of Hegelian and Marxist thought. For Arendt's own discussion, see Arendt, "A Reply to Eric Voegelin," in *Essays in Understanding, 1930–1954*, ed. Jerome Kohn (New York, 1994), 403; Arendt, "Understanding and Politics (The Difficulties of Understanding)," in *Essays in Understanding*, 319, 320. For

the perspectives of other scholars, see, for example, Margaret Canovan, "Arendt's Theory of Totalitarianism: A Reassessment," in *The Cambridge Companion to Hannah Arendt*, ed. Dana R. Villa (Cambridge, U.K., 2000), 30; Bernard Crick, "Arendt and *The Origins of Totalitarianism*: An Anglocentric View," in *Hannah Arendt in Jerusalem*, ed. Steven E. Aschheim (Berkeley, 2001), 94, 97, 99; Dana R. Villa, "Totalitarianism, Modernity, and the Tradition," in *Hannah Arendt in Jerusalem*, ed. Steven E. Aschheim (Berkeley, 2001), 125.

9. Arendt, *Origins*, 185.
10. India is cited as well, though not pursued.
11. Ibid., 186, 207.
12. Ibid., 207.
13. Ibid.
14. Ibid.
15. Ibid., 212.
16. Ibid., 216.
17. Ibid., 126.
18. Ibid., 107.
19. Ibid., 107, 108.
20. Ibid., 317.
21. Ibid., 150.
22. Ibid., 206.
23. Ibid., 152.
24. Ibid.
25. J. A. Hobson, *Imperialism: A Study* (Ann Arbor, 1965); V. I. Lenin, *Imperialism: The Highest Stage of Capitalism* (London, 1996).
26. Her marginal economic emphasis and her general critique of Marxism, seen also in her discussion of the Stalin regime, attracted critics. See, for example, C. H. Van Duzer, Review of Hannah Arendt, *The Origins of Totalitarianism*. *The American Historical Review* 57, no. 4 (1952): 934; Crick, "Arendt and *The Origins of Totalitarianism*," 99.
27. Africa's history had been studied prior to the postcolonial period, though it is commonly agreed that the contours and methodologies of the contemporary discipline emerged after decolonization. See, for example, Steven Feierman, "African Histories and the Dissolution of World History," in *Africa and the Disciplines: The Contribution of Research in Africa to the Social Sciences and Humanities*, ed. Robert H. Bates, V. Y. Mudimbe, and J. F. O'Barr (Chicago, 1993), 167–212. For an overview of South Africa's historiography, see Christopher C. Saunders, *The Making of the South African Past: Major Historians on Race and Class* (Cape Town, 1988).
28. Important work by these scholars include: Shula Marks, *Reluctant Rebellion: The 1906–8 Disturbances in Natal* (Oxford, 1970); Colin Bundy, *The Rise and Fall of the South African Peasantry* (Berkeley, 1979); Charles van Onselen, *Studies in the Social and Economic History of the Witwatersrand, 1886–1914*, 2 vols. (New York, 1982).
29. Marking this turn in the literature, see Shula Marks and Stanley Trapido, eds., *The Politics of Race, Class, and Nationalism in Twentieth-Century South Africa* (Johannesburg, 1986); Saul Dubow, *Racial Segregation and the Origins of Apartheid in South Africa* (London, 1989); Adam Ashforth, *The Politics of Official Discourse in Twentieth-Century South Africa* (Oxford, 1990); and Deborah Posel, *The Making of Apartheid, 1948–1961: Conflict and Compromise* (Oxford, 1991). For more recent work, see Saul Dubow, *Scientific Racism in Modern South Africa* (Cambridge, U.K., 1995); Aletta J. Norval, *Deconstructing Apartheid Discourse* (London, 1996); and Timothy Keegan, *Colonial South Africa and the Origins of the Racial Order* (Charlottesville, 1997). For commentary on the surprising absence of race from many discussions of South African history, see Deborah Posel, Jonathan Hyslop, and Noor Nieftagodien, "Editorial: Debating 'Race' in South African Scholarship," *Transformation* 47 (2001): i–xviii.
30. For discussion of apartheid's origins, see Posel, *Making of Apartheid*; Saul Dubow, "Afrikaner Nationalism, Apartheid, and the Conceptualization of 'Race,'" *Journal of African History* 33, no.

2 (1992): 209–237; Dubow, *Scientific Racism in Modern South Africa*. For general overviews, see William Beinart and Saul Dubow, eds., *Segregation and Apartheid in Twentieth-Century South Africa* (London, 1995); Nancy L. Clark and William H. Worger, *South Africa: The Rise and Fall of Apartheid* (New York, 2004).

31. One arguable difference is a focus on groups during the segregation period in contrast to a focus on individuals during the apartheid period, a reflection of the increased power sought by the apartheid government. For discussion, see Beinart and Dubow, eds., *Segregation and Apartheid*, 12; John W. Cell, *The Highest Stage of White Supremacy* (Cambridge, U.K., 1982); George M. Fredrickson, *White Supremacy: A Comparative Study of American and South African History* (New York/Oxford, 1981).

32. Ivan Evans, *Bureaucracy and Race: Native Administration in South Africa* (Berkeley, 1997), 1.

33. Ashforth, *Politics of Official Discourse*; Posel, *Making of Apartheid*.

34. Evans, *Bureaucracy*, 17.

35. Ibid., 20.

36. Ibid., 17.

37. Ibid, 17, 292. It is important to note here that Arendt did comment on the fulfillment of her ideas in South Africa in a 1967 preface to "Imperialism," writing that "white rule in South Africa where the tyrannical minority is outnumbered almost ten to one probably was never more secure than today." Ibid., xxi.

38. Mahmood Mamdani, *Citizen and Subject: Contemporary Africa and the Legacy of Late Colonialism* (Princeton, 1996), 9–11.

39. Lord Frederick Lugard, *The Dual Mandate in British Tropical Africa* (London, 1922).

40. Lugard, *Dual Mandate*, 193.

41. Mamdani, *Citizen and Subject*, 18.

42. Ibid., 8, 90.

43. Ibid., 90.

44. Mamdani, *When Victims Become Killers*, 14. Tutsis did, in fact, accrue some privileges and status during the precolonial period. For discussion, see Jan Vansina, *Antecedents to Modern Rwanda: The Nyiginya Kingdom* (Madison, 2004).

45. To read further on the 1994 genocide, beyond this overview, see, for example, Alison des Forges, *Leave None to Tell the Story: Genocide in Rwanda* (New York, 1999); Gérard Prunier, *The Rwanda Crisis: History of a Genocide* (New York, 1995); Philip Gourevitch, *We Wish to Inform You That Tomorrow We Will Be Killed With Our Families: Stories from Rwanda* (New York, 1998); Samantha Power, *"A Problem from Hell": America and the Age of Genocide* (New York, 2002).

46. Mamdani, *When Victims Become Killers*, 76.

47. Ibid., 78.

48. Ibid., 12, 13.

49. Ibid., 14.

50. Ibid., 13.

51. Ibid., 10.

52. Ibid., 270, 273.

53. Ibid., 266, 273. Mamdani suggests that South Africa needs societal reconciliation, whereas Rwanda needs a political solution, a position that can be argued. In his words, "Where beneficiaries are many, reconciliation has to be social to be durable, which is the same thing as saying there can be no durable reconciliation without some form of social justice. But where beneficiaries are few, the key to reconciliation is political reconciliation. The prime requirement of political reconciliation is neither criminal justice nor social justice, but *political justice*. It requires not only shifting the primary focus of reform from individuals to institutions, but also recognizing that the key to institutional reform is the reform of institutions of rule"(273). This perspective may be too schematic, given efforts at both political and social solutions in both countries.

54. Previously cited authors such as Dubow and Fredrickson discuss this, but see also Dan O'Meara, *Volkskapitalisme: Class, Capital and Ideology in the Development of Afrikaner Nationalism, 1934–1948* (Cam-

bridge, U.K., 1983); Peter Alexander, *Workers, War, and the Origins of Apartheid: Labour and Politics in South Africa* (Athens, OH, 2000).

55. Mamdani, *When Victims Become Killers*, 230.

56. Chapter 7 also demonstrates an uncritical use of derogatory language toward Africa. For a critique of Arendt's language, see Walter Laqueur, "The Arendt Cult: Hannah Arendt as Political Commentator," in *Hannah Arendt in Jerusalem*, ed. Steven E. Aschheim (Berkeley, 2001), 49.

57. For examples of this field, again see Hall, ed., *Cultures of Empire*; Burton, ed., *After the Imperial Turn*; Wilson, ed., *A New Imperial History*.

58. Arendt, *Origins*, 207.

59. Ann Laura Stoler and Frederick Cooper, "Between Metropole and Colony: Rethinking a Research Agenda," in *Tensions of Empire: Colonial Cultures in a Bourgeois World*, ed. Frederick Cooper and Ann Laura Stoler (Berkeley, 1997), 5. The expression "laboratory of modernity" is from Gwendolyn Wright, "Tradition in the Service of Modernity," *Journal of Modern History* 59 (1987): 291–316.

60. Immanuel Wallerstein, *The Modern World System*, 3 vols. (New York, 1974–1989).

61. Arendt, "A Reply to Eric Voegelin," 403; Arendt, "Understanding and Politics (The Difficulties of Understanding)," 319, 320.

62. See, for example, Lora Wildenthal, *German Women for Empire, 1884–1945* (Durham, 2001). In an earlier work, Mamdani has discussed how imperialism helped establish postcolonial autocracies. See Mahmood Mamdani, *Imperialism and Fascism in Uganda* (Nairobi, 1983).

63. On "radical evil," see Arendt, *Origins*, 459; Steven Aschheim, "Introduction: Hannah Arendt in Jerusalem," in *Hannah Arendt in Jerusalem*, ed. Aschheim, 12.

Chapter 5

ON PAIN OF EXTINCTION

Laws of Nature and History in Darwin, Marx, and Arendt

Tony Barta

> It is the monstrous, yet seemingly unanswerable claim of totali-
> tarian rule that, far from being "lawless," it goes to the source of
> authority from which positive laws received their ultimate legiti-
> mation, that far from being arbitrary it is more obedient to these
> superhuman forces than any government ever was before, and that
> far from wielding its power in the interest of one man, it is quite
> prepared to sacrifice everybody's vital immediate interests to the
> execution of what it assumes to be the law of History or the law
> of Nature.
>
> —Hannah Arendt[1]

These are not words that can be found in the first edition of Hannah Arendt's
great work *The Origins of Totalitarianism*, conceived during the Second World War
and published in 1951. In it, the continuities between the age of European imperialism and the age of fascism in Europe were traced through theories of race, notions of racial and cultural superiority, and the right of "superior races" to expand
territorially. An idiosyncratic history linking the failure of the bourgeoisie, "the
decline of the nation state," and "the alliance between mob and capital" provided
some brilliant insights into the newly baptized phenomenon of "totalitarianism."
The book ended with a pessimistic view of totalitarianism in power, a system of
"radical evil" marked by the elimination of masses of people considered superfluous. "It is inherent in our whole philosophical system that we cannot conceive of
a 'radical evil' . . . Therefore we actually have nothing to fall back on in order to
understand a phenomenon that nevertheless confronts us with its overpowering
reality and breaks down all standards we know."[2]

That the historical explanation fell short, and left her readers with a philo-sophical problem she was not about to solve, did not trouble Arendt as much as we might think. She declined to be regarded as an historian—though most of the book is clearly history—and she always rejected the title of political philosopher. Rather, she saw her work as directed to political decision making in the present: here, "between past and future," all of us should be deciding how to act and how to live. A political philosopher, she told Günter Gaus, did not have to act, nor did an historian. Her field, political theory, or political science, was about understanding processes at work historically, and to a degree philosophically, but always with a sense of personal engagement and responsibility.[3]

Yet she knew her book had stopped at a point she herself found unsatisfactory. Even before it appeared she began an essay that was published separately in 1953, and then added as chapter 13 to the revised 1958 edition of the *Origins:* "Ideology and Terror: A Novel Form of Government."[4] Her new concluding chapter points the whole argument of the book toward historical lineages only briefly indicated in the earlier edition.

Arendt returns with new intellectual energy to the question of totalitarianism and law. She notes that totalitarian rule "operates neither without guidance of law nor is it arbitrary, for it claims to obey strictly and unequivocally those laws of Nature or of History from which all positive laws have always been supposed to spring." This "higher form of legitimacy" in modern times derived either from Marx or Darwin, or (more interestingly and fatefully, as Arendt observes) from combining them. It has not been sufficiently recognized—nor does Arendt herself pursue the matter—that "Darwin's introduction of the concept of development in nature . . . means in fact that nature is, as it were, being swept into history, that natural life is considered to be historical."[5]

It is time to notice how this addition provides a stronger key to explicating Arendt's own grand theory, one that opens the way to fundamental connections be-tween colonialism, the "disappearance" of indigenous peoples, and the genocides of the twentieth century. Darwin fostered, rather than resolved, the contradiction between natural selection and intervention in nature, whether by controlled breed-ing of plants and animals, by colonizing (planting and supplanting), by eugenics, or by "extermination." The colonial project ("civilization" carried to every corner of the globe) he persistently cast as both biological and historic. Marx expounded the historical process with only a starting-point reference to biology, and without caring more than Darwin about the casualties of history as a dialectical evolution. History was the process of humans emerging from the necessities of nature to dom-inate nature for their own purposes.[6] In this global progress both Darwin and Marx accepted that millions far from Europe were dying. They did not foresee—nor did Engels, more humanly engaged with working-class suffering and more persistent in both historical anthropology and contemporary history—how in a Europe alienated both from nature and a universal humanity more millions would follow them.

Arendt is concerned to explain the emergence of "total terror" in the service of a totally justifying historical or biological law, which dictated the replacement of previous ideas of natural or human law. "Guilt and innocence become sense-less notions; guilty is he who stands in the way of the natural or historical process which has passed judgment over 'inferior races,' over individuals 'unfit to live,' over dying classes and decadent peoples."[7] The reassertion of law insisting on human responsibility and culpability is, I agree, essential to humanity's recovery from the era of "natural" genocide, but it does little to assist us in our historical understanding. For that we need to follow through how the modern amalgam of Nature and History—whether Law of Nature or Law of History—became a law of genocidal practice in the colonies, and then returned home. We also need to understand how the totalitarian variants produced in Europe contaminated each other: Nazism sold itself less as racial ideology than as the cure for the class division of Marxism, and Stalinism could target whole national groups with the help of a racism more endemic in Russia than it was in Germany.

None of this should surprise us. Evolution in nature, human history, and scientific endeavor after all share one basic law: the law of unintended consequences. In history, nevertheless, intentions matter, even where they go wrong. Neither colonialism nor genocide can be understood apart from the intentions they exhibit; nor can they be understood apart from the structures and dynamics within which intentions were formed.[8] If neither Darwin nor Marx intended the outcomes traceable in part to their ideas, we should still check whether their ideas contained the seeds of such future possibilities. For historical and biographical reasons, Arendt did not pursue an enquiry less urgent in her agenda. Half a century later it is clear that her historical achievement changed the agenda for all who return to her concerns.[9]

Darwin and the Laws of Nature

Is it fair to draw the gentle scientist Darwin into the history of genocide? I have argued that it is.[10] Darwin's scientific enterprise was inseparable from the mapping, settling, and supplanting of European colonialism. That is how he came to be on the five-year voyage of HMS *Beagle*. Europeans inserted themselves, their ideas, their social order, and their economy everywhere to create the global system of relations Marx said all peoples "on pain of extinction" would have to belong to. In South America and Australia Darwin observed that genocide was part of the process. Whether this fed directly into the theory of natural selection is hard to say; we certainly know he was influenced by Malthus, who commented directly on the extermination of other peoples.[11]

We know also that Darwin's theory was developed within the "extinction discourse" of the early nineteenth century and that Darwinism became a major ideological driver of it later in the nineteenth century.[12] The quality which made it supremely effective was one Darwin had a special difficulty in countering: was this after all not nature's way? Darwin could campaign against slavery, and be horrified by inhumanity toward American natives (or, more briefly, Irish ones), but he could find no ground for a stand against something that looked so very similar to the natural process he had made fundamental to all life. What I have called "the naturalizing of genocide" was—and is—almost invariably based on Darwin's law of "Natural Selection."[13]

Is it right to associate Darwin with such a "law"? Darwin had no qualms about that. He was by temper and conviction a Popperian kind of scientist: after all, only by the weight of evidence casting doubt on the invariability of species did he find creation disproved and move toward a new theory, and he was always prepared for variation in his own position. But in the meantime he did not mince words: when "facts," "principles," "observations," "relations," and "correlations" all pointed in a certain direction, a "law" could and should be stated.[14] His famous concluding paragraph to *On the Origin of Species* gives natural laws the firmest—and most poetic— status.

> It is interesting to contemplate an entangled bank, clothed with many plants of many kinds, with birds singing in the bushes, with various insects flitting about, and with worms crawling through the damp earth, and to reflect that these elaborately constructed forms, so different from each other, and dependent on each other in so complex a manner, have all been produced by laws acting around us. These laws, taken in the largest sense, being Growth with reproduction; Inheritance which is almost certainly implied by reproduction; Variability from the indirect and direct action of the external condition of life, and from use and disuse; a Ratio of Increase so high as to lead to a Struggle for Life, and as a consequence to natural Selection, entailing Divergence of Character and the extinction of less improved forms.

We know, most clearly from Darwin's survey twenty years later in *The Descent of Man*, that "the extinction of less improved forms" was something he accepted in relations between humans as well, and already here there is no attempt to shy away from the violence of the process. Rather, the "grandeur" of these laws, associated finally with the most widely accepted "fixed law of gravity" lent beauty and wonder to the continuing drama of evolution.

> Thus, from the war of nature, from famine and death, the most exalted object of which we are capable of conceiving, namely the production of the higher animals, directly follows. There is grandeur in this view of life, with its several powers, having been originally breathed into a few forms or into one; and while this planet has gone cycling on according to the fixed law of gravity, from so simple a beginning endless forms most beautiful and most wonderful have been, and are being, evolved.[15]

There is much here that Arendt might have taken issue with, not least Darwin's view of life. For Arendt, the birth of a child with the open possibilities of a completely new life was the greatest wonder and the closest she came to an absolute principle—not a natural law—of politics.[16] Darwin shared her wonder, and knew terrible grief at the death of a beloved child, but embraced within his worldview a degree of suffering and mortality that nature demanded.[17] In *The Descent of Man*, Darwin's poetic intertwined the ruthlessness of nature and the ruthlessness of competition for resources in a way that made laws of nature and laws of history inextricable. For most of human history, famine, nomadic hardships, and the consequent death of infants—natural means of keeping population in check—could put off conflict but not avoid it. So "the contest is soon settled by war, slaughter, cannibalism, slavery and absorption. Even when a weaker tribe is not thus abruptly swept away, if it once begins to decrease, it generally goes on decreasing until it is extinct."

Then follow the sentences in which Darwin faces the unequal contest of modern colonialism. As I have argued elsewhere, Darwin knew from his own observations that genocide occurred in the colonization of South America; he was more circumspect in his comments about Australia. In the *Descent* he is both circumspect and direct: either way he continues to confuse, deliberately and disastrously, nature and history. Clearly genocide was not natural but a determinedly human *intervention* in nature. It was in fact fundamental to the European conquest of nature that involved the elimination of countless species as well as many peoples. Yet Darwin had recognized in his own society and the agricultural revolution on which its power was founded that intervention in evolution of species was both possible and beneficial—and profitable. Here he plays down any element of profit or policy in the colonies but does not gloss over the effects of the encounter:

> When civilised nations come into contact with barbarians the struggle is short, except where a deadly climate gives its aid to the native race. Of the causes which lead to the victory of civilised nations, some are plain and some very obscure. We can see that the cultivation of the land will be fatal in many ways to savages, for they cannot, or will not, change their habits. New diseases and vices are highly destructive; and it appears that in every nation a new disease causes much death . . .

The vices included "the evil effects from spirituous liquors"; he also noted the importance of "changed habits of life" and reports of natives losing motivation to cope with new conditions. Darwin did not set out the historical developments creating the upheaval. His way was simply to point to "the grade of civilization" as "a most important element in the success of nations which come into competition."[18]

He is most unlikely to have read the paragraph (intended to be scientific, poetic, and political) published by some unknown German exiles thirty years before:

> The bourgeoisie, by the rapid improvement of all instruments of production, by the immensely facilitated means of communication, draws all, even the most barbarian nations, into civilization. The cheap prices of its commodities are the heavy artillery with which it forces the barbarians' intensely obstinate hatred of foreigners to capitulate. It compels all nations, on pain of extinction, to adopt the bourgeois mode of production; it compels them to introduce what it calls civilization into their midst, i.e., to become bourgeois themselves. In one word, it creates a world after its own image.[19]

Marx and Engels: Laws of History

While Darwin showed no interest in Marx and Engels, they most definitely admired him.[20] To them he was the unflinching scientist who (almost) completed the Enlightenment project of chasing out mysticism with the light of reason by revealing the workings of the material world. Understanding nature—and that meant nature's laws—was the only understanding that could count. Their own contribution (and here Engels always modestly deferred to Marx) was not so much to extend the laws of nature into history, as Darwin in later life tried to do, but to show history as subject to its own laws. Arendt quotes the famous line from Engels at Marx's funeral: "Just as Darwin discovered the law of development of organic life, so Marx discovered the law of development of human history."[21]

In their earliest joint writings Marx and Engels show themselves to be natural materialists long before Darwin could face the facts in front of him. The more dynamic view of human interaction with the material world might have fascinated him when he was working on the *The Descent of Man*. There was a large degree of correspondence between the first principles being established by two young Germans in reaction to Hegel and Feuerbach on nature and the laborious last reflections being ventured by the great English naturalist on human kind. The ambitious sketch of historical anthropology in *The German Ideology* could have helped Darwin in his reflections on why civilization can be so deadly, and it is hard to see where he would have taken issue with it.

> Man can be distinguished from the animal by consciousness, religion, or anything else you please. He begins to distinguish himself from the animal the moment he begins to *produce* his means of subsistence, a step required by his physical organization. By producing food, man indirectly produces his material life itself.

From this proposition all else in Marxian theory begins to follow: "The nature of individuals thus depends on the material conditions which determine their production." "This production begins with *population growth*, which in turn presupposes *interaction* among individuals. The form of such interaction is again determined by production." Indeed, all historical development depends on the basic law of human interaction with nature and other human groups.

> The relations of various nations with one another depend on the extent to which each of them has developed its productive forces, the division of labour, and domestic commerce. This proposition is generally accepted. [Darwin included it in his "degree of civilization."] But not only the relation of one nation to others, but also the entire internal structure of the nation itself depends on the stage of development achieved by its production and its domestic and international commerce. How far the productive forces of a nation are developed is shown most evidently by the degree to which the division of labour has been developed . . .

From the division of labor came different forms of ownership, different social groups—"'patriarchalism,' slavery, estates, classes"—and the politics appropriate to such power and property relations. All forms of consciousness are historical products, "directly interwoven with the material activity and material relationships of men." Very importantly, though, not everyone has equal power to determine consciousness: "The division of labor is a true division only from the moment a division of material and mental labor appears."[22]

In themselves these are stimulating rather than restricting propositions. Later formulations, whether in the 1859 Preface to *A Contribution to the Critique of Political Economy* or the *Communist Manifesto*, were not proscriptive of prescriptive. The danger lay in the division of labor that gave special privileges to scholars, historical interpreters, and ideologists. From Marx's own example as enforcer of orthodoxy in the first International, Lenin was inspired to enforce Bolshevik orthodoxy and then revolutionary discipline. The exact source for the idea of carrying through a law of history is hard to pin down. The idea would seem to owe more to the impulse to make revolution when the possibility arises, to liberate the oppressed even if some must suffer, than to any clear assertion of an inescapable historical necessity.

Certainly there are "laws" that restrict what is possible historically, though these tend to be as close to commonsense as they are to revolutionary ideology. The succinct, almost epigrammatic, explanation in the Preface of how revolutionary transformations come about—"Then occurs a period of social revolution"—is followed by the famous caveat pronounced as a universal rule:

> No social order ever disappears before all the productive forces for which there is room in it have been developed; and new, higher relations of production never appear before the material conditions of their existence have appeared in the womb of the old society. Therefore, mankind always sets itself only such problems as it can solve; since on closer examination, it will always be found that the problem itself arises only when the material conditions necessary for its solution already exist or are in the process of formation.[23]

Unfortunately, closer examination reveals that such a statement is a gift to any ideologist who claims to discern when conditions are right for mankind to make the necessary move: the ability to discern the historical moment and to lead mankind to the new world is the heart of Leninism. Under Stalin, it rapidly became the core of the totalitarianism that Arendt sought to define. Once the leadership was acting in the interests of everyone—mankind—for a historical purpose which it alone could clearly see, the *obligation* of serving "history" allowed no crossing of the leader's will, no deviation, no appeal to any other definition of human rights, legality, or conscience. Arbitrary determination now left historical determinism behind: the *will* to order the world could allow no room for discussion of what historical laws—let alone historical realities—might be. So to follow even the most sophisticated and fair reading of Marx on history, as Arendt provisionally decided, becomes pointless: all such discussion outside or inside a totalitarian society is beside the point.[24]

In the end, the effort to connect Marx with Stalinist totalitarianism defeated Arendt. It was her major project immediately after completing the *Origins*, and at an early stage the "Ideology and Terror" essay was to be part of a book on Marxism that was never written. She saw "the lack of an adequate historical conceptual analysis of the ideological background of Bolshevism" as the "most serious gap in *The Origins of Totalitarianism*." The omission, she said, "was deliberate."

> The shocking originality of totalitarianism, the fact that its ideologies and methods of government were entirely unprecedented and that its causes defied proper explanation in the usual historical terms, is easily overlooked if one lays too much stress on the only element which has behind it a respectable tradition and whose critical discussion requires a criticism of some of the chief tenets of Western political philosophy—Marxism.[25]

Arendt's insistence that totalitarianism was a rupture from all preceding tradition has to be taken seriously. There were personal and historical reasons for her inability to complete the task she had set herself. The political climate of the Cold War could not have been more unfavorable, and the important collaboration with her husband Heinrich Blücher (to whom *Origins* was dedicated) brought her very close to Marxist idealism and its many tragedies within Communist Party history.[26] We do not have to accept that something unprecedented "defied proper explanation in the usual historical terms." We should, though, attempt to follow Arendt in her explanations of a radical breach.

Obviously, the departure from positive law, designed from social experience to regulate individual conduct and societal judgment, was already disastrous. The challenge for Arendt was to distinguish how totalitarianism differed from any previous tyranny. The key, as she saw it, was not only in the appeal to a higher, or more fundamental law; it was in the mission to expedite the development of nature or history by human intervention. More than once, she employs the word "race" as a verb to indicate the drive of totalitarian "movements." The fundamental laws were no longer those of stability or constraint, but of an obligation to take part in something historically dynamic and to urge the process forward. Terror necessarily comes into play because "a device has to be found not only to liberate the historical and natural forces, but to accelerate them to a speed they never would reach if left to themselves."

> Practically speaking, this means that terror executes on the spot the death sentences which Nature is supposed to have pronounced on races or individuals who are "unfit to live," or History on "dying classes," without waiting for the slower and less efficient processes of nature or history themselves.[27]

It seems right that Darwin's science of biological history so closely paralleled, and influenced, scientistic interpretations of human history. Marx and Engels differed radically from Darwin in making human affairs and even human nature subject to purposeful human action rather than an apparently "natural" social and economic order. Their radicalism, however, had consequences beyond the rescue of the poor and oppressed from the condition Darwin's class would at best ameliorate. They were no better than Darwin at seeing what merciless struggle would mean in places where capitalism had been overthrown by their followers. If Stalin had more victims than Hitler, and Mao millions more again,[28] it was in part because Hegel's idea of transcendent progress added a history and a metaphysics to the scientific materialism Marx believed he shared with Darwin. Darwin could not have dreamed (or could he?) that Marx's historical variant of natural history would stand behind another epic nightmare of starvation edicts and firing squads.

On pain of extinction: superfluous peoples in history

Arendt's analysis of the logic employed by Hitler and Stalin carries devastating conviction. Yet it does not carry through the promise of her references to Darwin and Marx. We do not need to contest Arendt's thesis in "Ideology and Terror" to wonder whether the departure she outlines might not have been given a stronger historical basis by linking it more clearly to her earlier chapters about imperialism and bourgeois society. The violence within the metropolitan societies that outraged Marx and Engels, and the violence in the colonies observed by Darwin, were incontestably human products, allowed and in important respects promoted by laws serving class and national interests. The ideologies of progress employed laws of history and nature to sooth consciences aware of the casualties of progress; it was implicit, and sometimes explicit, that those acting in the name of progress were covered by such higher laws. Since Arendt insists on a very particular definition of ideology—ideologies claim to be scientific and appear only with the historical movements that put their logic into action—we are not encouraged to seek their equivalents before the nineteenth century.[29]

The genocidal combination of scientistic historical radicalism and biological social radicalism could scarcely be imagined in the lifetimes of Darwin, Marx, or even Engels. Yet they were all, most fatefully, born into the worldwide laboratory of colonialism and into assumptions that many would die so that human civilization could proceed. Within a very few decades the coming catastrophe in Europe could be seen brewing in the remote regions where the vast experiment of "progress" in displacing human populations had been underway before they began their analyses. In the twentieth century, when the Marxist idea of progress provoked an anti-Marxist radicalism of the right, the biological idea of progress was waiting to become a program of human engineering more radical than anyone could have foreseen. But the project began in the colonial program already underway before the nineteenth century.

Europe's colonies were the key to what happened in Europe in ways Arendt inspires us to explore. Some of these have recently been highlighted by Richard King, others by Dirk Moses.[30] Any reader now engaged with Arendt's historical tour de force should be alert to a complicated (or straightforward?) blockage about the Anglo-Saxon colonies displacing and destroying peoples living in the seized lands. America and Australia were the two continents "without a culture or history of their own." They had "fallen into the hands of Europeans" when they were "almost empty and had no serious population problem." In a footnote Arendt then acknowledges that these populations "suffered comparatively short periods of liquidation."[31]

Darwin was a staunch upholder of British civilization, but he would have taken more care over a sentence in which hundreds of distinct indigenous groups were heedlessly expunged. Arendt has her eyes on an extension of civilization without casualties. "Instead of conquering and imposing their own law upon foreign peoples, the English colonists settled on newly-won territory in the four corners of the world and remained members of the same British nation." The violent winning of territory from other people is exactly the point, and all the more surprising in that Arendt in this section—"Expansion and the Nation-State"—shows a sympathy for the conquered Irish (which Darwin certainly did not exhibit) and for the "brutal exploitation" of Africans by the French. The worst examples, however, serve only to heighten the contrast: "The unequalled atrocities committed in the Belgian Congo . . . would offer too unfair an example of what was generally happening in overseas possessions."[32] That is true. The death dealt out in Africa—"the Boers' extermination of Hottentot tribes, the wild murdering by Carl Peters in German Southeast Africa, the decimation of the peaceful Congo population" all deserve to be branded with the terrible slogan from *Heart of Darkness:* "Exterminate all the brutes."[33]

Arendt is much too determined to distinguish the British as "leaving the conquered peoples to their own devices as far as culture, religion and law were concerned"—which of them, I wonder, would have testified to that?—"by staying aloof and refraining from spreading British law and culture." It all sits a little uncomfortably with the recognition a few lines later that their aloofness "strengthened tremendously the new imperialist consciousness of a fundamental, and not just a temporary, superiority of man over man, of the 'higher' over the 'lower' breeds."[34] And she herself makes a point of where this superiority can lead. She quotes one of Britain's troublesome imperial heroes, T. E. Lawrence:

> There is a preliminary Arab success, the British reinforcements go out as a punitive force. They fight their way to their objective, which is meanwhile bombarded by artillery, aeroplanes, or gunboats. Finally perhaps a village is burnt and the district pacified. It is odd that we don't use poison gas on these occasions. Bombing is a patchy way of getting rid of women and children. . . . By gas attacks the whole population of offending districts could be wiped out neatly; and as a method of government it would be no more immoral than the present system.[35]

We can see that Arendt is historian enough, despite all disclaimers, to care how colonialism differed in *practice* and how the differences related to *ideology*. Indeed, she comes close to recognizing something like Marxian *praxis* in the dialectics of deeds and ideas. Lawrence is the subject of a three-page case study, and she later contextualizes him (and his irony) in the troubled generation of Great War soldiers and intellectuals that nurtured fascism, Nazism, and the nihilism of the SS murderers.[36] Colonies, she seems to imply, demonstrated how ruthless acquisition and cynical population policies could make genocide an unexceptionable "final solution."

Arendt insists—I think rightly—that only the logic of totalitarianism succeeded in making not only *some* people superfluous, but in effect *all* people: no one could be sure, since no one had exemption from arbitrary definition, that they might not be next. Prominent leaders, dedicated perpetrators, the most fastidious bystanders, could all find themselves dispensable and added to the vast pool of victims. That totally inclusive superfluity, I agree, marks the radical break from previous practice and ideology. But Arendt herself, I want to argue, leads us to contest the proposition that there was no ideology of superfluity in earlier times. Slaves, as she points out, were not superfluous, but almost in the same breath—certainly in the same paragraph—she again mentions kinds of killing that acted as precedents:

> Many things that nowadays have become the specialty of totalitarian government are only too well known from the study of history. There have almost always been wars of aggression; the massacre of hostile populations after a victory went unchecked until the Romans mitigated it by introducing the *parcere subjectis;* through centuries the extermination of native peoples went hand in hand with the colonization of the Americas, Australia and Africa...[37]

This "hand in hand" marks the limit of Arendt's pathbreaking attention to the larger historical relations of colonial genocide. She takes care to distinguish trade expansion from imperialism, and links "conquest, decimation of the native population and permanent settlement." She lights the way to more recent research when she says "perhaps worst of all" the racist attitudes associated with mass murder in the colonies "resulted in the introduction of such means of pacification into ordinary, respectable foreign policies."[38]

The turn into the twentieth century, as Arendt noted, brought a return of racist interventionism from the colonies to Europe. Exactly in 1900 the German variety of Social Darwinism, stimulated by Haeckel and others, was recognized in the governing classes as having potential for a new biologically based kind of social integration. *Lebensreform, Naturphilosophie,* and a physical—even medical—Social Anthropology combined to combat the hitherto popular incorporation of Darwinism into Socialism. From this mix, came the poisonous popularizers read by Hitler.[39] Less widely discussed, though dramatized by the German genocide of the Herero in Southwest Africa, was the return to Europe of a project for potential colonial genocide. Just in time to link up with the push for world power, to be as "well born" as the other Great Powers, Germany would soon have to move away from emulating the overseas colonialism of France and Britain and be inspired by the example of Russia and the United States, whose expansion had concentrated on conquering their own continents. The idea of European *Lebensraum* for Germans survived its defeat in the Great War to inspire Hitler's eastern ambitions.[40]

It can't be forgotten—Arendt doesn't let us—that the casualties of totalitarianism were the motivating concern in her project. In a sense, she needed to establish the nature of totalitarianism in the twentieth century before searching for the origins in earlier times. So we cannot fairly fault her for less attention to the casualties of earlier genocides. And if we regret that she did not follow up some of her own leads bringing colonial genocides closer to those of Hitler and Stalin, we have to remind ourselves that the "radical break" with everything going before was fundamental to her. At the end of her book, even more than at the beginning, she wants to emphasize that totalitarianism is a new phenomenon.

The establishing of historical relations across this break, or of demonstrating that the break was a less radical one, is now a task for us. For both Darwin and Marx, colonies marked the entry of new varieties of mankind into the historical realm. If their life in it was short, well, that demonstrated how the laws of nature and the laws of history worked. Arendt was unhampered by such "laws" and was appalled by their consequences. But by (understandably) avoiding discussion of their genesis and not connecting them to an historical context she had done much to illuminate, Arendt missed an opportunity to integrate important insights of Marx and Darwin with her own.

We have to return to the larger context, dynamic rather than structural, of the societal evolution in which Darwin pondered nature and (rather selectively) contemporary history. Marx, of course, was not backward in pointing out the historical matrix of natural selection: "It is remarkable how Darwin recognizes among beasts and plants his English society with its division of labor, competition, opening up of new markets, 'inventions' and the Malthusian 'struggle for existence.'"[41] Like Arendt, Marx points to the Hobbesian "war of all against all"—Arendt actually gives much more space to Hobbes than she does to Darwin. That may be because, while she made "the political emancipation of the bourgeoisie" fundamental to her analysis of modernity, she also made imperialism a major project of the new modernizing class in a way that Marx did not. Darwin was a true son of this class in every sense; it was as a representative of its progressive and scientific triumphs that he was buried in Westminster Abbey.

So the laws of nature were not the only ones Darwin had confidence in. His belief in the advance of civilization showed as much faith in the laws of history. He did not claim to know how the laws of natural selection would work out in the future, and least of all in relation to humans, because he knew that they were now subject to human powers over nature as much as nature's powers over humans. Marx and Engels hailed this transfer as the key to a fully human future, liberated from nature's necessities. Liberation, however, would only occur in the historical working out of the encounter with nature. The limit of Darwin's historical insight was to invoke natural laws exactly at the time when his own class, his own society, his own scientific work was proclaiming the domination over nature and in effect the end of natural laws in human history. The historical had replaced the natural, but as Marx saw and Darwin did not, the realm of natural necessity—competition for resources and for power—could make the historical struggle still look natural.

Engels was most incisive about this. The economic "laws" of his own time, he wrote in 1865, "are not eternal laws of nature but historical laws which rise and disappear. . . . To us, therefore, none of these laws, in so far as it expresses purely bourgeois relations is older than modern bourgeois society."[42] Darwin of course understood well that positive laws, the kind Arendt held up in comparison to "higher laws," were effective and necessary: he felt passionately about the legislative abolition of the slave trade. Whether he would also have followed Lord Diplock's principle—that British justice recognized in the foreseeable consequences of acts evidence of intention—is not clear.[43] Darwin cared more than many of his class about the moral content of civilizing projects, but did not proceed to connect the seemingly natural consequences of colonization with the historically and biologically natural drive to colonize. Contemporary historical analysis could have helped him, but he would have had to be less taken with Spencer and Bagehot and more curious about Marx.

It was the *practice* of colonization that could reveal both the historical and moral realities. Darwin wanted to deal with these only in optimistic terms, and so comprehensively retreated from his early engagement with the fate of the colonized: in this respect he swung more dramatically than most of his class. Few had his experience as a young man of seeing how indigenous populations surplus to labor requirements and competing for land were dealt with by settlers. He knew that some of the drive in colonization came from surplus population at home, from the poverty he saw in Malthusian rather than Marxian terms. He thought reforms such as abolition of the Corn Laws would alleviate poverty and later he became impressed with eugenics for breeding it out. There are sufficient indications in the *Descent* that he thought problems further from home would eventually be solved in the same way. So neither the Irish famine, where he was doubtful about short-term relief, nor the Indian Mutiny with its train of punitive massacres could long distract him from his researches. Superfluity of population would be solved one way or another, and most often by suffering and violence.[44]

Darwin's *Origin of Species* and Arendt's *Origins*, almost a century apart, bookend the fatal juncture of evolution, colonial genocide, imperialist society, and the apotheosis of genocide in Europe. How Darwinism became attached to varieties of competition and intervention that posed as natural when they were historical in origin and purpose, is most likely to be understood—current fashion notwithstanding—by a healthy infusion of Marxian insights. No Marxist "laws," which we could say "spooked" Arendt, are required; we need something closer (surely Arendt would approve) to Marxian commonsense.[45] Yes, the appeal to laws of nature and laws of history drove the hubristic effort to make nature and history conform to ideological conceptions of reality. This is one of Arendt's enduring contributions, and it should serve to reestablish the importance of conceptualizing totalitarianism. But such ideological appeals were practiced earlier than Arendt wanted to recognize, and their uncounted thousands of victims await historical recognition.[46]

We can now see that Arendt's own sense of historical trajectory, and her engagement in the crisis of her own time and place (mid twentieth century Europe and America) prevented her from taking this insight back into the world of the precursors. I am not about to dilute her historical analysis by suggesting Communist and Nazi forms of totalitarianism existed before their time, but I do think it important to look again at the context she established for their emergence. In all the elements—emancipation of the bourgeoisie, the alliance between mob and capital, anti-Semitism, racism, and imperialism—the ambition to make the world conform to an ideological image, *and the power to make the image reality*, were practiced as determinedly as a not yet totalitarian age would allow. European colonialism was the great triumph and unparalleled catastrophe of this first worldwide revolution, not exhaustively interpreted by Marx and only half understood by Darwin. Arendt brought us closer to historical understanding of the murderous progress of modernity, by relating—brilliantly but too briefly—genocide in the colonies to developments far away. Laws of nature and laws of history covered up the realities of policy and the relations of power. If we look for the realities and relations of genocide, rather than laws, we can come closer still.

It was in the total transformation of the world through European expansion that Darwinist and Marxist explanations of nature and history were created. Included in them were simple "laws" of surplus population and almost impenetrable ones of "surplus value." They pointed to ways that both practice and ideology denied natural value to any part of nature that could not be exploited, and withdrew human value from any population surplus to the requirements of the new local—and global—economy. Arendt's attention was not primarily directed to understanding how Darwinism and Marxism meshed with the violence she saw in colonialism. Her enquiry was into Europe's competing and intertwined political extremes. The extreme impact of Europe on the world, bringing new ways of life and new kinds of death, with unforeseen consequences for Europe, is an unfinished story. We should hope for new questions, new research, new theories, and an intellectual imagination that engages new perspectives with older ones—not least those of Darwin, Marx, and Arendt.

Notes

1. Hannah Arendt, *The Origins of Totalitarianism*, rev. ed (New York, 1958), 461–62. My thanks to Richard King, Dan Stone, and Dirk Moses for generous help with vexing questions raised (rather than resolved) in this chapter.
2. Arendt, *Origins*, 459. See also Institute of Historical Research at <http://www.history.ac.uk/reviews/paper/kingRichard.html> for review by Richard H. King of Michael Halberstam, *Totalitarianism and the Modern Conception of Politics* (New Haven, 1999.)
3. "What Remains? The Language Remains": A Conversation with Günter Gaus (1965), in Hannah Arendt, *Essays in Understanding* (New York, 1994) 1–23. Arendt, of course, always had to deal with the unedifying example of Heidegger, "whose enthusiasm for the Third Reich was matched only by his glaring ignorance of what he was talking about." "The Image of Hell" (1946), in *Essays in Understanding*, 202. See also Berel Lang, "Snowblind: Martin Heidegger

and Hannah Arendt," *The New Criterion* 14, no. 5 (1996), http://www.newcriterion.com/archive/14/jan96/lang.htm

4. Elisabeth Young-Bruehl, *Hannah Arendt: For Love of the World* (New Haven, 1982), 251–53, 285, 541. See also Jerome Kohn, Introduction to the *Social Research* issue on *Origins*, 69, no. 2 (Summer 2002): v–xv.

5. Arendt *Origins*, 461–64. Engels tried in an uncompleted labor to explain that nature was as much subject to dialectical laws as history was. Engels, *Dialectics of Nature*, (1872–1882), introduction and notes J.B.S. Haldane (London, 1940). Haldane pointed out that while Engels was well aware of the newness of science, his knowledge was in important matters being superseded even as he wrote. For instance, new work suggesting that chemical changes might affect global cooling made one of the most famous passages more poetry than science—or history. "The declining warmth of the sun will no longer suffice to melt the ice thrusting forward from the poles; when the human race crowding more and more about the equator will finally no longer find even there enough heat for life (20)." Finally perhaps, but we have a more pressing trial to survive first. See also Philip Moran, "In Defense of the Dialectics of Engels' *Dialectics of Nature*," in Alan R. Burger et al. (eds), *Marxism, Science, and the Movement of History* (Amsterdam, 1980), 57–75.

6. The best interpretation, in my view, remains Helmut Fleischer, *Marxism and History* (New York, 1973). First published in German as *Marxismus und Geschichte* (Frankfurt-am-Main, 1969), it is likely to have come to Arendt's attention, but I am not aware of any comments she may have made. Bikhu Parekh says Arendt misunderstood Marx's concept of "species-being" and the historical role he ascribed to labor in relation to nature. Bikhu Parekh, "Hannah Arendt's Critique of Marx," in *Hannah Arendt: The Recovery of the Public World*, ed. Melvyn A. Hill (New York, 1979), 67–100.

7. Arendt, *Origins*, 465. Arendt did not exclude "natural law" from "positive law." Canovan makes the point repeatedly that Arendt liked the idea of law promoted by Montesquieu: a set of agreed relations or connections rather than the commands of an authority. Law in this sense (or "spirit") was the best protection against tyranny. Margaret Canovan, *Hannah Arendt: A Reinterpretation of Her Political Thought* (Cambridge, 1992), 172, 195. Part of the "spirit" was a long-agreed on sense of natural law, rules which might be transgressed but which could not themselves transgress a supposed historical consensus about right and wrong, actions, and consequences. I am not sure that Arendt altogether resolves the place of natural law in modern times; as Baumann says, 'Modernity is an inherently transgressive mode of being-in-the-world.' Zygmunt Baumann, *Modernity and the Holocaust* (Ithaca, 2000), 229. Thus was made possible the radical transgression Arendt saw as the critical rupture in civilization, with new "laws" of nature or history replacing any appeal to natural law in the old sense.

8. For an example of dialectical discourse about such historical processes see Tony Barta, "Relations of Genocide: Land and Lives in the Colonization of Australia," in *Genocide and the Modern Age*, ed. Isidor Wallimann and Michael N. Dobkowski (New York 1987), and A. Dirk Moses, "An Antipodean Genocide? The Origin of the Genocidal Moment in the Colonization of Australia," *Journal of Genocide Research* 2, no. 1 (2000): 89–105.

9. John Beatty, "Hannah Arendt and Karl Popper: Darwinism, Historical Determinism and Totalitarianism," in *Thinking about Evolution: Historical, Philosophical and Political Perspectives*, ed. Rama S. Singh, Costas S. Krimbas, Diane B. Paul, and John Beatty (Cambridge, 2001), vol. 2, 62–76, is a compact and stimulating reminder of parallels between two writers on totalitarianism who apparently never commented on each other's works. Beatty elucidates problems in their readings of Darwin and Marx by reference to Richard Levins and Richard Lewontin, *The Dialectical Biologist* (Cambridge, MA, 1985), the most interesting attempt to integrate Darwinism and Marxism. Its dedication is "To Frederick Engels, who got it wrong a lot of the time but who got it right where it counted." In particular, while "Marx insisted that human history was part of natural history," Engels looked for evidence of dialectical interaction. "Despite, or because of, his Lamarckian biases, Engels captured the essential feature of human evolution: the very strong

feedback between what people did and how they changed" (253). An excellent concluding chapter on dialectics and the historical context of knowledge suggests the appropriate analogy is not to the laws of natural science, but rather to Darwin's principles of variability, heritability, and selection.

10. Tony Barta, "Mr Darwin's Shooters: On Natural Selection and the Naturalizing of Genocide," *Patterns of Prejudice* 39, no. 2 (2005): 116–37.

11. Darwin appears to have read (in 1838, "for entertainment" on the *Beagle*) the 1826 version of the essay Malthus first published in 1798. See Francis Darwin, ed., *The Autobiography of Charles Darwin and Selected Letters* (New York, 1958 [1892]), 200–1. Sven Lindqvist points out that Malthus clearly identified colonial genocide, and rejected it. *A History of Bombing* (London, 2001), excerpt 35, no page numbers. Quoted in Barta, "Mr Darwin's shooters," 126 n. 28.

12. See Patrick Brantlinger, *Dark Vanishings: Discourse on the Extinction of Primitive Races, 1800–1930* (Ithaca, 2003).

13. Barta, "Mr Darwin's shooters." In the first version of *Origins* Arendt made a point of putting Darwin and his political influence into a longer tradition. "As a matter of fact, the doctrine of Might is Right needed several centuries (from the seventeenth to the nineteenth) to conquer natural science and produce the 'law' of the survival of the fittest." She mentions Darwin early in the chapter "Race thinking before Racism" and affirms that "blame is not to be laid on any science as such," but leaves unclear whether he belongs among the "certain scientists who were no less hypnotized by ideologies than their fellow citizens." Arendt, *Origins*, 159–60.

14. All these terms are from Darwin's Introduction to *The Origin of Species by Means of Natural Selection* (New York, 2004) ["*On*" was removed from the title in all editions after the first in 1859].

15. Darwin, *The Origin of Species*, 384.

16. The importance of "natality" to Arendt is discussed briefly in Canovan, 130 and 190, and more intensively by Hans Saner, "Die politische Bedeutung der Natalität bei Hannah Arendt," in Hannah Arendt, *Nach dem Totalitarismus*, ed. Daniel Ganzfried and Sebastian Hefti (Hamburg, 1997), 103-19; Patricia Bowen-Moore, *Hannah Arendt's Philosophy of Natality* (Basingstoke, 1989); and Jonathan Schell, "A Politics of Natality," *Social Research* 69, no. 2 (Summer 2002): 461–471.

17. Are God and Nature then at strife,
    That Nature lends such evil dreams?
    So careful of the type she seems,
    So careless of the single life.
    . . .
    "So careful of the type?" but no.
    from scarped cliff and quarried stone
    She cries, "A thousand types are gone:
    I care for nothing, all shall go."
    These lines from Tennyson's *In Memoriam*, the poet laureate's 1850 response to the new laws of nature, were alas no comfort to the Darwins. Adrian Desmond and James Moore, *Darwin* (London, 1991), 383–84.

18. Charles Darwin, *The Descent of Man* (1871) facsimile edition (Princeton, 1981), 238–39.

19. Karl Marx and Friedrich Engels, "Manifesto of the Communist Party" (1848) in Karl Marx and Friedrich Engels, *Basic Writings on Politics and Philosophy*, ed. Lewis S. Feuer (London, 1969), 53. As I write, Chinese consumer goods are piling up in European ports while the original exporting nations cry unfair competition. Ah, the ironies of history.

20. Janet Browne finds scant evidence for the story that Marx asked if he might dedicate a future edition of *Capital* to Darwin but believes the copy sent by "his sincere admirer" in 1873 remained in Darwin's library, "uncut, unopened, and almost certainly unread." Janet Browne, *Charles Darwin: The Power of Place* (London, 2002), 403.

21. Arendt, *Origins*, 463, n.1. Other references, including Engels' preface to the 1888 English edition of the *Communist Manifesto*, can be found in Feuer, ed., *Marx and Engels Basic Writings*, 46, 126, 138. Engels was more interested in science than Marx was, and therefore paid more attention to

Darwin: Feuer, 254, 969. He also wrote more on anthropology and contemporary history, but in neither case did he show an interest in Europe's overseas colonies. Many on the right would have liked his view on German colonization: it was destined to dominate Eastern Europe, where most commercial activity was in the hands of Jews "whose native tongue is a horribly corrupted German," and where attempts to express a "dying Tschechian nationality" were destined to fall to the more progressive German advance. *New York Daily Tribune* (5 March 1852), in Engels, *The German Revolutions*, ed. Leonard Krieger (Chicago, 1967), 173–77.

22. Marx and Engels, "The German Ideology," as translated in Lloyd D. Easton and Kurt H. Guddat, *Writings of the Young Marx on Philosophy and Society* (New York, 1967), 403–23. The division of labor in Marx caused Arendt much (perhaps unnecessary) trouble. An inadequate distinction between *animal laborans* and *homo faber* and the supposed "victory" of the former in Marxism led her into strange territory, asserting that Marx's view came down to "a natural force . . . whose only aim, if it had an aim at all, was the survival of the animal species man." There is something sad in one of the great intellectuals building up to another defense of "the life of the mind" with the assertion, "What was not needed, not necessitated by life's metabolism with nature, was either superfluous or could be justified only in terms of a peculiarity of human as distinguished from other forms of life—so that Milton was considered to have written his *Paradise Lost* for the same reasons and out of the same urges that compel the silkworm to produce silk." Hannah Arendt, *The Human Condition* 2nd ed. (1958), introduction Margaret Canovan (Chicago, 1998), 320–5. Though Marx did say it himself—Arendt gives chapter and verse—he also said other rather more enobling things about human imagination. A further judgment also derives from her determinedly undialectical reading: "Marx's contention that economic laws are like natural laws, that they are not made by man to regulate the free exchange but are functions of the productive conditions as a whole, is correct only in a laboring society, where all activities are leveled down to the human body's metabolism with nature and where no exchange exists but only consumption (209)."

23. Karl Marx, "Preface" to "A Contribution to the Critique of Political Economy" (1859), in *Karl Marx: Selected Writings in Sociology and Social Philosophy*, ed. T. B. Bottomore and M. Rubel (London, 1970), 67–9.

24. This is not the place to recapitulate the long disputes within Marxism about dialectical materialism, scientific determinism, and human agency: an excellent overview is Andrzej Walicki, *Marxism and the Leap to the Kingdom of Freedom: The Rise and Fall of the Communist Utopia* (Stanford, 1995). Chapter 2, "Engels and 'Scientific Socialism,'" thoroughly reviews the case that Engels was more responsible than Marx for the deterministic "Marxism" later rejected by Gramsci, Korsch, Lukács, and most Western Marxists. Walicki agrees that Engels went further than Marx in conflating laws of history with laws of nature, and emphasizes his historical influence on both German Social Democracy and Soviet Communism, but does not see that Marx himself can be exempted from promoting the idea of a scientifically ascertainable "historical necessity" and with it "a misconceived view of human liberation." (207) "It goes without saying that totalitarianism was not a necessary consequence of Marxism;" that depended on "concrete historical circumstances." "Nonetheless, it is a fact that Marxism proved to be well-suited to the legitimization of the most consistent and long lived form of totalitarian regime known," one that could even be seen as " the predictable outcome of a Marxist-inspired revolutionary communist movement" (497-8). For the development of "Western Marxism"—with which Arendt generally had no more engagement than she had with Communism—see Martin Jay, *Marxism and Totality: The Adventures of a Concept from Lukács to Habermas* (Cambridge 1984).

25. Grant proposal to the Guggenheim Foundation, 1952, quoted by Young-Bruehl, in her important discussion of the project, *Hannah Arendt*, 276–280. See also Canovan, *Hannah Arendt*, especially chapter 3, "Totalitarian Elements in Marxism." Whether Arendt had the temperamental or intellectual engagement to carry her through analysis of the various lineages of Communism—Plekhanov and Lenin in Russia; Kautsky, Liebknecht, and Luxemburg in Germany—is another question.

26. Blücher had been close to the KPD leadership before 1933 but distanced himself first from Communism and then from Marx. Arendt always let it be known that she had never belonged to the Left in Germany, certainly not in any sense that meant links to a party. Marx makes only eight brief appearances in the correspondence between them, *Between Four Walls*, ed. Lotte Kohler (Orlando, 2000). For examples of how Arendt dealt with Marxism and Communism in the years after she published *Origins*, see "Religion and Politics" and "The Ex-Communists," *Essays in Understanding*, 368–90, 391–400.

27. Arendt, *Origins*, 466.

28. Arendt made a point, in her 1957 Epilogue on the Hungarian revolution, of adding a note on Mao's first casualties to the *Origins*. At that time she could write that China "has so far refused to follow the Russian depopulation policy; for great as the number of victims in the first years of dictatorial rule may appear—15 million seems a plausible guess it is insignificant in proportion to the population when compared with the losses Stalin used to inflict on his subjects." Arendt, *Origins*, 486.

29. Interestingly, she does see in kinds of deism the makings of an ideology that would become the totalitarianism of terror in the twenty-first century. *Origins*, 468–9. See also "'Religion and Politics" (1953 in *Essays in Understanding*, 368–390, on social science, secularism, and communism contrasted with religion; and Richard H. King, *Race, Culture and the Intellectuals, 1940–1970* (Washington, D.C. / Baltimore, 2004), 110–114.

30. King, 100–108, 115–119. Dirk Moses refers to a range of Arendt's statements in his important introductory essay to A. Dirk Moses, ed., *Genocide and Settler Society* (New York, 2004), 4–5. See also Enzo Traverso, *The Origins of Nazi Violence* (New York, 2003), chapter 2 ("Conquest").

31. Arendt, *Origins*, 182, 186, 187 note 4, 128.

32. Ibid., 130, note 16.

33. Ibid., 185. On Arendt's own figures the Congo genocide was much worse than "decimation." She cites "20 to 40 million people reduced to 8 million."

34. Ibid., 124–34.

35. T. E. Lawrence in an article written for *The Observer* in 1920. *Letters*, ed. David Garnett (New York, 1939), 311 ff., as cited by Arendt, *Origins*, note 80, 134.

36. Arendt, Origins, 218–20, 327–31. The front generation, she says, were influenced by passions rather than scientific demonstrations: "They read not Darwin but the Marquis de Sade. If they believed at all in universal laws, they certainly did not particularly care to confront them. To them, violence, power, cruelty, were the supreme capacities of men who had definitely lost their place in the universe and were much too proud to long for a power theory that would safely bring them back and reintegrate them into the world."

37. Ibid., 440.

38. Ibid., 185. Her example is from Kaiser Wilhelm II in 1900, referring to the Boxer rebellion in China, but the African connection, via colonialism and the Boer War was also the one that most shaped German attitudes.

39. Paul Weindling, *Health, Race and German Politics Between National Unification and Nazism, 1870–1945* (Cambridge, 1989) is an impressive history of the connections between German Darwinism and National Socialism, via eugenics and other politicized developments in science. See also Richard Weikart, *From Darwin to Hitler: Evolutionary Ethics, Eugenics, and Racism in Germany* (New York, 2004).

40. See Jürgen Zimmerer, "Colonialism and the Holocaust: Towards an Archeology of Genocide," in *Genocide and Settler Society*, ed. Moses, 49–76; and Zimmerer, "The Birth of the 'Eastern Land' out of the Spirit of Colonialism," *Patterns of Prejudice* 39, no. 2 (2005): 197–219.

41. Marx to Engels, 18 June 1862, in *Selected Correspondence* (Moscow, 1955), 128. Marx was in London and Engels in Manchester. Further telling comments are on 123, 171–72, 301–3. In his polemic against Dühring, Engels made great play of any primitive correspondence between Darwinism and social development. Dühring, he wrote, saw Darwin as simply importing Mal-

thus into natural history, and then creating a theory that was no more than "a piece of brutality turned against humanity." Friedrich Engels, *Anti-Dühring* (1878) 3d. ed., rev. ed. 1894 in Karl Marx, Friedrich Engels, *Ausgewählte Werke* (Berlin: 1984) vol. V, 77.

42. Engels to F. A. Lange, 29 March 1865, *Correspondence,* 172. The letter deserves attention, partly because of its references to colonization and the new global economy.

43. For the importance of Diplock's judgment in questions of genocide, see A. Dirk Moses "Conceptual Blockages and Definitional Dilemmas in the 'Racial Century': Genocides of Indigenous Peoples and the Holocaust," *Patterns of Prejudice* 36, no. 4 (2002): 7–36.

44. See the new introduction by Moore and Desmond to *The Descent of Man* (London, 2004), and their *Darwin,* 456, 668. For case studies of surplus population, including Ireland, see Richard L. Rubenstein, *The Age of Triage: Fear and Hope in an Overcrowded World* (Boston, 1982).

45. Not surprisingly, the kind of history I have in mind comes from that unique hybrid, British Marxism. See, as a relevant example, the elucidation of Darwin's mode of science in E. P. Thompson, "The Peculiarities of the English," in *The Poverty of Theory and Other Essays* (London, 1978), 56–74.

46. Brantlinger, who does not fail to notice the *Communist Manifesto's* claim that all nations are compelled "on pain of extinction" to adopt the bourgeois mode of production, adds: "The elimination of the primitive is not just a tragic side effect of modernization; as this passage suggests, it is its definition and destination." Brantlinger, *Dark Vanishings,* note 15, 203.

Part II

NATION AND RACE

Chapter 6

THE REFRACTORY LEGACY
OF ALGERIAN DECOLONIZATION
Revisiting Arendt on Violence

Ned Curthoys

While I was virtuously busy debunking the myths of colonization, could I complacently approve of the counter-myths fabricated by the colonized? (Preface, 11).

The leftist colonizer will accept all the ideological themes of the struggling colonized; he will temporarily forget that he is a leftist (81).

There is also a drama of the colonizer which would be absurd and unjust to underestimate (191).

As for the failure of assimilation, I do not derive any particular joy from it, especially since that solution carries a universalistic and socialistic flavor which makes it *a priori* respectable (193).
—Albert Memmi *The Colonizer and The Colonized* (1957)

In this chapter I discuss Hannah Arendt's critique of revolutionary and anti-colonial violence in her essay *On Violence* (1969), which makes a critical distinction between violence and legitimate political activity. It has often been assumed that Arendt's disquisition on the political dangers of violence was written in response to the growing militancy of the student movement and the appropriation of a rhetoric of violent revolution by the New Left in the United States, France, Germany, and other Western countries by the late 1960s. The Paris barricades of May 1968, the riots of that same year at the Democratic National Convention in Chicago, and the emergence of the separatist Black Power movement catalyzed Arendt's desire in *On Violence* to discern and distinguish the "authentic" political demands of the student movement from its violent manifestations and the extremism of its "criminal elements."[1]

However, Arendt's broader critique of violence, whose immediate foil is Frantz Fanon and Jean Paul Sartre's influential endorsement of revolutionary violence in the early 1960s, is informed by a vigorous debate within the French and Algerian Left about the ethics of the French-Algerian war that took place a decade earlier. Arendt's essay is in conversation with earlier Algerian, *pied noir*, and French responses to the challenges posed to leftist principles by the violence of the oppressed. This was an urgent issue considering the anti-colonial terrorist tactics of the indigenous National Liberation Front (FLN) in Algeria, which included shootings, bombings, and the massacre of civilians. Participants in the Algerian debate were confronted with difficult questions: is anticolonial guerilla violence truly emancipatory and efficacious? What is the responsibility of progressive intellectuals during liminal periods when the authority of previous democratic paradigms of nonviolence, humanism, and internationalism appear nugatory when compared to the exigent needs of colonized peoples? Should intellectuals court the danger of supporting or even fabricating Albert Memmi's "counter-mythology" of the oppressed, with all the risks of ideological distortion and authoritarianism such a mythology entails? Is violence a form of political praxis? What are the effects upon the governmentality of political movements, which succeed through violent means?

By the late 1960s Arendt was confronted by another liminal period for the Left, a crisis of cognition and ethics in the United States as the rhetoric of violence threatened to eclipse nonviolence as a discourse of critique, protest, and amelioration. By drawing on the skeptical energy and nonviolent disposition of liberal and reformist commentators on the Algerian war, Arendt vigorously critiques the rhetorical excesses of Fanon and Sartre's doctrinaire and portentous narration of dialectical emancipation that was proving so enabling for the more militant post-civil rights atmosphere in the United States. I suggest that the aphoristic wisdom, ironic awareness, and deflationary cynicism of *On Violence* invoke earlier critiques of colonial and anticolonial violence. Arendt's essay resonates with Albert Memmi's probing phenomenological exploration of the subjectivity of the colonizer and the colonized, and Albert Camus' principled humanist opposition to violence and chauvinism. The robust debates around the Algerian war, often drawing on eclectic rhetorical media and the pathos of historical experience to defuse the pretensions of revolutionary doctrine, enabled Arendt, in *On Violence*, to distinguish violence as an ephemeral source of inspiration from more durable political phenomena such as "authority" and "power." Arendt interprets violence as ultimately inimical to the authority of persuasive leadership and the power of acting in concert to achieve a pluralist body politic.

My purpose in invoking Arendt as a significant contributor to postcolonial theory is to enrich and historicize contemporary discussions of the legacy of decolonization. Arendt's philosophical distinctions and genealogical explorations of revolutionary theory can enable heterogeneous perspectives on anticolonial violence as a modality of nation formation. As the historian of French-Algeria James

Le Sueur argues, we need to begin to think of colonialism and decolonization as "dialogical processes," intertwining and mutually conditioned histories in which indigenous, metropolitan, and settler-colonial voices need to be respected as potential correctives of each other's parochialism for "as long as the legacy of decolonization remains in play."[2] However, while the dialogical interrogation of theories of decolonization I propose acknowledges Arendt's contribution to postcolonial theory, I also explore her conservative and Eurocentric anxieties about subaltern violence. Arendt's dismissive attitude toward the revolutionary desires of indigenous and oppressed peoples often neglects any sympathetic account of their particular histories, present conditions, and future aspirations.

On Violence

In *On Violence* Arendt contemplates the historical efficacy of violence as a mode of political activity, and discusses philosophies of violence from the perspective of the human catastrophe of the Second World War. She details the subsequent emergence of the nuclear age and an ominous era of total war endangering civilian life. Arendt writes that the "very substance" of violence is ruled by the means-end category and the necessity of instrumental reason to implement it. Yet the chief characteristic of violence applied to human affairs "has always been that the end is in danger of being overwhelmed by the means which it justifies." Therefore the "means used to achieve political goals are more often than not of greater relevance to the future world than the intended goals."[3] Arendt cautions that the nuclear age, with its guarantee of mutual destruction and diminution of the relevance of conventional warfare, reminds us of the "all-pervading unpredictability" one encounters "the moment we approach the realm of violence."[4]

Arendt's depiction of political violence as aleatory and uncertain rather than efficacious and predictable is illuminated by her earlier representation of political "action" in *The Human Condition* (1958) as intrinsically nonviolent. Arendt argues that genuine "action" in human affairs is "the only activity that goes on directly between men without the intermediary of things or matter, [corresponding] to the human condition of plurality."[5] In *The Human Condition* "action" is not a type of fabrication or goal-oriented instrumentality but an open-ended praxis whose hallmark is *natality*, the perpetual possibility of something new that occurs whenever human beings act in concert.

Arendt was enamored of the ancient Athenian democratic *polis* as a model for the political life or *bios politikos*. In Greek self-understanding, she writes, to "force people to violence, to command rather than persuade, were pre-political ways to deal with people."[6] The political life on this model requires two complementary activities, action (*praxis*) and speech (*lexis*). Arendtian political action requires a pluralist, rhetorically dynamic public sphere of unfettered communication where action and speech, the novel and the recursive, exemplary performance and prudent deliberation, heroism and sociability, coexist and reinforce each other.[7] For Arendt, the praxis of politics, preserving the capacity for natality in human affairs, should not be mediated by technocratic forms of instrumental reason or inhibited by violent coercion.

Arendt is just as emphatic in *On Violence* that "a gulf separates the essentially peaceful activities of thinking and laboring from all deeds of violence."[8] Her point is reinforced in her discussion of the fate of the concept of violence as "politics by other means" in the twentieth century. Acknowledging a generational crisis of confidence in capitalist modernity, the author of *The Origins of Totalitarianism* (1951) reasserts the "bankruptcy" of the European nation-state and its concept of sovereignty as an outcome of the conflagration of the Second World War. The Second World War did not issue in peace but the cold war, through which the United States has developed a military-industrial complex, a structural need for war making that has rapidly intensified the techniques of warfare and the possibility of total war where civilians are deliberately targeted.[9] In international relations today, Arendt suggests, one can no longer associate a capacity for violence with "political or economic continuity," a developing process determined by what preceded violent action.[10] Presciently, Arendt posits that violence can no longer be bound up with questions of sovereignty and security, given that neither conventional nor nuclear military strength is a "reliable guarantee against destruction by a substantially smaller or weaker power."[11]

It is therefore odd, Arendt observes, that the "more dubious and uncertain" an instrument violence has become in international relations, the more it has gained in reputation and appeal in domestic affairs as the preferred modality of revolution for substantial elements of the New Left.[12] Today, Arendt writes, adherents of nonviolence are on the defensive, and the Left's postwar revulsion against the genocidal violence of the twentieth century has transmuted into the cynical belief, inspired by Fanon and Sartre's glorification of emancipatory violence, that "only violence pays."[13] While acknowledging that Fanon's views on violence were tempered by his recognition of the exigency of quickly combating its brutality, Arendt is impatient with Sartre's flamboyant, modish faith in the autonomic capacity of violence, his asseveration that "violence . . . can heal the wounds it has inflicted." Surely if this were the case, she argues with demotic vigor, revenge would be the cure-all for most of our ills.[14]

Arendt is sympathetic to the student rebellion in the United States, France, and Germany, which, she thinks, is responding to the attenuation of university independence by the military-industrial complex, the cooptation of scientific research by the state, and the ominous threat of nuclear annihilation. In terms redolent of her praise of spontaneous revolutionary energy in *On Revolution* (1963) Arendt commends a generation of student activists characterized by "sheer courage, an astounding will to action, and by a no less astounding confidence in the possibility of change."[15] She is alert to the ambiguities of the student movement, exampled in May 1968, where the "moral character of the rebellion," imaginative, creative, passionate for justice, clashed with a "Marxian rhetoric" prone to prescriptive ideology and a doctrinaire philosophy of history.[16]

Arendt suggests that the "disinterested and highly moral claims of the white rebels" in the United States have been vitiated and coopted by the "serious violence" of the Black Power movement, supported by African American students admitted "without academic qualification." Encouraged by the ardent claims of the African-American community, these students have come to regard themselves as an interest group, whose "silly and outrageous demands" have intimidated the academic establishment and encouraged the New Left to embrace revolutionary theory.[17] Arendt intimates that the transcendental political imagination of Western students is being compromised and retarded by the self-interested, immanent concerns of a subaltern constituency.

It is not surprising that Arendt in *On Violence* holds Sartre's "irresponsible grandiose statements" glorifying the violence of the oppressed of the Third World as chiefly responsible for crudifying the salutary politicization of an anxious and idealistic generation of Western students.[18] As early as 1954 in a paper entitled "Concern with Politics in Recent European thought," Arendt distinguished two competing tendencies within postwar French existentialism, a philosophical movement which looked to politics for the "solution of philosophical perplexities." She suggests that for frustrated philosophers such as Sartre, the logic of revolution was that of theodicy, a deliverance from the philistinism of bourgeois society and the insufficiency of philosophical reason to overcome twentieth century nihilism. In response to these frustrations, Sartre and Merleau-Ponty "adopted a modified Hegelian Marxism as a kind of *logique* of the revolution" (438). On the other hand, the writer most closely associated with existentialism, Albert Camus, refused an "historical system and an elaborate definition of ends and means," preserving the original impulse of "man in rebellion" against the absurdity of the human condition in works such as *L'Homme révolté* (1954). Critical of the escapist desire for "political salvation" from nihilism implicit in Sartre's revolutionary theory, Arendt questioned whether febrile revolutionary desire could be "expected to formulate political principles in the most formal sense, let alone give direction to political choice."[19]

As Ronald Aronson suggests, Arendt preferred the ethos of Camus' *L'Homme révolté*, which critiqued revolutionary thought as an ideological *parti pris*, prone to forget the initial spirit of revolt, that of humane solidarity and measured protest based on individual experiences of injustice.[20] According to Jeffrey Isaac, Arendt was enamored with Camus the Resistance activist and intellectual, who articulated a post-national vision of freedom and justice.[21] It was the youthful post-Resistance Camus who had argued, in justification of his Resistance activities that, if violence can't be avoided, one must emphasize its scandalous character, refuse its legitimation, and its logic of reason or state, all the while reasserting its limitations.[22] In his *Letters To a German Friend* (1943, 1944) Camus was to point out that the Resisters resorted to violence only after much soul-searching, that their struggle was for the "nuance which separates sacrifice from mysticism, energy from violence, force from cruelty."[23]

Musing on the tension between the rebellious spirit and revolutionary dogma of the New Left, Arendt recuperates Camus' critique of historicism, arguing that progressive thought suffers from the inconsistency that while it rejects a glorified Hegelian and Eurocentric concept of history, it still seeks, like Sartre, to import the notion of human progress back into history via ideological slogans of subaltern emancipation.[24] Much of the remainder of *On Violence* is devoted to a heuristic analysis of violence as a form of political impotence, a sign that a political regime or faction lacks real *power*, the ability to generate activity in concert, or *authority*, durable respect for political leadership and institutional forms. Arendt has done us a great service in distilling a persuasive Camusian concept of politics as an imaginative and courageous activity of measured and preferably nonviolent rebellion against injustice. It remains to be seen how Arendt's high mindedness, her animus toward Sartre's revolutionary commitment, and her anxious desire to distinguish authentic forms of rebellion from "extremism," can be interpreted in light of the events of the Algerian war. For it was during the period of the French-Algerian war that the positions of both her nemesis and preferred interlocutor, Sartre and Camus, were thrown into urgent relief by a cycle of violence and a period of excessive colonial repression that continues to haunt France and Algeria to the present day.

Memmi's Situation

We can fruitfully compare Arendt's discussion of the crisis of the Left's orientation in the late 1960s with Albert Memmi's now classic analysis of the dilemmas of the leftist colonizer in *The Colonizer and the Colonized* (1957). Memmi is fascinated by the ambivalence of left-wing principles when confronted with anticolonial violence and its frequent corollaries of exclusive nationalism and ethnocentric chauvinism. Anticipating Arendt's *On Violence*, Memmi's famous chapter in that work, "The Colonist Who Refuses," explores a *mise en scene* of uncertain outcome, where ethical initiative and structural violence are in perpetual tension. As Memmi ruefully recognizes, the struggle to realize left-wing ideals of respect for the individual must perpetually confront the fatalistic realization that the colonial situation is based on the oppressive relationship between one group of people and another. Thus the "leftist colonizer" will be forced to share the colonizer's destiny, as "he shared its good fortune."[25]

Memmi's ironic, occasionally satirical, yet by no means unsympathetic exploration of the vacillations and aporias of the "colonist who refuses [colonialism]" is a rigorously conceived and composite portrait, by no means the caricature of Camus' isolated and ineffective *pied noir* liberalism described by Conor Cruise O'Brien in *Albert Camus: Of Europe and Africa* (1970), an influential postcolonial reading of Camus as betraying the Algerian independence movement.[26] Memmi offers an ambiguous and dialogically conceived evocation of two leftist European subjectivities responding to the outbreak of rebel violence during the French-Algerian war in the late 1950s. These portraits largely accord with the positions taken on the Algerian war by Camus and Sartre.

Written at the height of the French-Algerian war in 1957, Memmi acknowledges the "drama," the fears and bewilderment of the left-wing *colon* sympathetic to the emancipation of the colonized yet appalled and estranged by the emergence of a violent anticolonial nationalism that threatens his and his family's future existence in, and multicultural ideals for, his beloved *terre natal.* Here one recognizes the republican idealism of Albert Camus, for Memmi a figure of the internationalism and instinctive antiviolence of the post-War European Left. Memmi traces the ways in which the leftist colonizer initially adopts the cause of the colonized; as a radical reporter Camus wrote a series of articles for *Alger républicain* criticizing the appalling social and economic condition of the Kabyle people of Algeria.[27] The leftist colonizer, however, becomes more hesitant when confronted with the ideology and violent practices of the indigenous liberation movement, symptomatic of the way the "European left suffers from immense doubts and real uneasiness in the face of the nationalistic form of those attempts at liberation."[28] At around this period the leftist colonizer is "staggered" to learn that "he will have no place in the future nation," intensifying the gap between his theoretical commitment to the human community and the real distance he feels between his culture and ethical milieu and that of the colonized.[29]

The colonizer who refuses desires a future nation in which he would no longer be protected by the rule of his own army, but by the "fraternity of peoples," a nation renewed by the power of his idealism, his misty-eyed and nostalgic love of the land of his birth.[30] Yet as Camus' sonorous moralizing and complacent humanist nostrums make clear, the leftist colonizer often lacks the necessary imagination to conceive of a deep transformation of his own situation and of his personality, assuming the continuous domination of his culture and language in any future state.[31] Indeed, as late as 1955, Camus continued to assume that a reinvigorated republican French culture could repair the damage it had caused. He argued that a "French vocation" for the Mediterranean region, both historic and cultural, could "draw out the resemblance between the Orient and the West," and, therefore, federate the overseas territories with metropolitan France in a relationship of hybridizing association rather than economic and military domination.[32]

The political ineffectiveness and profound isolation of the leftist colonizer, unable to mobilize his or her demands for political ends, generates an identity crisis, an anomalous position, a retreat into idiosyncratic explanations of the self-evident injustices of colonialism, a lapse into self- mythology, and finally, when overtaken by events, silence.[33] As Memmi notes, the leftist colonizer reaches an aporia, a sense of insurmountable contradiction and uneasiness that, in Camus' case, either collapsed under the pressure of events into sectarian loyalty or found refuge in the clarity of an intrinsic morality and a retreat into sanctimonious posturing. Camus is now best known for controversially arguing in 1958 that he would defend his mother, residing in Algiers, "before justice" itself. For Memmi, Camus' downfall as one of the humanist Left's shining stars marks the perplexities and unsustainable ambivalence generated by the "colonial situation," where all hopes for intercommunal dialogue are shattered by the structural violence of colonialism.[34]

Sartre

Memmi's "drama of the colonizer" is in the generic tradition of Menippean satire, a journey of ideas and a juxtaposition of character types without comfortable resolution. His evocation of leftist angst delicately segues into a depiction of the metropolitan sympathizer with the colonized, recognizable in the imposing Parisian public intellectual Jean-Paul Sartre. It is Sartre who best represents Memmi's figure of the leftist colonizer who accepts and endorses the struggle of the oppressed *tout court*, regardless of its ideological form (perhaps nationalist or theocratic) or tactics (terrorist violence, propaganda, intimidation, and coercion). The Sartrean subject-position is acutely vulnerable to Frantz Fanon's essay, which first appeared in the FLN newspaper *El Moudjahid* in 1957, and asserted that "one of the first duties of intellectuals and democratic elements in colonialist countries is unreservedly to support the national aspirations of colonized peoples."[35] Responding to the charge that the FLN's moral authority was being undermined by acts of terrorism, in particular its probable culpability for the massacre of Algerian villagers loyal to a rival Algerian faction in the Kabylia village of Mélouza in May 1957, Sartre insisted that it was not an issue of supporting or not supporting the FLN: "Listen, whatever the FLN is, it is there, the Algerian Revolution is it. We have to take it how it is."[36] Confessing that he did not know what the FLN wanted, in resigned tones Sartre suggests that "we are only powerless intellectuals asking them to pay attention to moral values . . . they no longer have any confidence in us. . . . They want a rupture."[37]

Whereas Camus had attempted to apply traditional liberal and republican values to his judgment of the colonial situation, Sartre considered "the colonial juncture as being original," thus abandoning his values and usual habits of political thought, which induced him to support the cause of the colonized in the first place.[38] Sartre is Memmi's model of the now resolutely partisan, leftist, anticolonialist who will endorse all the ideological themes of the struggling colonized, supporting "the colonized's unconditional liberation, by whatever means they use, and the future which they seem to have chosen for themselves."[39] Memmi is mindful, however, that the decisiveness of the Sartrean type, his silencing of his own qualms, is an understandable reaction to the exigency of the situation for the colonized. Sartre responded to the colonial situation by internalizing and responding passionately to the plight of indigenous people:

> What! they tell him, a people is waiting, suffering from hunger, illness and contempt, one child in four dies before he is one year old, and he wants assurances on ends and means! . . . The only task at the moment is that of freeing the people. As for the future, there will be plenty of time to deal with it when it becomes the present.[40]

Memmi's Sartre has taken an irrevocable decision, a veritable oath of allegiance, to lend succor in any way possible to colonized and oppressed peoples. The result is a profound legacy of support for intellectuals from colonized countries including Fanon and Memmi himself; a series of devastating analyses of French colonial

exploitation, dispelling the myth of colonialism as a civilizing agent; a voice of
conscience that savagely rebuked the indifference and complicity of the French
population in respect of their army's hideous acts of torture, repression, and genocide during the Algerian war; and a lifelong and laudable commitment to critiquing the nexus of capitalism and imperialism from French colonialism to America's
"genocidal" assault on Vietnam.[41]

Colonialism: Not a Situation but a System

Sartre, the committed anticolonialist, was impatient with Memmi's phenomenology of the ethical tensions and passing hopes for a bicultural community generated
by a colonial situation. Sartre's introduction to Memmi's book tellingly critiques
the latter's interest in humanizing the colonial relationship: "The whole difference
between us arises perhaps because he sees a situation where I see a system."[42] The
difference between systemic analysis and Memmi's situated exploration of fissured
subjectivities and ethical dilemmas is a crucial one for Sartre. Sartre's dialectical
comprehension of "History" seeks to incorporate and then transcend, in Hegelian
fashion, a sociological, cultural, or subjective account of colonial relations. For
Sartre, a colonial "system" should be isolated as a homogenous collective whose
economic functioning and inert reproduction of its original violence transcends
the heterogeneity of historical events and the complexity of human agency. Sartre's
dialectical and historicist prism, predicated on the subordination and then revolutionary emancipation of social categories rendered Other throughout history,
cannot tolerate the anomalous possibility of a "colonist who refuses" and the conciliatory and reformist possibilities such a subjectivity reprises. Ironically, Sartre, the
great philosopher of existential voluntarism, renounces an ethics of choice and self-
transformation in his discussion of the historical necessity of anticolonial violence.

In his *Critique of Dialectical Reason* (1960), Sartre avers that "all the relations" between colonialist and native in the colonial system have originary "practico-inert"
characteristics conditioned by the genocidal invasion of Algeria in 1830 and the
capitalist system of indigenous exploitation it established. These inert conditions
can only be transmuted through a "developing History," that of the reciprocal
violence, the "impotence-revolt" of the masses. Reflecting on the Algerian war,
Sartre posits that "the violence of the rebel *was* the violence of the colonialist,
there was never any other."[43] Sartre transfigures anticolonial violence into revolutionary praxis, deriding liberal critics such as Camus as mere "Good Samaritans"
who refuse the responsibility of historical agency.

Fanon concurred with Sartre's reification of colonialism, affirming in *The Wretched
of the Earth* that "colonialism is only military domination" . . . "the conquest of a
national territory, and the oppression of a people: that is all."[44] For Fanon, French
colonialism in Algeria was coextensive with its initial invasion and occupation,
contrary to the myth of a Franco-Algerian community that he felt the French Left
were still beholden to. Therefore, Fanon concludes, colonialism in Algeria is not

a type of individual relation or a "pattern of relations between individuals. Every Frenchman in Algeria is at the present time an enemy soldier."[45] Fanon's political rhetoric on behalf of the FLN during this period is symbiotic with Sartre's quasi-Hegelian metaphysics of violence as a dialectical praxis of emancipation. Fanon enthuses that on the eve of independence, the Algerian "people are getting ready to begin to go forward again, to put an end to the static period begun by colonization, and to make history."[46] Anticolonial violence is now posited as transformative alchemy. Fanon argues that the realization of an Algerian nation through violence has summarily dispelled the nostalgic, superstitious, and defensive imaginary of the colonial era: the nation is now the very center of the "Algerian man," who has a "new dimension to his existence."[47]

Metropolitan Responses

Sartre's and Fanon's contempt for the residual possibility of Franco-Algerian conciliation, their countermythology of the colonial world as a Manichean polarity of colonizer and colonized, their failure to distinguish between the invading French of 150 years before and the contemporary *pied noir* Franco-Algerian settler community, and their reticence over FLN atrocities including the massacre of non-FLN aligned Algerians at Mélouza in 1957, garnered telling critiques from elements of the French democratic Left and from indigenous Algerians themselves.

These French metropolitan commentators, such as Jean Daniel, Jean-Marie Domenach, and Gilles Martinet were associated with the Comité d'Action, established in 1955, which condemned French colonialism in North Africa and sought a peaceful resolution to the Algerian conflict. Their now forgotten perspectives on the Algerian war remind us that Fanon's fighting words in *El Moudjahid* condemning French liberals in Paris for not unreservedly supporting the Algerian struggle were an often shrill attempt to recapture the moral high ground of a nationalist cause whose tactics were rapidly complicating the allegiances of sympathetic observers; rather than purveying a "transgressive and transitional truth" as Homi Bhabha's hagiographical reading would have it, Fanon, the zealous convert to militant Algerian nationalism, often derided ethical perspectives concerned for social democratic principles and an Algerian future deprived of a bicultural intelligentsia, and French economic capital and technological infrastructure.[48]

One such dissenter from Fanon's militant nationalist theodicy was Jules Martinet, the socialist cofounder of the left-wing news magazine *France observateur.* In January 1958, Martinet, an opponent of the war against Algeria, responded vigorously to Fanon's series of anonymous articles in *El Moudjahid* in 1957. Martinet criticized the polemical intransigence of Fanon the doctrinaire anticolonialist, who, like the French government before the close of the decade, refused to make the concessions necessary for peace. Whereas the FLN had initially communicated its respect for the individual rights of the *colons* living in Algeria, Martinet was dismayed that the FLN's "recent intellectual convert" was making a dangerous ontological leap, suggesting that all the French people living there were to be considered enemies of Algeria, with ominous results for French and Algerian civilians alike.[49] Martinet suggests that the French Left needed to reconcile the exigency of Algerian independence with its internationalist principles, that it was not a matter of indifference as to whether an independent Algeria would become a Nasserite military regime or a socialist republic. Tactical considerations and a patriotic interest in France's future socialism required a discerning interest in those factors that were likely to play in "favour of one or the other."[50]

Another riposte to Fanon's essays in *El Moudjahid* came from Jean Marie Domenach, editor of the progressive magazine *L'Esprit*. Domenach stressed that the FLN's turn towards violence, with its concomitant effacing of a conciliatory paradigm that had animated earlier forms of Algerian nationalism, had weakened the ability of the French intellectuals to help Algerians in their struggle for independence, alienating support for the Algerian cause in France.[51] Anticipating Arendt's analysis of terrorist violence as ephemeral in its political efficacy, Domenach remarks that violence, as celebrated by the FLN, was nothing but a "caricature of power": it testifies only to the absence of authority that sacrifices the final goal for instantaneous shock.[52]

Domenach also argued that the FLN idealization of its terrorist activities as somehow reprising the original heroic struggles of an always existent Algerian nation in dialectical warfare against its French invader tended to erase the social transformations in Algeria undergone in the last one hundred and twenty-five years.[53] Domenach countered that Fanon's resort to eternal definitions of Algeria and a monolithic French invader/colonizer prepared a "terrorism of essences," which was not revolution but its parody. Such an essentializing discourse "prepares generic murders, total war."[54] Domenach concludes that, in the debate over Algeria, greater clarity and political realism would have to replace dehumanizing abstraction.[55]

Bourdieu

Pierre Bourdieu's analyses of the Algerian revolution were written out of sympathy for the plight of the Algerian people in the midst of a chaotic period of spiraling violence. He shared Memmi's patient and cautionary investigation into the creative possibilities and tragic potential of decolonization for a society profoundly transformed by the colonial period. Unlike Fanon and Sartre, Bourdieu counseled against evacuating a sense of individual agency in interpreting the outcome of an unraveling colonial situation. Bourdieu's aim in his sociological studies of Algeria from the 1950s was to show that a whole ethnography was needed, rather than a revolutionary theory, to explain what had occurred in Algeria and the national dispositions this had bequeathed to the country.[56]

In *Algeria 1960*, a work meant to enhance a concrete perception of the conditions pertaining in revolutionary Algeria, Bourdieu implicitly challenges Fanon's enthusiasm for the militarization of the *déclassé* as a revolutionary avant-garde, stressing that the sufferings imposed by the inhuman situation of colonialism are not sufficient in themselves to conceive a new economic and social order.[57] Bourdieu makes a significant distinction between the demoralized, uprooted subproletariat, many of whom had been displaced from rural life by the French army, and what he describes as the "revolutionary disposition" of the organized workers who brought technological and cultural skills to a modern economy.[58] There are economic conditions for the awareness of economic conditions, and in the absence of reasonable expectations or an inability to calculate and predict an objective future, Bourdieu cautions that the subproletariat in Algeria shows a dangerous tendency toward revolutionary chiliasm and magical utopias.[59] Deftly refuting Fanon's intoxication with the "new man" born anew from the dregs of society by militant resistance, Bourdieu argues that the Algerian proletariat can be a truly revolutionary force, but not when they are positioned at the bottom, in the abyss, as "a certain eschatological vision of revolution as reversal would have it."[60]

Bourdieu emphasizes the importance of bilingualism and modern education as the best means for Algerian workers to integrate themselves into the economic and social order. The French language, according to his Algerian interviewees, is felt to be more secular, realistic, and "positive." In an essay written for *Esprit* in 1961, Bourdieu called on Algerians not to give in to the rule of old customs and traditional ancestral values, but to find a new "art of living" for edifying social harmony. In particular there is an urgent postcolonial need for mediators, dialogue, and education to replace the ephemeral unity of military resistance to the French army.[61] One is reminded of Arendt's assertion that "no human relationship is more transitory" than the fraternal solidarity of warfare, a comradeship that was so appealing to Fanon as a panacea for the degradations of the colonized.[62]

Addressing Algeria's postwar condition on the threshold of independence in *The Algerians* (1962), Bourdieu goes on to offer a supple and dynamic analysis of what he termed the "revolution within the revolution." By this he meant that the Algerian war, by its special form and its duration, had transformed the situation in which and by which it was brought into being, heralding a volatile state of affairs with mixed prospects.[63] Wary of the mythology of guerrilla warfare, Bourdieu argues in an optimistic vein that the declaration of open hostilities, ending a lengthy period of hypocritically espousing Franco-Algerian integration, has proved less unfavorable to cultural exchanges than the opaque nature of the FLN underground resistance. The conflict had brought the two sides together in some respects, because aspiring nationalists had necessarily borrowed the efficient means of their adversary, and because "war remains a dialogue when all is said and done."[64] Acknowledging the indebtedness of Algerian nationalism as a discursive construct to Western thought, Bourdieu intimates that the revolutionary situation has generated a "great thirst for learning, understanding, information, material progress" and that in affective sympathy with all former colonial possessions, "Algeria has become resolutely open to the world."[65]

Bourdieu's analyses cum gentle exhortations to Algerians to remain openminded were tempered by his recognition that Algeria contained such "explosive forces" that its real choice was between chaos and an "original form of socialism carefully designed to meet the needs of the actual situation."[66] He had taken note of another centrifugal dynamic within the revolution, the emergence of isolated and defenseless men torn from the organic social units in which they had formerly existed, unable to recall the honor and dignity they had now lost.[67] He was also mindful of a youthful generation "schooled by the war," adolescents often animated by a spirit of radicalism and negativism, which separated them drastically from their elders.[68] Bourdieu challenges Algerians to shirk off xenophobia and poses the question as to whether its creative and bicultural intelligentsia can renew its Islamic identity through transcultural mediation: "Will a personalized Islam emerge from a secularized Algerian intellectual 'between two worlds.'"[69]

While strongly critical of the European *pied noir*, a complacent and insular caste whose ignorance and indifference toward the misery of indigenous Algerians is buttressed by a parochial local press that sustains their "imaginary world" of racist privilege, Bourdieu offers a differentiated analysis of their ranks that neither denies the ethical interest of the "colonist who refuses," nor simply conflates the *pied noir* with metropolitan France. Doubtless with Camus in mind, whose liberal assimilationist rhetoric was wont to ascribe Algerian resentment to aberrant acts of colonial injustice that were capable of redemption through the institution of French republican ideals, Bourdieu stresses that the Algerian uprising is based on an objective situation, that its causes are partially rooted in the collapse of a world of traditional values and the necessary overthrow of an unjust and decaying colonial order.[70] He reminds the "colonizer who refuses" to recognize that:

> formal goodwill, though a thousand times preferable to cynical adherence to prevailing conditions, nevertheless tends to sanction the established order while appearing to be attempting to correct it. The goodwill of the colonizer allows the benefactor to hide from "himself" the fact that his many individual acts of generosity do not erase the injustice that is consubstantial with the existing state of affairs.[71]

Even the most heartfelt language of fraternization between French and Muslim Algerians, Bourdieu suggests, could, by the late 1950s, be complicit with a government policy of integration, pacification, and repression, and this was indeed the prism through which Camus' silence on the question of French torture and military "pacification" tended, with some justification, to be interpreted.[72] Bourdieu recognizes that anticolonialist European-Algerians often experience difficult contradictions, an oscillation between a deeply instilled paternalism and the desire for dialogue and understanding, between moral anguish and sanctimonious admonition.[73]

After the outbreak of civil war in Algeria in 1992 between an antisecularist and revolutionary Islamic party and an authoritarian state controlled by the army, Bourdieu articulated even more clearly his belief that only a careful ethnography explaining the logic of practice within a particular habitus can explain the national dispositions that both colonialism and then a near decade of warfare has bequeathed to Algeria.[74] In an ironic mode, recalling Memmi's discussion of the fatal repetitions generated by the colonial situation, Bourdieu suggests that the Algerian government has become masters in "retrospective revolution," which often acted as an alibi for establishing conservatism. In addition to an aggressive program of Arabization, the Algerian army had repeated what the French had done, with "the same phobias, mania, the same . . . reflexes of barbaric militarism . . . (where) the socialist rhetoric is used to mask and support the perpetuation of lineage privilege."[75]

Diaries of a War

Mouloud Feraoun's *Journal 1955–62: Reflections on the French-Algerian War* provides further insight into what Bourdieu has described as Algeria's "revolution within the revolution," its promise and extreme dangers. Feraoun was a Kabyle educator, French-educated and well respected, who joined the *Centres Sociaux*, a humanitarian educational institution, in 1960. Feraoun's diaries record both the intensification of Algerian nationalist feelings of solidarity and preparedness for sacrifice and the hellish consequences of a war between ruthless and authoritarian opponents. His early diary entries through 1955 readily dismiss the belated and paternalistic "integration" of indigenous Algerians as an autonomous community with equal electoral rights, a policy pursued by the Algerian governor-general Jacques Soustelle on behalf of a nervous metropolitan government from 1955. Describing the immense suffering of the people of his region of Kabylia, Feraoun, imbibing the revolutionary spirit of the early war period, avers in December 1955 that an "insurmountable gap separates us from the French, who are no longer models, or equals, but rather enemies."[76] He decries the hypocrisy of the French, including some of his closest colleagues, and the supposed goodness of the French as "essentially a veiled hatred" based on the colonialist polarities of civilized and barbaric, superior and inferior, Christian and Muslim.[77]

In the early stages of the war, Feraoun sometimes uses a revolutionary rhetoric not dissimilar to Fanon's intoxicated narrative of rupture. For example he repudiates the French designation of the nationalist leaders as criminals, bandits, and terrorists by acknowledging the revolutionary hopes of the Kabylia populations, who are with the "courageous and committed" nationalist rebels in spirit and desire to "wash away with their blood our shame at being inferior men."[78] Giving the lie to liberal *pied noir* homilies about fraternity and shared fate on a common land, Feraoun argues that there has never been a "marriage" between the two communities. The French have remained scornfully aloof, have always believed that they were Algeria, and have remained "foreigners on our land." The only possible option, Feraoun concludes, is to harvest this mutual indifference "that is the opposite of love."[79] For after all, Feraoun notes dryly, the French never seriously talked about integration when it was possible thirty to forty years ago; no French economist ever proposed a realistic plan to industrialize Algeria, and the French people have never welcomed Algerian workers, who, driven by dire need, have come to France.[80]

Feraoun's rhetorical mode is one of perpetual questioning, ironic detachment, syncopated rhythms, and the Socratic musings of an urbane educator willing to suspend all prejudices and acknowledge his own hybrid condition in the search for understanding. Speaking from a generational distance, as a teacher and a writer, he "cannot help but remain cautious, especially because I am well educated and know a little history."[81] The horrendous violence of the war raises difficult questions. In his own area of Fort-National in the Kabylia region the atmosphere has become cordial but tense. People are apprehensive and barely communicative, and this is not due simply to a fear of the French military repression. Rather the desire for freedom has evolved into the burden of partisanship, the necessity of obeying the aims of increasingly authoritarian nationalists. Upon hearing of secret assemblies between villagers and rebel delegates in local mosques in January of 1956, Feraoun states that the rebels' expectations are "both excessive and disappointing," including endless prohibitions that are dictated by the "most obtuse fanaticism, the most intransigent racism, and the most authoritarian fist," a mode of "true terrorism" in his words. Rejecting French introduced medical knowledge and technology, Feraoun reports that it is now forbidden in villagers for pregnant women to call for a doctor or a pharmacist.[82]

Feraoun is acutely aware of the dangers posed by a heroic nationalist mythology seeking to revive uncontaminated precolonial origins. He comments warily that the rebel visitors from their strongholds in the mountainous regions of Kabylia adopt the sanctified guise of heroes and apostles, "just as we would welcome the great saints of Islam one knows so well."[83] Meanwhile, Feraoun worries about the closing of schools in the local area, under threat from both the French military and the FLN, and a younger generation of nationalist youths. Like Bourdieu he is anxious about the aggressive assertiveness of militant young men, who, forgetting over a century of Franco-Algerian history, are scornful of their elders and prey to militant propaganda, wanting nothing more than to "avenge the first moudjahiddins."[84] People now think that it is time to avenge the ancestors of the Kabylias, who a century ago were ruthlessly crushed by a well-armed conqueror. Now the young, beardless French soldiers, whom the humane Feraoun expresses pity for, appear to Algerians as the first foreign legions.[85] We are gradually becoming insensitive to violence, he muses, while at the same time the FLN leaders stay hidden, refuse to declare their real intention, and yet impose their will ruthlessly on the local population. A derelict man and a crazy woman are killed by puritanical rebels; they were harmless, comments Feraoun, in no way can their murder have served the great cause of the rebels. Up to now the rebels were aiming to right grievous wrongs, but "now they are claiming to defend great principles."[86]

Feraoun's doubts continue to grow; the hubris of the nationalists and their desire to recolonize Algeria becomes more and more evident:

> We thought they wanted to liberate the country along with its inhabitants. But maybe they feel that this generation of cowards that is proliferating in Algeria must first disappear, that a truly free Algeria must be populated with new men who have not known the yoke of the secular invader.[87]

Discussing the massacre of poor French farmers, Feraoun questions whether those who kill in cold blood can be called liberators: "have they considered for a moment that their 'violence' will engender more 'violence,' will legitimize it, and will hasten its terrible manifestation?"[88]

Feraoun's diaries record his acute isolation in a nightmarish world bereft of dignity and compassion. He talks of the "desolation of war, the waste caused by an attack of raving madness." Discussing the massacre of seventeen young Parisians in the Kabylia area, Feraoun comments that, "this is the other side of a grotesque medal that we are minting with the flesh of innocent people in order to safeguard the right of the strongest." Feraoun comments bitterly that the *pied noir* newspapers only publish one side of this medal while ignoring the most hideous side, the devastation wrought by the French army, the systematic torture, relocation, the bombing of entire villages.[89]

And where do Feraoun's liberal French-Algerian friends, the writers Camus and Emmanuel Roblès stand on this, he asks. Do they truly dissent from the mendacity and silences of the *pied noir* toward the suffering of his people? They are wrong to talk to us, we Algerians, he says, when they cannot express their thoughts completely, when we Algerians are waiting for "generous hearts." Caustically rebuking Camus' self-serving rhetoric of fraternization, Feraoun observes that if leftist colonizers are to consider themselves Algerians, they must stand with those who fight for independence; they must "tell the French that this country does not belong to them, that they took it by force and intend to remain by force. Anything else is a lie, and in bad faith."[90] As Arendt, a German-Jew, would record of her German friends in the early years of Nazi rule, in a situation of gathering crisis, a vacuum forms around one, friends from the dominant group are notable by their silence.

Feraoun's panic grows; he is in the middle of hell; businesses fail and die; poverty is setting in. He senses that the thirst for military stripes only enhances warlike virtues, helps the villagers to commit injustices that diminish them today and will exhaust them tomorrow.[91] The French, the Kabylia, the soldier, and the rebel fellagha frighten him. He is afraid of himself. "The French are inside me, the Kabyle are inside me," he says, acknowledging the difficulties of maintaining bicultural attachments in an atmosphere of self-sacrificing national unity.[92] He feels disgust for those who kill, because they have the backbone to kill. Crimes are now rendered necessary, like acts of faith or worthy deeds.[93]

Feraoun feels that there is a general mania in the air, a distortion of human relationships. He notes with sorrow that a "century together has been deliberately forgotten." Instead a "metallic, ice-cold bridge" has been thrown over a century of Franco-Algerian history, a history that included cross-cultural friendships, the pluralist ideal of a multicultural Algeria, the arrival of dedicated French educators to outlying villages, and his own education into French language and literature. A "blade on fire" stands poised over this century now, he mourns; it is stained with the blood of men: that of the fighters and the victims. In the end, he feels, it will form a bloody line of retribution across a useless page.[94] Dismayed by a numbing cycle of violence that involves FLN attacks on French patrols, or attacks on isolated French farms, followed by French repression, relocation, and disappearances for the purposes of torture, Feraoun admits that, "it is true that 'violence breeds violence.' We live this cruel truth on a daily basis. It is the only truth that is left."[95]

A Phenomenology of Violence

We can consider Feraoun's diaries, his harrowing and increasingly despairing depiction of the atomization, ethical deterioration, and political instability generated by violence as consonant in many respects with Arendt's sober discussion of violence as an ephemeral, unpredictable, and destructive phenomenon, inimical to a stable and prudential political realm. Arendt herself could well have uttered Camus' denunciation of FLN terrorism as a "bloody error in itself and in its consequences," which, by the "force of events" became racist in its turn, ceasing to be the "instrument of controlled politics" but rather the "mad folly of an elemental hatred."[96] Her analysis reprises Bourdieu, Domenach, and Feraoun's insight that violence generates a self-perpetuating dynamic that convulses the social fabric, threatening to repeat, by a gesture of absolute reversal, the authoritarianism and invasive ideology of the original conquest. Arendt's interpretation of violence as exceeding any cognitive or ethical recuperation in an era of total war and the proliferation of technologies of mass destruction is a salutary reprise of Gandhi's habit of rigorously questioning the tactical wisdom and organic effects of anticolonial violence.

However, Arendt shares not only Camus' rejection of revolutionary theory and the philosophy of history that underpins it, but also the sterility of his liberal imperialism. Arendt enacts the ambivalences and evasions of the leftist colonizer when confronted by subaltern demands. Like Camus, from *Origins* to *On Violence*, Arendt adjudges the real tragedy of colonialism as its abrogation of European humanism and republican values, rather than its invasion and displacement of existing indigenous cultures. Unlike Sartre, Arendt refused to acknowledge those dimensions of colonialism and imperialism that constituted physical and cultural genocide, consistently failing to acknowledge the dignity and complexity of non-Western societies and the subjectivity of non-Western peoples. Anne Norton has commented on the ways in which Arendt's oeuvre prioritizes the "literary nation," ascribing world-historical importance to Western philosophical and political traditions alone.[97] Arendt praises the white student movement as inheriting Western traditions of civil disobedience, while constituting Africa and African Americans as outside of world history. African American demands are trivialized and infantilized as an "outlet into irrationality" or an "escape from reality."[98]

As with Camus on the Algerian question, when confronted by the detrimental impact of Zionism on the Palestinian people, Arendt acknowledges it but also dissembles. In her prescient essay of 1944, "Zionism Reconsidered," Arendt cautions against "Herzlian Zionism," the drive to establish an ethnocentric nation-state for the Jews in mandated Palestine. Rather, she argues, echoing Camus' idea that the pluralism of the Mediterranean should be respected, that a "Jewish homestead" should only be established on the basis of a "broad understanding that takes into account the region and the needs of all its peoples."[99] Yet, for Arendt, the Camusian leftist colonizer, the response of the Palestinian people is neither sought for nor even imagined as a potential interlocutor in this fraternal gesture. Arendt's desire for bicultural relations with Palestinians is comfortably buttressed by a powerful colonial enterprise and a Kibbutzim-oriented conception of the authentic Zionist vocation in Palestine that is carefully sequestered from its settler-colonial function.[100]

Arendt's valuable theoretical contribution to the ethics and political significance of violence is vitiated by her lack of interest in a colonized or subaltern perspective on the racist exclusions and colonialist inheritance of Western liberalism. The many voices we have discussed suggest the importance of dialogue rather than abstraction, along with a nuanced analysis of the texts and contexts of decolonization rather than an orthodox anticolonialism or a comfortable critique of revolutionary desire.

Notes

1. Hannah Arendt, *On Violence* (New York, 1970). See appendix III where she writes: "Even more alarming is the inclination of faculty as well as administration to treat drug addicts and criminal elements . . . with considerably more leniency than the authentic rebels" (91).
2. See James Le Sueur, "Introduction," *The Decolonization Reader*, ed. James D. Le Sueur (New York and London, 2003), 2.
3. Arendt, *On Violence*, 4.
4. Ibid., 4–5.
5. Hannah Arendt, *The Human Condition* (Chicago, 1973), 263.
6. Ibid., 26–7.
7. Ibid., 26.
8. Arendt, *On Violence*, 18.
9. Ibid., 6, 9.
10. Ibid., 9.
11. Ibid., 10.
12. Ibid., 11.
13. Ibid., 14.
14. Ibid., 20.
15. Ibid., 15.
16. Ibid., 23.
17. Ibid., 19.
18. Ibid., 20. Arendt credits the Algerian-based Fanon with managing to "stay closer to reality" than most speculative theorists of revolution (*On Violence*, 20), a barely disguised barb at Sartre.
19. Hannah Arendt, "Concern with Politics in Recent European Thought" (1954), in *Essays in Understanding 1930–1954*, ed. Jerome Kohn (New York, 1994), 438.

20. Ronald Aronson, *Camus and Sartre, the Story of a Friendship and the Quarrel that Ended It* (London and Chicago, 2004), 116. The following quotes from *The Rebel* exemplify Camus' interpretation of the "rebel's" commitment to communication and a sense of limitation: "when he rebels, a man identifies himself with other men and, from this point of view, human solidarity is metaphysical" and "in order to exist, man must rebel, but rebellion must respect the limits that it discovers in itself—limits where minds meet, and in meeting, begin to exist. Revolutionary thought, therefore, cannot dispense with memory." Albert Camus, *The Rebel* (London, 1960), 23, 27. Compare Camus' ideal of rebellion with Arendt's description of the plural and communicative conditions of political activity in *The Human Condition.*

21. Jeffrey C. Isaac, *Arendt, Camus, and Modern Rebellion* (New Haven and London, 1992), 17, 35.

22. See Albert Camus, *Réflexions sur le Terrorisme* (Paris, 2002), 27. The translation is my own. In May 1952, in a deliberate rebuff to the towering Parisian figure of Sartre, Arendt wrote to her husband Heinrich Blücher that Camus is the "best man now in France. He's head and shoulders above the other intellectuals." See Tony Judt, *The Burden of Responsibility: Blum, Camus, Aron, and the French Twentieth Century* (Chicago and London, 1998), 90. Arendt demonstrated her loyalty and sympathy for an increasingly embattled Camus in April 1952 when she wrote him a warm and admiring letter of praise for *L'Homme révolté.*

23. Camus, *Réflexions sur le Terrorisme,* 45.

24. Arendt, *On Violence,* 25.

25. Albert Memmi, *The Colonizer and the Colonized,* trans. Howard Greenfeld (London, 2003), 82.

26. Edward Said has been implacably hostile to Camus' stance on Algeria, describing his position as a hypocritical last ditch defense of French imperialism and Camus himself as paralyzed by a lack of empathy for indigenous Algerians. See Edward Said, *Culture and Imperialism* (London, 1994), 204–224. Said described a temporizing Camus as the "archetypal trimmer" in "Michael Walzer's *Exodus and Revolution*: A Canaanite Reading," in *Blaming the Victims: Spurious Scholarship and the Palestinian Question,* ed. Edward W. Said and Christopher Hitchens (London and New York, 1988), 174. David Schalk records that a letter by Memmi sent to the editors of the journal *La Nef* and published in 1957, notes that Camus does incarnate the colonizer of good will, but insists that the subject-position that he describes is "neither comical nor deserving of scorn." Quoted in David L. Schalk, *War and the Ivory Tower: Algeria and Vietnam* (Oxford and New York, 1991), 199.

27. See James D. Le Sueur, *Uncivil War: Intellectuals and Identity Politics during the Decolonization of Algeria* (Philadelphia, 2001), 91.

28. Memmi, *The Colonizer and the Colonized,* 73.

29. Ibid., 82.

30. For an example of Camus' desire to eternalize his conception of a pluralist and fraternal Algeria forged in the heyday of his period as a social activist on behalf of indigenous Algerians in the 1930s and immediately after the war, see his "Letter to an Algerian militant," addressed to the Algerian socialist leader Aziz Kessous in 1956: "we are united in the love that we carry for our country . . . we can live happily together on this earth that is ours." See Albert Camus, *Selected Political Writings* (London, 1981), 169. The translation is my own.

31. Memmi, *The Colonizer and the Colonized,* 84.

32. Quoted in Le Sueur, *Uncivil War,* 98.

33. Camus' now famous call in 1956 for a truce protecting civilian lives is a telling example of leftist colonizers' descent into idiosyncratic projection when confronted with their own ineffectiveness. Camus faced a mostly Algerian Muslim audience, including the important Algerian nationalist spokesperson and former moderate assimilationist, Ferhat Abbas. Many in the audience, such as Abbas, were now active on behalf of the FLN. Having to talk over the hate-filled invective directed towards him by European *pied noir* ultras outside, in the midst of a period of devastating French repression and intensifying FLN terrorism, Camus describes the cycle of violence, as he does in his writings of the period, as a "family quarrel," and speaks sanguinely of a "community of hope" founded on "different but rooted populations." See Camus, *Réflexions sur le Terrorisme,* 163, 165.

34. Quoted in Le Sueur, *Uncivil War,* 111. Camus, delivering a speech at the University of Uppsala four days after receiving the Nobel Prize for literature on December 10 1957, was responding to the heckling of an Algerian student, when he uttered these now infamous words.

35. Frantz Fanon, *Toward the African Revolution* (London, 1970), 86.

36. Jean Daniel, "Jean Paul Sartre," quoted in Le Sueur, *Uncivil War,* 195. This was from an unedited interview of 13 January 1958 in *Le Temps qui reste,* 251–55.

37. Ibid., 254.

38. Memmi, *The Colonizer and the Colonized,* 76.

39. Ibid., 81.

40. Ibid., 79.

41. See Sartre's insightful analysis of the colonization of Algeria in his introduction to *The Colonizer and the Colonized.* For Sartre's accusation of French silence, mutual suspicion, and bad faith in respect to events in Algeria, see the chapter "We are All Murderers" in Jean-Paul Sartre, *Colonialism and Neocolonialism,* trans. Azzedine Haddour, Steve Brewer, Terry McWilliams (London and New York, 2001). In *On Genocide,* written in 1968, Sartre describes the American attack on Vietnam as genocidal in its assault on the fabric and livelihood of a civilian population, and in its intended admonitory effect on other potential resistors against the neocolonialism of the United States. See Jean-Paul Sartre, *On Genocide* (Boston, 1968), 55–85.

42. Jean-Paul Sartre, "Introduction," *The Colonizer and the Colonized,* 21.

43. Jean-Paul Sartre, *Critique of Dialectical Reason* (London, 1991), 716, 725, 733.

44. See Frantz Fanon, "French Intellectuals and Democrats and the Algerian Revolution," in *Toward the African Revolution* (London, 1970), 91, which first appeared in *El Moudjahid* in 1957.

45. Ibid., 91.

46. Frantz Fanon, *The Wretched of the Earth* (London, 1973), 54.

47. Quoted in Le Sueur, *Uncivil War,* 245.

48. See Homi Bhabha, "Remembering Fanon," in *Remaking History,* ed. Barbara Kruger and Phil Mariani (Seattle, 1989), 132.

49. Le Sueur, *Uncivil War,* 189.

50. Ibid., 194.

51. Ibid., 190.

52. Ibid., 190.

53. Ibid., 191.

54. Ibid., 191.

55. Ibid., 192.

56. Michael Grenfell, *Pierre Bourdieu, Agent Provacateur* (London and New York, 2004), 52.

57. Pierre Bourdieu, *Algeria 1960: the Disenchantment of the World, the Sense of Honor, the Kabyle House or the World Reversed,* trans. Richard Nice (Cambridge, 1979), 60.

58. Ibid., viii.

59. Ibid., 56, 70.

60. In a similar vein Bourdieu rejects what he describes as a "mechanical image" of revolutionary violence as unfolding according to a Fanonian logic of, in Bourdieu's words, "compression and explosion." For Bourdieu, Fanon obscures the sociological insight that intense oppression does not usually coincide with the most acute awareness of oppression. This ignorance, according to Bourdieu, confounds the realistic apprehension of an "objective situation,"on which a successful revolutionary movement could be based. See *Algeria 1960,* 93.

61. Pierre Bourdieu, Quoted in Grenfell, *Pierre Bourdieu,* 51. It was originally in "Révolution dans la revolution," *Esprit* (January, 1961): 27–40.

62. Arendt, *On Violence,* 69.

63. Pierre Bourdieu, *The Algerians,* trans. Alan C.M. Ross (Boston, 1962), 155.

64. Ibid., 187.

65. Ibid., 188–90.

66. Ibid., 192.

67. Ibid., 184.
68. Ibid., 186.
69. Ibid., 118.
70. Ibid., 144.
71. Ibid., 148.
72. For a balanced historical analysis of Camus' position on the Algerian question, and its reception by the French Left at that time, see the chapter "The Question of Albert Camus" in Le Sueur's *Uncivil War*, 87–127.
73. Bourdieu, *The Algerians*, 149.
74. Grenfall, *Pierre Bourdieu*, 52.
75. See Pierre Bourdieu, Quoted in Grenfell, *Pierre Bourdieu*, 53. It is from *Interventions 1961–2001*, ed. T. Discepolo and F. Poupeau (Marseilles, 2002).
76. Mouloud Feraoun, *Journal, 1955–1962: Reflections on the French-Algerian War* (Lincoln, 2000), 25.
77. Feraoun, *Journal, 1955–1962*, 25.
78. Ibid., 39
79. Ibid., 42.
80. Ibid., 43.
81. Ibid., 69.
82. Ibid., 53.
83. Ibid., 54.
84. Ibid., 118.
85. Ibid., 60.
86. Ibid., 107.
87. Ibid., 85.
88. Ibid., 84.
89. Ibid., 107.
90. Ibid., 71.
91. Ibid., 118.
92. Ibid., 90.
93. Ibid., 90.
94. Ibid., 118.
95. Ibid., 78.
96. See Albert Camus, "Terrorisme et Répression," in *Reflexions sur Terrorisme*, 139.
97. Anne Norton, "Heart of Darkness: Africa and African Americans in the Writings of Hannah Arendt," in *Feminist Interpretations of Hannah Arendt*, ed. Bonnie Honig (University Park, 1995), 249, 253.
98. Arendt, *On Violence*, 65.
99. From Hannah Arendt, "Zionism Reconsidered" (1944), in *The Jew as Pariah: Jewish Identity and Politics in the Modern Age*, ed. Ron Feldman (New York, 1978), 133.
100. Arendt, *The Jew as Pariah*, 138.

Chapter 7

ANTI-SEMITISM, THE BOURGEOISIE, AND THE SELF-DESTRUCTION OF THE NATION-STATE

Marcel Stoetzler[1]

This chapter is about a series of contradictions in Hannah Arendt's writings, contradictions that she names and explores, and contradictions in her own discourse. Arendt's writings are a declaration of antipathy to the bourgeoisie by a thoroughly bourgeois writer, a defense of the nation-state based on dislike of nationalism, a defense of traditional bourgeois values from modern bourgeois domination, and an account of the modern state that granted the Jews emancipation at a point when, by becoming national, it was in the process of preparing the renewal of the Jews' exclusion and persecution.

Hannah Arendt "explained the centrality of anti-Semitism to modern European history" with reference to the "contradiction between society (reflected in such forms as nation, class and race) and the state."[2] This perspective was part of her wider theory that the destruction of what is reasonable and related to human freedom (represented as the political, the institutional, the state) is to be blamed on the dominance of "the social"—signifying necessity and non-freedom—as typical of the modern condition. This condition is determined essentially by the modern bourgeoisie. A discussion of the place anti-Semitism holds in Arendt's account of the self-destruction of the nation-state must therefore crucially include that of her vision of the bourgeoisie as a traditional as much as anti-traditional class. It entails a critique of capitalist modernity from what seems to be the perspective of the traditional values, as opposed to the modernizing dynamism, of the bourgeoisie. This is the larger framework in which Arendt explores anti-Semitism and nationalism.

Anti-Semitism

The gist of Arendt's position on anti-Semitism is that "modern antisemitism grew in proportion as traditional nationalism declined, and reached its climax at the exact moment when the European system of nation-states and its precarious balance of power crashed."[3] The link between both phenomena, and also for Arendt the key to understanding anti-Semitism, is the fact that "Jews received their citizenship from governments which in the process of centuries had made nationality a prerequisite for citizenship and homogeneity of population the outstanding characteristic of the body politic."[4] Jewish emancipation depended on the growth of a new type of state—independent from the existing groups and structures of civil society—that is usually referred to as bourgeois but from which the gentile bourgeoisie (with which Arendt typically means the *Wirtschaftsbürgertum*) stayed "aloof."

In all major nineteenth-century discourses on emancipation—the "Jewish question," the "workers' question," the "colonial question," and the "women's question"—admission to bourgeois society was made conditional on material as well as cultural adaptation to bourgeois standards. These included being a useful and productive member of society and loyal to the nation. The irony is that the liberal Enlightenment discourse that "economic merits or demerits" rather than religious affiliation should determine membership of the "Commonwealth"[5] became at the end of the nineteenth century as central to anti-Semitism as it had previously been to Jewish emancipation. Hertzberg writes for example that the readmission of Jews into France after 1500 "had been rooted in mercantilist considerations," i.e., the (traditional and at the time still quite accurate) notion that the presence of Jews would increase international trade.[6] Emerging "free trade" thinking among administrators and early economists also reduced their hostility to (irregular, especially Jewish) small-scale trade. Hertzberg names Colbert and Turgot whose fight against the guilds implied bringing "Jewish traders and artisans into the mainstream of the economy" as "the most important lineal ancestors" of the emancipation decrees of the Revolution.[7] Most importantly, these trends—as it were, the quasi-liberalism that was inherent to the *ancien régime*—were opposed not only by the traditionalism of peasants and guilds but also by a competing strand of modernizers: the "physiocrats" developed a theory of economic productivity (as opposed to the mercantilist theory that wealth derives from trade) according to which none of "the traditional Jewish trades" seemed "economically useful." Hertzberg points out that the implicit anti-Jewishness of physiocracy's concern with productivity—also one of the formative stages of modern political economy—left traces within the discourse of the Jacobins[8] and subsequently those of early nineteenth-century liberals, democrats, and socialists. This tradition is behind what Arendt calls "a brand of liberal antisemitism which lumped Jews and aristocracy together and pretended that they were in some kind of financial alliance against the rising bourgeoisie,"[9] promoted by early liberals in Prussia as in France. It far outlived the period when it had some point of reference in reality. It was mirrored, however, since the short period of antifeudal reform in Prussia between 1807 and 1815, by a form of *anti-liberal* anti-Semitism that expressed conservative aristocratic opposition to modernization and attacked reformed Prussia as a "new-fangled Jew-state."[10]

The configuration under French absolutism, in which the quasi-liberal policy of Turgot and Colbert found itself opposed on one side by the modern discourse on productivity, on the other by the social conservatism of the guilds, can be rediscovered similarly throughout the history of anti-Semitism. All of these have in the nineteenth century been elements of the liberal tradition. Populist, petty bourgeois (especially artisanal) anti-Semitism was rooted in anticapitalist and antimodernist moral sentiments[11] that often stigmatized capitalist modernity as "Jewish." To the extent that in the course of the nineteenth-century aristocratic as well as petty-bourgeois resistance to the capitalist mode of production crumbled, only the latter's openly destructive, extreme, and most unpopular aspects continued to be referred to as "Jewish." Anti-Semites from the second half of the nineteenth century onwards tended to blame what they would see as the "exaggerations" of modern capitalist development on the influence of the "Jewish spirit." Blaming the nasty sides of moneymaking on "the Jewish spirit" helped disappointed liberals and democrats bridge the gap between embracing industrial capitalism but at the same time being locked into an older, competing system of values that stemmed from petty bourgeois, small-scale commodity production. The "leftist movement of the lower middle class and the entire propaganda against banking capital turned more or less antisemitic."[12] Central to this development was the denunciation of Jews as unproductive appropriators of the wealth produced by the productive classes, which experienced themselves united as the national community. Anybody's notion of what constituted a healthy and desirable extent of capitalist modernity implied a complementary notion of what was *excessive* capitalist modernity—greed, materialism, usury, speculation, mammonization, predatory capital. The strategy of blaming that excess on "the Jews" fitted into socialist or liberal just as well as into conservative or reactionary frameworks.

The Bourgeoisie, the Social, and the Nation

One of my favorite Hannah Arendt quotes stems from her short essay, "The Eggs Speak Up":

> The material conclusion from true insight into a century so fraught with danger of the greatest evil should be a radical negation of the whole concept of the lesser evil in politics, because far from protecting us against the greater ones, the lesser evils have invariably led us into them.[13]

Arendt mocks in this essay "normally happy philistines"[14] whose normality, mediocrity, and smugness paved the road to hell. "Radical negation" of "lesser evils" is of course a tall order, and few people will be able to claim they never opted for a "lesser evil." Arendt certainly could not have made such a claim for herself: rejection of "lesser evils" is hardly compatible with the idea of "acting politically," which Arendt so vehemently defended and which almost by definition aims at reaching compromises. The radicalism and anger of "The Eggs Speak Up" seems to represent a subtext of Arendt's work that rarely comes to the surface of the text but points to a contradiction that is central to her work and is apparent most clearly in her account of the nation-state: the latter figures at the same time as one of those "lesser evils" that paved the road to (Nazi) hell, and as a normative ideal that seems worth defending as a weapon even against just that post nation-state hell.[15]

The figure of "the philistine" stands for the most despicable characteristics of the bourgeoisie according to Arendt. It is interesting to note that Arendt made frequent use of this concept, which comes straight from the heart of German early Romanticism: as Arendt herself reports, it was coined by Clemens von Brentano in a satire written for the anti-Semitic, nationalistic *Christlich-Deutsche Tischgesellschaft* in 1811.[16] These patriotic intellectuals tried to out-noble the nobility, if not in the real world then at least in the fields of imagination and *Bildung,* and created with the "true innate personality" in opposition to the shallow existence of "the philistine" a *topos* that has since then helped "the German bourgeois . . . to attribute to other peoples all the qualities which the nobility despised as typically bourgeois." These other, "philistine" peoples were, of course, the French, the English, and the Jews.[17] Arendt despises not only the anti-Semitism of these bourgeois intellectuals but most of all its motivation: the effort to emulate and flatter rather than to fight the nobility, a tendency that she writes became central in turn to *Bildungs*-philistinism especially in Germany. The people who coined the concept of the philistine were, or became, exactly that—philistines.

Further down in *The Origins of Totalitarianism,* though, Arendt defines her own version of the concept that is not too dissimilar from Brentano's, except that it is formulated as a social, not a national category:

> The philistine's retirement into private life, his single-minded devotion to matters of family and career was the last, and already degenerated, product of the bourgeoisie's belief in the primacy of private interest. The philistine is the bourgeois isolated from his own class, the atomized individual who is produced by the breakdown of the bourgeois class itself.[18]

This definition, and the polemic against liberal[19] philistines in "The Eggs Speak Up," even shares some characteristics with her own later depiction of the Nazi *über*-philistine, the indeed totally unromantic Adolf Eichmann.

The basically private and egoistic mindset of the bourgeoisie can be gleaned according to Arendt from cynical slogans such as "nothing succeeds like success" or "might is right," which she considers bourgeois home truths. She also sees them as late reflections of the logical "magnificence" of Thomas Hobbes who reduced the "publique interest" more consistently to the "private interest" than anybody else ever did, and who developed a concept of the (bourgeois) state as in its essence nothing but power in the service of combined egotisms—"the only great philosopher to whom the bourgeoisie can rightly and exclusively lay claim."[20] Rather prophetically, Hobbes was able to "detect in the rise of the bourgeoisie all those antitraditionalist qualities of the new class which would take more than three hundred years to develop fully."[21] "All so-called liberal concepts of politics"—that is, all preimperialist political notions of the bourgeoisie such as "unlimited competition regulated by a secret balance which comes mysteriously from the sum total of competing activities"—have in common that they

> simply add up private lives and personal behaviour patterns and present the sum as laws of history, or economics, or politics. Liberal concepts, however, . . . are only a temporary compromise between the old standards of Western culture and the new class's faith in property as a dynamic, self-moving principle. The old standards give way to the extent that automatically growing wealth actually replaces political action.[22]

This dichotomy between "the tradition" and the antitraditionalism of the new dominant class lies behind Arendt's understanding of republicanism.[23] The German tradition of republicanism differed from the one that started from Machiavelli and the Scottish Enlightenment insofar as the latter had rejected the agrarian presuppositions of Aristotelian republicanism with the notion that "commercial society" could be the basis of modern republics. Arendt (following the German republican tradition that included, as Springborg suggests, among others Kant, Nietzsche, and Weber) reemphasized a distinction which the proponents of the "commercial republic" had rejected, namely that of politics as the realm of freedom versus economics as the realm of necessity and non-freedom. Arendt sees the political sphere as "the stage for individual actions among peers" while "the social" is the extension of the patriarchal family (*oikos*) and the realm of public housekeeping (*oikonomia*).[24] This distinction is Janus-faced: it is, on the one hand, apologetic to the extent that it tends to naturalize and legitimize the existence of non-freedom in the social sphere, including slavery;[25] but it is also, on the other hand, critical insofar as it makes clear that political liberty based on the separation of the political from the social leaves the non-freedom of the social unchallenged. Arendt believed that the major shortcoming of the modern world was that the (social) realm of necessity was continually expanding into the (political) realm of freedom: the whole world seemed to turn into a big quasi-family, crushing the fragile realms of freedom with the naturalized inequality typical of despotism within the *oikos*.[26]

Arendt's idealized vision of the political life of the ancient Greek *polis* is based on a typical nineteenth-century misunderstanding: historians then projected the liberal idea of historical progress "from Savagery, through Barbarism to Civilization" onto their sources and misconstrued the ancient *polis* as the breakthrough of what they thought of as "Civilization." The transition to civilization in the form of the *polis* and "the creation of explicitly political forms," was assumed to involve "the transcendence [and renunciation] of primordial forms of association based on family, clan, tribe."[27] Here, in the idealist notion of progress from necessity to liberty lies also one of the historical backdrops of the distinction between "Western, political" (namely derived from the *polis*) and Eastern, not-so-political forms of the nation-state, that to an extent still underlie Arendt's account as well.[28] However, the persistence of traditional structures is far from incompatible with political society and has always been essential to it, including the case of the *polis*.[29] Arendt's enmity against "the social," which involves the non-freedom and necessities of bourgeois/civil [*bürgerliche*] society and enthusiasm for "the political" (liberty, reason, autonomous subjectivity), is driven by her concern with a lack of "the political" in modern society. It is out of this concern that she mobilizes the myth that before the nineteenth century, Western society enjoyed "a way of life that could be deemed political—urban, heterogeneous, entrepreneurial, face-to-face, highly participatory, and democratic—that they no longer do."[30] The critical impulse of this line of thought can, and must, be salvaged by doing away with the myth and the nostalgia: we did not lose liberty at the point of entering the nineteenth century; rather, we still need to find it in the first place.

The main point of reference in Arendt's historical framework is the "period of imperialism" (1884–1914, in Arendt's definition) which "led to an almost complete break in the continuous flow of Western history as we had known it for more than two thousand years."[31] Its "central inner-European event" was "the political emancipation of the bourgeoisie, which up to then had been the first class in history to achieve economic pre-eminence without aspiring to political rule." The takeover of the state by this class of nonpolitical egotists destroyed whatever was left of the "European tradition" and set the scene for a century of massacres. For Arendt, both the bourgeoisie's "early apathy" concerning politics and its later support for dictatorship "had their roots in a way and philosophy of life so insistently and exclusively centered on the individual's success or failure in ruthless competition that a citizen's duties and responsibilities could only be felt to be a needless drain on his limited time and energy."[32] Her dislike of the bourgeoisie went so far that it allowed her (not at all a Marxist) to make what is probably the most perceptive and empathetic remark anyone ever made on "Marx's antisemitism:" the "first generation of educated Jews" who "still wanted sincerely to lose their identity as Jews" and "longed for a country without either Christians or Jews"[33]—a group among whose heirs she seems to have counted herself—"were greatly hurt when they found out that governments which would give every privilege and honor to a Jewish banker, condemned Jewish intellectuals to starvation." If they were "worth their salt, all became rebels," as Arendt herself certainly did,

> and since the most reactionary governments of the period were supported and financed by Jewish bankers, their rebellion was especially violent against the official representatives of their own people. The anti-Jewish denunciations of Marx and Boerne cannot be properly understood except in the light of this conflict between rich Jews and Jewish intellectuals.[34]

Arendt's own criticisms of the "official representatives" of Zionism, to which she nevertheless somehow subscribed, and for which she was, again like Marx, denounced with the old chestnut of "Jewish self-hatred," was really motivated by a hatred of the bourgeoisie's tendency to betray the classical republican ideals of the "European tradition" (in Israel neither more nor less than anywhere else). If a person of rather high opinions about her own "self" can meaningfully be accused of any such thing at all, Arendt showed at the very most something like "bourgeois self-hatred," a phenomenon that would be described better, though, as an ambivalence between "classic" bourgeois and antibourgeois feelings.

Before looking at how and why, according to Arendt, the bourgeoisie is guilty of having destroyed the nation-state, and what this has to do with anti-Semitism, it is necessary to look more closely at how Arendt developed the concept of the nation-state in the first place. Her starting point was that

> [t]he fundamental political reality of our time is determined by two facts: on the one hand, it is based upon "nations," and, on the other, it is permanently disturbed and thoroughly menaced by "nationalism."[35]

Arendt applauds the French historian Delos for trying "to find a political principle which would prevent nations from developing nationalism and would thereby lay the fundamentals of an international community, capable of presenting and protecting the civilization of the modern world:"[36]

> A people becomes a nation when "it arrives at a historical consciousness of itself;"[37] as such it is attached to the soil which is the product of past labor and where history has left its traces. It represents the "milieu" into which man is born, a closed society to which one belongs by right of birth. The state on the other hand is an open society, ruling over a territory where its power protects and makes the law. As a legal institution, the state knows only citizens no matter of what nationality; its legal order is open to all who happen to live on its territory.[38]

Arendt operates here with two dichotomies, that of "nation" and "nationalism" and that between "nation" and "state." She affirms the existence of "nations" as a fact in sympathetic terms: a nation comes into existence when a people gains consciousness of itself. The existence of "peoples" seems presupposed as unproblematic. Nevertheless, the nation exists in a dynamic tension with the state. Significantly, while "the nation" is introduced as historical fact, the state is defined in highly idealist and normative terms: only at a time when the fight against feudalism and clerical domination was still not decided—as in the historical context in which Hegel was writing—could "the state" appear as the "open society," the instrument of political rationality and historical reason that opens up and transforms the "closed society" of the nation. Arendt's bottom line here is, in a rather Quixotic way, to defend the (German idealist) concept of the state against its reality.

But the battle—in the end equally Quixotic—fought by the state against the nation started quite early in the lifetime of either phenomenon: "The conquest of the state through the nation started with the declaration of the sovereignty of the nation."[39] In its course, the legal institutions of the state were reinterpreted as "means for the welfare of the nation"[40] rather than for that of its individual members. When Arendt writes that in the form of the nation-state, "the state was partly transformed from an instrument of the law into an instrument of the nation,"[41] she seems to imply a temporal succession. On other occasions, though, this transformation seems to be logical rather than temporal, and intrinsic to the nation-state from early on: already in the French Revolution, "the secret conflict between state and nation"[42] manifested itself in the simultaneous declamation of the "Rights of Man" and the demand for "national sovereignty." The nation was "at once declared to be subject to laws, which supposedly would flow from the Rights of Man, *and* sovereign," i.e., "acknowledging nothing superior to itself."[43] The claim for sovereignty robbed the state of its "legal, rational appearance"[44] and prepared the ground for subsequent reinterpretation of the state as the "nebulous representative of a 'national soul' which through the very fact of its existence was supposed to be beyond or above the law."[45]

Although the formulation of the "inalienable" Rights of Man seemed to suggest that these were rights possessed by human beings anywhere and under any circumstances, it was equally clear to the authors of their declaration that if "a tribal or other 'backward' community did not enjoy human rights, it was obviously because as a whole it had not yet reached that stage of civilization, the stage of popular and national sovereignty." For those who fought for "inalienable rights" in a situation of indeed violent conflict, it was obvious that the Rights of Man had to be actualized in specific institutional arrangements, which at the time most observers seemed to identify as "popular and national sovereignty." Straightforwardly universal human rights could not yet exist as humanity as a subject and master of its own history did not yet exist. Until the time it will, the Rights of Man, that are as yet only in their essence, or potentially, universal, seem to have to take the form of appearance of the rights of particulars such as national rights.

Paradoxically, the nationalist "conquest of the state was made possible through the liberal individualism of the nineteenth century:"[46] the national state was "called upon" to warrant the process of the "atomization" of society. It seems that for Arendt, individualism did to the individual what nationalism did to the nation-state. As the state "monopolized the whole of political life," the twin processes of social atomization and state formation destroyed any political life outside the sphere of the state. A longing for political life *within society itself* rather than merely within the state is one of the *leitmotifs* of Arendt's work. She understood nationalism as a cheap and inferior *ersatz* for true political life. The sovereignty of the state was complementary to that of the individual only as long as it was not "shaped after the model of the sovereignty of the individual." The state conquered by the nation came to be seen as "a kind of supreme individual before which all others had to bow."[47] This process meant the "perversion of the state into an instrument of the nation."[48]

> It seemed to be the will of the nation that the state protect it from the consequences of its social atomization and, at the same time, guarantee its possibility of remaining in a state of atomization . . . only a strongly centralized administration could counterbalance the centrifugal forces constantly produced in a class-ridden society. Nationalism, then, became the precious cement for binding together a centralized state and an atomized society.[49]

Political agency is for Arendt the supreme expression of the sovereignty, and thus liberty, of individuals. She does not want the political sphere (preferably, the full republican political society, or, in its absence, the second best version where politics is monopolized by the state) to be dominated by "the social"—economics, having to work, things that have to be done whether we like them or not. Her one-sided and unfair denunciation of "the social" as the pathetic and illiberal sphere of "housekeeping" is, against the first impression, one of the more inspiring aspects of her thinking: making politics is indeed much better than doing housework as everybody who ever had the choice will confirm, and the (collectively achieved) reduction of "economic" activity to the irreducible minimum on the societal level is without doubt a necessary precondition of the development of political as well as individual liberty.

Two complementary determinations of the concept of the nation can be discerned in Arendt's work: one is that of the nation as the community of productive citizens, formulated in opposition to parasitic, nonproducing appropriators. This vision has classically been formulated by Sieyes in his *What is the Third Estate*, arguably the most influential pamphlet of the period of the French Revolution, whose discourse was itself based on intensive study of Locke and the political economy of the Scottish Enlightenment.[50] The other determination is that of the nation as a cultural community that would undergird the modern society of (otherwise) egotistic individuals and the state they form. This "cultural turn," as it were, taken by the modern state, appears to be a political necessity that emerged in parallel with the concept of the nation as the community of producers, but was consistently fused with it only in the course of the nineteenth century. Both determinations can be antagonistic to each other—when "national culture" dictates measures that undermine productivity and profitability—but they can also reinforce each other such as in the case of anti-Semitism: "the Jews" not only represent cultural difference and endanger the homogeneity of the national culture on the levels of religiosity, morality, and taste, but they appear at the same time as unproductive, parasitic appropriators of the wealth produced by the nation. This coincidence is lethal.

Arendt considers a defining characteristic of the "body politic of the nation-state" that it was based on an equilibrium of societal forces that allowed the state to deploy a form of autonomous power, i.e., to assume "actual political rule which no longer depended upon social and economic factors."[51] As long as the "conquest of the state by the nation" was only "partially successful,"[52] there was a "precarious balance between nation and state, between national interest and legal institutions."[53] While it still bothered fighting its corner, the nation-state was at least a *lesser* evil:

> Insofar as the state, even in its perverted form, remained a legal institution, nationalism was controlled by some law, and insofar as it had sprung from the identification of nationals with their territory, it was limited by definite boundaries.[54]

Old-fashioned, typical nineteenth-century nationalists like Gladstone, Clemenceau, or Bismarck were the protagonists of "the battle fought by sanity," i.e., by the nation-state, against imperialism, which the former knew "by instinct rather than by insight" would destroy "the political body of the nation-state."[55] The notion of the relative sanity of nationalism seduced her also to the rather counterfactual claim that in Maoist China "nationalist sentiment, so prominent in all revolutionary upheavals in formerly colonial countries, was strong enough to impose limits upon total domination."[56] In Arendt's wishful thinking (probably reflecting Maoist positions encountered in the United States), Maoism would have limited Stalinist brutality before it would damage the national interest, more indebted as it was to nineteenth-century ideas than was proper, totalitarian Stalinism. Arendt admits, however, that "the nation" lost the battle against imperialism (and then, against totalitarianism) because its opposition was at best "half-hearted"[57]: "In theory, there is an abyss between nationalism and imperialism; in practice, it can be and has been bridged by tribal nationalism and outright racism."[58]

Despite her critical exploration of the self-destruction of the liberal nation-state, Arendt seems to maintain the belief in a benign form of the nation-state before anti-Semitic and imperialist nationalism conquered it. Arendt's notion that "the nation" and "nationalism" are opposed principles inherits nineteenth-century liberalism's opposition of "reasonable" to "exaggerated" nationalism.[59] Although she does not use these words, Arendt's notion of the nation-state before nationalism is similar to the more recent attempts to oppose "patriotism" to nationalism. While the critical edge of Arendt's perspective lies in her rather open and dialectical discussion, which leaves the contradiction unresolved, many more recent commentators on "patriotism" eliminate its critical value by arbitrarily adopting a neatly defined conceptual dichotomy.[60] The virtue of Arendt's account is that she acknowledges that the defining characteristic of modern nationalism is exactly its claim of a *congruence* of the political and the ethnic-cultural.

It seems safe to assume that Arendt's critique of nationalism was at least partly developed out of her struggle to come to terms with Zionism. She made a point of stating repeatedly that "the lesson" to be learned from the Holocaust was that a Jewish "homeland" had to be built in a way that would help avoiding the development the nation-state had taken in Europe. Jews should find a way to reap the benefits of the modern social order, which the modern nation-state helps to establish, but avoid its conquest by nationalism.[61]

Arendt's position on the question of the nation-state can be observed "in action," as it were, in *Eichmann in Jerusalem* (1963). To start with, her "report" is driven by her anger about the way the trial was used by the Israeli state to foster and consolidate an ethnic understanding of its statehood. Against this she argued that "one of the indispensable prerequisites for Israeli statehood," whose success she clearly presupposed was desirable, was that Jews abandon the "kind of 'Jewish consciousness'" that Ben-Gurion aimed to strengthen: the "conviction . . . that all Gentiles were alike" which prevented the Jews from "distinguish[ing] between friend and foe," the capacity of judgment most central to the activity of making politics.[62] She pointed out repeatedly in the text that the judges often managed to resist what she saw as the trial's nationalist instrumentalization. Triumphantly,

Arendt found in the trial evidence that "Justice, though perhaps an 'abstraction' for those of Mr. Ben-Gurion's turn of mind, proves to be a much sterner master than the Prime Minister with all his power."[63] The Zionism Arendt was ready to support would make "the Jews a people among peoples, a nation among nations, a state among states,"[64] i.e., equal and similar to all other peoples, nations, and states. Any particular "Jewish consciousness" seemed counterproductive to this goal and should certainly not detract from the search for "Justice."

Her understanding of nationhood also informed her interpretation of how the Holocaust was carried out, or not, in different European countries. Arendt names Denmark, Italy, and Bulgaria as examples of countries that "proved to be nearly immune to anti-Semitism."[65] In Denmark, this "immunity" resulted from "an authentically political sense, an inbred comprehension of the requirements and responsibilities of citizenship and independence," in Italy from "the almost automatic general humanity of an old and civilized people." These remarks clearly signal what kind of nations Arendt appreciated: very political ones and very old ones (the good old Hegelian category of the "historical peoples").[66] Explaining the case of Bulgaria required more dialectics. Arendt writes that in 1943 the Nazis found it impossible to execute the "final solution" in Bulgaria. She admits that no explanation is at hand and proceeds to tell the anecdote of Georgi Dimitrov's famous defense speech at the *Reichstagsbrand* trial in Berlin in 1933, in the course of which Dimitrov "questioned [Göring] as though he [Dimitrov] were in charge of the proceedings" and subsequently was released.

> His conduct was such that it won him the admiration of the whole world, Germany not excluded. "There is one man left in Germany," people used to say, "and he is a Bulgarian."[67]

This idiosyncratic conclusion to the section on the difficulties the Nazis encountered in Bulgaria is certainly somewhat tongue in cheek but nevertheless revealing: as the Bulgarian case does not fit in with the model of Western nation-states versus Eastern tribal nationalism that she usually presupposes, Arendt takes refuge in celebrating a specifically republican form of manliness: a real man, as opposed to a Nazi or a Quisling, is good at public speech. She suggests that this form of political virility is part of the Bulgarian national character and made the Bulgarians behave like Danes or Italians.

Benhabib summarized Arendt's position on Zionism like this:

> Reflecting on the weaknesses of the nation-system in central and eastern Europe, Arendt saw in Herzlian Zionism a recipe for repeating these follies in Palestine. Add to this the Eurocentric hubris of considering Palestine a "country without a people," as if the Arabs of Palestine did not exist, and Arendt saw in Herzlian Zionism a recipe for disaster.[68]

Arendt rejected the Western, Herzlian strand of the movement (as it was based on the typical late nineteenth-century combination of liberal nationalism *cum* colonialism), while the sympathies she had were with the social-revolutionary elements that she saw were at the core of Eastern European Zionism. While the former merely wanted "to establish the same set of conditions for their own people," the latter "rebelled against the social and political conditions of their time."[69] It should be noted that, in this context, Arendt rejected the vision of Israel becoming just another ordinary nation-state, which in *Eichmann in Jerusalem* (as argued above) she saw fit to defend against the more ethnic-cultural Zionism then prevalent. However, the more ethnic version of Zionism was rooted in labor Zionism—where Ben-Gurion came from—much more than in Herzlian Zionism, while in turn Arendt's polemics against Ben-Gurion in *Eichmann in Jerusalem* sound actually rather Herzlian. This contradiction points to a deeper ambivalence. Arendt sees a quasi-Blochian dialectic at work in the process by which the "unworldliness" and "romantic inwardness" of the Jewish (post-sixteenth-century) tradition of Eastern Europe turned into (twentieth-century) politics: "lack of realism, coupled with a tendency toward Messianic outbursts"[70] meant that the Jewish people "retired from the public scene of history."[71] But "by a curious dialectical twist, Arendt sees in Jewish mysticism the sources of popular action expressed through the hopes for world redemption and the return to Zion."[72] Arendt understands the power but also the weakness of politics driven by Messianic hopes: they do not easily translate into the negotiating and compromising (the choice of "lesser evils") that inevitably is at the heart of politics in the framework of the modern bourgeois world. Her ambivalence toward the Messianic roots of Eastern Jewish nationalism reflects that about "lesser evils": the rejection of "lesser evils" may itself be a late sprout from that Messianism.[73]

From Civilization to Race

In the last third of the nineteenth century, the bourgeoisie "turned to politics out of economic necessity" for "if it did not want to give up the capitalist system whose inherent law is constant economic growth, it had to impose this law upon its home governments and to proclaim expansion to be an ultimate goal of foreign policy."[74] Although the bourgeoisie "had developed within, and together with, the nation-state,"[75] during the imperialist period "imperialistically minded businessmen" remodelled international politics in "the competitive spirit of business concerns."[76] It is in this context that racism as Arendt understands it developed.

In the second chapter of Part Two of *Origins*, "Race-thinking before Racism," Arendt develops a conceptual history of "race" in eighteenth-century France and nineteenth-century Germany that ends with the conclusion that "thinking in terms of race" probably would have disappeared had it not been so convenient an "excuse" for the practices of imperialism in Africa.[77] Arendt's principal point is that these violently racist practices were utterly incompatible "with all Western political and moral standards of the past."[78] The concept of race, however, gave them the "appearance of national respectability or the seeming sanction of tradition." It is thus by helping to hide the radical novelty of racist politics that "race-thinking" contributed eventually to the destruction of "the comity of European nations" including that of the Jews. In the subsequent chapter, however ("Race and Bureaucracy") in which she discusses colonial racism, Arendt undermines her trademark distinction between venerable tradition and destructive bourgeois nontraditionalism by adopting the economistic categories of the bourgeoisie's discourse and developing her own usage of the concept of "race." Not incidentally, these are also the pages that contain her notorious racist comments on African "savages."

In the context of discussing the colonial history of South Africa, Arendt writes that the word "race" has "a precise meaning" only when it refers to "tribes[,] . . . which do not know any history of their own."[79] "Races in this sense" occur in particularly hostile natural environments and behave "like a part of nature." While the "native tribes" mimicked nature, the Boer settlers in turn mimicked the savages: they failed to form any "body politic" or "communal organization" and their "black slaves did not serve any white civilization."[80] Indeed, very much like Kurtz in *Heart of Darkness*, the Boers themselves became savages (which was certainly also the opinion of the British imperialists): "Ruling over tribes and living parasitically from their labor, they came to occupy a position very similar to that of the native tribal leaders whose domination they had liquidated." Having become *über*-chieftains, the Boers refrained from re-creating and spreading European civilization with all its blessings, such as law, a definite territory, and a body politic. "The black slaves in South Africa quickly became the only part of the population that actually worked." It was "absolute dependence on the work of others and complete contempt for labor and productivity in any form that transformed the Dutchman into the Boer."[81] "Lazy and unproductive, [the Boers] agreed to vegetate on essentially the same level as the black tribes had vegetated for thousands of years."[82] The inevitable result was "their own degeneration into a white race living beside and together with black races from whom in the end they would differ only in the color of their skin." More recently in South Africa, the "former slaves . . . are well on their way to becoming workers, a normal part of human civilization,"[83] while the poor Whites who continue to despise work and are granted "charity as the right of a white skin"[84] have now properly become "a race"—a degenerate, uncivilized, and unpolitical lot without any human dignity.

What Arendt has to say about the gold diggers is even less flattering than her portrayal of the Boers: they belonged to "a class of persons who prefer adventure and speculation to settled industry,"[85] seeking "permanent emancipation from work" in a "paradise of parasites."[86] The "new mob was as unwilling to work and as unfit to establish a civilisation"[87] as the Boers had been. According to Arendt the gold diggers resembled the Boers as much as the Boers resembled "the savages." Industrialization ("normal production") and civilization, however, "would . . . have destroyed automatically the way of life of a race society."[88] The structure of Arendt's argument here is uncannily similar to that of anti-Semitism: quite like "liberal antisemites," she constructs an image of "normal," peaceful capitalist development that is respectful of tradition, territoriality, and law and opposes it to the irresponsible, adventurous, greedy, parasitic behavior of those who want to get rich without working (gold diggers according to Arendt, the Jews according to anti-Semites).

Arendt develops here a concept of "race" as a cultural and economic category with a reasonable meaning: it is basically another word for people who refuse to take part in liberal progress and political economy. It works like a reflection of the French eighteenth-century aristocracy's fancy that they were a separate race from the *Gaulois* Third Estate. Here Arendt is as dismissive of the "savages" and the settlers who mimicked them as the bourgeoisie was of the unproductive, lazy, and prodigal nobility. Furthermore, she praises the antiracist credentials of "normal" capitalist progress and celebrates labor as the exit from savagery into humanity. She suggests that racism "is always closely tied to contempt for labor, hatred of territorial limitations, general rootlessness, and an activistic faith in one's own divine chosenness,"[89] all of which are exactly the opposite of what Arendt seeks to promote. She did not recognize that the bourgeois contempt for people who do not share the bourgeois concepts of time, labor, and history could also be racist; as Arendt knew well, even still at the beginning of the nineteenth century, this had been part of the rhetoric directed against the Jews.

*

The exploration of Arendt's position on nation-state and nationalism has shown a tension between a positive, almost nostalgic attitude toward the nation-state "before nationalism," on the one hand, and, on the other, a sense that a process of self-destruction was inherent to the nation-state. This tension is articulated within and through another, related one, between a utopian radicalism (fed by echoes of popular Jewish mysticism) that refuses to settle for "lesser evils," and a rationalism that celebrates political agency as dealing with and within the actual world, which almost by definition means seeking "lesser evils." Arendt vacillates between presenting the nineteenth-century nation-state as one of the "lesser evils" that paved the road to Auschwitz or as the republican, non-nationalist alternative that can almost serve as a normative ideal.

In this framework Arendt discusses anti-Semitism's ambivalent relationship toward modern society for which the observation that (modern) anti-Semitism is a reaction to emancipation is pivotal. The problem to which Arendt's discussion points without, however, being able to develop it fully, is that the grounds on which emancipation was granted were to a large extent the same on which it was revoked. Emancipation and anti-Semitism were antagonistic moments of the same process, the formation of modern society, its individuals, and its state. The notions of making society "productive" and "industrious," implying the "amelioration," marginalization, or elimination of unproductive ("parasitical") classes and groups of people, constitute a bridge between the discourse of the nation, that of Jewish emancipation and its rejection. The bourgeois class has been central to all of this and cannot be divided neatly into those of a classical republican mindset and unpolitical philistines. Arendt has given the best illustration of this when she embraced wholeheartedly the productivist agenda of the bourgeoisie in her polemic against South Africa's "race society." When Arendt writes that racists "consistently denied the great principle upon which national organizations of peoples are built, the principle of equality and solidarity of all peoples guaranteed by the idea of mankind,"[90] she brackets out to a large extent the more subtle dialectic whose unveiling is her principal and lasting merit.

Notes

1. The writing of this article was made possible by the generous support of an Economic and Social Research Council Postdoctoral Fellowship held at Goldsmiths College in 2004–5.
2. Eli Zaretsky, "Hannah Arendt and the Meaning of the Public/Private Distinction," in *Hannah Arendt and The Meaning of Politics*, ed. Craig Calhoun and John McGowan (Minneapolis, 1997), 216.
3. Hannah Arendt, *The Origins of Totalitarianism* (New York, 1973), 3.
4. Ibid., 11.
5. Jacob Katz, *Emancipation and Assimilation: Studies in Modern Jewish History* (Farnborough, 1972), 24.
6. Arthur Hertzberg, *The French Enlightenment and the Jews* (New York, 1968), 9.
7. Ibid.
8. Ibid., 10.
9. Arendt, *Origins*, 20.
10. Ludwig von der Marwitz, as quoted in Arendt, *Origins*, 31.
11. Eleonore Sterling, *Judenhass. Die Anfänge des politischen Antisemitismus in Deutschland 1815–1850* (Frankfurt-am-Main, 1969), 115.
12. Arendt, *Origins*, 37.
13. Hannah Arendt, "The Eggs Speak Up," in *Essays in Understanding 1930–1954*, ed. Jerome Kohn (New York, 1994), 271. The title of the essay alludes to the proverb that one needs to break eggs to make an omelette.
14. Ibid., 273.
15. Beiner writes that "the logic of her argument [in *Origins*] would seem to dictate a return to the nation-state rather than its supersession" in "Arendt and Nationalism," in *The Cambridge Companion to Hannah Arendt*, ed. Dana Villa (Cambridge, 2000), 46.
16. The word strictly speaking refers to a group of seafaring peoples who inhabited the coast of Palestine—which was named for them after they acculturated into its population—and who were early enemies of the Hebrews. For Brentano and his contemporaries, inhabitants of Palestine, Philistines, Semites, and Jews were all more or less the same suspect lot of people.
17. Arendt, *Origins*, 169.
18. Ibid., 338.
19. In "The Eggs Speak Up," Arendt mocks former Communists who turned into overzealous liberals.
20. Arendt, *Origins*, 139.
21. Ibid., 144–5.
22. Ibid., 145–6. "Automatically growing wealth" that subjects human agency is of course one of the Marxian determinations of capital. Arendt was familiar with Marx's writings including *Grundrisse*.
23. Patricia Springborg, "Hannah Arendt and the classical republican tradition," in *Hannah Arendt: Thinking, Judging, Freedom*, ed. Gisela T. Kaplan and Clive S. Kessler (Sydney, 1989), 9.

24. Ibid., 10.
25. The rejection of Aristotelianism by the Scottish Enlightenment reflects the struggle of political economy against the defenders of slavery and patrimonialism. This is a crucial aspect of the emancipatory merits of modern political economy.
26. The critique of the family as a social constellation, which is based on quasi-slavery (after all, this word that supposedly radiates so much warmth and intimacy stems from *famulus*, Latin for "servant") is also central to the Frankfurt School critique of the "authoritarian personality" and the more radical strands of feminist and gay theory.
27. Springborg, "Hannah Arendt and the republican tradition," 10.
28. Strangely, Arendt claimed that the political values of the West derived from the *polis* while she acknowledged that the state formation of the Western (subsequently national) states had its roots in feudal, medieval structures that were social, *not* political (in Arendt's sense). It had nothing to do with the classical *polis*, which is an Eastern phenomenon anyway as it originated in Mesopotamia, the Levant, and Asia Minor.
29. Springborg, "Hannah Arendt and the republican tradition," 13.
30. Ibid., 16.
31. Arendt, *Origins*, 123.
32. Ibid., 313.
33. Ibid., 64.
34. Ibid.
35. Arendt, "The Nation," in *Essays in Understanding*, 206. This is the 1946 review of a book by J.-T. Delos from 1944.
36. Ibid., 207.
37. I follow here the reformulation by Beiner (in Villa, ed., 53) of Arendt's less elegant translation from the French original.
38. Arendt, "The Nation," 208.
39. Ibid., 208–9.
40. Ibid., 209
41. Arendt, *Origins*, 230.
42. Ibid.
43. Ibid.
44. Ibid., 231.
45. Ibid.
46. Ibid.
47. Ibid.
48. Ibid.
49. Ibid.
50. William H Sewell, Jr. *A Rhetoric of Bourgeois Revolution: The Abbé Sieyes and WHAT IS THE THIRD ESTATE?* (Durham and London, 1994).
51. Arendt, *Origins*, 38.
52. Ibid., 354.
53. Ibid., 275.
54. Ibid., 231.
55. Ibid., 125.
56. Ibid., xxvi–xxvii.
57. Ibid., 132.
58. Ibid., 153.
59. For the German context, this *topos* can be observed paradigmatically in the Berlin Antisemitism Dispute of 1879–81; see my forthcoming "Cultural Difference in the National State: from trouser-selling Jews to unbridled multicultural society," *Patterns of Prejudice* 47, no. 3 (2008), and *The State, the Nation and the Jews, Liberalism and the Antisemitism Dispute in Bismarck's Germany* (Nebraska, forthcoming 2008).

60. Maurizio Viroli, *For Love of Country: An Essay on Patriotism and Nationalism* (Oxford, 1995) is an example of this rather woolly type of literature. A scholarly precise account of the development of the two concepts in the French context can be found in Brian Jenkins, *Nationalism in France, Class and Nation since 1789* (London and New York, 1990).

61. The "most plausible proposal" for the implementation of such a perspective was for Arendt "the creation of a Federation in the Near East or around the Mediterranean" starting with a federal and multinational Palestine. See Moshe Zimmermann, "Hannah Arendt, the Early 'Post-Zionist,'" in *Hannah Arendt in Jerusalem*, ed. Steven E. Aschheim (Berkeley, 2001), 187. Arendt's vision resembles that of the Balkan Federation originally envisaged by Tito.

62. Hannah Arendt, *Eichmann in Jerusalem: A Report on the Banality of Evil*, (Harmondsworth, 1964), 11

63. Ibid., 5.

64. Ibid., 11.

65. Ibid., 171.

66. In the chapter on Hungary, Arendt compares the Zionists favorably to "the gentlemen of the Jewish Council" (*Eichmann*, 198) because "the Zionist leaders knew they were outlaws," "acted accordingly," and "indulged less in self-deception"—in other words, they were good at political judgment. They were organized along political lines and had international connections, whereas the non-Zionist leadership relied on their wealth and the king's protection.

67. Ibid.

68. Seyla Benhabib, *The Reluctant Modernism of Hannah Arendt* (Thousand Oaks, 1996), 44.

69. Arendt quoted in Benhabib, *Reluctant Modernism*, 44.

70. Ibid., 45.

71. Arendt quoted in Benhabib, *Reluctant Modernism*, 45.

72. This imagery was also shared by late medieval and early modern heretical and subsequently Protestant movements.

73. The policy of exclusively employing "Jewish labor" was initially designed to prevent the Jewish settlers from becoming exploiters of Arab labor. The zeal to reinvent the Jewish people according to the Western European, Enlightenment notion of "turning the Jews into producers" helped prevent the labor Zionists from forming an alliance with the Arab peasants.

74. Arendt, *Origins*, 126.

75. Ibid., 123.

76. Ibid., 15.

77. Ibid., 183-4.

78. Ibid., 184.

79. Ibid., 192.

80. Ibid., 193.

81. Ibid., 193.

82. Ibid., 194.

83. Ibid., 195.

84. Ibid., 194.

85. Ibid., 198.

86. Ibid., 151.

87. Ibid., 199.

88. Ibid., 205.

89. Ibid., 197.

90. Ibid., 161.

Chapter 8

Post-Totalitarian Elements and Eichmann's Mentality in the Yugoslav War and Mass Killings

Vlasta Jalušič

In the large body of literature about the Holocaust and Nazi totalitarianism today, the extinction of the European Jewish population is treated as an unparalleled act that cannot and should not be repeated. "Never again" has become the motto of commemorations of the victims of Nazi terror in general and as such it represents the heart of the politics of memory, which, through awareness of the Holocaust's warning, has attempted to create conditions in which the repetition of such an unparalleled crime would be impossible. However, in spite of the persistent claims in the genocide scholarship of its uniqueness and in spite of the refusal to compare it to contemporary genocides, the Nazi Holocaust has inevitably been linked to the events in the former Yugoslavia and Rwanda. The Rwandan genocide, in particular—owing to the number of victims and the way the crime was accomplished—has emerged as the most suitable case for emphasizing a "crucial similarity,"[1] while the name "Srebrenica" has become associated with "the worst massacre in Europe after the Second World War." Conserving the Holocaust as a unique or paradigmatic case of genocide or using it as an ultimate standard of moral condemnation obviously has had no effect, since the new events have evinced similarities to the Holocaust, as well as their own uniqueness. The "never again" politics helped neither in the understanding nor the prevention of genocidal developments because one could not simply learn from the past to prevent future "repetitions."[2] In both these more recent cases it seemed as if the "unparalleled" had reappeared, except that the killings on the soil of the former Yugoslavia turned out to be exceptional in the European context.

After the reports of the massacre of Srebrenica in the summer of 1995, questions emerged reminiscent of those after the Second World War: How was such a thing possible? How could it have happened "again" (in the middle of "civilized" Europe)? Why would people kill their cocitizens, sometimes their neighbors and acquaintances? These disturbing questions implied a broader frame: Is it possible to explain and (eventually) understand such events? Could we possibly prevent them, if we knew their origins and recognized them in time? How can we help ourselves with the lessons from the Holocaust and totalitarianism?

These questions not only touch upon the issue of "definitions" of genocide, for example, or of the potential for a catastrophe such as the destruction of European Jews. They also struggle with the moral and political problem of how to make the conditions, "origins," or elements of such events "visible," how to "see" that they take place in order to make those who can or should prevent them "recognize" them, in the sense of providing adequate legal arrangements and/or initiating action. This chapter will engage with some of the above questions concerning the background of crimes and mass murders in the former Yugoslavia, while aiming at an understanding of the case through the perspective and the legacy of Hannah Arendt's thought.

The Arendtian Legacy and Post-Totalitarian Temptations

In spite of a growing literature on the "social construction" of both ethnicity and war in the former Yugoslavia, there still exist two interconnected and widespread explanations of the origins of war and mass killings. One is a thesis commonly voiced that people were "manipulated" by politicians, while the other involves the "in the beginning there were nationalisms" thesis that is partly connected to the former one. Manipulation and propaganda were seen as the reputed reasons for nationalist support, and the increasing emphasis on nationalisms, which erupted immediately after Tito's death, were then seen as the proper impetus for war. Social scientists have time and again fallen into the trap of seeing nationalism as a kind of biological, essential, or natural force, which, as some kind of an ever-present virus or contagious disease, "attacked" people in the former Yugoslavia or resulted from "ancient hatred," resulting in war and killing as their almost inevitable outcome.[3]

Such one-dimensional explanations are among the main reasons that I would like to point to some features of Arendtian political thought that might illuminate our understanding of some of the terrible events in the former Yugoslavia. The ideas about nationalism as "the origin" bear a resemblance to the presumption, rejected by Arendt, that an ancient hatred toward Jews—that is, an "eternal" anti-Semitism—was the main cause or a even a single explanation for the Holocaust and Nazi totalitarianism, a thesis which has been, in the case of German anti-Semitism, recently advocated zealously by Daniel Goldhagen.

Arendt refused monocausal explanations in attempting to create an understanding of the paths toward totalitarian domination and its novel crimes. On the one hand, she was *thinking in terms of elements* of totalitarianism, which she traced back to history, as she was trying to understand them, on the other hand, while *taking into account* something that mainstream social scientists' methods did not consider:

human action, human plurality, spontaneity, and the capacity to begin anew—exactly those elements of the human condition that totalitarianism was about to destroy.[4] This enabled her to argue about totalitarianism in a nondeterminist and noncausative way, to retrace and discuss the elements that she found to be crucial in its development, but to state clearly that it did not automatically spring from one single element, or even from a set of them, and that it (the tragedy) was thus not inevitable.[5] Anti-Semitism, imperialism, racism, and the decline of the nation-state were considered as important elements but not single causes. They would only "eventually crystallize into totalitarianism."[6] In the absence of causal relations, not only was the issue of individual guilt for the crimes strongly emphasized but also that of the individual and collective (political) responsibility for not preventing totalitarian developments as well. This approach, combining elements and underlining human agency in bringing about the political phenomena, resulted in a series of insights and lessons that are important for understanding the Yugoslav case.

Furthermore, Arendt did not consider totalitarianism and its threats—although they constituted an absolute novelty—to be a fixed and unchangeable evil structure. On the contrary, she immediately started to think about the possible "repetitions" and new, post-totalitarian predicaments.[7] Although it is true that the Holocaust and the most extreme forms of totalitarian domination have already passed, it remains a fact that totalitarian elements—for example racism, bureaucracy, the decline of the nation-state, and various forms of totalitarian solutions—"can survive the system in the form of several temptations."[8] Arendt thought that the "unparalleled" new crimes that happened under Nazi-totalitarianism (such as the constructed superfluity of humans and the destruction of plurality, exemplified in the extermination camps) became a precedent, and thus it was more likely than before that they would happen again,[9] once the "threshold" of "everything is possible" has been breached.[10] However, they will not necessarily appear in their cruellest form;[11] they will not "repeat" the identical event: "the true predicaments of our time will assume their authentic form . . . only when totalitarianism has become a thing of the past."[12]

This new situation and the new predicaments were closely connected with the new context emerging after totalitarian experience, with the broken tradition in all its senses, and especially with the impaired standards of political thinking and moral judgment. There are two important issues for the present analysis linked to this new context. One is related to *the role and the power* of ideologies—such as anti-Semitism, racism and, associated intrinsically with them, nationalism—and to the role of their transformed successors. The other applies to the *potential for new crimes,* brought about by totalitarianism, along with the *"nature" of evil* and the issue of responsibility.

Racism, Anti-Semitism, Nationalism, and the Power of Ideologies

Racism, anti-Semitism, and nationalism can be explained as interrelated modern ideologies: modern anti-Semitism is a special and principally a totalitarian variety, while the other two represent the ideologies of imagined communities (of race and of the nation-state). Basically, they each embody sets of attitudes, beliefs, and activities that produce and legitimize exclusions from, and inclusions into, imagined communities and are essentially linked to the establishment of boundaries between the imagined communities and "the Others." They are thus, as noted by Arendt, intrinsically connected to the rise (and decline) of the nation-state and its mechanisms of power. Though the ideas of race and nation can overlap, since, as noted by Balibar, "discourses on race and nation are never far apart," nationalism and racism do not represent the same or coderivable phenomena. There exists an ambiguous relation between them: nationalism can be seen as a determining condition for the production of racism, and racism might become a parameter to define nationalism.[13] This, however, does not necessarily imply that racism is an inevitable consequence of nationalism or that nationalism is impossible without latent racism.[14] The difference between them is not between the "normal" and "extreme" in terms of degree. Both being exclusive ways of human conduct, they nevertheless represent two different types of approach to the issue of political organization: if nationalism tends to articulate itself in terms of state objectives (either in state building or through an ideology such as "self determination") then racism attempts to overcome the state framework.[15]

This interrelation and opposition—namely, that racism can not be considered as a simple "intensification" of nationalism—was clearly observable in the relationship between Nazi racism and German nationalism, where racism exceeded and actually destroyed the nationalist project and became a goal in itself. Arendt has shown how the intersections between both phenomena in the German case and in other Pan-nationalisms and movements operate to form a new, "advanced" type of nationalism, the so called "tribal (*völkisch*) nationalism," with "race" as not only an indispensable part of its structure but its final target. This type of nationalism does not represent an "excessive" or "ultra" nationalism, but it shows a split between "traditional" nationalism, aiming at one's own state, and tribal nationalism, having as its goal an achievement of some kind of organic, racialized nation, transcending the boundaries of the nation-state. Tribal nationalisms were thus simultaneously an addition to and modification of nationalism: they were used as powerful ideologies by those peoples who understood themselves as rootless, but as an organic national body, surrounded by a world of enemies such as Germany or Russia and dispersed over the home country's borders. They believed in the chosen nature of their own race or people against others, adopted racism as the ideology of their national unity, and shared with overseas imperialism a hostility against their "narrow' (nation) state."[16]

This transformation of nationalism through the open establishment of a common ground between racism and nationalism, shown in the phenomenon of tribal nationalisms, was an ideal site for totalitarian policies themselves. It represented, together with anti-Semitism as its central component,[17] a superb means for the destruction of reality (in Arendt's terms the "world" itself) and thus for undermining the common ground of thinking and judgment. These movements have found an ideal "Other" in the fabricated image of the international Jew "in general," the "elusive enemy,"[18] representing the paradigmatic case of neoracism, "racism without race," and needing no pseudobiological concept of race or nature, since culture or some other type of ideological production can sufficiently replace it.[19] Only here anti-Semitism became a "pure" ideology, an "outrage to common sense,"[20] in the sense of total fabrication. However, totalitarian policies are "far from being simply anti-Semitic or racist or imperialist or communist." They "use and abuse their own ideological and political elements until the basis of factual reality, from which the ideologies originally derived their strength and their propaganda value . . . have all but disappeared."[21] This peculiar "self-manipulating" moment in the ideologies of racism and tribal nationalism, hardly comprehensible to those who see political action as above all an instrumental activity or manipulation of others, might cast light on the means by which totalitarian threats might adapt and become "ideologically" functional in the long run. They do so not by building an "instrumental" world where everything is "under control" but by creating what Arendt called "images," a "reality" frame, independent of the world, which starts to operate through its self-perpetuating logic as "truth."[22] These images function similarly to Erving Goffman's strong discourse, a frame that, once established, is very hard to resist, since it functions as reality ("The Truth") itself regardless of any "real basis" in truth. Since it is already permanently "in action," such an image can finally have perfectly real effects on the people's behaviour and actions. It can justify and normalize all possible deeds, including ethnic cleansing, or genocide. The "real" in respect to ideology is thus no longer its content or its attempt at indoctrination, but "self-manipulation," intense "social constructionism," productivity, and creativity. Modern ideologies adopt the mode of fabrication, without needing to "indoctrinate" or to constitute a "deep" conviction or belief. They seem rather to be a superficial set of fabricated policies of "everyday," "simple," and "obvious" truths. If we approach it this way, then such an "image" comes close to the Arendtian description of the evil as banal: it is nothing deep but is, as she once put it, after reconsidering her claim about radical evil in totalitarianism, "spreading like a fungus on the surface."[23]

Between "Structure" and "Intention": The Banality of Evil and the New Crimes?

These considerations are closely connected to the issue of the role played by ideologies in the motives of perpetrators, and in the attitudes of bystanders in instances of totalitarian temptations and mass murders. Arendt tackled this issue with the articulation of her "banality of evil" thesis and presumably reduced the role that she had previously attributed to ideology. She challenged the predominant interpretations of genocide and crimes against humanity in terms of anti-Semitic indoctrination and anticipated the later discussions and results of historical scholarship.[24] It is usually understood that the "banality of evil" thesis confirms and belongs to what is called the structural-functionalist Holocaust interpretation camp, which insists on modern structures as the origin for crimes "without motives" as a key factor. This stands in contrast to the ideological-intentionalist interpretation that insists on the power of indoctrination (presumably of ideologies) and on the evil intentions of the perpetrators.[25] However, taking a closer look at Arendt's analysis reveals the misunderstanding and misinterpretation behind such assumptions, which do not help us to think about the new experiences. With her analysis of thoughtlessness, Arendt in fact went beyond this dichotomy (although she insisted that she had abandoned the role of ideology in favor of the banality of the perpetrator).[26] I will try to show later how illuminating this can be for understanding the power of ideologies—racism and nationalism—in the case of the massive crimes in the former Yugoslavia.

In Eichmann, Arendt revealed a new type of perpetrator, one who committed a novel sort of crime, without traditional motives of hatred and without needing to be a monstrously fanatic, deeply indoctrinated anti-Semite. He appeared "banal" and "thoughtless" in the strict sense of the word, someone who was not able to think about what he was doing, although he "knew quite well what it was all about."[27] The main controversy provoked by this case became the issue of the intentionality or nonintentionality of his evil deeds, the question of whether Arendt, by detecting his thoughtlessness, had really absolved Eichmann of his deeds and, instead, blamed the victims (Jewish councils). In addition, there was the question of whether (and if so, why) she "changed her mind" and abandoned the concept of "radical evil" for that of "banality."[28] One of the recent (and paradigmatic) opponents of Arendt, Yaacov Lozowick, maintains that Arendt unjustifiably placed the main emphasis on the functional and not on ideological causes and completely overlooked the historic fact that Eichmann, together with his bunch of fellow bureaucrats, was an indoctrinated anti-Semite. Thus he was, contra Arendt, very much aware of his mission, and of what he was doing when sending transports of Jews to the concentration camps. This proves his evil motives and personality and the nonbanality of his deeds, and "cuts the ground from beneath" Arendt's thesis that he was a banal perpetrator.[29]

Arendt's point, however, was not at all that Eichmann was not conscious of the effects of his actions in the casual sense. On the contrary, she pointed to the fact that he was very much aware of the consequences of his deeds.[30] Her specific definition of "thoughtlessness" was not "mindlessness" or stupidity; it was rather based on the difference between knowing and thinking (analysed more closely in *The Life of the Mind*). Thoughtlessness represents a special kind of mentality—not the absence of rational and instrumental thinking but of the judging ability and activity, imagination itself. It emerges under conditions of inverted human order and represents a shield against reality—in fact, a constructed world of self-deception.

By raising the issue of banality and Eichmann's thoughtlessness, Arendt was not only pointing to a novel type of crime ("crime against humanity" or, beyond that, "against diversity" and not solely genocide)[31] and proclaiming Eichmann a "*hostis generis humani.*" She was also pointing to their universality and to the enormous potential for future repetition,[32] as the massive circumstances behind the development of such a type of thoughtless perpetrator could only spread and evolve on a global scale. Additionally, she stopped judging evil deeds by "intentions" and will but focused her attention on the factual *effects* of deeds.[33] Evil deeds and their new perpetrators do not necessarily have to look or be represented as monstrous in order to have immediate monstrous consequences. They do not have to be acts of an evil "will" or of any will at all. As our contemporary circumstances show, they might even present themselves as good and as fighting against presumably monstrous evils, which can be fabricated in the form of an elusive enemy.

Departing from the lessons about the power of ideologies, the banality of evil, and thoughtlessness I have outlined, there are two issues I would particularly like to tackle when turning to the Yugoslav case: first, the question of nationalism and the role of racism—as powerful ideological means for the mass mobilization and justification of violence and killings. Then, I would like to elaborate on the relation of racist and nationalist ideologies to the direct mobilization for the commission of crimes and to raise the question whether thoughtlessness represents a part of the general "structure" or frame that enables such crimes to happen in our time.

Elements of Racism: Yugoslavia

Yugoslavia was a paradigmatic new case in which race thinking, not directly connected to any assumed "biological" formulation, began to play an important role in the preparation for war, and where the combined elements of race production, mass mobilization, and terror influenced ethnic cleansing, mass murder, and post-conflict state building. However, racism in particular was overlooked or sidestepped by most analyses,[34] while mobilization, war, and genocide were debated in terms of excessive (ethnic) nationalism, ancient hatred, and elite manipulation. Except for a few authors, there are few references to racism in the literature about the war and the killings in the former Yugoslavia.[35] Even those analyses that account for elements of racism and refer to "racist dimensions" speak mainly about ethno-nationalism, ultranationalism,[36] extreme nationalism, or, like Branimir Anzulović in his book *Heavenly Serbia*, about ethnotribalism, which comes closest to noting racist elements and the issue of tribal nationalist mobilization.[37]

One reason for the prevailing omission of racism in this literature is certainly its nonconceptualization as a relevant explanatory moment for the Yugoslav case and the stress instead on biological racism, which thus does not link it with what is usually seen as nationalism or excessive nationalism.[38] Another incentive might resemble the academic avoidance of the question of massive popular participation in the Rwandan genocide, since it raises unpleasant questions about indifference, conformism, and collaboration[39] and does not tackle the issue of widespread racist thinking among intellectuals. Racism might thus be subsumed under the more "respectable" cover of nationalism or "culture." As Etienne Balibar has suggested, a strong emphasis on the distinction between nationalism and racism or Nazi-racism can conceal the racist elements within nationalism itself (especially underlining the difference between "normal" and "excessive" forms).[40]

In what sense can we speak of the power of racism in the 1980s and 1990s in the former Yugoslavia? It should be understood in relation to tribal nationalism as explained within its broader and transformative aspect and be tested against the above described role and power of totalitarian ideologies. Racism was, of course, not the "cause" of war/s in the sense of being the only element that led to the conflict.[41] Nonetheless, not unlike modern anti-Semitism, which, as Arendt noted, arose from a relatively unimportant political phenomenon to became a powerful transformative ideology, in the former Yugoslavia a new, transformed sort of racism emerged: it grew out of the nationalist soil and cemented various elements and discourses, including nationalist ones, together. Its mobilizing force and role are close to the tribal nationalism described in the first part of the chapter. It is a paradigmatic case of racism without race: race here is a social construction, a result of the essentialization of characteristics attributed to the group(s) (racialization) and primordialization of identities, rendering them natural and unchangeable. This process of racism was, to be sure, connected to nationalism, and it grew up on its own terrain.

Elements of racism in post-Tito Yugoslavia began to unfold with the help both of the masses and the rising elites, there being a need of popular support for their policies in the 1980s, and in view of the democratic multiparty elections in the 1990s.[42] These elements were crucial for the subsequent radical divisions. The consequences of race thinking and racism first came into view in connection with policies and police repression in the Serbian autonomous province of Kosovo (the Serbian "sacred land" that had an Albanian majority—a non-Slavic population) in the early 1980s, long before the beginning of the war. The Kosovo problem was the core of the process of the destruction of Yugoslavia, and during the process of escalation it became an "abstraction," a myth. It was there that the relations were first racialized and that the difference was framed in terms of quasi-biological differences and, so to speak, "written on the body." To understand the racialization of relations in the former Yugoslavia, one must consider the attitudes toward Kosovo Albanians, since the "Kosovization" of Serbian politics later spread to the whole of Yugoslav politics.[43]

Albanians were the target of Serbian race-thinking even at the beginning of the twentieth century: they were, on the one hand, dehumanized and represented as a wild, anarchic tribe without history and state—similar to apes and sleeping in trees—"European Redskins" who could not govern themselves, a sort of strange, resistant element that should be exterminated. On the other hand, they were treated actually as "lost Serbs," the worst converted characters, who had been assimilated through a process of Albanian violence, rape, killings, and property theft, since this was the only way to explain the preservation and even the demographic growth of Albanians.[44] In 1937, a Serbian academic, Vaso Čubrilović, prepared a memorandum to the "solution of the Albanian question." He raised the alarm regarding the "demographic explosion" of the Albanian population and suggested that all methods for marginalizing the Muslim-Albanian population had so far failed and that one should introduce methods which would correspond do the "Western approaches": the introduction of laws that would make the life of Albanians in Yugoslavia unbearable, followed by mass deportations.[45]

The proposed measures had the character of ethnic cleansing *avant la lettre,* and they point to a very problematic scholarly tradition from the first part of the twentieth century, which, based on racist premises, advocated population transfer and exchange as normal "policy solutions."[46] Not surprisingly, the discourse of "planned resettlement" was restored in the 1980s through intellectual and scientific discussions of the necessary demographic policies to hinder the supposed "demographic genocide" of Serbs in Kosovo. Dobrica Ćosić, a member of the Serbian Academia of Sciences, a novelist and confirmed dissident, who became president of Yugoslavia in 1992 and belonged among the intellectuals who formed the new Serbian Kosovo platform after Tito's death, stated in 1991: "Planned resettlement and population exchanges, while most difficult and most painful, are still better than a life of hatred and mutual killings."[47] In this process, Albanians were represented once more as dangerous, sly intruders who threaten "our" families, women, property, graves, and tradition and who can conspicuously misuse their own sexuality and rape or attempt to rape "our" women from sheer "separatist" motives. Here, the image of the "Other" was successfully combined with the image of an intruder, a settler, who is occupying and taking over "our land." This image of the intruder or settler acquired the status of an elusive enemy, which could later be applied easily to the Muslim population in Bosnia, who were targeted as "Turks."[48]

Through the prototype of the racialized Other, Albanians were not the only case of racialization. In the second half of the 1980s, the "clash of civilizations" loomed large—one could see derogatory images of a presumed Balkan and uncivilized enemy throughout Yugoslavia. The "Balkan man" was depicted as lazy, indifferent, and violent; and contrasted with images of a diligent, hard working, honest, civilized *non-Balkan* man. West-east and north-south divisions paved the way for the Europe-Balkans dividing line in these boundary drawings. They divided Yugoslavia itself and helped to reinforce the already existing Western racist-cultural prejudices and images that conditioned later problematic responses to the mass murders. The Slovenian and Croatian media and cultural elites tried to classify themselves as more civilized than the others and to place themselves on the "European" side of the demarcation line between Europe and Yugoslavia. They did so by enforcing an image of the "Balkans" as violent and macho, lazy and backward, fatalist, fraudulent, and cunning. The "North" or "West" saw itself as defending and cherishing European culture against the sinister backdrop of the wild, dark, orthodox, oriental, and Islamic Balkans. Yet the "eastern" part of Yugoslavia, on the other hand, worshipped its own putatively ancient, traditional, hospitable, and "anti-fascist" values. From that perspective, Slovenians were characterized as feminized, weak, exploitative, cunning, selfish, and calculating, whereas Croatians were positioned as more Western but also as Nazi-followers, and the supposed similarity of Croat and German characteristics of evil with bellicose traits emphasized

(Croats who "speak Croatian but think 'German'").[49] Albanians, Muslims, and Roma were in the worst position. In fact, to all those who shared a Slavic language, Albanians represented the "'Other' within."[50]

Tribal nationalism

The racialized picture created more room for the revivals of the old nationalist debates in the 1980s, with racial images assuming an inseparable part. The Memorandum of the Serbian Academy of Arts and Sciences, produced in 1986, was a paradigmatic example of such a problematic "national programme." It united racial and national components and declared that the federal organization of the Yugoslav state endangered Serbian national substance, and biological survival itself, claiming that the Serbs were victims of discriminatory policies and of an anti-Serbian coalition and conspiracy wherever they went. It demanded a change in the constitutional order by recalling the old historic and mythical ideas of Greater Serbia. Supposedly this would have enabled the unimpeded cultural unification of all Serbs, starting with the abolition of Kosovian autonomy. It was the basis for a mobilization of the Serbian population in all parts of the former Yugoslavia. The point of departure was created by the revival of conservative nationalist-organicist thought in Serbia.[51] This line of thought from the turn of the nineteenth century to the beginning of the twentieth century, following Charles Maurras and Joseph de Maistre's ideas and combining these with the race ideas of Gustave Le Bon, was amended by the works of new ideologists like Dobrica Ćosić. The result was combined with ideas of Christian collectivism, Pan-Slavism, "missionism," and the chosen nature of the Serbian people ("Christ's immortal people" in the words of the orthodox priests).[52] All this had an explicitly anti-Western perspective, since the history of Serbia has been seen as a conspiracy of the West against itself. But at the same time, it had as its aim the "salvation of the West." This reinvention of Serbian nationalism was crucial for the development of a specific "national revolution," the leading role of which was taken over politically by Milošević in 1987.

This prewar and interwar development would be more comprehensible, if we distinguished, as Arendt did, between two types of nationalisms, although—in the case of Yugoslavia we are discussing—the boundaries between these are not as clearly delineated as hers: between state-building nationalism and tribal or *völkisch* nationalism, which has Pan-national features, and presents itself as a continuously "unfinished" project, aiming at the extension of the national body against state-building. In the face of the assumed threats and seemingly enormous ethnic hatreds, in Yugoslavia it was constructed as a "defensive nationalism" and as a drive toward a "natural," organic community (*Volksgemeinschaft*), which would include all its members against any "artificial federation." As such, it had difficulty accepting the presence of the "Other." In fact, the advocates of "defensive" and "positive" nationalism demanded an "ethnically clean state"; and they accepted—through revivals of the old debates—the alleged "voluntary re-settlement." However, these old ideas became politically useful only when it seemed as if the enormous ethnic hatreds and "old hostilities" had "suddenly" recurred in Yugoslavia and when the politics of self-victimization and blaming others became everyday practice.[53] The consequence was that a solution could not be imagined without changing the ethnic composition or affecting "a humane, planned resettlement of population," or what came to be known as ethnic cleansing.[54]

Tribal nationalism is thus not the same as ethnonationalism. If we understand ethnonationalism as an endeavor for autonomy and/or independence on the part of the population/s, which is already part of a constituted "nation"—in the name of their own identity (already existing or in the process of construction),[55] then tribal nationalism does not have the same features as ethnonationalism. Ethnonationalism still represents a state- and polity-building endeavor, in spite of its homogenizing potential and exclusivist features. Though both these versions of nationalism include the potential for racist exclusion and do not have a "pure" appearance, they are to be distinguished in terms of their legitimization and their methods of understanding the state and citizenship. In the former Yugoslavia, tribal nationalism had to be seen as an addition to and modification of nationalism, which was, like German tribal nationalism at the beginning of Nazi-rule, successfully hiding its racist core and expansionist face under the "respectable cover of nationalism."[56] This is why it was—here as well—"rather difficult to distinguish between mere nationalism and clear-cut racism."[57] All seemed to be similar to the "general national feelings," and in the multinational state everyone had—finally— the possibility to express his or her feelings loudly and publicly. To distinguish between these elements was even more difficult in the case of Milošević's Serbia, where an additional "respectable cover" existed—not nationalism but the "saving" of Yugoslavia, which extending over the core of "Greater Serbia" provided him with international support. This kind of tribal nationalism with its racist kernel was misread to a large extent both by the international academic community and international actors as a "defense" of the Yugoslav state, although its propaganda was, almost from the inception, openly anti-state and genocidal.

To be sure, nationalist revivals and racist elements as parts of tribal or ethnonationalisms did not only exist in Serbia or among Serbs. Hierarchical images of "us" and "them" and myths of common origin and national mission, as described above, developed in Croatia, Slovenia, Bosnia and Herzegovina, and Macedonia as well. No one was "innocent" in this regard. In Croatia, where Tudjman and his Croatian Democratic Alliance came to power in the first multiparty elections in 1990, tribal nationalists, reviving national myths as well as Croatian fascist symbols (Ustaša symbols), completely overcame the state-building process and embarked on a total national revolution, thus representing an ideal confirmation of the correctness of Milošević's "pre-emptive" steps and Serbian mass mobilization across all of Yugoslavia. As Croatia was very soon dragged into war and lost nearly a third of its territory, the homogenization was almost unanimous. This brought about powerful mobilization and expansive military action (not defensive alone but military engagement in Bosnia) as well. Soon there were enemies all around who were demonized. Not only the Serbian enemy but the Muslims as well were acquiring clear racial features of the "Other," the "intruder," the "Turks," and the convert among other derogatory designations.[58]

However, to state that there were "universal" tribal nationalist and racist elements in the leadership goals and among parts of the population of all the republics at the time, and not only in Serbia, does not mean that they were all "identical" and that they all had equal weight or the same power. This would lead us to a type of relativist discourse (they were all "equally" bad), which was quite common among interpreters of the Yugoslav war. Such talk was basically connected to the alleged ancient hatreds among "Balkan men"—and probably accounted for many of the totally missed opportunities for intervention on the part of the international community. Not everybody was prepared for the war, and the least prepared were the Bosnian Muslims, who were viewed both by Serbs and Croats outside and within Bosnia either as an "artificial" ethnicity or as a group of national traitors, thus representing the most politically weak and potentially superfluous group in Bosnia and Herzegovina. The strongest and the most sustained mobilization of the population for war, and for processes that might be compared with those of totalitarian movements and developments, existed in Serbia; and the Serbian population in other places— such as Kosovo, Croatia, and Bosnia—was successfully mobilized for tribal nationalist goals as well. Together with the racist and *völkisch* ideology, this could bring about conditions for genocidal developments and outcomes. Military engagement and the bloody war in Bosnia, the partition of which was secretly agreed on between Milošević and Tudjman in 1991, started to function within a larger plan of "ethnic cleansing." As well, the strife between the two "nationalist" tendencies in Serbia (the dominant expansive tribal one and the other, promoting what is called a "modern Serbian state") could never really be resolved and left the Serbian question open, since many never had given up the tribal nationalist objectives.[59] By this, of course I do not mean to deny that similar developments took place in Croatia, for example, or that they would not have been be possible, under certain conditions, in any of the other Yugoslav nations (for example in Kosovo after 1999). On the contrary. But though the elements were present everywhere, they would not necessarily crystallize into the same murderous events.

Tribal nationalisms have used race thinking and racist endeavors to fix and naturalize hierarchic images of simple, logical race relations, the images of which were more than a product of "domestic" Yugoslav fabrication: such images were also nurtured by European and global clashes. They legitimized special demographic policies, exclusion, and subsequent ethnic resettlement as "lesser evils," and that paved the way for the ethnic cleansing and attempted annihilation of certain groups. Even the idea of legitimate "removals of populations" and ethnic cleansing itself created a condition of "inverse order," where one could first imagine, then easily "slip" into excesses and, finally, plan genocidal endeavors. Tribal nationalisms show a general trend: every nationalism, be it defensive or whatever, indulges in racism, in fact, if and when it denies universal equality and common humanity. Tribal nationalisms have their place among those policies and movements, which, from the position of "scientifically" supported race thinking, reorganize populations as separate bodies in the name of "cleanliness" and "purity." Such developments take place at all times when equality is perverted "from a political into a social concept," "the state into an instrument of the nation" and when parts of the population can be defined as "separate bodies."[60] Although the point of transgression—as shown by Arendt—is inherent in the sovereign structure of the nation-state itself, such a point of transgression does not play a decisive role as long as it is *limited politically.* Whether these elements are going to develop into genocidal events does not depend on the "nature" of nationalism—on its being "good" or "bad," "aggressive" or "defensive," Slovenian, Serbian, Albanian, or whatever it might be—but on its limitation by the state as a political institution, by the rule of law and constitutional government and by citizens' actions and judgment. As soon as we move out of the nation-state frame as a polity framework, one can expect the deadly fusion of racism and nationalism. In Yugoslavia the state, though authoritarian, ceased to exist. With the spreading of the tribal-nationalist shield against it, so did the ground for thinking and judgment. This had lethal consequences wherever the state could not be reconstructed, as was the situation in Bosnia, since nothing could have replaced it in time: neither the international community nor even less the UN protection.

Srebrenica and Banality

They told us that the Muslims were scum, more or less. That you would do well to have nothing to do with them. That actually the women and children were always nice . . . But the men with their big mouths, you should have nothing to do with them. The lads told us that Serbian men were better to deal with than Muslim men. They were much better disciplined.

—Dutch/ UN soldier in Srebrenica.

In 1993 a UN "safe area" with a few hundred peacekeepers was created in the eastern Bosnian town of Srebrenica to protect the remaining Muslim population gathered in that part of partitioned Bosnia after the Bosnian Serb Army occupation. In spite of this status, in July 1995, the enclave, together with more than 20,000 refugees, fell into the hands of Bosnian Serb troops under the leadership of General Ratko Mladić. Between 7,000 and 8,000 men aged twelve to sixty were killed within a very short time span. The weak UN battalion of Dutch soldiers was neither able nor willing, nor possessed of the mandate, to protect the enclave and the population. In that situation almost no one acted or judged, and the Dutch battalion commander, receiving no help from UN headquarters, under the circumstances even made an agreement with the Bosnian Serb general Mladić about the "transfer of the population." His soldiers stood by while Mladić's troops separated the men from the women and children. Before the well-organized executions of Muslim men, young and old, were carried out, Mladić proved efficiently the (non)earnestness and (non)willingness of the UN forces to protect the Muslim population. After kidnapping a group of Dutch soldiers, he threatened to kill the hostages if there were a NATO bombing. Air strikes ordered against him were cancelled by UN headquarters. Consequently, the unprotected enclave fell into the hands of Bosnian Serb militias, the Serbian secret police, and paramilitary troops. They immediately began the work of selection, transportation, and execution, under the pretext of organizing a "transfer of population" to the Muslim territories only. Those responsible in the UN did not take seriously warnings about the danger of a massacre, nor did they immediately report the early evidence of killings. The Dutch commander even evaluated Mladić's action as an "excellently planned military operation."[61] The probable estimate of the number of the genocide victims is 7,536, but only a few of them were identified.[62]

How was it possible that mass killings such as the one at Srebrenica took place? Why would people organize and mobilize for violence and killing? Were their motives racism and nationalism? The terrible role of the Serb Bosnian military leaders, professionals who "organized, planned and willingly participated in genocide or stood silent in the face of it"[63] must be queried along with the roles of immediate perpetrators like the soldiers, paramilitaries, and volunteers. Questions must be raised also concerning the role of the bystanders supposed to be protectors, such as the UN Dutch battalion, and the role of the international community as well. What happened to them? Why did they not act?[64]

There is no doubt that, after occupying the Srebernica territory, the Bosnian Serb military leaders under the command of General Mladić intended to kill eventually as many men as possible of fighting age and that the plan was carried out as a well-planned and rapidly organized military operation.[65] Overall, 17,342 members of military units and 1,988 members of the police, regardless of their function, were in one way or another involved in the events of Srebrenica's mass killings.[66] Also evident are the "unclear mission" of the UN peacekeepers, the grave mistakes, the absence of judgment, and the many omissions of the UN headquarters in Zagreb. Their situation as the supposed protectors of Srebrenica, yet who saw their mission as absurd, was obviously an impossible one. But this cannot answer the above questions.

An attempt to explain the involvement of direct perpetrators and collaborators in the organization of the massacres might oscillate between two interpretations. The dominant one is that people participated, used violence, and killed because of fanatical nationalism and hatred, and because they were manipulated by elites. Yet, despite the power of tribal nationalist ideologies and their persuasive effects on the elites and masses, analyses of the genocide and "ethnic violence" from Yugoslavia, Rwanda, Sri Lanka, Northern Ireland, Sudan, and Australia, suggests that ethnic hatred itself might not be as a powerful tool for direct mobilization as is usually maintained.[67] This reveals a contradiction in any explanation that insists on the ideological-intentionalist interpretation. Hatred, desire for vengeance, and a desire for ethnic cleansing might be involved here, though they are not in the initial plan.

On the one hand, there is no doubt that patterns of war, genocide, and rape in the former Yugoslavia were present in the public conduct—as described above—

before the real violence took place, and the war started. Tribal nationalisms with their neoracist features created a discursive script for violence and facilitated its normalization, crystallizing in practices of "ethnic cleansing." But these developments were neither natural nor the result of simple indoctrination. They emerged out of the transformation of reality itself. The belief that abuse, manipulation, and "evil" were on the side of the power elites and politicians only, who skilfully and consciously used racist and tribal ideologies, while the people (or "masses") were just obedient, innocent, naturally good and/or misled by leaders like Milošević in Serbia or Tudjman in Croatia is similarly questionable.[68] Too many facts contradict such a conclusion. First, among the crucial conditions for Milošević's successful policy in Serbia (as well as the effects—later, in the war—of Tudjman's policy in Croatia) were an elite-mob connection and a mob mobilization. The "meetings of truth" supporting Milošević in the second half of the 1980s were well-organized and -sponsored public rallies held all over Yugoslavia with the aim of removing noncoordinated party leaders. This was a pretext for the successful mobilization of the Serb population outside of Serbia and for the total division later in Bosnia. Something very close to the totalitarian manipulation of elements was generated "until reality vanished." The masses, as well as intellectuals, media, and the general public, participated in the fabrication of their own and ultimate "truths" and myths, and in a total reorganization of memory. Second, mobilization was perpetrated through the mobilization of thugs, hooligans, and football fans, who introduced violence, ritual, and symbolic warfare and, finally, served as a resource for the paramilitary troops for the war. They became the "weekend warriors."[69]

Similar to what Arendt described as the German case under Nazi rule, circumstances of "inverted order" were created, in which "the battle for destiny" of the Serbian people was at stake. In Bosnia, this caused the rapid development of total divisions and policies of ethnic separation, especially since, after the multiparty elections, power was divided exclusively along ethnic lines. Such self–deception was the reason that large parts of the Serbian intellectual and political elite could claim—by the middle of war—that Serbia was "not at the war," "that (war) was started by destiny, not by them" and "that it was a matter of life or death for them, who must annihilate (their) enemies or be annihilated."[70] For similar reasons after the war, there was a strong denial in Serbia of events like that at Srebrenica and a mass mobilization against the extradition of war criminals, both in Serbia and Croatia. The background for such an inversion was constructed by a racialized reality, and a majority mentality similar to Eichmann's thoughtlessness, or, as Primo Levi called it, the "will not to know."[71]

Contrary to the insistence on ethnic hatred, and racist and ideological indoctrination or blindness, studies of genocide and mass violence have suggested that "ethnic" violence was neither a "motive in itself" nor a development from the masses after being duped by the elites: "Rather... [it] can be a cover for other motivations such as looting, land grabs, and personal revenge, and the activities of thugs set loose by the politicians."[72] The personal motivations that lie behind genocidal violence between and among neighbors might have little to do with ideology as a "motivation resource." This has been proven in the context of collective violence in traditional warfare, where comradeship not hatred is the dominant battle motivation, and the main actors are "terrifyingly normal men" whose killing is "more or less a product of modern culture."[73] Within the inversion of order and rules (when killing is no longer necessarily a crime), there are certain "pleasures of war" that are inculcated, encouraged, and maintained in the tradition of warfare and killing to make warfare attractive and psychologically endurable.[74]

Concentrating on the way perpetrators and collaborators were mobilized for genocide, J. Mueller argues that the factual mechanism of violence in the former Yugoslavia was "remarkably banal" and that it did not reflect deep, historic passions and hatreds. It seems that the immediate violence was rather "the result of a situation in which common, opportunistic, sadistic, and often distinctly nonideological marauders were recruited and permitted free rein by political authorities."[75] The Hague criminal tribunal trials have provided much material in support of such claims. Not surprisingly, the usual attitude of the defendants was one of "not guilty," since they had had no "intention" of perpetrating mass murder or war crimes. Slavenka Drakulić, who belongs among those authors who have increasingly begun to think in terms of the "banality" of perpetrators, introducing terminology used by Arendt in *Eichmann in Jerusalem*,[76] has analysed profiles of the perpetrators convicted of genocide and war crimes in the Yugoslav war and the Srebrenica mass murders. She shows that there is nothing monstrous about the perpetrators as people and that they are not evil nor beasts. Rather, they are "ordinary people" who became involved with violence and organized executions through professional or other decisions and took small steps in their lives without much reflection. "Ordinary thinking man" was neither inevitably a nationalist nor a madman, just someone who, when "given a chance to kill on apparently legitimate grounds and, in addition, to enrich himself by looting his victims, . . . did not think twice."[77] In fact, not only were they not necessarily fanatics, their motives simply did not count. But this was no Balkan peculiarity. Other instances of collective violence show similar features. Such perpetrators exist in all societies, thus similar events could, under the right circumstances, happen almost anywhere, including in Western societies. Furthermore, being aware of this fact (and not demonizing the perpetrators), one can go on to claim that the tragedies that overcame Bosnia, Croatia, and Rwanda could have been avoided. They could perhaps have been manageable with "different policing and accommodation procedures," if there were no monstrous and fatal evil supposed to be hidden behind them but simply human action and omission, and if they were not inevitably seen as springing automatically from a single cause or origin. These tragedies were the result neither of "inevitable historic necessities" nor of "ancient hatreds," but were provoked by the human actions of political leaders, local extremists, or thugs whose violence got out of control.[78]

Yet, if the mechanism of violence itself is banal, if the perpetrators are not stimulated by their hate, what is the role of widespread and seemingly overwhelming ethnic hatred, racist images, and ideologies of tribal nationalism that I have also been discussing? What role does racism play in the process of mass killing and of crimes against humanity, if it is not the immediate trigger? The provisional answer might be that such tribal nationalisms, racist ideologies and images provide, above all, a rationalizing frame for perpetrators who have primarily banal motivations but not the immediate thrust to act. These bring about the idea of extinction of the "other," demonstrate his superfluity; but it is up to the "banally evil" agents to carry out the more or less dirty task. Perhaps one can assume that racism (like anti-Semitism) gets lost in the process of extermination, and the "movement" itself takes the lead.[79]

However the dilemma does not really consist of a necessary choice between evil intentions, fanatical beliefs, and banal, mindless perpetrators or coalitions of the elite-masses. Rather one might think about the fact that both the elite and the masses share a common "ontological ground" which is actually banal and banally produced as well.[80] This is not a fixed and unchangeable culture or "ancient hatred." On the contrary, it is a constructed reality, a fabricated framework, which includes discursively constructed "scripts," myths of common origin, and easy historic explanations about "Us" and "Them"—foreigners, evildoers, and thus our enemies—which can be employed in present situations not only to produce feelings of fear and danger but to be an effective shield against any other reality. Here, emotions of hatred need not be included in the common picture, which is taken for granted, although, to be sure, they might exist beyond the common picture. Such a shield, a fabricated truth or image, seems to function as a process of ideological interpellation. It is not an essentialist demiurge but reproduced and manipulated by the actors themselves, left, so to speak, for their own personal use. Individuals are not indoctrinated but eventually come to occupy the "common ontological ground," which they coordinate and reshape with their own actions and omissions. This fabricated reality, as I tried to indicate in the first part of the chapter when talking about the Arendtian notion of ideology, is itself "banal." It is superficial, "thought defying," as Arendt wrote to Gershom Scholem, and facilitates self-deception. Such a banal "reality" might, of course, be diverse, but the hierarchic images of racialized relations, established through the tribal nationalist engagement, are sufficiently convenient, especially as they do not have to show their straightforward racist face but can be hidden—these days—under the respectable cover of cultural differences.

Not only the perpetrators and their collaborators but also the international professionals and bystanders have been caught in the self-made trap of such realities. This element belongs to the overall picture of bystander indifference and the conduct of the Dutch battalion. The Dutch soldiers were trained to accept an incredibly rigid and homogenized image both of the situation in the "Balkans" and of Bosnian Muslims, who were shown as the worst of the "Balkan men"—depicted literally as "the Other."[81] Faced with a situation without resources and under threat of their lives, they could easily disavow not only their professional but also their human responsibilities. To be sure, not only the Dutch soldiers shared a well-established, differentiated image of the Balkan populations. The message of the UN and the Dutch government was clear: Bosnian Muslim lives were not as valuable as those of UN soldiers. This has made the event at Srebrenica—like the genocide in Rwanda one year before—"more than a crime" but an event that "shamed humanity."[82]

Conclusion: The Yugoslav Elements—Old and New

What happened at Srebrenica had elements both of administrative mass murder and features of face-to-face killing and massacre. In this sense, it reminds us of both the Holocaust and the administrative massacres from colonial times. The "administrative" aspect of the mass murder lies not only in the perfect planning and organization of the killings, which took place in a very short time span, but in the interwoven test of stories: of the deeds and guilt of the immediate perpetrators; stories of the deeds and nondeeds, responsibility, and guilt of those who were directly in charge of the situation in the UN protected area, and stories about the part played by the international military and administrative structure responsible for protecting the lives of the Muslim refugees. The path toward the mass murder of Srebrenica, called "the worst massacre in Europe after the second World War," demonstrates how in Bosnia, through silent or open agreement with policies of "ethnic cleansing" and step by step, conditions involving "holes of oblivion" were established for a dreadful "solution" to the problem of those who had been rendered superfluous (in this case the Muslim population), and how judgment, responsibility, capacity, and readiness for action to prevent the murders could simply retreat from sight. The mass murder had been organized in such a way that even ordinary people, the population in general, either supported the perpetrators or directly participated in the killings, and was thus organized into guilt in the Arendtian sense. Finally, the outcome, while taking place within regional borders, offers lessons much broader than local or regional ones, and poses questions similar to those arising from the crisis of the European nation-state in the first half of the twentieth century. The outcome crystallized worldwide changes in the global policies of superpowers: the dawning of the era of so-called "humanitarian interventionism" and of the wars against terror.

These events were not only "repetitions," since novel elements and new forms emerged: in Bosnia, mass rape was part of the enterprise of annihilation of the Other, and cases of forced impregnation of women from the other ethnic group demonstrated a post-racist imagery in the annihilation practices. The killings, as illustrated by the shelling of Sarajevo, took place either before the very eyes of the "international community" and millions of virtual witnesses or, as in the case of Srebrenica, even with the collaboration ("standing by") of international forces, who were supposed to protect the population under threat. Srebrenica and the siege of Sarajevo, where Bosnian Serbian soldiers and weekend fighters served eight hour shifts of shelling daily, before the eyes of the international community, were among the unprecedented examples of the functioning of post-totalitarian elements under new circumstances. They both reflect more than just a war and a crime perpetrated as a consequence of racist endeavour. Was the mass murder of Srebrenica in Bosnia not the test case of the potential universal features of tribal nationalisms, the banality of evil, thoughtlessness, and of Eichmann-mentality in the post-totalitarian age within Europe itself—despite their relegation to the Balkans? Only here, apart from the direct perpetrators, the global bystanders, Eichmann's children, in the words of Günther Anders,[83] have also been included in the common picture. As Arendt enlightened us, the new predicaments might not look like the cruellest, at least not at first sight, but they might have the cruellest consequences imaginable.

Notes

1. Mahmood Mamdani, *When Victims Become Killers: Colonialism, Nativism, and the Genocide in Rwanda* (Princeton, and Oxford, 2001), 5.
2. On the question of the difference between the Holocaust and genocide, and of the uniqueness of the Holocaust, concerning scholarly discourse, see A. Dirk Moses, "The Holocaust and Genocide," in *The Historiography of the Holocaust*, ed. Dan Stone (Basingstoke, and New York, 2004), 547. On the comparison of the Holocaust with the Rwandan genocide, see Nigel Eltringham, *Accounting for Horror: Post Genocide Debates in Rwanda* (London, 2004), 51–68.
3. There are too many examples to list to them all but one might be the following: "To a historian, today's Balkan crises are rooted in, above all, the crippling dependence of all Balkan peoples on the ideology and psychology of expansionist nationalism." See William W. Hagen, "Balkans' Lethal Nationalisms," *Foreign Affairs* 78, no. 4 (1999): 52.
4. Ernst Vollrath, "Hannah Arendt and the Method of Political Thinking," *Social Research* 44, no. 1 (1977): 166.
5. Arendt considered the title, given by the publisher to *The Origins of Totalitarianism*, to be inappropriate since it conveyed the wrong impression that her intentions were to clarify "origins" and "causes." Hannah Arendt, "A Reply to Eric Voegelin," in *Essays in Understanding 1930–1954*, ed. Jerome Kohn (New York, 1994), 403.
6. Ibid.
7. She started to think about possible new forms of totalitarianism in the essay "Ideology and Terror," included in the 1958 revised edition of *Origins*, and she continued with that on the basis of observations of post-Second World War changes in Germany, of the consequences of the "thaw" in the Soviet Union, of the experience of the Hungarian Revolution in 1956. and the experience in the United States with McCarthyism.
8. Hannah Arendt, *The Origins of Totalitarianism* (London, 1986), 459.
9. Hannah Arendt, *Eichmann in Jerusalem: A Report on the Banality of Evil* (New York, 1977), 273.
10. Giorgio Agamben, *Homo Sacer: Sovereign Power and Bare Life* (Stanford, CA, 1998), 181ff.
11. Perhaps, in the future, we will see "large sections of population become 'superfluous' even in terms of labour," or we will have to face "the use of instruments beside which Hitler's gassing installations look like an evil child's fumbling toys." See Arendt, *Eichmann*, 273.
12. Arendt, *Origins*, 460.
13. Etienne Balibar and Immanuel Wallerstein, *Race, Nation, Class: Ambiguous Identities* (London, 1991), 37–8 and R. Miles, *Racism after Race Relations* (London, 1993), 59.
14. Balibar and Wallerstein, *Race, Nation, Class*, 37–38.

15. Racism is thus not an "'expression' of nationalism, but a supplement to nationalism, or more precisely a supplement internal to nationalism, always in excess of it, but always indispensable to its constitution and yet always still insufficient to achieve its project, just as nationalism is both indispensable and always insufficient to achieve the formation of the nation or the project of the 'nationalization' of society." Ibid, 54.

16. See Arendt, *Origins*, 227–243.

17. Richard Bernstein, *Hannah Arendt and the Jewish Question* (Cambridge, MA, 1996), 67.

18. Omer Bartov, "Defining Enemies, Making Victims: Germans, Jews, and the Holocaust," *American Historical Review* 10, no. 3 (1998): 771–816.

19. Balibar and Wallerstein, *Race, Nation, Class*, 22–23.

20. Arendt, *Origins*, 3–10.

21. Ibid., xv.

22. In "Lying in Politics," she spoke about such an imaginary enterprise as "image making as global policy." In Hannah Arendt, *Crises of the Republic* (New York, 1972), 18–19. About image making as a policy see also "Home to Roost," in Hannah Arendt, *Responsibility and Judgment*, ed. Jerome Kohn (New York, 2003), 257–275.

23. Hannah Arendt, "Letter to Gershom Scholem," in *The Jew as Pariah*, ed. Ron H. Feldman (New York, 1978), 150.

24. Hans Mommsen, "Hannah Arendt's Interpretation of the Holocaust as a Challenge to Human Existence: The Intellectual Background," in *Hannah Arendt in Jerusalem*, ed. Steven E. Aschheim (Berkeley, 2002), 225–6.

25. This debate was renewed with the publication of Daniel Jonah Goldhagen's *Hitler's Willing Executioners* (New York, 1996) maintaining that the main cause of the Holocaust was the German ideology of anti-Semitism. For more about this debate, see A. D. Moses, "Structure and Agency in the Holocaust: Daniel J. Goldhagen and his Critics," *History and Theory* 37, no. 2 (1998): 194–219, 202ff.

26. Arendt apparently changed her mind regarding the role and power of ideology when reporting about the process against Eichmann. She claimed that in *Origins* she had overstated the influence of ideologies on the individual. In her letter to Mary McCarthy on September 20, 1963, she wrote that anti-Semitism itself gets lost in the process of extermination and instead the "movement" itself takes the lead. It seems, however, that Arendt unconsciously held two notions of ideology: the first concerns the role of ideology as indoctrination and is close to the Marxist notion; the second underlines ideological productivity—of totalitarian movements and policies, fabricating the frame of "reality" that is comparable to Foucauldian productivity and power of discourse. Later, she returned to this ideological productivity—as early as in *Eichmann in Jerusalem*—when claiming that Eichmann had been living in the world of "self-deception" common to millions of Germans and thus living in a kind of a "fabricated truth." She noticed the power of the image when trying to withstand incomprehensibly brutal attacks on her book about Eichmann. Many of those who attacked the Eichmann book were actually dealing with a fabricated image of it and not with what she really wrote. Hannah Arendt-Mary McCarthy. *Im Vertrauen: Briefwechsel 1949 – 1975* (Munich, 1995), 233–4, 238–9.

27. Arendt, *Eichmann*, 287.

28. Among recent critiques of the Arendtian "banality of evil" thesis, see Yaacov Lozowick, *Hitler's Bureaucrats: The Nazi Security and the Banality of Evil* (London and New York, 2002), and Richard Wolin, *Heidegger's Children: Hannah Arendt, Karl Löwith, Hans Jonas, and Herbert Marcuse* (Princeton, NJ, 2001), 31–69. An excellent clarification of the relation between radical and banal evil is given in Bernstein, *Hannah Arendt*, 137–153. For overviews of the reception of Arendt's book on Eichmann and the debates about the main issues, see: Richard I. Cohen, "A Generation's Response to Eichmann in Jerusalem," in *Hannah Arendt in Jerusalem*, ed. Aschheim, 253–277; Elizabeth Young-Bruehl, *Hannah Arendt: For Love of the World* (New Haven and London, 1982), 328–377; Jennifer Ring, *The Political Consequences of Thinking, Gender and Judaism in the Work of Hannah Arendt* (Albany, 1997); Hans Mommsen, "Hannah Arendt's Interpretation of the Holocaust

as a Challenge to Human Existence: The Intellectual Background"; Susan Neiman, "Theodicy in Jerusalem"; and Dana Villa, "Apologist or Critic? On Arendt's Relation to Heidegger," in *Hannah Arendt in Jerusalem*, ed. Aschheim, 224–232, 65–90, and 325–337. On the intellectual anchorage and universalist effects of the notion of the banality of evil, see Richard H. King, *Race, Culture and Intellectuals 1940–1970* (Baltimore and Washington, D.C., 2004), 173–195.

29. Lozowick, *Hitler's Bureaucrats*, 230. Lozowick repeats Yehuda Bauer's judgment, which, however, forgets that Arendt never claimed Eichmann's deeds as "banal" but the perpetrator himself (see King, *Race, Culture, and the Intellectuals*, 189).

30. Arendt, *Eichmann*, 212ff, 22, 277–8.

31. She considered the Holocaust a crime against humanity "committed on the body of the Jewish people." See *Eichmann*, 7.

32. See King, *Race, Culture, and the Intellectuals*, 192.

33. See Neiman, "Theodicy in Jerusalem."

34. Julie Mertus, "The Role of Racism as a Cause or Factor in Wars and Civil Conflict," in *International Council on Human Rights Policy: Consultation on Racism and Human Rights* Geneva, (December 3–4), 1999, (http://www.ichrp.org/ac/excerpts/50.pdf), accessed 13 May 2005, 1.

35. Michael A. Sells' *The Bridge Betrayed: Religion and Genocide in Bosnia* (Berkeley, Los Angeles, and London, 1998) explores "religious mythology, extreme nationalism, and racialist theory" in the case of Bosnia (xv). See also David Bruce MacDonald, *Balkan Holocausts? Serbian and Croatian Victim-Centred Propaganda and the War in Yugoslavia* (Manchester and New York, 2002), 122ff. and Aleksa Djilas, *The Contested Country: Yugoslav Unity and Communist Revolution, 1919–1953* (Cambridge, MA, 1991), 107, who both underline the importance of racial differences in the process of distinction making between the Serbian and the Croatian groups.

36. See J. A. Irvine, "Balkan Authoritarian Ultranationalist Ideology and State-Building in Croatia, 1990–1996," in *Problems of Post-Communism* 44, no. 4 (2001): 30–44.

37. See Branimir Anzulović, *Heavenly Serbia: From Myth to Gencide* (London, 1999). Other exceptions besides Julie Mertus's writings are Branka Magaš's reflections on Milošević's Serbia as a fascist state in terms of the only remaining "post-Stalinist" state (among the post Yugoslav republics) that "remained largely intact to be turned to a racist, even genocidal project"; in Magaš, "Milosevic's Serbia and Ethnic Cleansing: The Making of a Fascist State," *Against the Current* 52 (September/October, 1994). Similarly, some analyses speak about chauvinism, "bordering on racism," "racist reasoning," and about depictions of the Other that are linked to racist metaphors. See Robert M. Hayden, "The Triumph of Chauvinistic Nationalism in Yugoslavia: Bleak Implications for Anthropology," *Anthropology of East Europe Review* 11, nos. 1–2 (1993). As well as the exceptions, one must enumerate the problem of Orientalist approaches toward the Balkans. See Maria Todorova, *Imagining the Balkans* (New York, 1997) and Dušan I. Bjelić and Obrad Savić, ed., *Balkan as Metaphor: Between Globalizaton and Fragmentation* (Cambridge, MA, 2002).

38. Such an approach keeps nationalism and racism strictly apart and insists on the fundamental difference between them. On the basis of the claim that the Holocaust was about biological racism, one can then refuse all comparisons and claims, for example, that the "Balkan ethnic cleansing" was "fundamentally different" from the Holocaust, which was a "program of biological extermination based on racist eugenic theories." The fundamental difference is that it "does not require mass extermination but rather mass removal." See Hagen, "Balkans Lethal Nationalisms," 8 (my emphasis). Such "particular" treatment of "ethnic cleansing" as a local peculiarity and a "lesser evil" actually legitimizes it and its methods of annihilation—similar to a very problematic scholarly tradition from the first part of the twentieth century.

39. Mamdani, *When Victims become Killers*, 8.

40. Balibar and Wallerstein, *Race, Nation, Class*, 46–7.

41. Mertus, "The Role of Racism," 1.

42. In an apparent paradox, they coincided with the opening of the public space and the emergence of wide press and other media freedom and made possible the public revival and competition

of the old debates about the voice and standing of particular nations. This shows that—contrary to the common liberal belief that governments are the foremost producers of nationalist propaganda and that free speech is the best "antidote"—under conditions of incipient democratization and openness of public debate, nationalist mythmaking and ethnic conflict can be fostered and that nationalist and racist ideas can be sold successfully in the "marketplace of ideas." The instances of the media in the Yugoslav and Rwandan cases demonstrate that the impact of nationalist and racist propaganda depends on the "demand," and the masses are not just the innocent victims of elites. See a convincing analysis by Jack Snyder and Karin Ballentine, "Nationalism and the Marketplace of Ideas," *International Security* 21, no. 2 (1996): 5–40.

43. See Julie Mertus, *Kosovo: How Myths and Truths Started a War* (Berkeley, 1999), 8–9.

44. See the chapter on Albanians in Ivo Banac, *The National Question in Yugoslavia* (Ithaca, 1984) and Olivera Milosavljević, *U tradiciji nacionalizma ili stereotipi srpskih intelektualaca XX veka o 'nama' i 'dru-gima'* [*In the Tradition of Nationalism, or Stereotypes of Serbian Intellectuals about 'Us' and 'Others' in the XX Century*] (Belgrade, 2002), 218ff. It is significant that the so-called "race betrayal" is also a key theme of the famous epic poetry written by Njegoš, *The Mountain Wreath*. The Slavic Muslims were seen as "turkified" by having converted to Islam, and this "was not simply to adopt the religion and mores of a Turk, but to transform oneself into a Turk. To convert to a religion other than Christianity was simultaneously to convert from the Slav race to an alien race." Sells, *The Bridge Betrayed*, 45.

45. Wolfgang Petritsch, Karl Kaser, Robert Pichler. *Kosovo, Kosova: Mythen, Daten, Fakten* (Klagenfurt, 1999), 113–128.

46. The measures—the agreed transfer of the 200,000 Albanians, Turks, and Muslims from Kosovo and Macedonia to Turkey—were not carried out, owing to the outbreak of the Second World War and for other reasons. However, between 90.000 and 150,000 Albanians left Kosovo at that time. Petritsch, et al,. *Kosovo*, 128. On the issue of "ethnic cleansing," see Tone Bringa, "Averted Gaze: Genocide in Bosnia and Herzegovina," in *Annihilating Difference: The Anthropology of Genocide*, ed. Alexander Laban Hinton (Berkeley, 2002), 204–5 and Milosavljević, *U tradiciji nacionalizma*. Bringa rightfully problematizes the terms "ethnic cleansing" and "genocide" in the Yugoslav conflict, showing how the use of "ethnic cleansing" (denoted as a "lesser evil") supported nonintervention policies and the relativization of crimes and how the term genocide was misused by the Serb leadership and propagandists. Ibid., 203–4.

47. Olivera Milosavljević, "The Abuse of the Authority of Science," in *The Road to War in Serbia: Trauma and Catharsis*, ed. Nebojša Popov (Budapest, 2000), 302.

48. Mamdani shows how the Rwandan genocide took place as a "native genocide" and how the Tutsi were constructed as "settlers" to be targeted as intruders and not neighbors. Mamdani, *When Victims*, 10ff.

49. Milosavljević, *U tradiciji nacionalizma*, 252ff.

50. See Slavenka Drakulić, "We Are All Albanians," *The Nation* 268, no. 21 (June 7, 1999); Franke Wilmer, *The Social Construction of Man, The State and War: Identity, Conflict and Violence in Former Yugoslavia* (New York and London 2002), 101.

51. For an exhaustive elaboration on this, see Mirko Đorđević, *Srpska konzervativna misao* [*Serbian Conservative Thought*] (Belgrade, 2003).

52. Radmila Radić, "The Church and the 'Serbian Question,'" in *The Road to War in Serbia*, ed. Popov, 251.

53. In the words of Radovan Karadžić, Bosnian Serb leader, "We cannot live with the Muslims and the Croats, for there is too much hatred, centuries of hatred. Serbs fear the Muslims. They cannot live together. Because of genocide committed against them (the Serbs), they have to defend themselves." These words have been picked up by the Western media, and "ancient hatred" has become a mantra of which the consequence has been the fatalistic notion that the war cannot be stopped (see Bringa, "Averted Gaze," 197).

54. Olivera Milosavljević, "New and Old Nationalisms," *Helsinki Files 11. The Balkans Rachomon.* (http://www.helsinki.org.yu/files.php?lang=en), accessed June 20, 2005, 42–5.

55. *Dictionary of Race, Ethnicity and Culture*, ed. Guido Bolaffi, Raffaele Bracaletni, Peter Braham and Sandro Gindro (London, 2003), 103–4.

56. Arendt, *Origins*, 167.

57. Ibid., 165.

58. Tudjman suggested to Western diplomats that Croatia was fighting its war against Muslim fundamentalism. Bringa, "Averted Gaze," 241. For more about the development of Croatian nationalism, the Ustaša legacy and extremist developments, including racist dimensions, see Irvine, "Balkan Authoritarian Ultranationalist Ideology and State-Building in Croatia."

59. This is one of the reasons that the prime minister, Zoran Djindjić, who had been the representative of "modern liberal nationalism," was assassinated in 2003. Latinka Perović, "The Sociopolitical and Ethno-religious Dimension of Wars in Yugoslavia," in *The Violent Dissolution of Yugoslavia: Causes, Dynamics and Effects*, ed. Miroslav Hadžić (Belgrade 2004), 123–4.

60. Arendt, *Origins*, 138, 231.

61. Samantha Power, *"A Problem from Hell": America and the Age of Genocide* (London, 2003), 417.

62. Helge Brunborg, Torkild Hovde Lyngstad and Henrik Urdal, "Accounting for Genocide: How Many Were Killed in Srebrenica?" *European Journal of Population* 19 (2003): 244. About the Srebrenica case, see David Rhode, *Endgame: The Betrayal and Fall of Srebrenica* (New York, 1997); Michael N. Barnett, "The Politics of Indifference at the United Nations and Genocide in Rwanda and Bosnia," in *This Time we Knew: Western Responses to Genocide in Bosnia*, ed. Thomas Cushman and Stjepan Meštrović (New York, 1996), 128–162, Jan William Honig and Norbert Both, *Srebrenica: Record of a War Crime* (Harmondsworth, 1996); David Rieff, *A Bed for the Night: Humanitarianism in Crisis* (New York, 2003); Julija Bogoeva and Caroline Fetcher, *Srebrenica. Ein Prozess, Dokumente und Materialien aus dem UN-Kriegsverbrechertribunal in Den Haag* (Frankfurt-am-Main, 2002). For detailed research into the UN Dutch battalion role in Srebrenica, see the report of The Netherlands Institute for War Documentation (NIOD), *Srebrenica – a 'safe' area. The fall of a Safe Area Reconstruction, background consequences and analyses of the fall of the Safe Area.* (http://213.222.3.5/srebrenica/), accessed September 5, 2005. A deeply shocking BBC documentary about the mass atrocities in Srebrenica is *A Cry From the Grave.*

63. Slavenka Drakulić, *They Would Never Hurt a Fly: War Criminals on Trial in The Hague* (London, 2004), 75.

64. These issues were thoroughly worked out by Arne J. Vetlesen, who develops a typology of bystanders to genocide and defines groups of bystanders: those directly in charge of the situation and those responsible in the loose sense of being cognizant of genocide through television, radio, newspapers, and other public media, but not directly involved in it (neither by profession nor by formal appointment) and then asks a question about the status of (non)action in such cases. See his "Genocide: A Case for the Responsibility of the Bystander," *Journal of Peace Research* [Special Issue on Ethics of War and Peace] 37, no. 4 (2000): 519–532.

65. *Srebrenica – a 'safe' area* (http://213.222.3.5/srebrenica/toc/p2_c02-s003_b01.html)

66. The preliminary data is from *Republika Srbska*, published by the Bosnian Working Group for Srebrenica in October 2005.

67. See James D. Fearon, and David D. Laitin, "Violence and the Social Construction of Ethnic Identity," *International Organization* 54, no. 4 (2000): 845–878.

68. Mamdani, who made a detailed analysis of the Rwandan mobilization for genocide, sees such reasoning as a great problem in academic writing, which likes to see genocide as "designed from above" and hesitates to acknowledge the action and initiative from below. Mamdani, *When Victims become Killers*, 8.

69. Such was the case of the Belgrade Red Star football club fans, who became the real "warriors," the so called "Arkan's Tigers," and engaged in the war in Bosnia. See Ivan Čolović, "Football, Hooligans and War," in *The Road to War*, ed. Popov, 373–396.

70. See Arendt, *Eichmann*, 52,

71. Primo Levi, *If this is a Man/The Truce* (London, 2003), 386.

72. Fearon and Laitin, "Violence and the Social Construction," 874.

73. Glenn Gray, *The Warriors: Reflections on Men in Battle*, Introduction Hannah Arendt (Lincoln and London 1970; reprint 1998), xviii.

74. See Joanna Bourke *An Intimate History of Killing: Face-to-face Killing in Twentieth-Century Warfare* (London, 1999), 13ff.

75. John Mueller, "The Banality of Ethnic War," *International Security* 25, no. 1 (2000): 43.

76. For example: Tim Judah, *The Serbs: History, Myth and the Destruction of Yugoslavia* (New Haven, 1997), 228–238 and Mueller, "The Banality of Ethnic War," *International Security* 25, no. 1 (2000): 42–73.

77. Drakulić, *They Would Never Hurt a Fly*, 167.

78. See Mueller, "The Banality of Ethnic War," 67ff.

79. See footnote 27.

80. Fearon and Laitin, "Violence and the Social Construction," 86

81. NIOD, *Srebrenica – a 'safe' area*, (http://213.222.3.5/srebrenica/toc/p2_c08-s003_b01.html), accessed September 5, 2005.

82. See Mark Huband in Roy Gutman and David Rieff, *Crimes of War: What the Public Should Know* (New York and London 1999), 314, and Vetlesen, "Genocide: A Case," 531.

83. This is the title of Günther Anders's (Stern) not widely known book in German, *Wir, Eichmannsöhne, Brief an Klaus Eichmann* (Muenchen, 1988) [*We, Sons of Eichmann: A Letter to Klaus Eichmann*]. Anders, Arendt's first husband, closely analyses the procedures of self–deception within a modern society of unlimited fabrication. He describes this problem in terms of a discrepancy between *Herstellen* (fabrication, the technically feasible) and *Vorstellen* (imagination), whereby the unimaginable (*Unvorstellbare*) always tends to be fabricated if we fear to think about the consequences of our actions. See 24 ff.

Part III

INTELLECTUAL GENEALOGIES
AND LEGACIES

Chapter 9

HANNAH ARENDT ON TOTALITARIANISM
Moral Equivalence and Degrees of Evil in Modern Political Violence

Richard Shorten

To be found at the interstices of the current academic literatures on the relation between history and memory, on the nature and sources of modern political violence, and on the problem of totalitarianism is an idiosyncratic series of questions that has the effect of making the thought of Hannah Arendt acutely relevant. One of these questions—or, at least, the broad question that I have in mind—concerns how the historical experiences of imperialism, Nazism, and Stalinism might be both understood and situated *vis-à-vis* one another, and how their status and relation might be clarified.

This question arises at the intersection of each of the aforementioned literatures for the following reasons. First, the ever-expanding literature on history and memory has, as its orbit, the experience of the Nazi genocide, moreover contained—as it tends to be—within an "inverted kind of Eurocentrism" that privileges this (specific) site of memory, while rendering its sources nearly exclusively indigenous.[1] Arendt's thought—germane in this context for her thinking on political evil, particularly in *The Origins of Totalitarianism*—is set off by precisely this event. Equally, though, it takes her into an attempt to engage with its extra-European antecedents—and especially late nineteenth-century imperialism. Second, within an area of research often designated as "genocide studies," the status of that discipline's core concepts are frequently debated with the Holocaust as the primary point of reference.[2] Nonetheless, this is increasingly a source of concern for those who consider this focus on the Holocaust—and, it should be said, the focus on communist violence also—to confine attention disingenuously to the twentieth century. The upshot of this, as one commentator has explained it, is to "throw a convenient cloak on the carnage created by colonial and imperial expansion prior to the century just passed."[3] Arendt's thought, again, is relevant here, both for the reason given above and in light of her efforts, continuing throughout her intellectual career, to conceptualize the nature of "radical evil." Third, much of the current work on totalitarianism can be said to serve as a contextualization of Nazi violence that places it in an exclusive relationship to communism/Stalinism. Once more, it is the peculiarity of Arendt's thinking on totalitarianism to lend its emergence a broader context.

As such, in the course of this chapter I intend to touch on each of these issues at various points. Namely, how does memory impact on our thinking about political evil? By what criteria might (specific) historical events be assigned uniqueness or otherwise? And what is at stake in the contextualization of Nazi violence? Somewhat less ambitiously, however, the aim in raising these issues—in close connection with *Origins*—is to think through what is, admittedly, a rather opaque problem, one which surfaces as a curiously recurrent concern in much present thinking on modern political violence and that is frequently expressed in the terminology of "moral equivalence." Accordingly, the aim is to seek to tease out from Arendt's thought a set of criteria, which might serve to resolve this problem. To lend clarity to what is under contestation here requires, at the outset, a brief survey of some current and recent controversies.

The Problem of Equivalency: Nazism, Stalinism, and imperialism

The question of "moral equivalence," within the broad literature on totalitarianism, usually surfaces in connection with the issue of whether communism/Stalinism—in comparison to Nazism—constitutes a "lesser evil." Indeed, a recent volume of essays takes this trope as its title as it seeks to work through the "systematic imbalance" in the chronicling of these two historical experiences and the putatively different responses to them.[4] The broad context to all of this has been stated tersely by Slavoj Žižek: "Till now . . . Stalinism hasn't been rejected *in the same way* as Nazism."[5] The reasons that intellectual discourse—particularly in Western Europe—has hitherto been resistant to a sense of moral equivalence between Soviet and Nazi practices conceivably are manifold: communism's rootedness in the Enlightenment tradition, the role of the Red Army in the Third Reich's downfall, the remoteness of Russia from Western modernity, an incapacity to engage empathetically with the victims of communism, and/or the gulf that separates a political project that failed to live up to its ideals from one that all too successfully delivered on its (perverse) aims. The latter position has arguably been the most influential. Moreover, it was the one given most coherent expression by Raymond Aron in 1965 and has, thereafter, been much cited. "There is a difference," stated Aron, "between a philosophy whose logic is monstrous, and one which can be given a monstrous interpretation."[6] The contention here, however, is that for some time, this position has been in the process of undergoing an inversion. Drawing on the metaphor of disease deployed in this context by Steven Lukes, one may propose that whereas an earlier wave of scholarly interpretations of communism saw it as having been *contracted*—its failure lying in the nature of its implementation—a more recent wave has cast it as *congenital*—intrinsic to the very theory behind it.[7] Further, this move to subvert a widely-accepted paradigm that affords Nazism a "unique status as 'absolute evil'" can be traced across various national contexts.[8]

In Britain, for instance, the application of a moral double standard was the theme of the novelist Martin Amis's *Koba the Dread*, published in 2002. Supposed ignorance of the crimes of Stalinism is one of the primary targets here ("Everybody knows of the 6 million of the Holocaust. Nobody knows of the 6 million of the Terror-Famine"). Amis goes about attacking the stance of liberal intellectuals whom he accuses—in the past as much as in the present—of having shied away from this reality for fear that wholesale condemnation of the Soviet utopian "experiment" might be a concession that detracts, bizarrely, from the "progressive" agenda in British politics.[9]

In Germany the theme of moral equivalence has been documented most notably in the case of the *Historikerstreit* in the mid 1980s, although the key proponent of equivalence in this debate, Ernst Nolte, has since developed further a theory of totalitarianism that turns on equivalency. At the time of the *Historikerstreit*, Nolte caused the greatest stir with an inelegantly constructed and acrimoniously received observation that he put in the form of the following rhetorical question: "Was not the Gulag Archipelago more original than Auschwitz?"[10] He has since attempted to qualify this observation as merely a "metaphorical abbreviation" [!] of a more sophisticated interpretation, one which he suggests "might also be formulated" thus:

> The Bolsheviks' enterprise, unprecedented in modern European history, to destroy socially Russia's "ruling class" (particularly the bourgeoisie and the "old intelligentsia," and later, the independent peasantry, as well) which, to a considerable extent, actually resulted in physical destruction ("class murder") drew the fascist and National Socialist enterprise of counter-destruction in its wake.

It is worth noting in the present context that, as a contextualization of Nazism, this "historical-genetic" account of totalitarianism does two things. First, it performs a kind of relativization. Hence Nolte, inveighing against a long-entrenched consensus in Western moral discourse, at the same time remarks that the "interpretation which endeavors to see an 'absolute evil' in National Socialism is not an interpretation but a quasi-religious mythology."[11] Second, in the chronological sequence that it abstracts, and drawing once more on Lukes' pathological metaphor, communism now becomes the "original sin"—the causal context without which Nazism is a non-starter, given that its own practices are both a reaction to and an imitation of practices already displayed in the Soviet polity: no Gulag, no Holocaust.

In contemporary France too the moral equivalence of the crimes of Hitler and Stalin has been an especially prominent theme, specifically so in a post-Marxist context where the settling of accounts with Marxism and Leninism has been a belated concern. Under this rubric, most accounts start out from the claim that the crimes of communism have long been ignored in French political culture. For this reason, in the late 1990s, two texts in particular prompted debate there about the nature of the appropriate comparison to be made between communism and Nazism.[12] François Furet's argument in *The Passing of an Illusion* did much toward redressing the imbalance held up by a series of "illusions" concerning communism that, for parochial reasons, were peculiarly deep-seated in France.[13] It was another text, though, the coauthored and provocatively titled *The Black Book of Communism: Crimes, Terror, Repression* that placed the problem of equivalency center stage. Above all, Stéphane Courtois' introduction to this collection of essays stated the thesis of equivalency unambiguously, in terms that were at the same time quantitative and qualitative. At the quantitative level, it estimated the total number of victims of communist crimes globally at 100 million and compared this with the 25 million victims of National Socialist crimes. In the qualitative sense it deduced first an equivalency of these crimes from an "equality" of the suffering of their victims: "the deliberate starvation of a child of a Ukrainian kulak as a result of the famine caused by Stalin's regime 'is equal to' the starvation of a Jewish child in the Warsaw ghetto as a result of the famine caused by the Nazi regime." Second, it flattened any available distinctions between what it formulated in terms of the "genocide of a 'race'" and the "genocide of a 'class.'"[14]

We might add finally that a third text to come out of the French context—Tzvetan Todorov's *Hope and Memory*—queries Aron's point from a more strictly philosophical angle. Unconvinced by Aron's distinction between communism and Nazism at the level of their respective ideals—the former "universal," "inspired by humanitarian values" with its "noble aspirations;" the latter "nationalistic, racial and anything but humane"—Todorov sees the entire universalism/particularism dichotomy as unsustainable. "The ideals of both regimes jettison universal ambitions," writes Todorov, since each seeks "the happiness of humanity" only "once the 'bad guys' have been separated out from it": in the case of communism, the bourgeoisie, the kulaks, and so forth.[15]

In sum, one might say that the combined effect of these specific yet related revisions of an "absolutizing discourse" on Nazism[16] is to foster a morally unattractive, not to say rather tasteless, hierarchical ordering of forms of modern political violence. At the extreme there is a peculiar logic at work, whereby different events are set up as equivalent (i.e., events that might *rightly* be differentiated) and whereby the sequential order in which these events occur is attributed significance: it is with the construction of a *chain* of equivalences that the hierarchy emerges. The effect is symptomatic of a more general feature of discourse, that statements which express an equivalence (x "as well as" y, x "not just" y, etc.) in practice create an implicit antithesis: x "rather than" y. In this particular case x and y are constituted as interconnected equivalences—with the effect that a strong impression is conveyed that communism renders Nazism inevitable.[17] Accordingly, one consequence, among others, is that any serious treatment of the questions of causality and responsibility is elided; they are merely insinuated by casual sleight of hand.

My claim here, however, is that the concerns that arise in connection with the problem of equivalency are not without relevance for thinking about Arendt's own contextualization of Nazism. In the abstract sense, Arendt's effort to probe the "origins" of totalitarianism brings her thought into this orbit, for origins insinuate questions of cause, responsibility, provenance, beginnings, comparison, uniqueness, and so on.[18] To put this differently, Arendt's interpretation of totalitarianism is more than a structural account—i.e., one that simply draws attention to commonalities between systems of rule—and seeks rather to locate it, from a temporal perspective, in terms of its genocidal dynamic. In the more substantive sense there is also relevance with regard to the terrain upon which Arendt fleshes out her specific conception of "origins," centrally insofar as she brings imperialism into focus as a background factor in the rise of totalitarianism. As such, the present aim is to transpose Arendt's thought to the context just mapped out, and to work through the implications of what she might have to say.

To be sure, from the vantage point of Arendt's thinking on totalitarianism, several of the claims advanced within the current debates appear dubious. With regard to the parameters of the historical comparison involved, whereas the *Black Book* takes Stalinism (or rather, strictly speaking, "the pattern elaborated in Moscow in 1917") to be the model for the practice of communism worldwide—thereby providing Nazism with a *global* kind of comparison—Arendt argues against the applicability of "totalitarianism" to all communist regimes.[19] Similarly, it is Nazism "far more than the Soviet experience"[20] that animates Arendt's thinking on totalitarianism, and her repeated emphasis on the "unprecedented" nature of the event of totalitarianism is her characteristic way of expressing the historical *caesura* effected by the Nazi extermination project.

Nonetheless, in other senses, the *Black Book*'s move away from an exclusively Eurocentric focus, in surveying the global balance sheet of communism in the twentieth century, suggests affinities with Arendt to the extent that it too brings the colonial context into focus—if not the earlier history of colonial violence that she narrates, then at least a subsequent history of violent (and global) decolonization during the period of the Cold War. Likewise, the less the Nazi project of extermination comes to be conceived as the "paradigmatic" experience of modern political violence, the more significant becomes the space in which arguments such as that of Vinay Lal might be evaluated: that Nazi genocidal policies "visited upon the peoples of Europe the violence that colonial powers had routinely inflicted on the 'natives' all over the world for nearly five hundred years."[21] Such arguments—while they can be imagined to elicit far greater sympathy than those of Nolte, for instance—nevertheless give rise to the same concerns as they constitute a restated version of the equivalency thesis. Specifically, the danger becomes that the analogy to and, indeed, precedent of the violence of European imperialism threatens to overshadow the singular aspects of Nazism; and that, once more, the construction of a chain of equivalences serves not merely to draw attention to previously overlooked and potentially significant connections between events, but rather to pit one historical atrocity against another.[22]

In point of fact, these concerns are touched on in Enzo Traverso's recent, and rather modish, attempt to reconsider "the origins of Nazi violence." Traverso argues that the origins of Nazism are to be located in the synthesis of various forms of violence integral to modernity—ranging from the guillotine to the Fordist factory—in which (and here he is consciously paraphrasing Nolte) "the 'logical and factual precedent' for Nazi crimes is to be found in colonial wars, not in Bolshevik Russia."[23] Clarification of how Arendt herself came to make this latter connection requires some exposition of the circumstances that informed the composition of *Origins*.

The Context of Arendt's Theory of Totalitarianism

Despite its ostensible division into three sections (Antisemitism, Imperialism, Totalitarianism), *Origins* is really comprised of only two discrete parts. The final part is separated from the others by Arendt's decision—prompted by the unfolding of events and arising out of her conviction that a new political reality rendered obsolete the typologies of classical political thought—to elucidate the structural similarities of the Nazi and communist movements and regimes under the conceptual rubric of "totalitarianism" itself. In this, Arendt initially spent no time at all in justifying the term, "simply accept[ing] its existence, both as a worthwhile concept and as a phenomenon of our times."[24] Yet as late as 1946 she still conceived of the work in progress as a historical investigation into what she termed, instead, "'racial imperialism,' the most extreme form of the suppression of minority nations by the ruling nation of a sovereign state."[25] That is to say, *Origins* was initially conceived as a theoretical inquiry into the crisis of the modern nation-state in connection with imperialism, which only subsequently became displaced by a primary focus on Nazism, which itself was only lastly incorporated with an analysis of Stalinism.

The term "racial imperialism" Arendt derived originally from Franz Neumann—though she cites him only twice—who, in a Marxian account of the rise of National Socialism, pointed to the masking of class antagonism by racial theory and to the way in which imperial expansion was provided with a basis in mass support by theories of racial superiority.[26] In fact, commentators often view Arendt as drawing on a wider Marxist tradition in the first part of *Origins*—in places lending Nazism a somewhat capitalist genealogy—which then gives way to a different conceptual framework in the second part.[27] It is incorrect, though, to understand Arendt to be moving from a "leftist" interpretation of totalitarianism—principally indicting imperialism, toward a "rightist" account (*à la* Hayek and Talmon)—indicting the revolutionary tradition itself, and identifying the roots of totalitarianism in the supposedly organicist ideology of Marx or Rousseau.[28] Rather, the subject matter changes: in the second part of the text, her concern is no longer with the "origins" of the totalitarian regime but with the totalitarian edifice itself, its organizational structure and so forth.

It is Arendt's increasing identification of the centrality of the concentration camp to totalitarian rule that frames this shift of emphasis. Like Primo Levi, who described the concentration camp system as "pre-eminently a gigantic biological and social experiment," she arrives at the judgment that totalitarianism "finally erects concentration camps as special laboratories to carry through its experiment in total domination." The transgressive extremities of totalitarianism were such that their most radical possibilities could only be fully tested there. Specifically, Arendt sets out the case that, via a three-stage process, the camp system completed totalitarianism's enactment of the destruction of the human status, by attacking in turn the juridical, moral, and individual persons in man: man who is a bearer of rights, man who owns and acts upon a conscience, and man who possesses a unique identity.[29] Yet, to return to the problem in hand, what this begs is the purpose that the discussion of "racial imperialism"—which now becomes, as it were, totalitarianism's "pre-history"—is meant to serve. How, in other words, is it meant to illuminate the "event of totalitarian domination" without setting up an undesirable case of equivalence? This issue becomes evident when one considers some of Arendt's statements. For instance, she writes: 'There are no parallels to the life in the concentration camp . . . all parallels create confusion and distract attention from what is essential. Forced labor in prisons and penal colonies, banishment, slavery, all seem for a moment to offer helpful comparisons, but on closer inspection lead nowhere.'[30] From this reconstruction of the background to the completion of *Origins* at least two points can be inferred as relevant to the present purpose. First, the "origins" in question refer to those of Nazism, not Stalinism. And second, the ordering of the two parts of *Origins*—despite the haphazard route to publication—is intended to be both logical and chronological. Next, to grasp how and what Arendt conceives as the relation between the event of Nazism and its antecedents requires undertaking an examination, in turn (in the two sections below), both of the form that her origins take and their substantive content. What is called for, in other words, is some elucidation of what she means by origins and, thereafter, of what she identifies these origins as consisting in.

Origins, Crystallization, Beginnings, and Narrative

To ascertain the formal conception of "origins" that Arendt is working with requires carefully unpacking her intentions. Certainly, the contemporary reception of *Origins* among historians and political scientists was marked by a degree of scepticism regarding its method: reviewers, for instance, were dismissive of its "over-reliance on deductive reasoning."[31] Largely, however, this was to miss the subtleties of Arendt's approach. While Richard Bernstein writes that, "Arendt's remarks about her 'method' are casual, metaphoric, and frequently confusing," Ira Katznelson has more recently commented that *Origins* is informed by a "methodological self-consciousness."[32] The apparent tension between these two views is to be reconciled in the fact that Arendt's own statement on method is to be found outside of her text. The methodological clarifications she *does* make initially, in the preface to the original edition, are indeed unclear. This is evident where she distinguishes "comprehension" both from "deducing the unprecedented from precedents" (which is to ascribe to events a kind of false necessity) and the insufficient kind of explanation achieved by mere analogy. This "comprehension," she says, must entail "the unpremeditated, attentive facing up to, and resisting of, reality—whatever it may be." These comments revisit her earlier theme of the event of totalitarianism having thrown into high relief all received conceptual frameworks, though they fall short of articulating an adequate conception of historical change.[33]

Instead, then, one must look to other sources for illumination on Arendt's method. Much is resolved in her rejoinder to Eric Voegelin's review of *Origins*. In it Arendt makes the distinctive claim that she had sought to give "a historical account of the *elements* which *crystallized* into totalitarianism," prior to undertaking "an analysis of the '*elementary structure*' of totalitarian movements and domination itself."[34] And this claim she makes in the spirit of correcting Voegelin's misreading of her interpretation of totalitarianism as unfolding—chronologically—out of the eighteenth century. The implications that flow from her attempt to correct Voegelin are as follows. What stand out, before everything else, are the crystallization metaphor and the broader "physics language" that she makes use of.[35] While some of this is apparent in the text itself, it is in tension with the conventional causal analysis signaled in the deployment of the term "origins." By way of sharpening this point, her "elements" there are anti-Semitism, the decline of the nation-state, racism, expansion, and the "alliance between capital and mob,"[36] with anti-Semitism also serving as the "catalytic agent" for the entire totalitarian edifice.[37] Yet this "vocabulary for contingency"—which she goes some way toward developing—is mixed with the "evolutionary metaphor" that totalitarianism evolved from some primary cause, such that her account runs the risk of the specific phenomenon at hand being reduced to what came before it.[38] The imagery of crystallization, conversely, implies a configuration of what we might surmise to be an array of preconditions—necessary but, in themselves, insufficient—which, viewed as such, she fleshes out liberally in terms of a mixture of currents of thought, political outlooks, events, and institutions.

Next, this restatement of method leads to a related point. Implicit in this framework is the privileging of the retrospective vantage point in narrating the story of "those subterranean elements that crystallized into totalitarianism." This she makes clear in another essay, where she writes as follows: "Whenever an event occurs that is great enough to illuminate its own past, history comes into being. Only then does the chaotic maze of past happenings emerge as a story which can be told, because it has a beginning and an end."[39] In this regard, rather than rejecting the idea of "origins," insofar as they are conceived as inexorably bound up with the evolutionary metaphor, Arendt now lends them a very specific sense, one in which "origins" refer to "elements that become constitutive in a historical phenomenon only *after* having been condensed within it."[40] By this token it is possible to understand Arendt as having been driven by a conviction, *in retrospect*, that there were significant connections between Nazism and the imperialism of the late nineteenth century. Interestingly, she actually expresses this as a concern at one stage in

Origins, when she locates the point of separation of the twentieth century from the nineteenth in the three decades from 1884 to 1914: "We can hardly avoid looking at this close and yet distant past with the too-wise eyes of those who know the end of the story in advance, who know it led to an almost complete break in the continuous flow of Western history as we had known it for more than two thousand years."[41] In other words, there is a double danger here: of an arbitrary aspect in the backward selection of "elements" and an interpretation of those elements that is highly colored by subsequent historical experience. Of all Arendt's commentators, Julia Kristeva couches this danger in the strongest terms—though by no means critically—when she contends that the "crystallization" Arendt discovers at the core of totalitarianism is "essentially an imaginary process."[42] This itself is an extension of a problem expressed long ago by Marc Bloch; namely that if for the historian "origins" is taken to mean *beginnings* (rather than, in the stronger conception, *causes*), then it remains acutely problematic even so, since "for most historical realities the very notion of a starting point remains elusive."[43]

The broader issue finally, then, is that of historical periodization. This requires the identification of a particular antecedent that fixes meaning to a particular historical epoch in an unavoidably selective way, thereby providing the "necessary fiction" of a beginning.[44] Indeed, Katznelson ventures that what Arendt wants to effect in writing *Origins* is to draw attention to "the existence of a qualitatively dark time."[45] As Charles Maier has suggested, this kind of periodization consists in the effort "to assign a meaning to historical phenomena by relating them either to sequential chains of other events or to webs of relationships, including institutions, social groups of one sort or another, or even mentalités that endure across a significant length of time."[46] Arendt's own hand in organizing these relevant sequential chains and webs of relationships thus raises the issue of the limits to the available range of legitimate contextualizations or, perhaps, *narratives.* From this perspective, and in the last analysis, Arendt is intimately involved in the construction of a narrative directed at the moral appraisal of (specific) events, a process which—for her—begs the question of the selection of the relevant aspects of historical reality, to which she gives expression in the form of a configuration of currents of thought, political outlooks, events, and institutions that lends sense to a historical period. The aim is thus emblematic of a purpose more generally characteristic of narrative; specifically, to "render the exceptional comprehensible."[47] However, if one of the characteristic features of those present debates on modern political violence is the (retrospective) projection of Nazism back onto Stalinism/communism, the concern to be voiced here is that Arendt's own project engenders this kind of equivalence or, more accurately, entails the projection of Nazism back onto imperialism.

Arendt and the Dark Continent

The above reconstruction of the meaning that Arendt ultimately ascribes to the "origins" of totalitarianism in the formal sense suggests the following about the substantive content she gives to the idea of "origins" in the earlier part of her book. First, in search of a necessary fiction for the beginning of an historical epoch that terminates in full-blown Nazi totalitarianism, she looks essentially to the "period of Imperialism." While she places anti-Semitism at the head of her narrative, it is clear from her account that, whereas nineteenth-century anti-Semitism only *made possible* the later atrocities, the period of imperialism was both *accompanied by* atrocities on a colossal scale and *prefigured* the political violence of totalitarianism—"the whole period a preparatory stage for coming catastrophe."[48] The second point, however, comes with a caveat. Namely, Arendt's emphasis on contingency in historical understanding suggests that, whatever else she is doing, she is emphatically *not* seeking to construct a chain of guilt that leads back to imperialism as in some sense the original sin, whatever might be the lesser degree to which she means to implicate imperialism in totalitarianism. A third point concerns Arendt's deployment of the tools and techniques of narrative. Her use of theatrical metaphor, for instance, is consistent with her rather speculative conception of origins; hence, in the light of her reconstruction of the events of imperialism, she writes that, "the stage seemed to be set for all possible horrors."[49] Moreover, the story that Arendt has to tell at the heart of the second part of *Origins* can in fact be read in terms of a narrative sequence of motive, encounter, and effect.

What encloses this story is at one end the Scramble for Africa and, at the other, the development of the early twentieth-century pan-movements (Pan-German and Pan-Slav) that, for Arendt, provide the more immediate stimulus to the totalitarian movements, the move from the one to the other being a process that Arendt explains by quite a circuitous route. The initial *motive* for the land grab among European powers is economic interest. By Arendt's reckoning, the colonial expansion beginning in the 1880s parts company with earlier kinds of empire building in that it was born out of the realization of "national limitations" to the expansion of capitalism and a concomitant crisis of overproduction—necessitating the search for alternative investment opportunities for "superfluous money." Yet although by origin an economic phenomenon it is, by degrees, increasingly political, its "central political idea" steadily revealed to be that of "expansion as a permanent and supreme aim of politics." Furthermore, in the peculiar "alliance between capital and mob" that Arendt casts as the fundamental support for imperialism, there is psychological fuel as well, since unhappy and disillusioned types—"the scum of the big cities"—take flight to the Dark Continent, together with prospectors, in search of adventure and upward mobility.[50]

The *encounter* that ensues, as Arendt continues her account, is between these Europeans and the natives. It is here that Arendt implies that the ideology of imperialism emerges, from which, in turn, the exploits of the imperialists derive, with the consequence that the discussion of the expansion of late capitalism now fades entirely from view. Arendt's key theme fundamentally is that of the confrontation between civilized and uncivilized worlds, where—in her terms—"civilized" has to do with the distinction of developing and sustaining political institutions and public spaces as potential realms of individuality and creativity, elevating (or hu-

manizing) the world above what is biological and natural.[51] It is from this particular background assumption that she arrives at what is, by now, a generally accepted
claim: specifically, that aspects of the colonial experience reinforced notions of
racial superiority and established a legitimizing framework for the use of violence
by one race against another. What she has to say of the initial confrontation, however, is characteristically distinctive of her particular account:

> [the Europeans] were confronted with human beings who, living without the future
> of a purpose and the past of an accomplishment, were as incomprehensible as the
> inmates of a madhouse. . . . What made them different from other human beings
> was *not at all the color of their skin* but the fact that they behaved like part of nature, that
> they had not created a human world. . . . They were, as it were, "natural" human
> beings who lacked the specifically human character, the specifically human reality, so
> that when European men massacred them they were somehow not aware that they
> had committed murder.[52]

"Not at all the color of their skin." Rather, as Arendt has it, race is "the emergency
explanation" concocted by the Europeans to make sense of the strangeness of what
they encountered on the Dark Continent. And its result is the perpetration of horrific "administrative massacres" in which bureaucracy too becomes race's corollary
device for political organization. It is in patterns of race-thinking, however, that
effect is most far-reaching. Racism—one of those "irresponsible opinions of the nineteenth century" Arendt thinks otherwise liable to have disappeared—is not only
reinvigorated, but its grounding in cultural difference displaced by that in biological difference.[53] Thus, already edging at this point toward an account of Nazism
as "colonialism come home," her next move renders this account explicit. Shifting
ground from "overseas imperialism" to "continental imperialism," she locates the
latter geographically at the heart of Europe in the form of the "frustrated ambitions" of those nations left behind in the earlier wave of expansion.[54] This is a
phenomenon based even more on reinvigorated race-thinking, for it offers the mob
a distinctive form of integration through an "enlarged tribal consciousness" pre-
mised on superiority and, since it lacks any grounding in experience—even of the
most primitive kind symbolized in the European confrontation in Africa—it is entirely divorced from reality. In sum, therefore, Arendt's real argument is that imperialism effects a "preparatory stage" for Nazism because it prepares the ground both
for *thinking* in terms of race, and for *acting* in ways terrifyingly consistent with this.[55]

To reiterate the point expressed earlier, our concern must be whether anything
of Arendt's account of imperialism is overly colored by the retrospective projection of an interpretation of Nazism back onto it. Something commensurate, it is
important to stress, is certainly a symptom of the current debates surrounding the
character of modern political violence. The *Black Book*'s emphasis on the "genocide
of a 'class'" supposedly enacted by Soviet-style totalitarianism is a case in point.
Although this idea is, from one perspective, etymologically incoherent—unless the
state-directed destruction of a *genos* (race, tribe) is taken to encompass the destruction of particular economic groups—it is nonetheless consistent with a broader

trend in the literature.[56] Sometimes the claim is that "genocide" can be committed even against groups which have no reality other than in the imagination of the perpetrator—typically gathered together amorphously under the category "enemies of the people."[57] At other times the claim is that the target of Soviet violence was, indeed, a "biologized" other, either constructed as such through the deployment of a language of "purification," or else having become so via an understanding of class as a hereditary condition.[58] What is common to both claims, however, is that the role of *categorization* in communist/Stalinist violence is evaluated very much with the case of Nazism in mind.

Now, Arendt, as we have seen, certainly works with a notion of the "biologized" other, which—in the light of the earlier analysis—we can only imagine was drawn out of her reflection on the Nazi experience, before she located it as present in imperialism. However, regarding the question of the extent to which she wants to implicate imperialism in totalitarianism, the answer in the view of her critics is, paradoxically, that she does not go as far as the evidence actually warrants. Conversely, a common charge is that she actually fails to give due weight to the significance of the crimes committed during the imperialist period. She is dismissive, for example, of the capacity of the concept of genocide to capture the "unprecedented" nature of the crimes perpetrated by Nazism precisely *because* "massacres of whole peoples . . . were the order of the day in antiquity," as they were common in a longer-term history of "colonization and imperialism."[59] In *Origins* she makes passing reference to the scale of the "decimation" of the population of the Congo under the dominion of King Leopold II of Belgium—"from 20 to 40 million reduced to 8 million people"—but later makes it clear that "suffering . . . is not the issue, nor is the number of victims."[60]

The broader charge against Arendt here is, needless to say, Eurocentrism, which constitutes more than the matter of the somewhat detached tone she adopts. Once again, this charge can be framed in terms of the terminology of moral equivalence manifest in the current debates. In them, a frequent point of contention is that the appraisal of the unique status of Nazism is largely explicable in terms of the *cultural reception* of political violence.[61] Typically, it is mooted that there are barriers to identifying with the victims of communist violence; and not only because collective memory provides an unclear conception of who the victims of communism *were* exactly (*contra* those of Nazism),[62] but because of their uncivilized "otherness." The *Black Book* formulates this point provocatively: there is something reprehensible, states Courtois, in our inability to empathize with the deliberate starvation of "the child of a Ukrainian peasant." Seen in this light, the charge against Arendt is her inability to empathize with the African natives. At issue is the refusal of her narrative to give voice to the native experience, its refusal to extend the "empathetic imagination" to the viewpoint of the Other, its reluctance to widen the scope of the interpretative "generosity" afforded to the imperialist adventurers (who after all, she writes, were "not aware they had committed murder").[63] Indeed, from this perspective, it is indicative that she makes heavy use of that phrase—"the Dark Continent"—that says "much more about the seer than the seen," suggestive of an anachronistic Eurocentric perspective that saw Africa as "faceless, blank, empty, a place on the map waiting to be explored."[64]

A closer reconstruction of Arendt's meaning, however, reveals the point at stake to be a significantly different one. At one level, the Eurocentric aspect to Arendt's narrative is clear enough. It is present to the extent that her analysis of imperialism—intentionally oriented at illuminating Nazism—seeks "to understand what happened there, *amongst 'civilised,' western people*, not between Europe and its colonized populations on their periphery."[65] Yet in this case it is peculiarly the antithesis of celebratory. She engages with the point of view of the imperialist adventurers while leaving the African silent, Benhabib and other sympathetic commentators rightly aver, because she looks at events from the standpoint of the influence of the scramble for Africa upon "the perversion of European morals, manners and customs."[66]

But there is, in addition, a more salient point. In this sense, the metaphors of the dichotomy of dark/light, natural/civilized that she deploys here—though they may have the side-effect of reifying ideas about civilizational hierarchy—are significant primarily in the terms by which they prefigure the *private/public* dichotomy she elucidates in her later political theory. To expand on this point, because the background assumption that Arendt brings to bear on her analysis of imperialism is that the natives "had not created a human world"—the achievement of a framework of politics itself, which alone is capable of affirming and sustaining *plurality* as the human condition—the Europeans in Africa were not engaged in the same attack on the human status that Arendt considers to be the hallmark of totalitarianism, especially as enacted in the Nazi Holocaust. That is to say, the atrocities committed by the imperialists (administrative massacres, slavery, the destruction of whole populations) did not entail—strictly-speaking—the systematic deprivation of the self, which proceeds with the destruction of the self as the bearer of rights, insofar as rights in the abstract have merely a phantom existence, being in reality only the fragile achievement of the political community. Accordingly, it is in the attack on the achievement of human plurality—what she sometimes renders as "the right to have rights"—that the unprecedented nature of the Nazi crimes arises, which thereby negates any final equivalency.[67]

Arendt on Degrees of Evil

Current and recent attempts to invoke the moral equivalence theme in thinking about modern political violence in comparative perspective are intentionally targeted, from a rather *fin de siècle* perspective, at redressing a perceived dearth of condemnations directed at atrocities committed in the name of communism. Conversely, Arendt's view is, as it were, the view from the concentration camp. With this contrast in mind, we need to consider finally what might be teased out of the reconstruction of Arendt's thought by way of working toward a set of criteria from which it may prove possible to establish gradations of evil embodied in discrete sets of events. Several plausible criteria for evaluation seem to recommend themselves as: intention, scale, process, perpetrator/victim status, and chronological priority. We might test these, in turn, against Arendt's account.

With respect to intention, rather than to ascribe either greater or lesser valuation to mass murder in the name of a noble ideal, Arendt is well-known for having suspended the idea that motives—good, bad, or otherwise—are central to the assessment of evil deeds.[68] Concerning scale, we have already seen that Arendt refuses to privilege quantitative distinctions of this kind. In terms of process, at times she articulates a particular revulsion at the nature of industrialized killing—the "mass production of corpses." Regarding perpetrator/victim status, Arendt's account indeed seems to afford this some salience. In particular, the above discussion of her analysis of imperialism appears to lend some force to Shiraz Dossa's synopsis of Arendt's characterization of the Holocaust as the paradigmatic case of "the murder of eminently 'civilized' victims by equally 'civilized' killers."[69]

However, there would appear to be grounds for supposing that more thought should be given especially to the implications of the final plausible criterion. Chronological priority, of the kind given prominence in Ernst Nolte's argument, is a disingenuous category, as we have seen, conflating causality with the sequential ordering of historical events. Nonetheless, it is from something approximating this viewpoint, concerned with the task of historical periodization that locates beginnings and endings, which Arendt takes up in *Origins* and from which she might have something consequential to say about gradations of evil. Arendt's narrative is, I have argued, oriented toward illuminating the sources of Nazi violence in retrospect and at the same time directed toward the moral appraisal of a specific set of events. The implication therefore is that other events with claims to equivalence require a similar exercise in understanding. Furthermore, in the case of her own narrative, Arendt sends out two retorts to the would-be proponents of moral equivalence. Arendt's identification of imperialism as a "preparatory stage" for Nazi totalitarianism gives it a particular place in the story she has to tell of the rise of moral and political nihilism—from which it finally became possible that human beings could be treated as if they were "superfluous"—but does not have the effect of collapsing the distinctions between these two sets of events. The narrative arrangement of *Origins*, moreover, and the view from the concentration camp, is such that the distinction between the Gulag and the Nazi camps respectively is between "Purgatory," neglect combined with forced labor, and "Hell in the most literal sense."[70]

Notes

1. Steven E. Aschheim, "Imagining the Absolute: Mapping Western Conceptions of Evil," in *The Lesser Evil: Moral Approaches to Genocide Practices*, ed. Helmut Dubiel and Gabriel Motzkin (London,

2004), 75. On the history and memory literature, see Jan-Werner Müller, ed., *Memory and Power in Post-War Europe* (Cambridge, 2002).

2. See, for instance, Uwe Makino, "Final Solutions, Crimes against Mankind: on the Genesis and Criticism of the Concept of Genocide," *Journal of Genocide Research* 3, no. 1 (2001): 49–73; and Mark Mazower, "Violence and the State in the Twentieth Century," *American Historical Review* 107, no. 4 (2002): 1158–78.

3. G. Jan Colijn, "Carnage Before Our Time: Nineteenth-Century Colonial Genocide," *Journal of Genocide Research* 5, no. 4 (2003): 617.

4. Dubiel and Motzkin, eds., *The Lesser Evil*, vii. While a hard and fast definition of "evil" is difficult to come by, Claudia Card defines it in terms of "foreseeable intolerable harms produced by culpable wrongdoing." Card, *The Atrocity Paradigm: A Theory of Evil* (New York, 2002), 3. More broadly, while the problem of evil is traditionally a preoccupation of the philosophy of religion, recent attempts to think it through have tended to be occasioned by a concern with political themes. In particular, see Richard Bernstein, *Radical Evil: A Philosophical Interrogation* (Oxford, 2002) and Susan Neiman, *Evil in Modern Thought: An Alternative History of Philosophy* (Princeton, 2002).

5. Slavoj Žižek, "The Two Totalitarianisms," *London Review of Books* 27, no. 6 (17 March 2005), italics added. For the most robust statement of the "uniqueness" of the Holocaust see Steven T. Katz, *The Holocaust in Historical Context*, vol. 1: *The Holocaust and Mass Death before the Modern Age* (New York, 1994).

6. Raymond Aron, *Democracy and Totalitarianism* (London, 1968), 203–4. It should be added that Aron later changed his position. See Aron, *Fifty Years of Political Reflection: Memoirs* (New York, 1990), 471.

7. Steven Lukes, "On the Moral Blindness of Communism," in *The Lesser Evil*, 155.

8. Martin Malia, "The Lesser Evil? Obstacles to Comparing the Holocaust and the Gulag after the Opening of the Soviet Archives," *Times Literary Supplement* (27 March 1998): 3–4.

9. Martin Amis, *Koba the Dread: Laughter and the Twenty Million* (London, 2002), 257.

10. Ernst Nolte, "The Past That Will Not Pass Away," in *Forever in the Shadow of Hitler? Original Documents of the 'Historikerstreit,'* ed. James Knowlton and Truett Cates (Atlantic Highlands, 1993), 22. On the *Historikerstreit* see especially Charles S. Maier, *The Unmasterable Past: History, Holocaust, and German National Identity* (Cambridge, MA, 1988).

11. Ernst Nolte, "The Three Versions of the Theory of Totalitarianism and the Significance of the Historical-Genetic Version," in *The Totalitarian Paradigm after the End of Communism: Towards a Reassessment*, ed. Achim Siegel (Amsterdam, 1998), 124, 127.

12. Henry Rousso, ed., *Stalinism and Nazism: History and Memory Compared*, (Lincoln, 2004), xi. For a dissenting view that emphasizes a longer history of critiques of communism, see Michael Scott Christofferson, *French Intellectuals Against the Left* (Oxford, 2004).

13. François Furet, *The Passing of an Illusion: The Idea of Communism in the Twentieth Century* (Chicago, 1999).

14. Stéphane Courtois, "Introduction: The Crimes of Communism," in *The Black Book of Communism: Crimes, Terror, Repression*, ed. Stéphane Courtois, Nicolas Werth, et al. (Cambridge, MA, 1999), 4, 15, 9.

15. Aron, *Democracy and Totalitarianism*, 197, 198; Tzvetan Todorov, *Hope and Memory: Reflections on the Twentieth Century* (London, 2003), 35–6.

16. Aschheim, "Imagining the Absolute," 74.

17. See Norman Fairclough, *New Labour, New Language?* (London, 2000), 52. Of course, in itself the effect of any "list" is to obscure differences. And it is simply a case of false reasoning to posit that merely because two events take place in sequence that one caused the other—or, moreover, that the two are necessarily related. Indeed, moral equivalence need not entail any notion of causality—it is rather that Nolte, in particular, deliberately constructs his story as such, the rationale being animated by what critics with some force construe to be apologetics for the Third Reich.

18. Ira Katznelson, *Desolation and Enlightenment: Political Knowledge after Total War, Totalitarianism, and the Holocaust* (New York, 2003), 49.

19. Courtois, "Conclusion: Why?" in *Black Book*, 754; Hannah Arendt, *The Origins of Totalitarianism* (London, 1973), xxiii–xl.

20. Steven Aschheim, "Nazism, Culture and *The Origins of Totalitarianism*: Hannah Arendt and the Discourse of Evil," *New German Critique* 70 (1997): 126.

21. Vinay Lal, "Genocide, Barbaric Others, and the Violence of Categories: A Response to Omer Bartov," *American Historical Review* 103, no. 4 (1998): 1188.

22. The case of the trial of Klaus Barbie is a particularly apt example here. Notoriously, Jacques Vergès, Barbie's defense attorney, deployed an argumentative strategy that bears close affinities with Nolte's revisionism. Vergès attempted—with some degree of success—to connect French war crimes committed in Algeria to crimes committed during the Nazi occupation, with the implicit intention of downplaying the latter and accentuating the more recent of the two events. See esp. Alain Finkielkraut, *Remembering in Vain: the Klaus Barbie Trial and Crimes against Humanity* (New York, 1992). On the singular aspects of Nazism see Ian Kershaw, "Hitler and the Uniqueness of Nazism," *Journal of Contemporary History* 39, no. 2 (2004): 239–254.

23. Enzo Traverso, *The Origins of Nazi Violence* (London, 2003), 73. Nolte uses this expression in "The Past That Will Not Pass Away," 22.

24. Bernard Crick, "On Rereading *The Origins of Totalitarianism*," *Social Research* 44, no. 7 (1977): 109.

25. Elizabeth Young-Bruehl, *Hannah Arendt: For Love of the World* (New Haven, 1982), 158, 203.

26. Alfons Söllner, "Hannah Arendt's *The Origins of Totalitarianism* in its Original Context," *European Journal of Political Theory* 3, no. 2 (2004): 222. See Franz Neumann, *Behemoth: The Structure and Practice of National Socialism, 1933–1944* (New York, 1963), 184–221.

27. For examples, see Furet, *The Passing of an Illusion*, 434; Aschheim, "Nazism, Culture and *The Origins of Totalitarianism*," 127. Arendt does, however, give a characteristic twist to Lenin's famous argument: "Imperialism must be considered the first stage in political rule of the bourgeoisie rather than the last stage of capitalism." *Origins*, 138.

28. E.g., Domenico Losurdo, "Towards a Critique of the Category of Totalitarianism," *Historical Materialism* 12, no. 2 (2004): 25–55.

29. Primo Levi, *If This is a Man/The Truce* (London, 1987), 93; Arendt, *Origins*, 392, 456, 447–57.

30. Arendt, *Origins*, 444.

31. Robert Burrowes, "Totalitarianism: The Revised Standard Version," *World Politics* 21 (1969): 280.

32. Richard J. Bernstein, *Hannah Arendt and the Jewish Question* (Oxford, 1996), 50; Katznelson, *Desolation and Enlightenment*, 59.

33. Arendt, *Origins*, vii. See also Arendt, "Social Science Techniques and the Study of Concentration Camps," in *Essays in Understanding*, 232–47.

34. Arendt, "A Reply to Eric Voegelin," in *Essays in Understanding*, 403.

35. Lisa Disch, "More Truth Than Fact: Storytelling as Critical Understanding in the Writings of Hannah Arendt," *Political Theory* 21, no. 4 (1993): 676.

36. Margaret Canovan, *Hannah Arendt: A Reinterpretation of her Political Thought* (Cambridge, 1992), 28.

37. Arendt, *Origins*, vii.

38. Disch, "More Truth than Fact," 675, 676.

39. Bernstein, *Hannah Arendt*, 51; Arendt, "Understanding and Politics," in *Essays in Understanding*, 319.

40. Traverso, *Nazi Violence*, 17; italics added.

41. Arendt, *Origins*, 123.

42. Julia Kristeva, *Hannah Arendt* (New York, 2003), 102.

43. Marc Bloch, *The Historian's Craft* (Manchester, 1992), 25.

44. Edward Said, *Beginnings: Intention and Method* (London, 1997), 50.

45. Katznelson, *Desolation and Enlightenment*, 65.

46. Charles E. Maier, "Consigning the Twentieth Century to History: Alternative Narratives for the Modern Era," *American Historical Review* 105 (2000): 809.

47. Jerome Bruner, *Acts of Meaning* (Cambridge, MA, 1990), 52.

48. Arendt, *Origins*, 123.

49. Ibid., 220.

50. Ibid., 126, 125, 151.

51. Ibid., 160. The discussion anticipates the theory of politics Arendt elaborates in *The Human Condition* (Chicago, 1958).

52. Ibid., 190, 192; italics added.

53. Ibid., 185, 133, 183. See Arendt's discussion of Gobineau, Burke, and German nationalism, 158–85.

54. Ibid., 227.

55. It is important to stress that, in another strand of Arendt's argument, continental imperialism also brings to a head the decline of the nation-state, sounding out the intrinsic tension between "nation" and "state" in the compound idea of the nation-state.

56. One significant point at stake here is that the UN Genocide Convention excludes economic groups from the categories it does cover ("national," "ethnical," "racial" and "religious" groups). See, for instance, Peter Singer, *One World: The Ethics of Globalization* (New Haven, 2002), 123–4. Though there are, of course, aspects of communist violence, which were transparently "ethnic" if one considers, say, the treatment of the Chechens, Tatars, Balts, Poles. See Anne Applebaum, *Gulag: A History of the Soviet Camps* (London, 2004), 21.

57. See Frank Chalk and Kurt Jonassohn, *The History and Sociology of Genocide: Analyses and Case Studies* (New Haven, 1990), 26; Makino, "Final Solutions, Crimes against Mankind." The idea that (modern) genocide is to be understood in terms of "social engineering" in general leans on Zygmunt Bauman's account. See Bauman, *Modernity and the Holocaust* (Oxford 1989), 88–93.

58. See Eric Weitz, *A Century of Genocide: Utopias of Race and Nation* (Princeton, 2003); Peter Holquist, "State Violence as Technique: The Logic of Violence in Soviet Totalitarianism," in *Landscaping the Human Garden: Twentieth-Century Population Management in a Comparative Framework*, ed. Amir Weiner (Stanford, 2003), 19–45; Weitz, "Racial Politics without the Concept of Race: Re-evaluating Soviet Ethnic and National Purges," *Slavic Review* 61, no. 1 (2002): 1–29; Amir Weiner, "Nature, Nurture, and Memory in a Socialist Utopia: Delineating the Soviet Socio-Ethnic Body in the Age of Socialism," *American Historical Review* 104 (1999): 1114–55.

59. Arendt, *Eichmann in Jerusalem: A Report on the Banality of Evil* (London, 1994), 288.

60. Arendt, *Origins*, 185, 458–9.

61. Aschheim has argued that the level of civilization ascribed to a culture often structures the reception of violence perpetrated by that culture. Aschheim, *Culture and Catastrophe: German and Jewish Confrontations with National Socialism and Other Crises* (Basingstoke, 1996), 9–10.

62. For this argument see Motzkin, "The Memory of Crime and the Formation of Identity," in *The Lesser Evil*, 196.

63. Anne Norton, "Heart of Darkness: Africa and African Americans in the Writings of Hannah Arendt," in *Feminist Interpretations of Hannah Arendt*, ed. Bonnie Honig (Philadelphia, 1995), 247–61; Kateb, *Hannah Arendt*, 61–63; Shiraz Dossa, "Human Status and Politics: Hannah Arendt on the Holocaust," *Canadian Journal of Political Science* 13, no. 2 (1980): 309–23.

64. Adam Hochschild, *King Leopold's Ghost: A Story of Greed, Terror and Heroism in Colonial Africa* (London, 2000), 18.

65. Katnelson, *Desolation and Enlightenment*, 70.

66. Seyla Benhabib, *The Reluctant Modernism of Hannah Arendt* (London, 1996), 86.

67. It is important to note a further point here. This reading of Arendt's meaning is obscured in that she runs together a series of quite distinct characterizations of totalitarianism in *Origins*. Another of these—which recurs when she emphasizes the role of *deterministic ideologies*—accentuates rather the centrality of categorization in totalitarianism and, as such, is far more suggestive of its affinities with imperialism. That is, when Arendt takes totalitarian ideologies

to be repositories of knowledge of "the mysteries of the whole historical process" reduced to a single idea, rendering political action as the reshaping of reality in accordance with the *logic* of this idea (the execution of the judgments of Nature and History, as she sometimes puts it) she accentuates a characterization of totalitarianism as the kind of political violence that derives from a pseudo-scientific process of categorization. Here, genocide follows logically from submission to a pseudo-Darwinian, biological Law of Nature that separates the healthy from the unhealthy races, and the elimination of all classes other than the proletariat follows logically from submission to the Law of History. Arendt, *Origins*, 469.

68. See Arendt, *Eichmann in Jerusalem*. While in *Origins* she works with the concept of "radical evil" rather than the "banality of evil," they are in many ways consistent. See especially Richard J. Bernstein, "Did Hannah Arendt Change Her Mind?: From Radical Evil to the Banality of Evil," in *Hannah Arendt: Twenty Years Later*, ed. Jerome Kohn and Larry May (Cambridge, MA, 1996), 127–46.

69. Arendt, *Origins*, 415; Dossa, "Human Status and Politics," 319–20.

70. Arendt, *Origins*, 445.

Chapter 10

HANNAH ARENDT, BIOPOLITCS, AND THE PROBLEM OF VIOLENCE
From animal laborans to homo sacer

André Duarte

> Since Auschwitz, nothing has ever happened that could be lived as a refutation of Auschwitz. . . . To live with the sensation of helplessness: today, probably this is the moral state in which, by resisting, we could be faithful to our times.
>
> —Imre Kertész

The contemporary experience of the political "as" violence

It would be hard to find another thesis in political theory less questioned than the traditional identification of violence and politics. This is true to such an extent that the possibility of a nonviolent politics may seem chimerical, likewise that of tracing a conceptual distinction between power and violence. Even if it is true that not all violent phenomena are political phenomena, we tend to feel quite certain that there could be no politics without violence. As we know, Hannah Arendt is among those very few thinkers in contemporary political theory who refuse the strict identification of politics and violence, arguing that violence is not necessarily inherent to the political, and that violence and power are not the same. In works such as *The Human Condition* and *On Violence*, Arendt sought to demonstrate that while power is spontaneously generated by concerted action among a plurality of citizens, violence is mute; its effect is to disperse, silence, and isolate people, disrupting the civic bonds between them. While power is not a means to some further end, being the very stuff that unites political actors in a public realm, violence is paradigmatically instrumental. While power may generate a provisional consensus, one that does not prevent the possibility of dissent and contestation, pure violence is destructive, being incapable of creating new relationships and free agreement.

In this paper, however, I do not intend to discuss Arendt's analysis of the philosophical equation of politics and violence, nor to explore the implications of her distinction between power and violence for a radically democratic politics.[1] I want to explore, instead, Arendt's diagnosis of the present, in which politics tends to be transformed into a wide variety of violent phenomena, so that, nowadays, we almost always experience the political "as" violence. After all, Arendt's thesis that power and violence are not the same does not contradict her view that, throughout Western history—and perhaps even more so in the present day—politics has been experienced frequently as violence. Preventive wars have been declared, for example, by countries that represent themselves as absolute good fighting against absolute evil, in order to prevent possible future evil deeds. The United States, among other countries, has disregarded previous international juridical agreements, asserting its political and economic hegemony in an ever more violent and insecure world. Suicidal fundamentalists, secret organizations, and even the regular armed forces of states launch terrorist attacks. The twentieth century began with the deployment of chemical and bacteriological weapons, which rapidly became more and more lethal, culminating with nuclear weapons able to destroy all life on the planet. States have enacted repressive policies against immigrants and refugees, as well as against political movements that organize the unemployed, nonconformists of all sorts, displaced and homeless people, among many other "undesirable" social groups. Last but not least, consider the whole mass of human beings who cannot be integrated into the capitalist system of globalized production and consumption. Considering these different contemporary experiences of politics "as" violence, I want to ask: is there any connection between them? Has Arendt anything to say in order to render these phenomena more comprehensible?

I believe that the answer is positive. To start answering these questions I would like to propose that we consider the notion of biopolitics—by no means an Arendtian category.[2] My suggestion is that this notion provides a missing link that can help us connect Arendt's reflections concerning the tragic fate of the political in the modern age in *The Human Condition*, with her analysis of totalitarian regimes in *The Origins of Totalitarianism*. In other words, I think that the notion of biopolitics can allow the Arendtian diagnosis of the present to illuminate the contemporary spread of violence and the growing meaninglessness of the political in our bureaucratized, mass-, and market-oriented representative democracies, that is, our actually existent democracies.

My interpretive approach is inspired by Giorgio Agamben's work, *Homo Sacer: Sovereign Power and Bare Life*, in which he argues that Arendt and Foucault were the first contemporary thinkers to understand the radical changes undergone by the political in modern times.[3] According to Agamben, these changes culminate in the Nazi and Stalinist extermination camps with the reduction of citizens to the "bare life" (*nuda vita*) of *homo sacer*, the prototype of a man whose murder would not be a crime. According to Agamben's research, the *homo sacer* was an old and rather obscure juridical figure of Roman law, designating a man excluded from both divine and human legislation. In other words, the *homo sacer*—the sacrificial man—embodied the paradox of belonging to the code of the Roman law only by virtue of his total exclusion from it. As such, the *homo sacer* was deprived of any legal protection against anyone who attempted to murder him, providing that this murder was not supported by legal procedures or religious rites. Thus, the paradox of simultaneously pertaining to and being excluded from the political domain is the paradigmatic structure of biopolitics, a feature that would also explain the reason why at the very moment that the enforcement of life became the focus of political affairs, political genocides became increasingly augmented, as noticed by Michel Foucault. Surely, this is not the place for extensive commentary on Agamben, nor will I attempt to compare thinkers as different as Arendt and Foucault. Rather, I would like to stress a convergence in Arendt's, Foucault's, and Agamben's reflections in terms of a biopolitical diagnosis of the present. I believe that the introduction of the notion of biopolitics into Arendt's thinking enables us to understand better the correlation between the most important manifestations of contemporary political violence: the extraordinary violence of totalitarian disaster, and the ordinary violence of our mass- and market-democracies, corroded by the loss of any radical political alternative to both capitalism and socialism. Although this involves the risks of reading Arendt beyond Arendt, I believe that I remain faithful to the core of her own thinking in interweaving her thought with decisive political experiences of the present.

To justify introducing the notion of biopolitics where it does not originally appear, we need to understand the sense in which biopolitical violence has become the common denominator of contemporary politics, establishing tragic continuities between modern mass representative democracies and totalitarian regimes. This idea has to be developed carefully since Arendt considered totalitarianism to be an unprecedented form of government, one that broke with all previous forms such as dictatorship, tyranny, or despotism. Arendt's account of Nazi and Stalinist totalitarianism analyzes the structural characteristics they shared, which distinguished them from all other political regimes. Without challenging Arendt's distinctions, I want to argue that biopolitical violence has become the common factor underlying our contemporary political experiences—that is, to *refuse* too simplistic an opposition of totalitarianism and mass democracies. Slavoj Žižek has aptly described the ideological use of the concept of totalitarianism as a specter whose possible resurgence is used to undermine any radical political alternative. The misuse of this notion results in a sort of political blackmail: it is better to accept the inequalities and absurdities of capitalism than to abolish it through what is figured as the only alternative, totalitarian politics.[4] However, I believe Žižek goes too far when he detects this ideological misuse of the notion of totalitarianism in Arendt's reflections; after all, her own critical analysis of totalitarianism was never meant to be an uncritical endorsement of liberal democracy. Arendt was never dismissive of what orthodox Marxists call "bourgeois liberties," much to the contrary; however, it is also clear that her sympathies relied on the so-called "council system," which sprang up each time politics was fully embraced by active citizens in the core of modern revolutions. In other words, if the council system is not intrinsically contradictory to democracy, to the rule of law and to the system of rights, nevertheless it is not identical to liberal and representative democracy, as we know it today. Therefore, analyzing treacherous continuities in the historical situation of both totalitarianism and liberal democracies, a crucial aspect of Arendt's and Agamben's analyses, does not imply that liberal democracy equals totalitarianism, nor does it mean that actual liberal democracy is the only antidote to totalitarianism. In other words, I believe that the concept of totalitarianism still provides a fundamental way of understanding the totalitarian dangers that surround our actually existing democracies, and this should help us to rethink and reconsider the meaning of democracy. Accordingly, what matters at the present time is to understand the perverse biopolitical mechanisms through which human beings have been incorporated into, *and* excluded from, the political and economic spheres in contemporary democracies and in totalitarian regimes.

Moreover, to consider totalitarianism as a disruptive event in Western history is by no means to deny the possibility of understanding it as a historical phenomenon—in Arendt's terms, as the crystallization of different historical elements that have become constitutive of late modern politics and, therefore, also have something to do with liberal democracies. In other words, although totalitarian regimes should not be considered as the necessary culmination of modernity, neither are they mere accidents. To recall Zygmunt Bauman's Arendt-inspired analysis, totalitarianism has to be understood in a historical context involving the conjunction of modern science and technology, bureaucratic administration and mass murder, all of which may be united by the desire to purify and embellish the so-called "garden of politics."[5] One should not forget that if such a desire is much less present in liberal democracies than in totalitarian regimes, both of them share a substantially similar historical background. It is not a matter of bluntly refusing democracy and modernity, but of considering that it is not by chance if many of the historical elements that crystallized in totalitarian regimes still remain present in our actually existing democracies: racism, xenophobia, political apathy and indifference, economic and territorial imperialism, the massed use of lies and violence to dominate whole populations, the multiplication of the displaced and the stateless, the political and economic superfluousness of huge masses of human beings. Under these conditions we should be attentive not only to the possible appearance of new totalitarian regimes, but also to quasi-totalitarian elements at the core of our mass democracies, as observed by Agamben. At the end of her analysis of totalitarianism, Arendt herself warned of the standing danger of totalitarian measures to "solve" contemporary political dilemmas:

> The danger of the corpse factories and holes of oblivion is that today, with populations and homelessness everywhere on the increase, masses of people are continuously rendered superfluous if we continue to think of our world in utilitarian terms. Political, social, and economic events everywhere are in a silent conspiracy with totalitarian instruments devised for making men superfluous. . . . The Nazis and

the Bolsheviks can be sure that their factories of annihilation which demonstrate the swiftest solution to the problem of overpopulation, of economically superfluous and socially rootless human masses, are as much of an attraction as a warning. Totalitarian solutions may well survive the fall of totalitarian regimes in the form of strong temptations which will come up whenever it seems impossible to alleviate political, social, or economic misery in a manner worthy of man.[6]

Toward the notion of biopolitics in Arendt's thought

What does it mean to characterize the present equation of politics and violence in terms of biopolitics? And how can this non-Arendtian notion make sense within Arendt's work? Let us begin with the first question. My contention is that the distinguishing mark of the political from the beginning of the nineteenth century to the present day is the following paradox: the elevation of life to the status of the supreme good combined with the multiplication of instances in which life is degraded to the utmost. I believe, therefore, that the constitutive element of the political in the present is the reduction of citizenship to the level of "bare life," as Agamben understands it. Human life is thus politicized, divided between life included and protected by the political and economic community and life excluded and unprotected, exposed to degradation and death.[7]

Investigating changes in the way power was conceived of and exercised at the turn of the nineteenth century, Foucault realized that when life turned out to be a constitutive political element, managed, calculated, and normalized by means of biopolitics, political strategies soon became murderous. Paradoxically, thinks Foucault, when the sovereign's prerogative ceased to be simply that of imposing violent death, and became a matter of promoting the growth of life, wars became more and more bloody, mass killing more frequent. Political conflicts now aimed at preserving and intensifying the life of the winners, so that enmity ceased to be political and came to be seen biologically: it is not enough to defeat the enemy; the enemy must be *exterminated* as a danger to the health of the race, people, or community. Thus Foucault on the formation of the modern biopolitical paradigm at the end of the nineteenth century:

> death that was based on the right of the sovereign is now manifested as simply the reverse of the right of the social body to ensure, maintain or develop its life. Yet wars were never as bloody as they have been since the nineteenth century, and all things being equal, never before did regimes visit such holocausts on their own populations. But this formidable power of death . . . now presents itself as the counterpart of a power that exerts a positive influence on life that endeavours to administer, optimize, and multiply it, subjecting it to precise controls and comprehensive regulations. Wars are no longer waged in the name of a sovereign who must be defended; they are waged on behalf of the existence of everyone; entire populations are mobilized for the purpose of wholesale slaughter in the name of life necessity: massacres have become vital. It is as managers of life and survival, of bodies and the race, that so many regimes have been able to wage so many wars, causing so many men to be

killed. And through a turn that closes the circle, as the technology of wars have caused them to tend increasingly toward all-out destruction, the decision that initiates them and the one that terminates them are in fact increasingly informed by the naked question of survival. . . . If genocide is indeed the dream of modern powers, this is not because of a recent return of the ancient right to kill; it is because power is situated and exercised at the level of life, the species, the race, and the large-scale phenomena of population.[8]

Expressed in terms of biopolitics, the death of the Other does not imply only my own security and safety; inasmuch as the death of the Other is the "death of the bad race, of the inferior race (or the degenerate, or the abnormal)", it has to be understood as "something that will make life in general healthier, healthier and purer."[9] In *On Violence*, Arendt argued a similar thesis concerning the violent character of racist and naturalist conceptions of politics: "Nothing could be theoretically more dangerous than the tradition of organic thought in political matters"; if power and violence are interpreted in terms of biological metaphors this can only produce more violence, especially where race is involved. Racism as an ideological system of thought is inherently violent, indeed murderous, because it attacks natural "biological" data that, as such, cannot be changed by any power or persuasion, so that when conflicts become radicalized all that can be done is to "exterminate" the Other.[10]

As to the second question—how the notion of biopolitics may fit into Arendt's work: we find an answer encapsulated in Arendt's thesis regarding the "unnatural growth of the natural," a peculiar formula meant to capture the main historical transformations of the modern age.[11] This notion comprehends a range of different historical phenomena stemming from the Industrial Revolution, such as the transformation of man into a beast of burden, a living being attached to the activities of laboring and consuming; the widening of the realm of human "life processes" (that is, laboring and consuming), to the point that life itself becomes the supreme good and the furtherance of these processes (which center on the private interests of *animal laborans*) the most important object of politics; the requirement of the continuous production and consumption of goods in ever increasing abundance, so that nature is reduced to a stock of natural resources—a stock abused to the point where its self-reproducing character is endangered; the promotion of laboring activity to the status of the most important human activity. In this process the public sphere is transformed into a social one, that is, a market for economic exchanges based on a cycle of ceaseless production and consumption. From the nineteenth century onward, then, the political realm has been overrun by individual, social, and economic interests, which today we see massed in the form of international corporations, coercive international trade regimes, financial globalization, and free market ideologies. This results from politics becoming the activity of managing the production and reproduction of the life and happiness of *animal laborans*. To put it in Antonio Negri and Michael Hardt's terms, the industrial and financial powers of the present produce, not only commodities but also subjectivities, needs, social relations, bodies, and minds, since they actually produce the producers.[12] Arendt does not mean to affirm that before the nine-teenth century there was a still intact public sphere, uncorrupted by social needs or economic interests and not tainted by sheer violence. The point of the matter is to specify that after the Industrial Revolution politics became almost exclusively concerned with the life and interests of *animal laborans,* a shift that redefined the character and the intensity of political violence. Most importantly, it should be noticed that these political changes are not exclusive to capitalism, but also applied fully to socialist regimes.[13]

Politically, perhaps the most salient consequence of this historical process is that we do not know if there is even any space left for the establishment of new and radical political alternatives, since all state policies—above all in underdevel-oped countries—are always subject to the decidedly unstable flows of interna-tional financial investments, stock-exchange fluctuations, and global financial insti-tutions such as the World Bank. The changes associated with the development of global capitalism imply many specifically contemporary losses, if we follow Arendt: the loss of the political as a space of freedom, replaced by requirements of eco-nomic necessity; free and spontaneous action replaced by predictable, conformist behavior;[14] the subordination of public and shared interests to those of private lobbies and other hidden pressure groups, freed from public vigilance by the with-ering of the public realm; the submission of all political opinion to the supposedly inexorable laws of market economics; the substitution of violence for the power won through persuasion; the weakening of the citizen's ability to consent and to dissent, our ability to act in concert replaced at best by the solitary experience of voting; the reduction of the political arena to disputes among bureaucratic and oligarchic party machines; with a compliant media depicting those who do not ac-cept their game-rules as "anarchists," "rioters," even "terrorists." The "citizen" con-sumes in the democratic–"supermarket": choose from a strictly limited variety of political brands, with no option to question the political options on offer. (And what would the question be when all political parties declare that their aim is to protect citizens' interests and quality of life?) As Agamben argues, to question the limitations of our political system has become more and more difficult since poli-tics has been declared as the task of caring for and administering bare life. In this situation, traditional political distinctions (right-left, liberal-totalitarian, private-public) have lost their intelligibility, since all political categories are subordinated to the demands of bare life.[15] Since "capitalism has become one with reality," we are condemned, in Marina Garcés' words, "to make choices in an elective space in which there are no options. Everything is possible, but we can do nothing."[16] Even the practices and discourses of the so-called anti-globalization movements— "another globalization is possible" and the like—are largely unable to create real alternatives to the economic realities they are intent on confronting.[17]

These historic transformations have not only brought more violence to the core of the political but have also redefined its character by giving rise to biopolitical violence. As stated, what characterizes biopolitics is a dynamic both of protecting and abandoning life through its inclusion and exclusion from the political and economic community. In Arendtian terms, the biopolitical danger is best described as the risk of converting *animal laborans* into Agamben's *homo sacer*, the human being who can be put to death by anyone and whose killing does not imply any crime whatsoever.[18] When politics is conceived of as biopolitics, as the task of increasing the life and happiness of the national *animal laborans*, the nation-state becomes ever more violent and murderous. If we link Arendt's thesis from *The Human Condition* to those of *Origins*, we can see the Nazi and Stalinist extermination camps as the most refined experiments in annihilating the "bare life" of *animal laborans* (although these are by no means the only instances in which the modern state has devoted itself to human slaughter). Arendt is concerned not only with the process of the extermination itself, but also the historical situation in which large-scale exterminations were made possible—above all, the emergence of "uprooted" and "superfluous" modern masses, what we might describe as *animal laborans* balanced on the knife-edge of "bare life." Compare her words in "Ideology and Terror" (1953), which became the conclusion of later editions of *Origins:*

> Isolation is that impasse into which men are driven when the political sphere of their lives . . . is destroyed. . . . Isolated man who lost his place in the political realm of action is deserted by the world of things as well, if he is no longer recognized as *homo faber* but treated as an *animal laborans* whose necessary "metabolism with nature" is of concern to no one. Isolation then becomes loneliness. . . . Loneliness, the common ground for terror, the essence of totalitarian government, and for ideology or logicality, the preparation of its executioners and victims, is closely connected with uprootedness and superfluousness which have been the curse of modern masses since the beginning of the industrial revolution and have become acute with the rise of imperialism at the end of the last century and the break-down of political institutions and social traditions in our own time. To be uprooted means to have no place in the world, recognized and guaranteed by others; to be superfluous means not to belong to the world at all.[19]

Thus, the conversion of *homo faber*, the human being as creator of durable objects and institutions, into *animal laborans* and, later on, into *homo sacer*, can be traced in Arendt's account of nineteenth-century imperialism. As argued in the second volume of *Origins*, European colonialism combined racism and bureaucracy to perpetrate the "most terrible massacres in recent history, the Boers' extermination of Hottentot tribes, the wild murdering by Carl Peters in German Southeast Africa, the decimation of the peaceful Congo population—from 20 to 40 million reduced to 8 million people; and finally, perhaps worst of all, it resulted in the triumphant introduction of such means of pacification into ordinary, respectable foreign policies."[20] This simultaneous protection and destruction of life was also at the core of the two world wars, as well as in many other more local conflicts, during which whole populations have become stateless or deprived of a public realm. In spite of all their political differences, the United States of Roosevelt, the Soviet Russia of Stalin, the Nazi Germany of Hitler, and the Fascist Italy of Mussolini were all conceived of as states devoted to the needs of the national *animal laborans*. According to Agamben, since our contemporary politics recognizes no other value than life, Nazism and fascism, that is, regimes which have taken bare life as their supreme political criterion, are bound to remain standing temptations.[21] Finally, it is obvious that this same logic of promoting and annihilating life persists both in post-industrial and in underdeveloped countries, inasmuch as economic growth depends on the increase of unemployment and on many forms of political exclusion. Of course, the notion of biopolitics implies that the economical *per se* is not the main or the unique factor in explaining human wastage, since genocides also depend on racism, religious beliefs, national rivalries, and the like. Rather, the argument is that under biopolitical conditions contemporary human slaughter is implemented and justified on the basis of strengthening and securing the life and values of the *animal laborans*, to which purpose huge parcels of human masses are reduced to the underprivileged status of *homo sacer*.

When politics is reduced to the tasks of administering, preserving, and promoting the life and happiness of *animal laborans*, it ceases to matter that those objectives require increasingly violent acts, both in national and international arenas. Therefore, we should not be surprised that under a biopolitical paradigm the legality of state violence has become a secondary aspect in political discussions, since what really matters is to protect and stimulate the life of the national (or, as the case may be, Western) *animal laborans*. In order to maintain sacrosanct ideals of increased mass production and mass consumerism, developed countries ignore the finite character of natural reserves and refuse to sign International Protocols regarding natural resource conservation or pollution reduction, thereby jeopardizing future humanity. They also launch preventive attacks and wars and disregard basic human rights, for instance, in extra-legal detention camps such as Guantánamo.[22] Some countries have even considered imprisoning whole populations, physically isolating them from other communities, in a new form of social, political, and economic apartheid. In short, in a biopolitical age states permit themselves to impose physical and structural violence against individuals and regimes ("rogue states"[23]) that supposedly interfere with the security and growth of their national life process.

If, according to Arendt, the common world consists of an institutional in-between meant to outlast both human natality and mortality, in modern mass societies we find the progressive abolition of the institutional artifice that separates and protects our world from the forces of nature.[24] This explains the contemporary feeling of disorientation and unhappiness, likewise the political impossibility we find in combining stability and novelty.[25] In the context of a "waste economy, in which things must be almost as quickly devoured and discarded as they have appeared in the world, if the process itself is not to come to a sudden catastrophic end,"[26] it is not only possible, but also necessary, that people themselves become raw material to be consumed, discarded, annihilated. In other words, when Arendt announces the "grave danger that eventually no object of the world will be safe from consumption and annihilation through consumption,"[27] we should also remember that human annihilation, once elevated to the status of an "end-in-itself" in totalitarian regimes, still continues to occur—albeit in different degrees and by different methods, in contemporary "holes of oblivion" such as miserably poor Third World neighborhoods[28] and penitentiaries, or in underpaid and slave labor camps, always in the name of protecting the vital interests of *animal laborans.*

To talk about a process of human consumption is not to speak metaphorically but literally. Heidegger had realized this in his notes written during the late 1930s and mid 1940s, later published under the title of *Overcoming Metaphysics.* He claimed that the difference between war and peace had already been blurred in a society in which "metaphysical man, the *animal rationale,* gets fixed as the laboring animal," so that "labor is now reaching the metaphysical rank of the unconditional objectification of everything present."[29] Heidegger argued that once the world becomes fully determined by the "circularity of consumption for the sake of consumption" it is at the brink of becoming an "unworld" *(Unwelt),* since man, who no longer conceals his character of being the most important raw material, is also drawn into the process. Man is "the most important raw material" because he remains the subject of all consumption.[30] After the Second World War and the release of detailed information concerning the death factories, Heidegger took his critique even further, acknowledging that to understand man as both subject and object of the consumption process would still not comprehend the process of deliberate mass extermination. He saw this, instead, in terms of the conversion of man into no more than an "item of the reserve fund for the fabrication of corpses" *(Bestandestücke eines Bestandes der Fabrikation von Leichen).* According to Heidegger, what happened in the extermination camps was that death became meaningless, and the existential importance of our anxiety in the face of death was lost; instead, people were robbed of the essential possibility of dying, so that they merely "passed away" in the process of being "unconspicuously liquidated" *(unauffällig liquidiert).*[31] The human being as *animal laborans* (Arendt), as *homo sacer* (Agamben), or as an "item of the reserve fund" (Heidegger)—all describe the same process of dehumanization whereby humankind is reduced, by means of contemporary technological implements, to the bare fact of being alive, with no further qualifications. As argued by Agamben, when it becomes impossible to differentiate between bios and zoē, that is, when bare life is transformed into a qualified or specific "form of life," we face the emergence of a biopolitical epoch.[32] So, when States promote the animalization of man by policies that aim both at protecting and destroying human life, we can interpret this in terms of the widespread presence of the *homo sacer* in our world: "If it is true that the figure proposed by our age is that of an unsacrificeable life that has nevertheless become capable of being killed to an unprecedented degree, then the bare life of *homo sacer* concerns us in a special way . . . If today there is no longer any one clear figure of the sacred man, it is perhaps because we are all virtually *homines sacri.*"[33] Biopolitical violence is the result of a naturalized conception of the political, found both in totalitarianism and the quasi-totalitarian elements of modern mass democracies. For Arendt, all forms of naturalizing the political threaten the political artifice of egalitarianism, without which no defense and validation of human freedom and dignity are possible. Arendt's analysis of the terrible experience of refugees, of those interned in different kinds of concentration camps, of those left with no home, and all those who have lost a secure place in the world, showed her that nature—and, of course, human nature—cannot ground and secure any rights or, indeed, any democratic politics. This revealed the paradox inherent in a naturalistic understanding of the Rights of Man, since once those rights ceased to be recognized and enforced by a political community, their inalienable character simply vanished, leaving unprotected the very human beings that most needed them: "The Rights of Man, supposedly inalienable, proved to be unenforceable . . . whenever people appeared who were no longer citizens of a sovereign state."[34]

The loss of the Rights of Man *qua* rights of the citizen did not itself deprive a human being of his/her life, liberty, property, freedom of expression, or freedom to pursue happiness. The real predicament for people in these circumstances is that they "no longer belong to any community whatsoever. Their plight is not that they are not equal before the law, but that no law exists for them."[35] The core of her argument is not that man outside the political sphere automatically loses the character of humanity, but that without the political decision to protect and enforce human rights under egalitarian political conditions there can be no other outcome than the devaluation of human life. In other words, nationalistic and racialized biopolitics has produced a huge mass of people denied what Arendt termed the "right to have rights," that is, the "right to belong to some kind of organized community": "Man, it turns out, can lose all so-called Rights of Man without losing his essential quality as man, his human dignity. Only the loss of a polity itself expels him from humanity."[36] The "abstract nakedness" of merely being a human being is no substitute for the artificial character of the pacts freely entered into by active citizens. By analyzing the dynamic of the extermination camps, Arendt understood that *humanity* is an attribute that categorically goes beyond the notion of the human being as a mere natural living being: "man's 'nature' is only 'human' insofar as it opens up to man the possibility of becoming something highly unnatural, that is, a man."[37] Humanity, politically speaking, does not reside in the sheer natural fact of being alive; politically, humanity depends on artificial legal and political institutions to protect it. The Arendtian rejection of understanding the human being as a living being in the singular, as well as her postulation of human plurality as the condition of all genuine politics, depend on her thesis that politics has to do with the formation of a common world in the course of people's acting and exchanging opinions. Politics depends on the human faculty of *opinion*, our capacities to agree and disagree, so that what is mysteriously given to us by nature ceases to be politically decisive. For Arendt, equality is not a natural given, but a political construction oriented by the "principle of justice." It is the result of agreement to grant one another equal rights, based on the assumption that equality can be forged by those who act and exchange opinions among themselves and thus change the world in which they live.[38]

Agamben's thesis goes even further than Arendt's. He finds that modern biopolitics is contained already in the Declaration of the Rights of Man, inasmuch as these rights constitute the very inscription of naked life into the political-juridical order. According to Agamben, in the 1789 Declaration natural bare life is both the foundational source and the carrier of the rights of man, since a man's bare life—or, more precisely, the very fact of being born in a certain territory—is the element that effects the transition from the *ancien régime*'s principle of divine sovereignty to modern sovereignty concentrated in the nation-state:

> It is not possible to understand the "national" and biopolitical development and vocation of the modern state in the nineteenth and twentieth centuries if one forgets that what lies at its basis is not man as a free and conscious political subject but, above all, man's bare life, the simple birth that as such is, in the passage from subject to citizen, invested with the principle of sovereignty.[39]

Conclusion

To conclude this chapter, I would like to underline how much Arendt's principal reflections on totalitarianism still remain relevant today, especially when we remember the feeble character of actually existing democracies. Rephrased in biopolitical terms, the core of Arendt's diagnosis of the present is that whenever politics has mostly to do with the maintenance and increase of the vital metabolism of affluent nation states, *animal laborans* is on the verge of being degraded still further: to the status of *homo sacer*, bare and unprotected life that can be delivered to oblivion and death. Our common sense understanding of politics as the administrative promotion of abundance and the happiness of the human being as *animal laborans* is in fact correlated with economic and political exclusion, racialized prejudice, violence, and even genocide against the naked life of *homo sacer*. Arendt thus sheds light on our current dilemmas, providing us with theoretical elements for a critical diagnosis of the present, as well as for opening new possibilities for collective action in the world. Arendt was a master of chiaroscuro political thinking, never blind to always open possibilities of radically renovating the political, nor, by brutal contrast, to the intrinsic connection between political exclusion and violence under a biopolitical paradigm. If we wish to remain with Arendt and the hope of a politics of freedom and equality, then we must reflect on and pursue new spaces and forms of political association, action, and discussion, wherever and whenever they may subvert the tedious multiplication of the same in our administered, covertly, and overtly violent present.

Arendt proposed no political utopias, but she remained convinced that our political dilemmas have no necessary outcome, that history has not and will not come to a tragic end. Neither a pessimist nor an optimist, she wanted only to understand the world in which she lived and to stimulate our thinking and acting in the present. It is always possible that radically new political constellations will come into our world, and responsibility for them will always be ours. If we wish to remain faithful to the spirit of Arendt's political thinking, then we must think and act politically without constraining our thinking and acting in terms of some predefined understanding of what politics "is" or "should" be. In other words, I believe that the political challenge of the present is to multiply the forms, possibilities, and spaces in which we can act politically. These may be strategic actions destined to further the agendas of political parties concerned with social justice. They can also be discrete, subversive actions favored by small groups at the margins of the bureaucratized party machines, promoting political interventions free of particular strategic intentions, since their goal is to invite radical politicization of existence. Finally, there are also actions in which ethical openness toward Otherness becomes political: small and rather inconspicuous actions of acknowledging and welcoming, of extending hospitality and solidarity toward others.

Notes

1. Arendt was most interested in nonviolent politics, such as civil rights movements, civil disobedience, and passive resistance. See "Civil Disobedience" and "Thoughts on politics and revolution" in *Crises of the Republic* (New York, 1972).
2. The concept of "biopolitics" was proposed by Michel Foucault in his *History of Sexuality*, vol. I (New York, 1990). With this concept, Foucault aimed at clarifying the political shift that occurred at the beginning of the nineteenth century, according to which bare life became the core of multiple state policies whose aims are to enforce and stimulate the life of the citizens or plainly to destroy it.
3. Giorgio Agamben, *Homo Sacer: Sovereign Power and Bare Life* (Stanford, 1998).
4. Slavoj Žižek, *Did Somebody Say Totalitarianism? Four Interventions in the (Mis)use of a Notion* (London, 2001), 3.
5. Zygmunt Bauman, *Modernity and the Holocaust* (Oxford, 1989), 113.
6. Hannah Arendt, *The Origins of Totalitarianism* (New York, 1973), 459.
7. I do not espouse Agamben's thesis of biopolitics as the ontological core of the political in the Western world. See Andrew Norris, "'The Exemplary Exception': Philosophical and Political Decisions in Giorgio Agamben's *Homo Sacer*," *Radical Philosophy* 119 (2003).
8. Foucault, *The History of Sexuality*, vol. I, 136–7.
9. Michel Foucault, *Society Must Be Defended* (New York, 2003), 255.
10. Hannah Arendt, *On Violence* (New York, 1970), 75–6.
11. Hannah Arendt, *The Human Condition* (Chicago, 1958), 47.
12. Antonio Negri and Michael Hardt, *Empire* (Cambridge, MA, 2000), 22ff.
13. According to Arendt, "Expropriation, the initial accumulation of capital—that was the law according to which capitalism arose and according to which it has advanced step by step. . . . But if you look at what has actually happened in Russia, then you can see that there the process of expropriation has been carried further. And you can observe that something very similar is going on in the modern capitalistic countries, where it is as though the old expropriation process is again let loose." *Crises of the Republic*, 211–12.
14. Arendt, *The Human Condition*, 321.
15. Agamben, *Homo Sacer*, 122.
16. Marina Garcés, "Possibilidad y Subversión," in *Archipiélago, Cuadernos de Crítica de la Cultura* 53 (2002): 15. See also *En las prisiones de lo posible* (Barcelona, 2003).

17. Santiago Lopez Petit, *El Estado guerra* (Hiru, 2003); see also *El infinito y la nada. El querer vivir como desafio* (Barcelona, 2003).
18. Agamben, *Homo Sacer,* 86.
19. Arendt, *Origins,* 474–5.
20. Ibid., 185. With such horrifying precedents, one should not be surprised if genocides still happen in Rwanda as elsewhere.
21. Agamben, *Homo Sacer,* 10.
22. Giorgio Agamben, *State of Exception* (Chicago, 2005).
23. Jacques Derrida, *Rogues: Two Essays on Reason* (Stanford, 2003).
24. Arendt, *The Human Condition,* 126.
25. Ibid., 134.
26. Ibid.
27. Ibid., 133.
28. Brazilian extermination groups do not target their victims for political, criminal, or any other particular reason: it suffices that these are poor and helpless people on the fringes of society, with no means to claim justice and whose murder is usually taken to be statistically predictable anyway. On the evening of 29 March 2005, 29 people were randomly murdered in Nova Iguaçu, a poor metropolitan area of Rio de Janeiro.
29. Martin Heidegger, "Overcoming Metaphysics," in *The Heidegger Controversy,* ed. Richard Wolin (Cambridge, MA, 1993), 68. At 85, he states that, "War has become a distortion of the consumption of beings which is continued in peace."
30. Heidegger, "Overcoming Metaphysics," 87 and 84.
31. Martin Heidegger, *Bremer und Freiburger Vorträge,* Gesamtausgabe vol. 79 (Frankfurt am Main, 1994), 56. According to Arendt, "The concentration camps, by making death itself anonymous . . . robbed death of its meaning as the end of a fulfilled life. In a sense they took away the individual's own death, proving that henceforth nothing belonged to him and he belonged to no one. His death merely set a seal on the fact that he had never really existed." *Origins,* 452.
32. Agamben, *Homo Sacer,* 2, 4.
33. Ibid., 114–5.
34. Arendt, *Origins,* 293.
35. Ibid., 295–6.
36. Ibid., 297.
37. Ibid., 455.
38. Ibid., 301.
39. Agamben, *Homo Sacer,* 128.

Chapter 11

THE "SUBTERRANEAN STREAM OF WESTERN HISTORY"
Arendt and Levinas after Heidegger

Robert Eaglestone

What sort of a book is *The Origins of Totalitarianism*? One of Arendt's strongest defenders, Seyla Benhabib, writes that it is too "systematically ambitious and over-interpreted" to be strictly history, "too anecdotal, narrative and ideographic" for social science, and is "too philosophical" for political journalism.[1] In this chapter I will argue that the work is not only, as others have argued, an act of storytelling, but also an attempt to reframe the stories we tell. I use the word "reframe" precisely because of its Heideggerian echoes. As Arendt's extraordinarily abstruse fable "Heidegger the Fox" suggests and as much scholarship has established, her intellectual relationship with Heidegger is complex. Her work is not simply developing or filling in a "Heideggerian politics" nor is she to be understood as a "left Heideggerian."[2] I will argue that *Origins* is written in an implicitly Heideggerian vein, enabled by his pre-War thought, and, while developing that path of thought, is at the same time a critique of it. Arendt's vision of the inextricable interrelationship between the phenomena of totalitarianism, racism, empire, anti-Semitism, and genocide, what she names in the 1951 preface as the "subterranean stream of Western history," stems from her Heideggerian intellectual inheritance, and her views on these matters develop and highlight two central failures in this inheritance.[3]

In order to throw this into relief, I contrast Arendt's work with the thought of Emmanuel Levinas. Like Arendt, Levinas was a student of Heidegger, and his work records the impact of Heidegger's philosophy: "a debt that [modern thinkers] often owe to [their] regret."[4] Making explicit what Arendt left implicit, Levinas argued that his own work is "governed by a profound need to leave the climate of [Heidegger's] philosophy and by the conviction that we cannot leave it for a philosophy that would be pre-Heideggarian."[5] I suggest that Arendt's and Levinas's work complement each other: while Arendt's work "looks out," as it were, to the effects of this subterranean stream, Levinas's "looks in" to explain and critique its internal dynamics. Together, they reveal the complex matrix of deeply grounded philosophical ideas that are central to Arendt's new framing of the "burden of our times."

A partial consensus has arisen among scholars, with support from her own published and unpublished writing, that Arendt's work can be best understood as "storytelling." Apart from reflecting the particular stylistic driving force of Arendt's writing, this claim has numerous advantages. It is a "get out of jail free card" in relation to many forms of criticism from more traditionally minded empiricist historians and political scientists. But others have seen more than a sleight of hand in this commitment to narrative. For Benhabib, it represents a redemptive power, "redeeming the memory of the dead, the defeated and the vanquished by making present to us once more their failed hopes, their untrodden paths and unfulfilled dreams."[6] For Agnes Heller, narrative is "a vehicle of political interventions" which does not "merely tell readers something philosophical about political actions . . . but also instructs them that there is the possibility to act."[7] And, while suggesting that Arendt's apologies for "story telling" were "disingenuous," Lisa Jane Disch finds much in them for "marginal critical theory."[8] While there is a great deal of force to these arguments and descriptions, they are not, however, complete. A narrative cannot exist in and of itself. In order to be comprehensible, to work as a story, it needs a framework within which to be understood. Great works, as readers of Walter Benjamin know, both destroy and remake these very frameworks, end and begin genres, and it is this "reframing" that is central to *Origins*. The importance and relevance of the book today lies not so much in the facts it conveys but in the links and associations that it makes which in turn stem from its reframing of "deep history."

"Deep History"

Heidegger asked:

> What did the Second World War really decide? . . . This World War has decided nothing—if we use here "decision" in so high and wide a sense that it concerns solely man's essential fate on this earth.[9]

This sounds like a very odd remark, as it seems obvious that the War was decisive in many respects. On the largest scale, it decided which political systems survived and which perished, while on a smaller scale, it decided the lives of hundreds of millions of individuals at the time and thereafter. However, Heidegger is discussing the events at a different level, as it were. Tim Clark argues that where Heidegger expounds his ideas on the nature of history, he makes use of the difference between the German terms *Historie* and *Geschichte*. The former, Clark suggests, names "the familiar sense of history as the study and narrating of the past," which finds its apotheosis in the discipline of history.[10] This "defines entities as entities" and traces them "back in their origin to other entities."[11] However, in contrast, Heidegger also "names something less familiar and more profound" with *Geschichte* which

> means "history" as when we say in English that such or such an event or decision was "historical": i.e., that it altered things in such a way that we are still living inside the space it opened up, just as, say, the modern West still inhabits a world in which Christianity has been a decisive 'historical' force, whether one believes in Jesus or not.[12]

This, for Heidegger, is the "history of being." Not a "*longue durée*" history, nor a history of "mentalities," but rather a deep tracing of the experience of being in the West. Clark, adapting a term from work by Heideggerian scholars on "deep ecology," calls this "deep history." However, Heidegger really only marks three events in this Western history of being. First, he believed that the Romans transformed Greek thought. Heidegger argued that Greek thought was an authentic engagement with the world as it is, and that the imperialist metaphysics of the Romans usurped this thought and turned it into one which saw the world and its contents simply as made up of tools to be used. Second, Heidegger marked the integration of this Roman worldview into Christianity in the medieval period. And third, he argued that the birth of technoscience in the Enlightenment finalized this movement by framing everything (including the human being) as a thing in terms of use.

Of course, this sort of "deep history," or the idea of the "history of being" raises empiricist and, in another way, materialist hackles. In the Anglo-American historical tradition, it is echoed by debates in historiography between empiricists and idealists. But in Heidegger's work, these two ways of thinking about history are not supposed to be opposites. As with many of Heidegger's interlocking arguments, his view does not negate, challenge, or dispose of more standard history or histories. Rather, he seeks the larger frames, which, in fact, empower these arguments and discourses. For Heidegger, this "deep history" is what so profoundly shapes our existence. Moreover, it is so close to us that we are hardly able to see it, like the glasses through which we look. Without a sense of "deep history" the discipline of history would be impossible: it is only in light of the development of the Enlightenment, for example, that empiricist historical methodology comes to be and to make sense.[13] The concept of "deep history" has been terribly influential on a range of thinkers. It is clearly what inspired Foucault's accounts of profound historical shifts and changes, for example. It also underlies Agamben's recent work on the figure of the *Homo Sacer*. However, before these two thinkers, the idea of "deep history" also laid the groundwork for Arendt's work in *Origins*.

The aim of *Origins* is not only to chart a history, to tell a story, or offer a "genealogy."[14] Rather, it is an attempt by Arendt to show how there has been a new turn in the "history of being," a turn for which Heidegger himself failed to account.

Either through a lack of interest in the political or because he thought it already enfolded into his primordial enquiry or, at worst, through a culpable political choice, Heidegger did not address explicitly what many have taken to be the central moment of his age. As Emil Fackenheim argues, "the Holocaust world—or *Un-welt*—should have been for him—but was not—an *Ereignis*": that is an "event" in the "history of being."[15] It is precisely this, which Arendt is trying to account for, and in so doing she both uses Heidegger's thought and critiques it.

This event in the "history of being," for Arendt is named "totalitarianism." If Heidegger traces the ways in which productionist metaphysics turns the world into a world of use, Arendt shows how this goes another step. For Arendt, experience itself, and the authentic judgment that arises from experience, is extirpated by ideology. This is not simply a "contingent event" but something in the "subterranean stream of western history" that "has finally come to the surface and usurped the dignity of our tradition. This is the reality in which we live."[16] Arendt, like Orwell in *1984*, the twin of *Origins*, makes clear that what is being shaped and changed under this new system of government is what it is *to be*: "What totalitarian ideologies . . . aim at is not the transformation of the outside world or the revolutionizing transmutation of society, but the transformation of human nature itself."[17] Arendt is not positing some force beyond the human, such as the divine or Spirit or so on. (Indeed, a belief in such a thing is precisely one of the factors that empowers totalitarianism. She writes that, "Terror is lawfulness, if law is the law of the movement of some suprahuman force, Nature or History."[18] All Arendt's work is motivated by the desire to drive thought back to authentic human judgment rather than simply to follow an axiomatic program or submit to what Adorno and Horkheimer called "ticket thinking").[19] Rather, it is to account for what she felt to be a caesura in human history, to illuminate the "dark times," which seem to change who we are. The book is an attempt to reframe the terms of reference for the times in which we find ourselves.

This idea of a change in what it is *to be* is commonly invoked in relation to the Holocaust whether by survivor witnesses like Elie Wiesel, philosopher/theologians such as Emil Fackenheim, or more prosaic historians like Christopher Browning who writes, "I believe that the Holocaust was a watershed event in human history."[20] For Arendt in the late 1940s, while the horror was fresh but the full extent of the genocide was only understood hazily, the "concentration camps" were a "true central institution of totalitarian organizational power" and "the most consequential institution of totalitarian rule."[21] For her, the "event in being" was caused not only by the death camps, which only revealed most authentically and clearly the face of the "radical evil," but by the way the death camps brought to the fore the

realization that something seems to be involved in modern politics that should never be involved in politics as we used to understand it, namely all or nothing—all, and that is an undetermined infinity of forms of human living-together, or nothing, for a victory of the concentration-camp system would mean the same inexorable doom for human beings as the use of the hydrogen bomb would mean the doom of the human race.[22]

Of course, Theodor Adorno and Zygmunt Bauman, heavily influenced by Adorno, have also argued that the camps are a development of modernity. However, Arendt's understanding has perhaps a crucial difference from Adorno's. Arendt does not see the camps and totalitarianism as an *inevitable* result of modernity. While the dark times are an event in the "history of being," they are not necessarily an all-consuming disaster. This means that she is able to avoid Adorno's pessimism, both philosophical ("All post-Auschwitz culture, including its urgent critique, is garbage . . . Not even silence gets us out of the circle") and personal ("the question of whether one can *live* after Auschwitz. This question has appeared to me, for example, in the recurring dreams which plague me, in which I have the feeling that I am no longer really alive, but am just the emanation of a wish of some victim of Auschwitz").[23] It also means that she is more able than Adorno, say, to see how various particular "ignominious deeds" and their motivations led to the death camps: for example, how "fundamental aspects" of imperialism "appear so close to totalitarian phenomena of the twentieth century that it may be justifiable to consider the whole period a preparatory stage for coming catastrophes."[24] That is, she is able to consider these as the "subterranean stream" of Western thought, not as an all-engulfing flood.

Totalitarianism and Western Thought

And it is to the content of that stream that I now turn. While *Origins* was about "the hidden structure of totalitarianism," and sought to show how this had come to dominate twentieth century life even in defeat, this structure in turn, as an event in "deep history," relied on an element in all Western thought.[25] In order to cast light on this element, I want to turn to the work of Emmanuel Levinas.

A superficial overview of their biographies might suggest that Arendt and Levinas had much in common. Both were philosophers and early students of Heidegger and both their oeuvres are marked by a struggle with his thought; both were diasporic Jews with intellectual investments in the Diaspora; both were involved in the Holocaust (Arendt as a refugee, while Levinas had been in a POW camp for French Jewish soldiers). However, there are marked and profound differences. Where Arendt focused on the political, Levinas's focus is on ethics and religion. Moreover, Levinas's biographer suggests that there was, from Levinas's side at least, a sense of rivalry over their interpretations of Heidegger, as well as an animus over her views on Israel and the United States.[26] While there is not space to do this conjunction justice here, I suggest that their accounts usefully complement each other in terms of coming to understand the "subterranean stream."

In her discussion of Heidegger in "What is Existential Philosophy?" Arendt "discerned a hidden functionalism" in his thought.[27] His use of the term *Dasein*,

Arendt argues, while aiming only to "resolve man into several modes of being that are phenomenologically demonstrable," in fact strips the human of characteristics such as "freedom, human dignity and reason".[28] Thus, for Arendt, Heidegger betrays a

> functionalism not unlike Hobbes's realism. If man consists in the fact that he is, he is no more than the modes of Being or functions in the world (or in society, Hobbes would say)....The crucial element of Man's being is its being in the world, and what is at stake for his being in the world is quite simply survival in the world.[29]

This leads, Arendt argues, to the fundamental alienation of *Dasein*, and so to its "absolute isolation" from others in the world.[30] Indeed, her praising excoriation of Hobbes (and so, to some extent, of Heidegger) lies at the core of the "Imperialism" section of *Origins*. Arendt highlights how Hobbes, "the only great philosopher to whom the bourgeoisie can rightly and exclusively lay claim," constitutes the state not in relation to some wider authority such as natural law, but on the basis of individual interests in term of contracts.[31] This analysis "which in three hundred years has never been outdated or excelled" envisages a person as "without reason, without the capability of truth and without free will—that is without the capability for responsibility," simply in competition with the others in the world.[32] Thus, since a person's worth is determined by his or her power, power is "the fundamental passion of man"; and it is this that lies at the bottom of each individual's contract with others.[33] Community, established through contracts, is then temporary, an inessential. This "picture of man," she argues, is not "an attempt at psychological realism or philosophical truth," but an "unmatched insight into the political needs of the new social body of the rising bourgeois . . . a picture of man as he ought to become and ought to behave if he wanted to fit onto the coming bourgeoisie society," constantly needing to expand his possession and so power.[34] If this picture is true, if the "idea of humanity" is jettisoned, then "all together are predestined to war against each other until they have disappeared from the face of the earth."[35] However, at least in *Origins*, Arendt does not offer an ethically based challenge to this view of the human. While commenting that "men are neither ants nor bees" and stressing our unity as species, she does not develop in that book a model of the human self, of the ethical commitment one to another.[36]

However, and from much the same philosophical starting point, Emmanuel Levinas, does aim to do precisely this. As part of this investigation, he analyses the same "underground stream" as Arendt. For Levinas, this "stream" is not a basic human inclination (power, *pace* Hobbes), nor simply the result of the interests of a particular class, but lies within Western metaphysics. Levinas's first major work, *Totality and Infinity*, begins with a Hobbesian vision of each warring against each:

> Everyone will readily agree that it is of the highest importance to know whether we are not duped by morality. Does not lucidity . . . consist in catching sight of the permanent possibility of war? . . . The state of war suspends morality . . . it renders morality derisory.[37]

Levinas's argument against this vision, made painstakingly over the course of that book, is that the nature of subjectivity itself reveals a responsibility to the other, which comes before the self. As he writes in a later work, "in the 'pre-history' of the ego posited for itself speaks a responsibility; the self is through and through a hostage, older than the ego, prior to principles."[38] However, the ways in which subjectivity has been understood in the West have always worked to cover up this responsibility in its very attempt to grasp the other. He argues that Western thought, in its attempt to come to terms with otherness, always posits it via a third, neutral term. That is, the other is not understood as an Other, but as what can be grasped as an example of some universal concept. For example, an other is not encountered as an Other, but as an example of "man" and so judged by that culturally weighted yardstick. "Western Philosophy," he writes "has most often been an ontology: a reduction of the other to the same by interposition of a middle and neutral term that ensures the comprehension of being."[39] This comprehension or grasping, both in the sense of seizing and our more metaphorical use of "grasp" in the way one grasps a solution to a mathematical problem, means that for Levinas "'I think' comes down to 'I can'—to an appropriation of what is, to an exploitation of reality."[40]

For Levinas, then, Western thought is all consuming of otherness. While Levinas gives almost no examples of this process, remaining at an abstract level, it is possible to read *Origins* as a very detailed account precisely of this. Arendt's account of the very logic of totalitarianism makes this clear. Totalitarianism is an "-ism, which to the satisfaction of its adherents can explain everything and every occurrence by deducing it from a single premise."[41] It is the idea of a "neutral term" taken to its furthest degree, to the point where it "becomes independent of all experience," because, for Arendt, the content of the idea mattered less than the "the logical processes which could be developed from it."[42] These processes are the logic of argument and reason developed from a central assertion or axiom which aimed to "to organize the infinite plurality of human beings as if all humanity were just one individual" and, in so doing, consumed all Otherness into its own system.[43] Thus, it is not only the "idea," such as the Party and the movement of History, or the Führer-Principle that is at issue, but its logical application. This logical application depends less on the founding "idea" and more on the whole panoply of Western thought and logic, which allow it to be applied. (Thus, perhaps, the importance of judgment for Arendt: knowing how and when and why to apply particulars to general categories, rather than simply and blindly following axioms). Arendt's account of imperial expansion, as well as her account of totalitarian systems, demonstrates this same structure. Cecil Rhodes, her 'leitmotif' figure, writes that expansion "is everything . . . I would annex the planets if I could."[44] The whole process of colonial expansion, especially in Africa, relies on this axiom of expansion conjoined to what Arendt analyzes as the so-called "new key to history," the race-thinking and racism which reduces particular others to examples of universal categories of race.[45] Arendt writes that when Englishmen have all turned into "white men," as already for a disastrous spell all Germans became Aryans, then this change will signify the end of Western man. . . . Race is not the natural birth of man but his unnatural death.[46]

However, neither Levinas nor Arendt is always so pessimistic. Levinas's thought is structured by a doubleness. He is constantly moving between what he sees as Greek and Hebrew, between the secular and the religious, the true and the good, the transcendental and the empirical. He finds this echoed in the rhetorical figure of the "amphibology," a sentence that may have two very distinct meanings without changing its actual words. This doubleness allows Levinas to see on the one hand the imperialism in the ontology of Western thought, its basis in possession and control, and at the same time to find a space from which to question this. Indeed, in the very encounter between the same and the other, Levinas argues that the same is called "into question" by the other and that we "name this calling into question of my spontaneity by the presence of the other ethics."[47] Ethics here means the way that the "strangeness of the Other, his irreducibility to the I, to my thoughts and possessions" occurs.[48] This inability to comprehend and to grasp the other leads to the way that ethics critiques knowledge. Western thought simultaneously attempts to reduce the other to the same and is troubled by the other, and it is exactly in this troubling that Levinas finds the ethical moment. If Western thought is the place from which this oppressive power stems, for Levinas it is also the place from which it can be opposed.

It is widely acknowledged that despite his comments on political matters, Levinas's ethical phenomenology does not necessarily offer moral or political decisions, that is, judgment. In contrast, despite the range of Arendt's writing, and her insistence on political and social judgment, she does not offer an explicit and well-supported ethical theory. I suggest that, in this context at least, these two former students of Heidegger have complementary positions over the "subterranean stream." It is through an ethical account of the political story told in *The Origins of Totalitarianism* that its location in post-phenomenological thought is clearest. The work is an account of how this long running part of Western metaphysics erupted from its underground stream and so effected a change in "deep history," in who we are.

Namibia, Totalitarianism, and *Peter Moor*

How, then, might the churning of the waters from the "subterranean stream" be shown, or at least illuminated, in the historical world? Clearly this sort of description is not susceptible to empirical proofs. One of the major legacies of *The Origins of Totalitarianism* is in its strikingly different approach to the past and the present and how we understand them. The term "methodology" is perhaps inappropriate, as Arendt never developed one explicitly, though various scholars have usefully drawn out methodological elements from her work.[49] Seyla Benhabib argues it works by "configuration and crystallisation of elements," seizing on crucial moments, stories, phrases, anecdotes, documents to shine light on her wider conception.[50] If it were just this, however, it would resemble, perhaps, the avant garde historiographical experiments of, say, Sven Lindqvist. [51] I have suggested that it does more than this in the way that it offers an implicit reframing of "deep history," which I have argued is usefully illuminated by Levinas's conception of ethics. Thus it is a *philosophical* history. It is possible, in the light of its analysis, to uncover moments where this stream emerges and clashes with the other channels of Western thought and experience.

Following Arendt's approach, and while heeding her warning that there "is an abyss between the men of brilliant and facile conceptions and men of brutal deeds and active bestiality which no intellectual explanation is able to bridge," I want to conclude by briefly analyzing Gustav Frenssen's *Peter Moor,* an adventure story for boys from pre-War Germany which parallels the British Imperialist stories of G. A. Henty.[52] Frenssen's book concerns the colonial war in Southwest Africa and the genocide of the Herero, and was very widely read in Germany before 1945, passing through several editions.[53] Adorno writes that children's books "like *Alice in Wonderland* or *Struwwelpeter,* of which it would be absurd to ask whether they are progressive or reactionary, contain incomparably more eloquent ciphers of history than the high drama of Hebbel" and this is clearly the case here.[54] In contrast to Uwe Timm's more sophisticated novel *Morenga,* which covers the same ground and period and has a wider focus, and which offers more staged examples of the horrors and contradictions of colonialism, Frenssen's book is crude and straightforward.[55]

In at least two places in his book, different traditions clash, and, while there are resolutions of a kind, the clash itself remains uppermost. This reflects the conflicted doubleness that Levinas analyses, where the mixture of the surface and subterrenean streams comes to the fore. In the first, the narrator, the young soldier Peter Moor, overhears conversations about the cause of the revolt.

> The matter stood this way: there were missionaries here who said [to the Herero]: "You are our dear brothers in the Lord, and we want to bring you these benefits— namely Faith, Love and Hope." And there were soldiers, farmers and traders, and they said: "We want to take your cattle and your land gradually away from you, and make you slaves without legal rights." Those two things didn't go side by side . . . Either it is right to colonize—that is deprive others of their rights, to rob and makes slaves—or it is just and right to Christianize, that is to proclaim and live up to brotherly love. One must clearly desire the one and despise the other. [56]

The role of conversion in the colonies was complex, and not always simply in support of the imperial process (indeed, in India, for example, the British government explicitly stopped officially supporting evangelism). Some of the earliest writers seen as anticolonial, Las Casas, for example, are religious in origin. However, in this passage the conflict between possession, and a recognition of otherness and equality, is very clear. Two streams of thought are clearly in conflict, and while the passage goes on to blame the missionaries for giving the Herero "ideas above their station," the uneasy sense that there is a mixed message internal to the colonial pro-cess is explicit. In fact, it is only by denigrating one part of the Western tradition (a respect for others, even if phrased and veiled in the language of "faith, love and hope") that the other, the grasping comprehension and destruction of otherness, is possible. This is even more explicit in a second moment.

After the major battle of the war, the narrator discusses matters with his Lieu-tenant after shooting a straggler who "says he has not taken part in the war."[57] The Lieutenant argues that the "blacks have deserved death before God and man" not for their revolt but because

> they have built no houses and dug no wells . . . God has let us conquer here because we are the nobler and more advanced. This is not saying much in comparison with this black nation, but we must see to it that we become better and braver before all the nations of the earth. . . . To the nobler and more vigorous belongs the world.[58]

However, later, after reflection, the Lieutenant says, "but the missionary was right when he said all men are brothers."[59] Peter then points out that they have, in fact, killed their brother, and in an attempt to resolve this paradox, the Lieutenant re-plies, "For a long time we must be hard and kill, but at the same time strive towards high thoughts and noble deeds so that we may contribute our part to mankind, our future brothers."[60] The similarity between these speeches from popular writing and Nazi accounts is obvious. Moreover, the Lieutenant squares the circle (killing the Herero/all men are brothers) by projecting the fraternal links into the future, a typical totalitarian ideological move, so that the current killing is absolved in the eye of the future. Here again, it is possible to see the "subterranean stream" of ontological possession emerging and taking over other Western traditions. More-over, in this last extract, the destruction of otherness is taking place by positing a neutral term (the "nobility" which will make mankind "future brothers") against which it is possible to judge people in the present (those less noble and advanced). In these little vignettes, in a book read and reread by pre-War German youth, the conflict between different yet contiguous streams of thought is played out. It is one of Arendt's achievements, perhaps, that even such small exchanges, frozen in a children's book, can illuminate the "deep history" that underlies the burden of the post-War years.

I have argued that Hannah Arendt's work stems from a Heideggerian perspec-tive on the nature of the "history of being," but, where Heidegger did not engage with the moment of his own time, Arendt developed his thought to reframe the "history of being" in an age of totalitarianism. It was this that allowed her an in-sight into the origins of totalitarianism and its linkages with other phenomena as well as with Western thought itself. This is an implicit criticism of Heidegger's re-lation to the sphere of the political. Moreover, complemented by Levinas's analysis of Western thought, Arendt offers an ethical critique of Heidegger's thought, too. Both of these responses to failures in Heidegger's work provide a crucial reframing to "deep history." Our times are still burdensome, but their burdens have changed and developed: to come to terms with our burdens, we would do well to try to gain the same sort of vision Arendt achieved.

Notes

1. Selya Benhabib, *The Reluctant Modernism of Hannah Arendt* (London, 1996), 63.
2. For a detailed accounts of the intellectual relationship see Dana Villa, *Arendt and Heidegger: The Fate of the Political* (Princeton, 1996); April Flakne, "Beyond Banality and Fatality: Arendt, Heidegger and Jaspers on Political Speech," *New German Critique* 86 (2002): 3–18; Michael Jones, "Heidegger the Fox: Hannah Arendt's Hidden Dialogue," *New German Critique* 73 (1998): 164–92; L. P. Hinchman, and S. K Hinchman, "In Heidegger's Shadow: Hannah Arendt's Phenomenological Humanism," *Review of Politics* 46 (1984): 183–211. For a more rhetorical account, see Richard Wolin, *Heidegger's Children* (Princeton, 2001).
3. Hannah Arendt, *The Origins of Totalitarianism* (London, 1973), ix.
4. Emmanuel Levinas, *God, Death and Time*, trans. Bettina Bergo (Stanford, 2000), 8.
5. Emmanuel Levinas, *Existence and Existents*, trans. Alphonso Lingis (London, 1978), 19.
6. Seyla Benhabib, "Hannah Arendt and the Redemptive Power of Narrative," *Social Research* 57 (1990): 167–196, 196.
7. Agnes Heller, "Hannah Arendt on Tradition and New Beginnings," in *Hannah Arendt in Jerusalem*, ed. Stephen E. Aschheim (Berkeley, 2001), 27.
8. Lisa Jane Disch, *Hannah Arendt and the Limits of Philosophy* (Ithaca, 1994), 4, 9.
9. Martin Heidegger, *What is Called Thinking?* trans. J. Glenn Gray (New York, 1968), 66.
10. Tim Clark, *Martin Heidegger* (London, 2002), 27.
11. Martin Heidegger, *Being and Time*, trans. John Macquarrie and Edward Robinson (Oxford, 1962), H. 6.
12. Clark, *Heidegger*, 28
13. I offer an extension of this argument in my book *The Holocaust and the Postmodern* (Oxford, 2004).
14. Heller, "Hannah Arendt," 23.
15. Emil Fackenheim, *To Mend the World: Foundations of Jewish Thought* (New York, 1982), 190.
16. Arendt, *Origins*, ix.
17. Ibid., 458.
18. Ibid., 465.
19. Theodor Adorno and Max Horkheimer, *Dialectic of Enlightenment*, trans. John Cumming (London, 1997), 200–208.
20. Christopher Browning, *Nazi Policy, Jewish Workers, German Killers* (Cambridge, UK, 2000), 32.
21. Arendt, *Origins*, 438, 441. On this, see also Dan Stone, "Ontology or Bureaucracy? Hannah Arendt's Early Interpretations of the Holocaust," in *History, Memory and Mass Atrocity: Essays on the Holocaust and Genocide* (London, 2006), 53–69.
22. Arendt, *Origins*, 443.
23. Theodor Adorno, *Negative Dialectics*, trans. E. B. Ashton (London, 1973), 367; Theodor Adorno, *Metaphysics: Concepts and Problems*, ed. Rolf Tiedemann, trans. Edmund Jephcott (Cambridge, UK, 2000), 110.
24. Arendt, *Origins*, 123.
25. Richard J. Bernstein, *Hannah Arendt and the Jewish Question* (Cambridge, MA, 1996), 89.
26. Marie-Anne Lescourret, *Emmanuel Levinas* (Paris, 1994), 289–90.
27. Hinchman and Hinchman, "In Heidegger's Shadow," 204.

28. Hannah Arendt, *Essays in Understanding 1930–1954* (London, 1994), 178.
29. Arendt, *Essays*, 178, 179.
30. Ibid., 181.
31. Arendt, *Origins*, 139.
32. Ibid., 139.
33. Ibid.
34. Ibid., 140, 142, 143.
35. Ibid., 157.
36. Ibid., 145.
37. Emmanuel Levinas, *Totality and Infinity*, trans. Alphonso Lingis (London, 1991), 21.
38. Emmanuel Levinas, *Otherwise than Being: or, Beyond Essence*, trans. Alphonso Lingis (The Hague, 1981), 117.
39. Ibid., 43.
40. Ibid., 46.
41. Arendt, *Origins*, 468.
42. Ibid., 470, 472.
43. Ibid., 438.
44. Ibid., 124.
45. Ibid., 170.
46. Ibid., 157.
47. Levinas, *Totality and Infinity*, 43.
48. Ibid.
49. See, for example, Elisabeth Young-Bruehl, *Hannah Arendt: For Love of the World* 2ᵈ ed. (London, 2004), 320 ff; Disch, *Hannah Arendt and the Limits of Philosophy*, 107 ff.
50. Benhabib, *The Reluctant Modernism*, 64.
51. Sven Lindvist, *"Exterminate all the Brutes,"* trans. Joan Tate (London, 1997); Sven Lindvist, *A History of Bombing*, trans. Linda Haverty Rugg (London, 2001).
52. Arendt, *Origins*, 183.
53. For more on this, see Jürgen Zimmerer, "The birth of the *Ostland* out of the spirit of colonialism: a postcolonial perspective on the Nazi policy of conquest and extermination," *Patterns of Prejudice* 39, no. 2 (2005): 197–219. There are at least two English translations of *Peter Moor* (1908, 1914).
54. Theodor Adorno, *Minima Moralia*, trans E. F. N. Jephcott (London, 1978), 151.
55. Uwe Timm, *Morenga: A Novel*, trans. Breeon Mitchell (New York, 2003), with thanks to Dan Stone for this point of comparison.
56. Gustav Frenssen, *Peter Moor: a Narrative of the German campaign in South-West Africa*, trans. Margaret May Ward (London, 1914), 79. On this issue of missionaries, see also Horst Drechsler, *"Let us die fighting": The Struggle of the Herero and Nama against German Imperialism* (London, 1980), 133 ff.
57. Frenssen, *Peter Moor*, 236. "In Hereroland itself German death squads made little effort to distinguish between Hereros, berg-Damaras and Bushmen": David Soggot, *Namibia: The Violent Heritage* (London, 1986), 11.
58. Frenssen, *Peter Moor*, 236. In *Morenga*, by contrast, Uwe Timm stresses the Herero's success in breeding cattle.
59. Frenssen, *Peter Moor*, 37.
60. Ibid.

Chapter 12

HANNAH ARENDT AND
THE OLD "NEW SCIENCE"

Steven Douglas Maloney

Hannah Arendt's political writings are frequently analyzed through the lenses of her German-Jewish identity or her tutelage under *existenz* philosophers like Martin Heidegger or Karl Jaspers. This approach has been useful in understanding much of what Arendt was trying to offer in her writings, but it also restricts our understanding of Arendt in very significant ways. Too much focus on Arendt's direct influences (teachers, identity, place in history) has created an environment where academic work on Arendt has tried to dig into every possible historical clue it can to "come to terms" with her thought, in the same way that Victor Farias' book on Heidegger forced many to have to "come to terms" with Arendt's famous professor. This scholarly fascination is transposed in Richard Wolin's *Heidegger's Children.* Wolin takes the relatively recent scholarly fascination of coming to terms with the character and biography of Heidegger and projects this fixation as a dominant feature of the academic efforts of students like Arendt. What is missing in Wolin's accounts of Arendt, among those of many others, is that her "impressionableness" is not to be found strictly in her direct relationships, like with Heidegger and Karl Jaspers. Instead, we need to see that Arendt possessed a rather vivid imagination that allowed her to be quite impressed by a great many great minds that she only knew through reading books. Arendt leaves many not-too-subtle clues as to who these influential writers are who have left this lasting impression upon her, and yet some of these influences still are underemphasized for the most part in Arendt scholarship.

   In this chapter, I make the case that any understanding of Arendt's views on political topics cannot be understood properly without understanding the contributions of political theorists, such as Montesquieu and Tocqueville, on Arendt's own understanding of the various political topics that she wrote about. Arendt's *On Revolution* (1963) commends Montesquieu's understanding of political regimes as flowing from the realities of a diverse and often contradictory set of forces that people find themselves having to navigate effectively and practically in order to govern. Perhaps the best example of the type of political science Montesquieu was trying to describe is Tocqueville's *Democracy in America.* Tocqueville's two-volume work can be seen as a massive account of all of the various forces that comprise the "general spirit" of which Montesquieu speaks as they played out in mid-nineteenth century America. The scholarship of these two theorists in particular plays a critical role in Arendt's *On Revolution,* perhaps Arendt's most concentrated effort to comment on the politics of the world at the time she was actually writing.

If we read Arendt with an eye toward these republican influences, we allow ourselves a broader understanding of Arendt's writing that incorporates all of the ideas and influences she has drawn upon to make her arguments. In her biography of Arendt, Elisabeth Young-Bruehl claims that:

> In the early 1950s Hannah Arendt began to envision a new science of politics for a world in which political events—world war, totalitarianism, atomic bombings—demand serious attention from philosophers. "A new science of politics is needed for a new world," wrote de Tocqueville in *Democracy in America,* and with each decade both the necessity and the potential scope of such a science have grown.[1]

This new science that Arendt envisions takes the dangers of the modern age seriously and is not a very different kind of "new science" than the one Tocqueville was writing about a hundred years earlier. Arendt's "new science" is partially comprised, at least, of the research into the etymology and the reconstitution of various important definitions and terms that we commonly come across in political theory and philosophy, which are more or less understood when they are written and read in today's academic environment.

As an example, Arendt writes in *On Violence* (1970): "It is, I think, a rather sad reflection on the present state of political science that our terminology does not distinguish among such key words as 'power,' 'strength,' 'force,' 'authority,' and, finally, 'violence.'"[2] Beyond thinking that the definitional distinctions of these words was important, Arendt also believed that she was not alone in practicing this more nuanced vocabulary for describing the political world. Arendt writes that Montesquieu fashioned a unique understanding of power for his age, "and this discovery stands in so flagrant a contradiction to all conventional notions on this matter that it has almost been forgotten, despite the fact that the foundation of the Republic in America was largely inspired by it."[3] The importance of Montesquieu's "unique understanding" is not simply that it provides an intellectual alternative, but it also carries a pragmatic value that seems immeasurable when contrasted with the understanding of power used in the French and Russian revolutions. Arendt implies that such a distinction is still of practical value in understanding the world, and she aims for her work to contribute to this distinction as much as possible.

A few things should be noted before proceeding. In no way are the contents of this chapter an attempt to create a strict genealogy of thought. This is an examination of what Arendt learned from Montesquieu and Tocqueville and then developed into her political writings. Also, this chapter does not intend to suggest a complete understanding of topics such as genocide, racism, imperialism, and slavery, but instead is aiming to bring out some considerations that more traditional treatments of these topics may not give as much attention to. In this way, it is intentionally overemphasizing certain connections and aspects of issues that Arendt uniquely saw in them. The purpose is to show the types of analysis that her approach to studying these topics captures and that other means of analysis do not. She herself did not believe in essential understandings of things, and this chapter contends that Arendt's methods add to the scholarship without claiming to replace or crowd out other methods or other work on the various subjects she examined that we will use as examples here.

In a similar vein, analyzing the distinctions between Arendt and mainstream liberal political theory is not done with the intention of implying that she is illiberal. Rather, she sees liberalism, like all concepts that pass through many people's hands, as something which needs "redemption from the predicament of irreversibility—of being unable to undo what one has done though one did not, and could not, have known what he was doing."[4] Arendt wants no part of constructing a new ideological grand narrative. She is a critic of modernity and of liberalism, but her criticisms, if we are to take her at her own word, are for the purpose of generating a better understanding and nothing more.[5]

The Connection with Montesquieu as an Alternative to the Liberal Canon

Arendt states in her published lectures on Kant: "If we want to study philosophy of law in general, we certainly shall not turn to Kant but to Pufendorff or Grotius or Montesquieu."[6] This statement confirms the importance that Arendt placed on Montesquieu. In order best to understand the ways in which Montesquieu earned this place of importance for her and how she put his, and later Tocqueville's, approach to good use, we should turn to Arendt's commentary on law.

When Arendt praises American constitutional devices, such as the balance of powers, she formulates this praise by writing, "How well this part of Montesquieu's teaching was understood in the days of the foundation of the republic!"[7] In her controversial "Reflections on Little Rock," it is Alexis de Tocqueville's interpretation of Montesquieu's "general spirit" in America that she turns to in order to provide a theoretical justification for her arguments:

> Tocqueville saw over a century ago that equality of opportunity and condition, as well as equality of rights, constituted the basic 'law' of the American democracy, and he predicted that the dilemmas and perplexities inherent in the principle of equality might one day become the most dangerous challenge to the American way of life.[8]

Here, the term "law" is perhaps understood differently than our common contemporary understanding. Arendt explains this alternative understanding of law by tracing its lineage, "The original meaning of the word *lex* is 'intimate connection' or relationship, namely something which connects two things or two partners whom external circumstances have brought together."[9] This is consistent with Tocqueville's "law" from the earlier quotation and with what Montesquieu has in mind when he talks about the "spirit of the law." Montesquieu concisely summarizes the "spirit of the law" when he writes, "Many things govern men: climate, religion, laws, the maxims of the government, examples of past things, mores, and manners; a general spirit is formed as a result."[10] This idea of "spirit of the laws" in Montesquieu is an understanding of politics as, in Arendt's parlance, part of the human condition. Specifically, politics is the condition humans have to face as they relate to a world of physical reality and a world inhabited by other human beings.

While Montesquieu's understanding is certainly not the same as the political existentialism that Arendt develops, the two conceptions are close enough to be kindred. Both are more expansive in scope with regard to the well spring of human opinion and the necessary role of what we might roughly call "good society" than most liberal political theory would be. Consider Robert Nozick's own analysis of what we should conclude from his famed *Anarchy, State, and Utopia:*

> Our main conclusions about the state are that a minimal state, limited to the narrow functions of protection against force, theft, fraud, enforcement of contracts, and so on, is justified; that any more extensive state will violate persons' rights not to be forced to do certain things, and is unjustified; and that the minimal state is inspiring as well as right.[11]

While they are thought of as intellectual opposites in many ways, we could just as easily have drawn the same general idea from John Rawls:

> The most fundamental idea in this conception of justice is the idea of society as a fair system of social cooperation over time from one generation to the next . . . This central idea is worked out in conjunction with two companion fundamental ideas. These are: the idea of citizens (those engaged in cooperation) as free and equal persons; and the idea of a well-ordered society.[12]

These two concepts of liberal politics share a common theoretical backbone that rests on the understanding that the aim of the state is to allow citizens to act upon their reason as "free and equal persons" in an environment that protects and empowers them, without violating some understanding of what constitutes natural rights. While liberals may disagree on the amount and nature of minimalist regime interference, their arguments, generally speaking, are predicated on the conception that once the right balance is found between protection of the state and free exercise by citizenry, a state that is "inspiring as well as right" is what naturally follows.

Jeffrey Isaac wrote that Arendt—and Albert Camus as well—"are important because they point the way toward a more satisfactory political orientation" and that "although both writers were suspicious of the justifications and programs entailed by liberal and Marxist versions of universalism, neither was willing to abandon the idea that there is a common human condition."[13] This common human condition—in Arendt, as well as in Montesquieu—is set apart from the organization of the human condition as described by the liberal tradition, and yet it is not fundamentally an "anti-liberal" mode of political argument. The disagreement with liberalism here is diagnostic and prescriptive in nature.

One of the differences with liberal political theory is that it often seems to ignore the importance of how a detail such as climate could impact the creation of a state's constitution. Montesquieu writes, "If it is true that the character of the spirit and the passions of the heart are extremely different in various climates, *laws* should be relative to the differences in these passions and the differences in these characters."[14] Furthermore, Tocqueville does not begin his massive *Democracy in America* with a conversation about institutions or a description of the people, but instead devotes his first chapter to such geographic characteristics of North America as, "The space enclosed between the two chains of mountains comprises 228,843 square leagues. Its area is therefore around six times greater than that of France."[15] Arendt notices that the Founders looked for a way to cope with the effects that geography and climate have on the founding of a regime. Specifically, they worried about how to make a good regime out of so large a territory. Arendt writes, "What the founders were afraid of in practice was not power but impotence," and she frequently cited Montesquieu's view "that republican government was effective only in relatively small territories."[16]

Arendt believes that the founders turned to Montesquieu not just to understand the problem, but to consider its solution as well:

> Hamilton and Madison called attention to another view of Montesquieu, according to which a confederacy of republics could solve the problems of larger countries under the condition that the constituted bodies—small republics—were capable of constituting a new body politic, the confederate republic, instead of resigning themselves to mere alliance.[17]

From this, it follows that she saw Hamilton and Madison's view of constituting free republics as a combination of theoretical understanding combined with various practical concerns, and *not* as an establishment and unyielding obedience to some *a priori* universal principle of rational human organization. Her own writing echoes this sentiment repeatedly, and Elisabeth Young-Bruehl notes that Arendt's understanding of human action is "not tied to particular hierarchical ideal or standard, but must vary from particular instance to particular instance."[18]

Arendt believed that there was danger in any hierarchical ideal or standard mode of political thinking, even the traditional liberal ones. This is evidenced by the fact that Arendt traces the West's journey into imperialism through Thomas Hobbes. She calls Hobbes, "the only great philosopher to whom the bourgeoisie can rightly and exclusively lay claim, even if his principles were not recognized by the bourgeois class for a long time."[19] Arendt argues that Hobbes's reconstruction of man, power, politics, and the state created permission for the new and more exploitative behaviors of the age:

> Since power is essentially only a means to an end a community based solely on power must decay in the calm of order and stability; its complete security reveals that it is built on sand. Only by building more power can it guarantee the status quo; only by constantly extending its authority and only through the process of power accumulation can it remain stable.[20]

This system exhausts itself until, "the accumulation of capital has reached its natural, national limits."[21] Once this happens, Arendt believes that "the bourgeoisie understood that only with an 'expansion is everything' ideology . . . would it be able to set the old motor into motion again."[22] The state's takeover of household interests in the affairs of the political is what she calls the "rise of the social."[23] The state has then created a practical demand to fulfill the needs of the private interests of its citizens.

The nature of these forces did not mean that imperialism was an inevitable next step; but it was certainly an obvious one. The origin of the term social, as Arendt notes in *The Human Condition*, comes from the Roman *societas*, and it was meant to represent people gathering together not as equals, but conspiratorially in order to fulfill some sort of material objective.[24] Only later did the term become enlarged to encompass society as a "conspiracy of all men." In the case of the French Revolution, this trick was turned by engaging another set of fixed, hierarchical liberal standards. In this instance, it was the combination of Rousseau's idea of general will, which was "a highly ingenious means to put a multitude into the place of a single person"[25] and the masses of impoverished citizens who "carried with them necessity, to which they had been subject as long as memory reaches, together with the violence that has always been used to overcome necessity."[26] The French had unleashed a monster in bringing the poor to the political scene *en masse*, because "Nothing, we might say today, could be more obsolete than to attempt to liberate mankind from poverty by political means; nothing could be more futile and dangerous."[27]

Redefined Terms

It was mentioned briefly that Arendt and Montesquieu both seemed to have an uncommon understanding of the term "law." Arendt highlights her understanding of "law" with an American historical example in the following passage about those who formed the Mayflower Compact, "They obviously feared the so-called state of nature, the untold wilderness, unlimited by any boundary, as well as the unlimited initiative of men bound by no law."[28] Her reference to the Mayflower Compact shows that it was not historical process or institutions that formed the covenant by the Pilgrims. Instead it was that "their obvious fear of one another was accompanied by the no less obvious confidence they had in their own power, granted and confirmed by no one and as yet unsupported by any means of violence, to combine themselves into a 'civil Body Politick.'"[29] It is important for the validity of Arendt's definition of "law" that the Mayflower Compact "quickly became a precedent" that spread across New England. So much so that when Connecticut was granted its official royal charter, "it sanctioned and confirmed an already existing form of government."[30] This is to say that the elements of the spirit of the laws had already been tied together by contractual promise well in advance of any royal charter.

The use of the term "power" in describing the Mayflower Compact comes from the definition that Arendt gives to the term in *On Violence*, "Power corresponds to the human ability not just to act, but to act in concert. Power is never the property of an individual; it belongs to the group and remains in existence only so long as the group keeps together."[31] This definition of power also fits into Montesquieu's understanding of power, particularly with regard to the value Montesquieu places in the separation of powers. According to Arendt, Montesquieu's great insight, on a theoretical level, is that,

> Power can be stopped and still be kept intact only by power, so that the principle of separation of power not only provides a guarantee against the monopolization of power by one part of the government, but actually provides a kind of mechanism, built into the very heart of government, through which new power is constantly generated, without, however, being able to overgrow and expand to the detriment of other centers or sources of power.[32]

Arendt explains that no one understood the practical importance of this insight better than James Madison. She comments on Madison:

> Had he believed in the current notions of the indivisibility of power—that divided power is less power—he would have concluded that the new powers of the union must be founded on powers surrendered by the states, so that the stronger the union was to be, the weaker its constituents were to become. His point however, was that the very establishment of the Union had founded a new source of power which in no way drew its strength from the powers of the states, as it had not been established at their expense.[33]

Arendt draws a direct comparison between those who formed the Mayflower Compact and the states, which formed the new union under the Constitution. She notes that the understandings of law, power, and the pursuit of public happiness were concepts that became dividing lines in thought between those who anticipated the great revolutions of the 18th century and those who could not. The erosion of "the old Roman trinity of religion, tradition, and authority" weakened the prevailing forces behind law and order so that, "what could be foreseen, what Montesquieu was only the first to predict explicitly, was the incredible ease with which governments would be overthrown."[34] Montesquieu was anticipating the changes in *fortuna* that seemed to be coming in the age ahead of him as the power of institutions which had formed many of the accepted habits and values of the age started to wither. As the dynamics shifted between the various forces that made up the spirit of the laws, Montesquieu foresaw an age where the old laws were no longer vested in the hearts and minds of the people, and thus were no longer binding.

Tocqueville's *Democracy in America* explores the creation of a new political order built in the wake of the withering away of the old institutions and values, which Montesquieu had predicted would happen. While Arendt has one eye on the theoretical clashes between the legacies of the French and American revolutionary traditions in this wake, she keeps her other eye fixed on the rapid and dynamic changes in the world that threaten what order has been established and maintained to this point in the modern age. The introduction to *On Revolution* contains the warning that the changes in the technological capacity for destruction in twentieth century warfare are changing the rules of political conflict so that, "those who still put their faith in power politics . . . may well discover in the not too distant future that they have become masters in a rather useless and obsolete trade."[35] The point is that changes in technology have to some degree altered the reality of politics in our age, and coming to terms with this new reality means altering our normative views as to what is to be valued from our politics (and our understanding of politics).

Arendt tried to put this alternative understanding to work when she approached topics such as slavery, and genocide. She cites the ancient belief that, "To labor meant to be enslaved by necessity, and this enslavement was inherent in the conditions of human life."[36] Thus, slavery was "not a device for cheap labor or an instrument of exploitation for profit, but rather an attempt to exclude labor from the conditions of man's life."[37] This definition of slavery is important to keep in mind when Arendt writes about political movements based upon the social question, "it is only the rise of technology, and not the rise of modern political ideas as such, which has refuted the old and terrible truth that only violence and rule over others could make some men free."[38] In the absence of adequate technology, any revolution promising liberation for all from the necessity of the household can at best only shift the burden from one set of people to another.

The non-citizen status of slaves and colonials made it impossible for them to appear in public to argue their case. This was even true of American colonists, who eventually grew wary of their political invisibility to England, and took up arms when they realized that their English citizenship did not mean what they believed it had. For those who were so unfortunate as to live in non-white colonies, rebellion would come late, for they did not have the same means to organize a resistance, nor did they have the same access to appear before other Western nations and plead their case for assistance. Arendt has this perspective to offer us, "Persecution of the powerless or power-losing groups may not be a very pleasant spectacle, but it does not spring from human meanness alone."[39] Such spectacles emanate from the fact that, "Even exploitation and oppression still make society work and establish some kind of order."[40]

The lack of a political realm where one can participate is perhaps exemplified by looking at genocide in the twentieth century. Hitler once remarked, "Who today still speaks of the massacre of the Armenians?"[41] The moral was that the Turks had gotten away with mass murder, and that such an activity was not the concern of a political realm where all are held as equals. Instead, the Westphalia system defined the relationships between countries as belonging purely in a social realm, where strength and resources are bandied back and forth so that the material ambitions of nations can be fulfilled. In such a realm, there is little room for the concerns of the victims of genocide, imperialism, or slavery.

Arendt's view of genocide is that it, too, is only possible in the absence of a political realm where one ought to exist. The move Nazi Germany made against its Jewish population was at least partially a result of its ability to exert its strength to eliminate a people already politically invisible, using bureaucracy, authority, and violence. Arendt writes that, "Antisemitism reached its climax when Jews had similarly lost their public functions and their influence."[42] If one wishes to engage in violence and eliminate a group of people, an absence of politics, and thus the political invisibility of the victims, while not the cause of genocide, is probably crucial in facilitating the process. One thing that separates genocide from slavery or imperialism is that the component of fulfilling any particular private or social need is also absent for the dominated group. Arendt seems aware of this critical distinction when she notices that, "When Hitler came to power, the German banks were already almost *judenrein* (and it was here that Jews had held key positions for more than a hundred years)."[43]

Tocqueville's Influence on Arendt's Comments on Racism

In "Reflections on Little Rock," possibly her most controversial writing, Arendt reiterates something she believed was said first by William Faulkner, that "forced integration is no better than forced segregation."[44] For Arendt, this criticism is rooted in a firm belief that forced integration had no real hope of attacking the root problems of racial inequality in America. Her commentary on the history of racial inequality in the United States is really, in terms of the text itself, overshadowed by a more generalized theoretical account of such forces as discrimination and political equality on the ability of the public and private realms to function properly in their assigned roles.

Arendt's larger point here is often obscured by inflammatory comments about her essay and what seem to be just plain bad arguments that are contained within them. Her implication that the NAACP and African-American parents involved in the Civil Rights movement were somehow cowardly individuals who "intend to have our political battles fought out in the school yards" is still criticized as an insultingly gross mischaracterization, and it is difficult to see such statements as anything else.

However, we can glimpse a bit of the "Montesquieu-ian" Arendt via one criticism that she did receive well. Ralph Ellison responded to Arendt by saying "that one of the important clues to the meaning of the Negro experience lies in the idea, the *ideal* of sacrifice."[45] Ellison said that her failure to understand this "caused her to fly way off into left field"[46] in her analysis of the situation. Yet Ellison's argument centers on the idea that Arendt misunderstood the forces, and not the means of analysis. Ellison claimed that she "has absolutely no conception of what goes on in the minds of Negro parents when they send their kids through the lines of hostile people."[47] This sending of children has the "overtones of a rite of initiation" where the child faces a "confrontation of the terrors of social life with all of the mysteries stripped away."[48] Arendt writes that when we leave the private realm "we enter first, not the political realm of equality, but the social sphere."[49] Ellison's central dispute with her argument is that the children sent out into this situation are destined one day to confront the realities of the social sphere. Ellison seems sympathetic to Arendt's idea that "psychologically, the situation of being unwanted is more difficult to bear than outright persecution."[50] yet still in disagreement when he says, "It is a harsh requirement, but if he fails this basic test, his life will be even harsher."[51]

Arendt believed that outside of the schools of Little Rock was a moment where people could have walked out of the "protective four walls of our private homes" and directly into a sphere that asserted the principle of equality, which is the "innermost principle of the body politic."[52] Ellison's criticism implies that Arendt misreads the situation. Where she sees African-American parents sending children out to fight a political battle for them, Ellison argues that this action is strictly a lesson in teaching the realities of the social sphere that Arendt herself claims has discrimination as its innermost principle. Young-Bruehl writes that Arendt sent a letter to Ellison saying that, "It is precisely this ideal of sacrifice which I didn't understand" and that she "abandoned her judgement that parvenu social behavior was being demanded of black children."[53]

While Ellison was certainly highly critical of Arendt's remarks, they were essentially engaged in a discussion over whether or not the situation regarding "Little Rock" was a public or social matter and what Arendt called her "first question" regarding the essay, "what would I do if I were a Negro mother?"[54] Ellison's critique was not so much arguing with Arendt's analytical construction as it was addressing the fact that she had fundamentally misread the situation in the first place.

Arendt claims that she asked herself two more questions that motivated her writing in this essay. The second question merely asks the same question as the first with the race of the mother changed to White, which makes the flaws Ellison exposes in her first question apparent as well. Her third question, however, returns us to an understanding of the convergence of thought with Tocqueville and Montesquieu, as she asks a question we could envision them also posing about this situation, "what distinguishes the so-called Southern way of life from the American way of life with respect to the color question?"[55]

According to Arendt the answer to this question is "that while discrimination and segregation are the rule of law in the whole country, they are enforced by legislation only in the Southern States." The South had a different relationship to law than does the rest of America, because it has merged the characteristics of

society with the political. This relationship to law includes passing laws that enforce segregation in social and political situations such as marriage and voting
rights. At the same time, Southern society turned its back on the force of law
when it came to commands from the national government to desegregate. Arendt
notes that a public opinion poll conducted in Virginia showed "that 79% denied
any obligation to accept the Supreme Court decision as binding . . . The so-called
liberals and moderates of the South are simply those who are law abiding, and they
have dwindled to a minority of 21%."[56] These results lead Arendt to say:

> The sorry fact was that the town's law-abiding citizens left the streets to the mob,
> that neither white nor black citizens felt it their duty to see the Negro children safely
> to school. That is, even prior to the arrival of Federal troops, law-abiding Southern-
> ers had decided that enforcement of the law against mob rule and protection of
> their children against adult mobsters were none of their business. In other words, the
> arrival of troops did little more than change passive into massive resistance.[57]

Forced integration led to a switch from "passive" to "massive" resistance because
there was no political realm where the issue could be mediated. There was no
hope of a concerted effort from either party. Arendt writes that, "Power and violence are opposites; where the one rules absolutely, the other is absent. Violence
appears when power is in jeopardy, but left to its own course it ends in power's
disappearance."[58] In Little Rock, violence appeared on the stage both in the form
of intimidation by segregationists and with the appearance of armed Federal Law
enforcement agents.

When Arendt writes, "Strictly speaking, the franchise and eligibility for office
are the only political rights, and they constitute a modern democracy and the quin-
tessence of citizenship,"[59] she is making a statement about what she feels is truly
the missing ingredient that cures the political ill of segregation. It is not simply
to acquire equal access to certain public places, but to try to guarantee that this
flows from the reality of equal citizenship. This idea of "massive resistance" to
combat the "passive resistance" of much of the white population's indifference to
segregation echoes Tocqueville's concern about the relationship between equality
and despotism. Tocqueville wrote, "I believe that it is easier to establish an absolute
and despotic government in a people where conditions are equal than in any other,"
and then a few sentences later, "Despotism therefore appears to me particularly
dreaded in democratic ages."[60] The common theme in the way that Arendt and
Tocqueville are treating equality appears to be a long-term fear about what a lack
of regard for the means to reaching equality can do to a people.

Robert S. Boynton writes about Arendt's "Reflections:" "While in the short
run classrooms would become integrated, Arendt believed that America would do
itself irreparable future harm by failing to make African-American political equality its first priority."[61] This reasoning, Boynton concludes, persists in the wake of
what many have considered a disappointing fifty-year legacy of *Brown v. Board*. He
notes that scholars of school integration like Orlando Patterson today advocate,

"some very Arendtian positions, arguing that it 'makes more sense in many cases to concentrate on those measures that will first integrate neighborhoods and occupations and let the integration of schools follow from them.'"[62]

What remains valuable from Arendt's "Reflections" to contemporary analysis of the problem of integration is twofold. First, there is Arendt's desire to understand and emphasize the importance of the "public sphere," the space in which we appear to one another as equals. Second, there is a weariness of grabbing the so-called "other end of the stick" and starting with remedying what should flow from political equality as opposed to establishing the latter as the source. This emphasis on the equality of outcomes as opposed to the freedom to appear before others was a theme emphasized by Tocqueville as well. "In times of equality, each individual is naturally isolated . . . In our day a citizen who is oppressed has therefore only one means of defending himself; it is to address the nation as a whole, and if it is deaf to him, the human race."[63] This appeal, which Tocqueville believes can be achieved through the freedom of the press, requires the ability to appear before those being appealed to as equals, regardless of the medium. Arendt makes it clear through her insistence on emphasizing voting rights and marriage rights that the commonality that allows us to appear to one another as equals must come from the fact that we approach each other equally as citizens in equal standing.

The problem of racism in America was not, and is not, strictly limited to the domain of Southern States, but what was troubling to Arendt was that the racism in the South had soaked through so much as to be incorporated into the law in ways that made African Americans diminished citizens. Segregation in education and in access to other public facilities were seen by Arendt as symptoms, and equality in terms of citizenship, which is to say equality in the possibility and the ability to act, that she proposes as a means to lessening their effects.

Conclusion

There is no panacea for such problems as racism, imperialism, slavery, and genocide, which is not to say that the intellectual history of the twentieth century has not considered many potential cure alls. Arendt's work allows us to reject the idea that there is some sort of magic in progress, self-interest, or even enlightenment. She notes that, "the idea that one can change the world by educating the children in the spirit of the future has been one of the hallmarks of utopias since antiquity."[64] This idea that education can somehow create a new "spirit of the future" divorced from the spirit of today could only conceivably work, "if the children are really separated from their parents" or other similar measures are taken such as "what happens in tyrannies."[65] There is no one thing that can be done to set the task of solving these great problems on an automatic path because such a change, like the hypothetical children in this argument, would not stand alone in the world apart from all of the other swirling forces and actors who are continuously remaking the world picture.

Arendt believes that miracles do not simply happen, but instead "we know the author of the 'miracles.' It is men who perform them."[66] The "men" she is talking about are at least as complex as the world in which they find themselves, and the problem of politics, the problem of navigating the relationships between these complex people and their complex worlds and realms, remains an immensely difficult challenge. The recognition of this fact is an important first step to gaining an understanding of politics, and it does not seem wide of the mark to acknowledge the role of Montesquieu and Tocqueville in guiding Arendt to this understanding. Much of this chapter can be captured in the quotation, "force can, indeed must, be centralized in order to be effective, but power cannot and must not." This quotation comes from Arendt, but it would not be shocking in the least to have found it in Montesquieu. In the next sentence Arendt goes on to note, "If the various sources from which it springs are dried up, the whole structure becomes impotent."[67] She is referring to integration in the American South, but her sentence can be widely applied to these sorts of struggles throughout the world.

Lieutenant General Dallaire summarized a profoundly simple yet deeply challenging concept when he said, "to be quite candid and soldierly, who the hell cared about Rwanda?"[68] The victims of racism, imperialism, slavery, and genocide have stood outside of the societies that have persecuted them, and have no means to appear in the political arena to plead their case, as Tocqueville wrote, either to the nation or the human race. Beyond this, the public realm carried significance for Arendt because it is, "reserved for individuality; it was the only place where men could show who they really and inexchangeably were."[69] Tocqueville worried about a democratic despotism, free of a place to appear, that "not only would it oppress men, but in the long term it would rob each of them of the principal attributes of humanity."[70]

There is rightful concern that deemphasizing the social question can manifest itself as uncaring for the miserable conditions of those in need. There is also rightful concern that there is no apparent means to create changes in the mores, laws, memories, and so on, of people who can effectively create any hope for reconstituting ourselves with an orientation toward more successfully facing the problems of racism. These concerns, however, at least deserve to be considered in conjunction with the problems of the day. Today, much of the public in the West receives a fragmented account of what is happening in Sudan, just as much of the public is largely unaware of the tenuous regimes in Central Asia which, like the monarchies that Montesquieu predicted would fall, are witnessing their sources of legitimacy crumble beneath their feet, while the masses of the impoverished gather in resistance groups and wait to burst onto the scene. When problems like this spring forth in the world, we will again be forced to the same choice as always: we may seek to find a solution, or we may continue to hide the dead bodies.

Notes

1. Elisabeth Young-Bruehl, *Hannah Arendt: For Love of the World* (New Haven, 1982), 322.
2. Hannah Arendt, *On Violence* (San Diego, 1970), 43.
3. Hannah Arendt, *On Revolution* (London, 1990), 151.
4. Hannah Arendt, *The Human Condition* (New York, 1958), 212–13.
5. Gunter Gauss, "What Remains? The Language Remains," in *The Portable Hannah Arendt*, ed. Peter Baehr (New York, 2000), 5.
6. Ronald Beiner, ed., *Hannah Arendt: Lectures on Kant* (Chicago, 1992), 8.
7. Arendt, *On Revolution*, 152.
8. Hannah Arendt, "Reflections on Little Rock," in *The Portable Hannah Arendt*, ed. Baehr, 234.
9. Arendt, *On Revolution*, 187.
10. Montesquieu, *The Spirit of the Laws*, ed. Raymond Geuss and Quentin Skinner, (Cambridge, UK, 1989), 310.
11. Robert Nozick, *Anarchy, State, and Utopia* (New York, 1974), ix.
12. John Rawls, *Justice as Fairness: A Restatement* (Cambridge, MA, 2001), 5 (Part I, Section 2.1).
13. Jeffrey Isaac, *Arendt, Camus, and Modern Rebellion* (New Haven, 1992), 11.
14. Montesquieu, *The Spirit of the Laws*, 231.
15. Alexis De Tocqueville, *Democracy in America* (Chicago, 2002), 20.
16. Arendt, *On Revolution*, 153.
17. Ibid., 153–54.
18. Elisabeth Young-Bruehl, "From the Pariah's Point of View: Reflections on Hannah Arendt's Life and Work," in *Hannah Arendt: The Recovery of the Public World*, ed. Melvyn A. Hill (New York, 1979), 24.
19. Hannah Arendt, *The Origins of Totalitarianism* (San Diego, 1968), 139.
20. Ibid., 142.
21. Ibid., 144.
22. Ibid.
23. Arendt, *The Human Condition*, 35–45.
24. Ibid., 24.
25. Arendt, *On Revolution*, 77.
26. Ibid., 114.
27. Ibid.
28. Ibid., 167.
29. Ibid.
30. Ibid., 167–68.
31. Arendt, *On Violence*, 44.
32. Arendt, *On Revolution*, 151–52.
33. Ibid., 153.
34. Ibid., 117.
35. Ibid., 18.
36. Arendt, *The Human Condition*, 74.
37. Ibid.
38. Arendt, *On Revolution*, 114.
39. Arendt, *Origins*, 5.
40. Ibid.
41. Samantha Power, *"A Problem from Hell": America and the Age of Genocide* (New York, 2002), 23.
42. Arendt, *Origins*, 4.
43. Ibid.
44. Arendt, "Reflections on Little Rock," 235.
45. Young-Bruehl, *Hannah Arendt: For Love of the World*, 316.
46. Ibid.

47. Ibid.
48. Ibid.
49. Arendt, "Reflections on Little Rock," 237.
50. Ibid., 244.
51. Young-Bruehl, *Hannah Arendt: For Love of the World,* 316.
52. Arendt, "Reflections on Little Rock," 237.
53. Young-Bruehl, *Hannah Arendt: For Love of the World.*
54. Hannah Arendt, "Reflections on Little Rock: A Reply to Critics," in *The Portable Hannah Arendt,* ed. Baehr, 244.
55. Ibid., 245.
56. Arendt, "Reflections on Little Rock," 235.
57. Ibid.
58. Arendt, *On Violence,* 56.
59. Arendt, "Reflections on Little Rock," 237.
60. De Tocqueville, *Democracy in America,* 666.
61. Robert S. Boynton, "F for Effort," *Bookforum* (2004).
62. Ibid.
63. De Tocqueville, *Democracy in America,* 668.
64. Arendt, "Reflections on Little Rock," 246.
65. Ibid.
66. Hannah Arendt, "What Is Freedom?" in *Between Past and Future* (New York, 1993), 171.
67. Arendt, "Reflections on Little Rock," 241.
68. Philip Gourevitch, *We Wish to Inform You That Tomorrow We Will Be Killed with Our Families* (New York, 1998), 168.
69. Arendt, *The Human Condition,* 38.
70. De Tocqueville, *Democracy in America,* 666.

Chapter 13

THE HOLOCAUST AND "THE HUMAN"

Dan Stone

Two worlds face one another—the men of God and the men of
Satan! The Jew is the anti-man, the creature of another god. He
must have come from another root of the human race. I set the
Aryan and the Jew over against each other; and if I call one of them
a human being I must call the other something else. The two are as
widely separated as man and beast. Not that I would call the Jew a
beast. He is much further from the beasts than we Aryans. He is a
creature outside nature and alien to nature.

—Adolf Hitler

We are segregated and separated from the world and the fullness
thereof, driven out of the society of the human race.

—Chaim Kaplan

At Auschwitz, not only man died, but the idea of man.

—Elie Wiesel[1]

It may or may not be the case, as an eminent literary critic wants us to believe, that
Shakespeare is to be credited with inventing our notion of "the human."[2] It is,
however, apparently clear who destroyed it. "It seems," Jacob Talmon wrote forty
years ago, "that nazism achieved considerable success in stifling in many of its
adherents the sense of the unity of the human species."[3] On the one hand, then,
we should not be surprised to find critics such as Aimé Césaire talking of "pseudo-
humanism" in the wake of colonialism and the Holocaust. Césaire says of humanism that "for too long it has diminished the rights of man," and is thus tempted
to dismiss any notion of "the human" as "sordidly racist." On the other hand, one
might be justified in arguing, with Martha Nussbaum, that the Nazis' attempt to
exclude certain groups from its purview should lead us back to the search for a

minimal definition of "the human" from which no one can be excluded.[4] Despite being sympathetic to the first view, in what follows I argue that after Auschwitz, and following Arendt, rather than rejecting humanism *tout court*, a notion of "the human" needs to be found that is neither divisible nor imperialist, racist, or paternalist. This is what Paul Gilroy calls "planetary humanism," a humanism that seeks to mediate between the local or culturally sensitive and the universal.[5]

At the heart of Nazism lay a radical philosophical anthropological challenge: a calling into question of what it means to be human. In this chapter, I respond to this challenge by showing what it is about the Holocaust that demands our continued attention; in other words, what it means to take the "post" in "post-Auschwitz" seriously. I will do so by appealing to the notion of "the human." In the process, I will not trawl comprehensively through all recent Holocaust historiography but will range widely but selectively through some of that literature, applying to it concepts borrowed from Hannah Arendt.

For Arendt, one of the most insightful critics of Nazism, it was precisely the fact that the totalitarian regime destroyed the possibility of political action, depriving its victims of the anthropological status of human beings, which constituted the awful uniqueness of the Holocaust.[6] Sadly, Arendt's view was achieved only at the price of a certain ethnocentrism, which meant that she valorized the sufferings of the Jews over earlier genocides, particularly those of antiquity. In Queensland, colonial settlers regularly referred to the Aborigines as "pests" to be "got rid of" and, as George Carrington put it in 1871, the Aborigine "has come to be considered in the light of a troublesome wild animal, to be shot and hunted down, whenever seen in the open country."[7] And Henry Morgenthau, U.S. ambassador to Turkey, had already described the genocide of the Armenians in similar terms: "When the caravans first started, the individuals bore some resemblance to human beings; in a few hours, however, the dust of the road plastered their faces and clothes, the mud caked their lower members, and the slowly advancing mobs, frequently bent with fatigue and crazed by the brutality of their 'protectors,' resembled some new and animal species."[8] More disturbingly, this ethnocentrism left Arendt apparently less moved by the treatment of colonial subjects during the nineteenth and twentieth centuries. Colonialism's victims fell, in her terminology, into the category *animal laborans*, "natural" men who had not developed the capacity for political activity, and whose murder therefore lacked the same poignancy as that of civilized people.[9]

Nevertheless, Arendt's insight that the essence of the Holocaust lay neither in the number of victims nor even in the use of modern technology and bureaucracy to implement it but in its anthropological assault, "making human beings as human beings superfluous,"[10] carries great weight, and need not be reserved exclusively for the genocide of the Jews. In what follows I argue that the reason for the Holocaust's enduring power to fascinate and repel, to draw us recurrently into the depths of depravity even as it forces us away, lies precisely in this all-out war against the notion of "the human" that had characterized Western thought since the days of Shakespeare (whether or not he was the major architect of this new creature—a claim, it has to be admitted, which stretches the imagination somewhat). I will make this argument, however, in the light of other such attacks, in particular the 1994 Rwandan genocide, in order not to follow Arendt's ethnocentric presumptions. For while I believe that the Holocaust does demand our special attention, it should not do so at the expense of other victims of Western duplicity.

In a famous letter to Jaspers written shortly after the war, Arendt first put forward an insight that she would develop in her subsequent works: "Perhaps what is behind it all is only that individual human beings did not kill other individual human beings for human reasons, but that an organized attempt was made to eradicate the concept of the human being."[11] Although in *The Origins of Totalitarianism* (1951), Arendt set out an argument that was meant to apply equally to Nazi Germany and the Soviet Union, her claims have stood the test of time far better where her analysis of Nazism is concerned, as the following discussion will show. Although Arendt's claims about both systems carrying out terror in the name of Laws of History is correct,[12] her analysis turns again and again to the death camps, a feature not of the Soviet Gulag (whose atrociousness lies elsewhere—this brief discussion is not meant to downplay its significance or horror) but of the Nazi regime.

Arendt's basic claim, then, is that the camps lie at the heart of the Nazi project, for they were the places where human nature was to be reshaped according to "the very realistic totalitarian attempt to rob man of his nature under the pretext of changing it."[13] Thus, it is not actually so much a question of 'reshaping' human nature as attempting to deny it altogether to certain categories of people.

> Both [totalitarian systems] mean to make human beings in their infinite variety and their unique individuality superfluous. . . . the camps serve, among other purposes, as laboratories in which human beings of the most varied kinds are reduced to an always constant collection of reactions and reflexes. . . . The concentration camps not only eradicate people; they also further the monstrous experiment, under scientifically exacting conditions, of destroying spontaneity as an element of human behavior and of transforming people into something that is even less than animal, namely, a bundle of reactions that, given the same set of conditions, will always react in the same way.[14]

There are two slightly different arguments at work here. One concerns the inmates of the camps, those who were being "re-educated" or "taught" to behave and think differently; this applies both to Nazism and Stalinism. Here Arendt observes the ways in which the two regimes tried to mold human beings so that they conformed to the same laws or norms of behavior and thought. The other concerns the death camps, which applies only to the Third Reich, and in which Arendt observes the Nazis' attempt to rid the world of certain people, primarily Jews, in order to redefine what it is to be human. The first may be summarized by Arendt's claim that:

> Totalitarian lawfulness, executing the laws of Nature or History, does not bother to translate them into standards of right and wrong for individual human beings, but applies them directly to the "species," to mankind. The laws of Nature or His-

tory, if properly executed, are expected to produce as their end a single "Mankind," and it is this expectation that lies behind the claim to global rule of all totalitarian governments.[15]

The second may be summarized as follows:

> it is surprising to see how, for all practical political purposes, these ideologies always result in the same "law" of elimination of individuals for the sake of the process or progress of the species. . . . this mankind which is the end and at the same time the embodiment of either History or Nature requires permanent sacrifices, the permanent elimination of hostile or parasitic or unhealthy classes or races in order to enter upon its bloody eternity.[16]

Both, however, come together to the extent that "[t]he purity of the experiment would be compromised if one admitted even as a remote possibility that these specimens of the species *homo sapiens* had ever existed as real human beings."[17] Thus, whether through the harsh regimes of the concentration camps or the policy of annihilation carried out at the death camps, Nazism sought to realize the "Laws of Nature"—that is, to bring about the triumph of the Aryan race, thus ending the struggle between the forces of good and evil that drove History—by redefining "the human." The final goal of both Nazism and Stalinism, according to Arendt, was not a "traditional" one of territorial or imperial domination or of revolutionizing political systems; rather, it was something more frightening: "What totalitarian ideologies therefore aim at is not the transformation of the outside world or the revolutionizing transmutation of society, but the transformation of human nature itself."[18]

✻

From a historian's perspective, Arendt's insights are useful where they reveal the conceptual limits of the current historiography of the Holocaust. Although the detailed empirical research on the Holocaust continues to expand and to make imaginative and innovative use of previously unused archives, especially in the former Communist countries of Eastern Europe, it is often undertaken with scant regard to broader interpretations of the Holocaust, the reasons that have given rise to such enormous interest in the subject in the first place. Arendt's theorizing about the Holocaust and "the human" provides a helpful theoretical supplement to much of the empirical scholarship.

Recent historical research has started uncovering in great detail the "mundanities" of the genocide of the Jews. It seems that the murder of the Jews in the occupied eastern territories was first begun under "economic" pressures: the necessity of feeding an occupied population *and* a huge occupying force in the autumn and winter of 1941. Only later, in this reading, with the declaration of war against the United States, was the step taken to full-scale murder of all the European Jews.[19] Hence the Wannsee Conference of 20 January 1942 has, in the eyes of at least one scholar, regained its historiographical status as the vital meeting to determine the course of the "Final Solution," that most historians have long denied it.[20] Yet while this pattern of events is clear enough—and it is, of course, open to dispute—it does not really explain the choice of the Jews as the victims. Only a more "traditional" emphasis on *Judenpolitik*— that is, on Nazi ideology (without necessarily seeing the command structure of genocide in the anarchic occupied territories as the rigid pyramid of the *Führerprinzip*)—can help in showing why the Jews became the victims of this "rationalizing" decision-making process. Once one sees this fact, it is also clear that the emphasis on the economic or logistic aspects of the decision for genocide omits something vital.

Although the—mainly German—scholars who have undertaken this research in the newly available Eastern European archives are to be applauded for expanding our knowledge of the course of events in 1941–1942, they do a disservice to understanding the origins of the Holocaust if they take these logistical problems to be the *cause* of the murders in anything but the most limited, short-term sense. One does not need to think of ideology in terms of a monolithic propaganda machine bearing down on the subjects and soldiers of the Third Reich, as in a typical 1950s understanding of totalitarianism. Rather, the workings of fantasy, of the desire to murder the Jews, or even the belief that the world would be a better place without them, with no accompanying feelings of enjoyment, purification, or ecstatic participation in the community's destiny, are all essential to understanding the background to the decision to murder the Jews (and not some other dispossessed group), and *precede* any problem of military supplies or occupation economics.

In the context of the Rwandan genocide, Philip Gourevitch write that, "For those who set about systematically exterminating an entire people . . . blood lust surely helps. But the engineers and perpetrators of a genocide . . . need not enjoy killing, and they may even find it unpleasant. What is required above all is that they want their victims dead. They have to want it so badly that they consider it a necessity."[21] We know that only a minority of the perpetrators of the Holocaust were fanatical Nazis. For most, murder became something they felt had to be done, as the numerous letters and diaries written by the participants testify. Peer pressure to participate may, as Christopher Browning asserts, have played a role,[22] but without a sense that what they were being asked to do was in some sense right, the "ordinary men" of the Holocaust would have surely taken longer to become used to their work. When one member of *Sonderkommando* 4a (a subdivision of the *Einsatzgruppen*) testifies that, " [i]t's almost impossible to imagine what nerves of steel it took to carry out that dirty work there. It was horrible,"[23] it becomes clear that participation in murder must have been with the feeling that one was serving a greater good, not simply obtaining for oneself and one's colleagues larger food rations. One must remember that, for the Nazis, "all roads lead to the Jew."[24]

The same applies to the later, so-called industrial stage of the genocide, the use of gas chambers to murder the Jews *en masse* without the killers having to involve themselves in nasty, face-to-face operations. But there is more to the camps than simply the final developmental stage of Nazi murder, "the place in which the most absolute *conditio inhumana* that has ever existed on earth was realized," the "anus mundi."[25] They embody the Nazi understanding of the world, as Alain Finkielkraut, following Arendt, explains:

> In such a system, the concentration camps are perhaps not economically useful, but they are ontologically necessary. Because, in order to assure the reign of the single will *[la volonté unique]*, it is at the same time necessary to liquidate the Enemy of man, and to liquidate in man spontaneity, singularity, the unforeseeable, in short everything which makes up the unique character of the human person. The mills of death are equally *laboratories of humanity without human beings.*[26]

It is necessary to back up these claims. I will do so in two ways: first, by referring to the writings of Holocaust victims—diarists and survivors—in order to establish how they perceived themselves during the period of the genocide, and how the perpetrators viewed them. Second, I will develop what these testimonies reveal about the concept of "the human" by framing it in a discussion of the Holocaust's implications for the concept of anthropology. This discussion will, of necessity, be no more than a pointer to future work, work which will need to consider the anthropological implications of the Holocaust in the light of other genocides, especially that in Rwanda.

✣

In his description of Treblinka, Jankiel Wiernik paints many horrific scenes, of which the following is typical:

> One of the Germans, a man named Sepp, was a vile and savage beast, who took special delight in torturing children. When he pushed women around and they begged him to stop because they had children with them, he would frequently snatch a child from the woman's arms and either tear the child in half or grab it by the legs, smash its head against a wall and throw the body away. Such incidents were by no means isolated. Tragic scenes of this kind occurred all the time.[27]

Wiernik's description is of the variety that often gets dismissed in Holocaust literature as an "exception," an interruption by a rare moment of sadism to the relentless rhythm of industrial murder. But murder in the death camps was not self-sustaining, mechanical; it required the brutal participation of many guards, often Balts and Ukranians, and SS-men. Sepp's murderous activities were in fact part of the everyday reality at Treblinka just as they were of the other concentration and death camps. What permitted such outbursts of rage and destructive violence?

There are many psychological studies of aggression which show that violence need not be instrumental, that in an environment where the usual, "civilized" checks on behavior are withdrawn, whether through personal choice or through state decree, people will exercise "barbaric" instincts (a word we still insist on using, as if to comfort ourselves, despite all that happened in the twentieth century, that there is something atavistic about violence, that it surely cannot be typical of modern societies[28]). Nevertheless, in the case of sustained murder, there must be more to the killings than a sudden outburst of energy or repressed rage. Perpetrators must also believe that their victims are unworthy of life. In the case of the Holocaust there is much to be said—especially in the face of the academically successful interpretation of the murders as industrial and somehow "neat"—for seeing the genocide as an outburst of excess energy.[29] However, without the years of Nazi ideology portraying the Jews as "anti-human" (*Gegenmenschen*), it is not possible to understand why the outburst, when it occurred, focused especially on the Jews.[30]

The first thing to note is that, in contrast to the scholars who are fascinated by the concept of "factory-line death," Holocaust testimonies are pervaded by this atmosphere of violence, an all-encompassing mood which regularly breaks open into actual acts of violence, like those described above by Wiernik, a "work-Jew" in Treblinka. The contrast is equally noticeable in the difference between the photographs taken by the SS of the killing process in Auschwitz-Birkenau in 1944 (the so-called Lili Jacob Album), which depicts the scene as orderly and tightly-controlled, and the drawings made after his liberation by child survivor Thomas Geve, whose innocent eye reveals far more about the chaotic reality that actually prevailed.[31] Most importantly, many of them voice the profound feeling—the feeling that broke so many of their comrades or fellow-*Häftlinge*—that they are no longer human, or will shortly cease to be so. A few examples will suffice to illustrate this point.

Many survivors testify to the feeling of being excluded from the ranks of humanity, or to the fact that others were so excluded. Primo Levi knew his work-mate *Null Achtzehn* only by number: "He is Null Achtzehn. He is not called anything except that, Zero Eighteen, the last three figures of his entry number; as if everyone was aware that only a man is worthy of a name, and that Null Achtzehn is no longer a man."[32] Rudolf Reder, one of the two known survivors of the Bełżec death camp, noted of the "work-Jews" in his 1946 testimony that, "We moved around like people without a will of their own: like one body. . . . We were just carrying on this dreadful existence mechanically."[33] The writings of the *Sonderkommando* men in Auschwitz, known as the "Scrolls of Auschwitz," also testify to this denial of human status to the victims and to their own sense of dehumanization. For example, Zalman Gradowski, the most eloquent of the writers, invited his future readers to "[f]orget your wife and children, your friends and acquaintances, forget the world you came from. Imagine that what you are seeing are not people, but despicable animals, animals which must be eliminated, for if not—your eyes will grow dim."[34]

And this perception applied just as much to the ghettos as it did to the camps. In Łódź, for example, the young diarist Dawid Sierakowiak noted on 20 May 1942, that, "We are not considered humans at all; cattle for work or slaughter."[35] Or, as the Polish underground courier Jan Karski said of the Warsaw ghetto, which he had visited after being smuggled in by two Jewish leaders: "It was not a world. It was not a part of humanity. I was not part of it. I did not belong there.—I was told that these were human beings—they didn't look like human beings."[36] Karski's testimony in Lanzmann's *Shoah* actually follows very closely what he had written over thirty years earlier in *Story of a Secret State*, the book he published on his arrival in the United States in 1944. There he wrote of how hard it was to describe the ghetto: "A cemetery? No, for these bodies were still moving, were indeed often violently agitated. These were still living people, if you could call them such. For apart from their skin, eyes, and voice there was nothing human left in these palpitating figures."[37]

Jews in all circumstances during the Holocaust experienced this same sensation of fighting to hold on to their human status. Naomi Samson has recounted how, in hiding in a small underground shelter in Poland, she began to feel as if she were becoming an animal. Through a crack in the shelter, she could see animals eating on the farm in which she and her family were being hidden:

> My eyes nearly popped out watching them chew and drool over the food as they were eating. As I felt my tears and my saliva dripping onto my cold hands, I licked my hands without taking my eyes from those animals, "Lucky animals!" I thought. Why couldn't I be one? (Actually, I felt I *was* an animal in those days—an underprivileged animal.)[38]

Of course, many of the Jewish victims realized what was being done to them, and testified to it later on. In Warsaw, Adina Blady Szwajger, a nurse in the children's home, understood what the ghetto was doing to its inmates. Recounting a conversation with Fajgele, one of the children, she writes: "Somehow it turned out that we were talking like equals. That we were all equally afraid and that we, too, didn't have much to eat but if we wanted to survive, we had to try to live like human beings, we had to remain human because they wanted to turn us into animals."[39] Or, as another survivor put it, "from the instant I grasped the motivating principle . . . it was as if I had awakened from a dream . . . I felt under orders to live. . . . And if I did die in Auschwitz, to die as a human being. . . . And a terrible struggle begun which went on day and night."[40] No more proof is needed of the truth of Arendt's claim that, "Extermination happens to human beings who for all practical purposes are already 'dead.'"[41]

These quotations then are not mere metaphors; rather they are literal descriptions of the victims' condition. The figure of the *Muselmann* is the ultimate proof of this process of dehumanization, for the *Muselmann* is the archetypal image of the "not-yet-dead." Although the image of the *Muselmann* has had to serve as a trope, especially in the work of Giorgio Agamben, in actual fact the existence of these "dead on leave" testifies to the extent to which the Nazis realized their ambition of creating human beings without human status and annihilating human beings as if they were not part of the species.[42] Indeed, the Nazis, who referred to the Slavs as *Untermenschen* (subhumans) but to the Jews as *Gegenmenschen* (antihumans) were all too aware of this aim. Goebbels, for example, noted in his diary: "We travel through the ghetto. We get out and observe everything in detail. It's indescribable. These are not human beings any more, they are animals. Therefore, we have not a humanitarian task to perform, but a surgical one. One must cut here, in a radical way. Otherwise, one day, Europe will perish of the Jewish disease."[43] Nazi ideology envisaged redeeming the world from the threat posed by Jews masquerading as human beings.[44]

*

I have so far chosen to back up Arendt's claims with reference to the Holocaust, since it was Nazism that Arendt herself examined (more compellingly than her analysis of Soviet Communism) in order to arrive at her claims about the nature of the camps. But the genocide of the Jews is no longer the only example of such anthropological refashioning, if it ever was. The 1994 genocide in Rwanda is equally instructive in this regard. Advocates of the uniqueness of the Holocaust must surely run up against the strongest challenge to their claims in the slaughter, in 100 days, of over 800,000 Tutsis by their Hutu neighbors in the spring of 1994. Although on the one hand the Rwandan genocide seems to fit the pattern of most "conventional" genocides—interethnic competition flaring up in the context of longstanding political and economic rivalry—there are, on the other, many similarities with the Holocaust (apart from the fact that in the Holocaust there were not, as in most genocides, two warring factions).

Take, for example, the language used. Just as the Nazis referred to the Jews as vermin (*Ungeziefer*), so the Hutus called the Tutsis "cockroaches" (*inyenzi*): "A cockroach gives birth to another cockroach . . . The history of Rwanda shows us clearly that a Tutsi always stays exactly the same, that he has never changed. The malice, the evil are just as we knew them in the history of our country." Just as the Nazis used euphemisms like "special treatment" to mean murder, so the Hutu *génocidaires* spoke of "work," setting the murder process into a familiar cultural framework of village labor service (*umuganda*).[45] Take also the fact that the genocide was organized at the highest levels of state, something which Holocaust scholars such as Eberhard Jäckel or Steven Katz see as unique to the murder of the Jews. Take, as a corollary to this, the network of guilt established throughout Rwanda. In Germany, scholars have shown the extent to which knowledge of the murders was widespread, even if direct participation was not (nor required to be).[46] Hutu Power took this a step further, declaring over national radio (RTLM) all those who refused to take part as themselves likely to be murdered.[47] A large proportion of the population thus became an accomplice to genocide, and the country accordingly is still facing the appallingly difficult task of trying the *génocidaires*, or having local communities do so using the traditional village system of *gacaca*, since only a few very high level perpetrators can be tried at the International Criminal Tribunal in Arusha, Tanzania. Or take, finally, the *jusq'au boutiste* nature of the killing. Unlike genocides, such as in East Timor, where mass murder is of the "pacification" variety, designed to achieve a territorial-political goal, but not to murder every member of the targeted group, the Rwandan Tutsis were *all* marked out to die, *because* they were Tutsis: "at the heart of what happened in Rwanda is the fact that Tutsis were killed for having been born."[48] No wonder then that one Rwandan journalist refers to Hutu Power as "tropical Nazism."[49]

These similarities between Rwanda and the Holocaust should not blind us to the differences. In Rwanda the history of Hutu-Tutsi conflict goes back long before 1994. It should come therefore as no surprise that the occurrence of the genocide is tangled up in a murky moral grey area, not least the genocide of Hutus by Tutsis in neighboring Burundi in 1972 or the atrocities committed by the RPF troops after their overthrow of the Hutu Power regime.[50] In the Holocaust, by contrast, despite Levi's "grey zones," we have a case in which, as one scholar notes, "the distinction between victims and perpetrators is surely as clear and as simple as it is possible to be in the realm of human affairs."[51] Furthermore, while the Nazis targeted Jews all over Europe, the Interahamwe did not envisage extending its operations into Burundi in order to target Tutsis there (although the RPF did subsequently become embroiled in a regional conflict in Zaire (subsequently the Democratic Republic of Congo)—though this owed as much to control of natural resources as it did to freeing Rwanda from the threat still posed by former *génocidaires*).[52] Nevertheless, far from being the actions of "natural men," the genocide carried out by Hutu Power was based on a strong belief in the need to rid Rwanda of Tutsis, and was justified with a an ideological program (in its most basic version, the "Hutu Ten Commandments"[53]) that not only resembled Nazi anti-Semitism in terms of fantasies and phobias about the "polluting race," but that required the removal of Tutsis from the category of "human" in order to bring "peace" to Rwanda.

As in the Holocaust, this aspect of the Rwandan genocide was recognized by the victims and the perpetrators. One perpetrator refers to his victims in terms reminiscent of Agamben's "bare life" when he says that, "They had become people to throw away, so to speak."[54] Another says: "We no longer saw a human being when we turned up a Tutsi in the swamps."[55] Yet another says: "We no longer considered the Tutsis as humans or even as creatures of God."[56] A witness to a so-called "pacification" meeting in Kinyamakara reported the way in which the killings were discussed: "At the meeting, some asked, 'Is it time to stop the killing while there are still Tutsi alive?' They had no shame asking that, even in public. It was the time to kill. They did not even see that it was a human being that they were busy killing."[57] Furthermore, in Rwanda, the discourse of "the human" has also been used to criticize the failings of the international community:

> When UNAMIR was withdrawn, I heard that there were people at the United Nations who were saying that they couldn't send their soldiers to be killed at the end of the earth without a good reason. This leads me to wonder about what humanity is, about who is included in humanity and who is excluded. Why didn't the United Nations consider the people of Rwanda to be part of the humanity it is bound to protect? I haven't found an answer to this question yet.[58]

Finally, it should be noted that the opposite applies as well; that is, that recognizing the humanity of the victims is disastrous for the self-assurance of the genocidal killer:

> Still, I do remember the first person who looked at me at the moment of the deadly blow. Now that was something. The eyes of someone you kill are immortal, if they

face you at the fatal instant. They have a terrible black color. They shake you more
than the streams of blood and the death rattles, even in a great turmoil of dying.
The eyes of the killed, for the killer, are his calamity if he looks into them. They are
the blame of the person he kills.[59]

✻

Arendt's claim about the camps as laboratories for the reshaping of "the human"
can easily be illustrated, as I have shown above. But what are the consequences of
viewing the Holocaust and genocides such as that in Rwanda as having at their
heart this ill-fated dream of refashioning human nature or redefining who counts
as human in the first place? There are two points that need addressing. The first
concerns the balance to be struck between the universal and the particular, the
second the implications of this "anthropological project" for assessing the guilt of
the perpetrators. In order to make these points clearer I will turn to an important
essay by Françoise Dastur, in which she put precisely these questions to Jacques
Derrida in response to the argument in his *Of Spirit* about Heidegger's relationship
to Nazism. There are no simple answers, but in this section I seek to problematize
the use of "the human" as a guiding concept, to note its shortcomings as well as
its benefits.

The first problem, then, is this: by talking of "the human" do we not inappropriately use an all-embracing category to talk of a situation that demands careful
attention be paid to specificity, of perpetrators and victims, of time and place, and
of ideologies? By using the concept of "the human" in this way do we end by sup-
pressing difference and thus inadvertently revictimizing the victims? By seeking to
extinguish the differences that animated the perpetrators, do we also accidentally
do away with notions of difference that sustain any group's identity?[60] In Robert
Antelme's famous analysis of the SS—that they will never be all-powerful and in
fact that their dream of changing the human race means that they are "mad," does
this blanket category smother far more than it protects?[61] Is it, in Arendt's term,
"hardly consoling" to cling to a notion of an unchangeable human nature, since it
leads to the conclusion "that either man himself is being destroyed or that freedom
does not belong to man's essential capabilities"?[62] Do we, by contrast, need not a
humanist ethic, but an "antihumanist" one? Or does seeing Nazism as a humanism
only compound the problem?[63]

The second problem concerns how the crime of the Holocaust is understood
by talking in anthropological terms. Although Arendt's claims appear to provide
us with compelling insights into the nature of the Nazi project, by referring to a
"project" to redefine "the human," do we not thereby ascribe to the Holocaust a
somewhat mystical sense of grandeur, precisely the feeling that the Nazis wished
to generate in order to convince themselves that they were undertaking a work of
great importance for the future of the Aryan race?

There have been responses, of course, to the attack on "the human" carried out
by Nazism, as the UNESCO statements on race and the whole thrust of postwar
biological anthropology shows.[64] But these have been aimed at racism as such, and

not at understanding why it is that Nazism has come to acquire such a perverse fascination for the Western (and not only the Western) mind as the embodiment of evil. Perhaps the fascination comes not only from the enormity of the crime but from the problem that however one tries to conceptualize it is inadequate. As Arendt said, "The Nazi crimes, it seems to me, explode the limits of the law; and that is precisely what constitutes their monstrousness."[65] If one sees Nazism as an attack on humanism, one reinstates a potentially difference-denying universalism under the rubric of equality and "the human"; if one sees Nazism as a humanism, since it made (a certain, restricted definition of) man the "measure of all things," one perhaps facilitates the removal of all checks on human behavior, under the guise of either antihumanist ethics or social constructivism. Can one reinstate a humanism that does not permit racism, that is, the claim that some people are "more human" than others? Furthermore, the fact that Nazism can be seen as a humanism does not mean that the Nazis were in any sense relativists; rather, their stress on "the human" was the result of very clear ideas of who was and who was not fit to inhabit the earth. Arendt's notion of human nature as characterized by freedom (the "right to have rights") is perhaps an answer here, since it makes no claims about physical or cultural essences, therefore does not preclude group specificities, but nevertheless remains at the level of universal (species) applicability.[66]

Here it is necessary to turn to Dastur's essay, "Three Questions to Jacques Derrida," to seek some clarification. Dastur's paper is a response to the book *Of Spirit*, in particular to the metaphysics of evil that Derrida sketches there. While sympathetic to Derrida's attempt to understand evil, following Heidegger, as inscribed "in the profundity of the history of spirit as its internal duality or dissension *[Zwietracht]*," Dastur notes that, by doing so, one ascribes to Nazism "a properly demonic dimension," and this is what worries her.[67] It does so because seeing Nazism as demonic means that "it will become impossible for us to identify and judge those who were guilty, and we will be irresistibly inclined to take refuge in that 'spiritual' construction named 'the collective guilt of the German people' or even in 'the guilt of the whole Platonic and Christian Occident.'"[68] As she goes on:

> What will be lost is the idea that crime is always singular and individual, so that the metaphysics of *Geistlichkeit*—of a spirit that unfolds its essence in the internal possibility of evil—will inevitably fall back into a mere metaphysics of *Geistigkeit*, that is, into a metaphysical construction that cannot account for the always individual deeds and that appeal to metaphysical entities in order to explain what factually happened.[69]

The question here is whether we can talk about the Nazi assault on "the human" yet still see the singular, individual crime. Dastur's questions are: is it possible to think about Nazism without employing "metaphysical" constructions—such as "the human"—which we have tried to denounce in the context of the Holocaust as essentializations? And, by naming Nazism as demonic, do we not thereby reassure ourselves that all European thought has not been contaminated? Yet if we do not, does evil become merely banal—as is implied in the work of historians such as Götz Aly—with the result that we abandon the attempt to *understand* what happened?[70]

The challenge is to be aware of both sides of the coin and try to talk of the Nazi assault on "the human" yet still be able to see the singular, individual crime. Here Arendt can be of service, for rather than simply beginning by attributing to Nazism a "satanic greatness," as Jaspers accused her of doing,[71] and then changing her mind to affirm the "banality of evil" in the wake of the Eichmann Trial, she points to a possible way out of Dastur's impasse. Arendt did, as is well known, describe Eichmann as an example of the banality of evil, but at the same time she sought to dissociate Nazism from the Western tradition, denying that it had any affiliation with the history of Western thinking, even with nineteenth-century race-thinking, and arguing that it came "from the gutter."[72] That is to say, Arendt did not seek to understand Nazism by using "metaphysical" concepts, but she also did not "take refuge in the limits of the ethical point of view" as a result and thus "renounce the effort to understand what happened."[73] Whether her disavowal of Nazism's links with the Western tradition convinces, however, is another matter.[74] Simply asserting the banality of evil (even if this was meant only with reference to Eichmann) and denying that Nazism is linked to the Western tradition is really to suppress rather than to answer the question. Nevertheless, if one cannot say that Arendt satisfactorily deals with Dastur's concern that focusing on a "metaphysical" explanation of Nazism leads one to overlook individual guilt, at least we are made more strikingly aware of the risks involved in trying to understand the Holocaust in terms of an assault on "the human."

✳

That this attack on the human lay at the heart of the Nazi genocidal impulse has been recognized by scholars since soon after the war. So too has its implications. In his pioneering study, *Harvest of Hate* (1953), Léon Poliakov wrote that the "deep essence" of Hitlerism was:

> the fact that it was an explosion of hatred and blind fury which, in venting itself on others, in the last analysis turned against itself. From this, one may conclude that over and beyond the revolt which he led against the Judeo-Christian spirit and morality, the German *Führer* also sought to attack and destroy an essential component of all human society. It is inherent in man's nature to recognise himself in others and to revere in them his own image and essence (the double meaning of the word "humanity," which we find in all languages, can have only this significance). Mass slaughters of human beings are perpetrated on the battlefield, but by soldiers running the same risks in accordance with the rules of warfare—when one group of men slaughters another, not as adversaries and men, but as noxious insects, the price it pays for this is its own humanity.[75]

Fifty years later, in his book, *The Open*, Giorgio Agamben has noted that Linnaeus' great achievement was to define man, *Homo*, as "the animal that *is* only *if* it recognizes that it *is not*." In other words, there being no "generic difference" between man and the apes as far as Linnaeus could tell, the definition of man rested not on a scientific description (as for all the other species), but on an injunction: *nosce te ipsum* (know yourself). Agamben explains: "man has no specific identity other than the *ability* to recognize himself. Yet to define the human not through any *nota characteristica*, but rather through his self-knowledge, means that man is the being which recognizes itself as such, that *man is the animal that must recognize itself as human to be human*."[76] Perhaps what the Nazis did was to put the Jews in the place of the apes, thereby seeking to *know themselves* as human. What they did not realize was that—as in medieval iconography, in which "the ape holds a mirror in which the man who sins must recognize himself as *simia dei* (ape of God)"—they thereby made themselves into something less than human, by "sinning" against the indivisible unity of the human species. The Nazis did not simply object to cultural or ethnic differences; rather, they sought—following to its logical conclusion the thrust of nineteenth-century race-thinking—to divide the human species into separate races, and even, in the case of the Jews, to remove certain people from the category of human altogether. That they dehumanized themselves in the process shows both the extraordinariness of the ambition and its impossibility, its abject and horrific failure. "Just as the victims in the death factories or the holes of oblivion are no longer 'human' in the eyes of their executioners, so this newest species of criminals is beyond the pale even of solidarity in human sinfulness."[77]

Notes

1. Hermann Rauschning, *Hitler Speaks: A Series of Political Conversations with Adolf Hitler on his Real Aims* (London, 1939), 238. Chaim A. Kaplan, *Scroll of Agony: The Warsaw Diary of Chaim A. Kaplan*, ed. and trans. Abraham I. Katsh (New York, 1965), 225, entry for 17 November 1940. Elie Wiesel, *Legends of Our Time* (New York, 1968), 1. My thanks to Joel Isaac, Richard King, and Angie Simon for their comments on earlier versions of this chapter.
2. Harold Bloom, *Shakespeare: The Invention of the Human* (London, 1999).
3. J. L. Talmon, "Mission and Testimony: The Universal Significance of Modern Anti-Semitism," in his *The Unique and the Universal: Some Historical Reflections* (London, 1965), 163.
4. Aimé Césaire, *Discourse on Colonialism* (New York, 1972), 15; Martha C. Nussbaum, "Human Functioning and Social Justice: in Defense of Aristotelian Essentialism," *Political Theory* 20, no. 2 (1992): 202–246.
5. Paul Gilroy, *Between Camps: Nations, Cultures and the Allure of Race* (Harmondsworth, 2000), 327–356. See also Kenan Malik, *The Meaning of Race: Race, History and Culture in Western Society* (Basingstoke, 1996); idem., "Making a Difference: Culture, Race and Social Policy," *Patterns of Prejudice* 39, no. 4 (2005): 361–378; Kwame Anthony Appiah, *The Ethics of Identity* (Princeton, 2005).
6. See my "Ontology or Bureaucracy? Hannah Arendt's Early Interpretation of the Holocaust," in *History, Memory and Mass Atrocity: Essays on the Holocaust and Genocide* (London, 2006), 53–69.
7. Cited in Alison Palmer, *Colonial Genocide* (Adelaide, 2000), 44.
8. Henry Morgenthau, *Ambassador Morgenthau's Story* (Garden City, NY, 1919), 313, cited in Debórah Dwork and Robert Jan Van Pelt, *Holocaust: A History* (London, 2002), 39.

9. Shiraz Dossa, "Human Status and Politics: Hannah Arendt on the Holocaust," *Canadian Journal of Political Science* 13, no. 2 (1980): 309–323. For the term *animal laborans,* as well as the other human types described by Arendt—*homo faber,* and *animal rationale*—see Hannah Arendt, *The Human Condition* (Chicago, 1958). See also Mary G. Dietz, "Arendt and the Holocaust," in *The Cambridge Companion to Hannah Arendt,* ed. Dana Villa (Cambridge, 2000), 86–109 for a convincing discussion of the importance of the terms developed in *The Human Condition* as a response to the Holocaust, and Richard Shorten's chapter in this volume for a demonstration of the fact that Arendt's categories developed with reference to Stalinism and Nazism can be used to think about nineteenth-century imperialism. It is also worth noting, as Ira Katznelson points out, that Arendt's Eurocentrism was "not celebratory," but was meant to act as an impetus for Europe to set its house in order. See his *Desolation and Enlightenment: Political Knowledge after Total War, Totalitarianism, and the Holocaust* (New York, 2003), 70. See also Alfons Söllner, "Hannah Arendt's The Origins of Totalitarianism in its Original Context," *European Journal of Political Theory* 3, no. 2 (2004): 219–238, and Pascal Grosse, "From Colonialism to National Socialism to Postcolonialism: Hannah Arendt's *The Origins of Totalitarianism,*" *Postcolonial Studies* 9, no. 1 (2006): 35–52.

10. Hannah Arendt to Karl Jaspers, 4 March 1951, in *Hannah Arendt / Karl Jaspers Correspondence 1926–1969,* ed. Lotte Kohler and Hans Saner (San Diego, 1992), 166. For discussions see Richard J. Bernstein, *Hannah Arendt and the Jewish Question* (Cambridge, 1996), 88–100; Dana R. Villa, *Politics, Philosophy, Terror: Essays on the Thought of Hannah Arendt* (Princeton, 1999), 11–38.

11. Arendt to Jaspers, 17 December 1946, in *Arendt / Jaspers Correspondence,* 69.

12. See Tony Barta's essay in this volume.

13. Hannah Arendt, "Understanding and Politics (The Difficulties of Understanding)," in *Essays in Understanding 1930–1954,* ed. Jerome Kohn (New York, 1994), 316.

14. Hannah Arendt, "Mankind and Terror," in *Essays in Understanding,* 304.

15. Hannah Arendt, "On The Nature of Totalitarianism," in *Essays in Understanding,* 340.

16. Ibid., 341.

17. Arendt, "Mankind and Terror," 305.

18. Hannah Arendt, *The Origins of Totalitarianism,* rev. ed. (San Diego, 1979), 458. It is important to note here Eric Voegelin's criticism of Arendt in his important review of *Origins:* "A 'nature' cannot be changed or transformed; a 'change of nature' is a contradiction of terms; tampering with the 'nature' of a thing means destroying the thing." For Voegelin this suggested that Arendt had adopted the same "immanentist ideology" as the "totalitarians." See "The Origins of Totalitarianism," *The Review of Politics* 15, no. 1 (1953): 74–75. However, Arendt's response seems to me entirely justified, not just when she argued that the "problem of the relationship between essence and existence in Occidental thought seems to me to be a bit more complicated and controversial than Voegelin's statement on 'nature' (identifying a 'thing as a thing' and therefore incapable of change by definition) implies," but also in her assertion that she was not advocating such a change, but only recognizing that the attempt to change human nature (irrespective of whether this is possible) was the aspiration of totalitarian regimes. Arendt's "A Reply to Voegelin" is in *The Review of Politics* 15, no. 1 (1953): 76–84, and is reprinted in *Essays in Understanding,* 401–408.

19. Ulrich Herbert, ed., *Nationalsozialistische Vernichtungspolitik 1939–1945: Neue Forschungen und Kontroversen* (Frankfurt am Main, 1998); Christian Gerlach, *Krieg, Ernährung, Völkermord* (Hamburg, 1998); Götz Aly, *'Final Solution': Nazi Population Policy and the Murder of the European Jews* (London, 1999).

20. Christian Gerlach, "The Wannsee Conference, the Fate of German Jews, and Hitler's Decision in Principle to Exterminate all European Jews," *Journal of Modern History* 70, no. 4 (1998): 759–812. See also Gerlach's response to critics in *Krieg, Ernährung, Völkermord,* 155–166, and, for a different approach, Christopher R. Browning, *Nazi Policy, Jewish Workers, German Killers* (Cambridge, UK, 2000), 26–57. See also Bogdan Musial, "The Origins of 'Operation Reinhard': The Decision-Making Process for the Mass Murder of the Jews in the Generalgouvernement,"

Yad Vashem Studies 28 (2000): 113–153; Mark Roseman, The Villa, the Lake, the Meeting: Wannsee and the Final Solution (Harmondsworth, 2002).

21. Philip Gourevitch, We Wish to Inform You That Tomorrow We Will Be Killed With Our Families: Stories from Rwanda (London, 1999), 17.

22. Christopher R. Browning, Ordinary Men: Reserve Police Battalion 101 and the Final Solution in Poland (London, 1992).

23. Statement of Kurt Werner in "Those Were the Days": The Holocaust as seen by the Perpetrators and Bystanders, ed. Ernst Klee, Willi Dressen, and Volker Riess (London, 1993), 67. For more examples, see Omer Bartov, Hitler's Army: Soldiers, Nazis, and War in the Third Reich (New York, 1992),

24. Alain Finkielkraut, L'Humanité perdue: essai sur le XXe siècle (Paris, 1998), 69. See also Alon Confino, "Fantasies About the Jews: Cultural Reflections on the Holocaust," History & Memory 17, nos. 1/2 (2005): 296–322.

25. Giorgio Agamben, "The Camp as the Nomos of the Modern," in Violence, Identity, and Self-Determination, ed. Hent de Vries and Samuel Weber (Stanford, 1997), 106.

26. Finkielkraut, L'Humanité perdue, 110–111.

27. Jankiel Wiernik, "One Year in Treblinka," in Art from the Ashes, ed. Lawrence L. Langer (New York, 1995), 30–31.

28. See my "Modernity and Violence: Theoretical Reflections on the Einsatzgruppen," in History, Memory and Mass Atrocity, 1–14. For useful studies on the social psychology of genocide, see Steven K. Baum, "A Bell Curve of Hate?" Journal of Genocide Research 6, no. 4 (2004): 567–577; Herbert C. Kelman, "Violence Without Moral Restraint: Reflections on the Dehumanization of Victims and Victimizers," Journal of Social Issues 29, no. 4 (1973): 25–61; John M. Darley, "Social Organization for the Production of Evil," Psychological Inquiry 3, no. 2 (1992): 199–218; Albert Bandura, "Moral Disengagement in the Perpetration of Inhumanities," Personality and Social Psychology Review 3, no. 3 (1999): 193–209.

29. See my essays "Georges Bataille and the Interpretation of the Holocaust" and "Genocide as Transgression," in History, Memory and Mass Atrocity, 70–92 and 196–216.

30. Jews were of course not the only victims of the Nazis. Among the many other victim groups, Europe's Gypsies (Roma and Sinti) were also victims of genocide. But the peculiar drive to destroy Jews, a result of the "metaphysical" way in which the Nazis regarded them, can make this conceptual difference meaningful.

31. See the drawings in Thomas Geve, Guns and Barbed Wire: A Child Survives the Holocaust (Chicago, 1987).

32. Primo Levi, If This is a Man and The Truce (London, 1987), 48.

33. Rudolf Reder, "Bełżec," Polin: Studies in Polish Jewry 13 (2000): 282.

34. Zalman Gradowski, "Writings," in The Scrolls of Auschwitz, ed. Ber Mark (Tel Aviv, 1985), 175

35. The Diary of Dawid Sierakowiak, ed. Alan Adelson (London, 1996), 170.

36. Claude Lanzmann, Shoah: An Oral History of the Holocaust. The Complete Text of the Film (New York, 1985), 174.

37. Jan Karski, Story of a Secret State (Boston, 1944), 330.

38. Naomi Samson, Hide: A Child's View of the Holocaust (Lincoln, 2000), 74–75.

39. Adina Blady Szwajger, I Remember Nothing More: The Warsaw Children's Hospital and the Jewish Resistance (New York, 1990), 45.

40. Pelagia Lewinska, Twenty Months at Auschwitz (1968), cited in Emil Fackenheim, "The Spectrum of Resistance During the Holocaust: An Essay in Description and Definition," Modern Judaism 2, no. 2 (1982): 123.

41. Hannah Arendt, "Social Science Techniques and the Study of Concentration Camps," in Essays in Understanding, 236. See also the discussion in Robert Eaglestone, The Holocaust and the Postmodern (Oxford, 2004), 317–338; and Amos Goldberg, "If This is a Man: The Image of Man in Autobiographical and Historical Writing During and After the Holocaust," Yad Vashem Studies 33 (2005): 381–429.

42. On the Muselmann see Giorgio Agamben, *Remnants of Auschwitz: The Witness and the Archive* (New York, 1999). While Agamben inappropriately makes the Muselmann the figure for the Holocaust survivor on the basis of far too small a selection of texts, this is nevertheless one of the few works that have attempted a theoretical analysis of the meaning of the Muselmann. For a critique of Agamben see Dominick LaCapra, *History in Transit: Experience, Identity, Critical Theory* (Ithaca, 2004), 144–194.

43. *Die Tagebücher von Joseph Goebbels: Sämtliche Fragmente*, ed. Elke Fröhlich (Munich, 1987), vol. 3, 628 (entry for 2 November 1940). One should note here the tension that often occurs in Nazi rhetoric between describing Jews as "animals," as Goebbels does here, and describing them, as Hitler does in my epigraph, as "anti-humans," i.e., something other than animals. Similarly, Himmler referred to Slavs but not to Jews as "human animals." See his speech of 4 October 1943, in *Nazism 1919–1945*, ed. J. Noakes and G. Pridham (Exeter, 1988), vol. 3, 920.

44. On the Holocaust as "salvation" see Michael Ley, *Genozid als Heilserwartung: Zum nationalsozialistischen Mord am europäischen Judentum*, 2nd ed. (Vienna, 1995); idem, *Holokaust als Menschenopfer: Vom Christentum zur politischen Religion des Nationalsozialismus* (Münster, 2002); Klaus Vondung, "National Socialism as a Political Religion: Potentials and Limitations of an Analytical Concept," *Totalitarian Movements and Political Religions* 6, no. 1 (2005): 87–95.

45. Alison Des Forges, *Leave None to Tell the Story: Genocide in Rwanda* (New York, 1999), 73 ("cockroaches"); 258 ("work").

46. Robert Gellately, *Backing Hitler: Coercion and Consent in Nazi Germany* (Oxford, 2001); Eric Johnson and Karl-Heinz Reuband, *What We Knew: Terror, Mass Murder and Everyday Life in Nazi Germany* (London, 2005); and the controversial Götz Aly, *Hitlers Volksstaat: Raub, Rassenkrieg und nationaler Sozialismus* (Frankfurt am Main, 2005).

47. See Darryl Li, "Echoes of Violence," in *The New Killing Fields: Massacre and the Politics of Intervention*, ed. Nicolaus Mills and Kira Brunner (New York, 2002), 117–128. For the numbers involved, see Scott Straus, "How Many Perpetrators Were There in the Rwandan Genocide? An Estimate," *Journal of Genocide Research* 6, no. 1 (2004): 85–98.

48. John A. Berry and Carol Pott Berry, "Introduction: Collecting Memory," in *Genocide in Rwanda: A Collective Memory*, ed. John A. Berry and Carol Pott Berry (Washington, D.C., 1999), 5.

49. Faustin Kagame, "The Artificial Racialization at the Root of the Genocide," in *Genocide in Rwanda*, ed. Berry and Berry, 73.

50. See Mark Levene, "Rwanda: The Aftermath," *Patterns of Prejudice* 35, no. 2 (2001): 87–94.

51. Steven E. Aschheim, *In Times of Crisis: Essays on European Culture, Germans, and Jews* (Madison, 2001), 55. For further discussion see Jonathan Petropoulos and John K. Roth, eds., *Gray Zones: Ambiguity and Compromise in the Holocaust and its Aftermath* (New York, 2005).

52. The Cambodian genocide too provides many examples of this attack on "the human," not just on individual human beings. A satisfactory analysis of Cambodian survivor testimonies requires a separate study; but for a starting point, see Jean-Louis Margolin, "L'amémoire du génocide cambodgien, ou comment s'en débarrasser," *Revue d'histoire de la Shoah* 181 (2004): 317–337.

53. See the discussion in Christopher C. Taylor, *Sacrifice as Terror: The Rwandan Genocide of 1994* (Oxford, 1999), 174–175, and Berry and Berry, ed., *Genocide in Rwanda*, 113–115.

54. Ignace Rukiramacumu in Jean Hatzfeld, *Machete Season: The Killers in Rwanda Speak* (New York, 2005), 47.

55. Pio Mutungirehe in *Machete Season*, 47.

56. Léopord Twagirayezu in *Machete Season*, 144.

57. Cited in Alison Des Forges, *Leave None to Tell the Story: Genocide in Rwanda* (New York, 1999), 347–348.

58. Thomas Kamilindi, journalist, "Witness Testimony," in *Genocide in Rwanda*, ed. Berry and Berry, 16. On the international community, see Linda Melvern, *A People Betrayed: The Role of the West in Rwanda's Genocide* (London, 2000); Romeo Dallaire, *Shake Hands with the Devil: The Failure of Humanity in Rwanda* (London, 2003).

59. Pancrace Hakizamungili in *Machete Season*, 21–22.

60. Or, as Seyla Benhabib notes in her work, "Arendt does not examine the philosophical step which would lead from a description of the equality of the human condition to the equality which comes from moral and political recognition. . . . The path leading from the anthropological plurality of the human condition to the moral and political equality of human beings in a community of reciprocal recognition remains philosophically unthematized." Seyla Benhabib, "Arendt's Eichmann in Jerusalem," in *The Cambridge Companion to Hannah Arendt*, ed. Villa, 82.

61. Robert Antelme, *The Human Race* (Marlboro, 1992). Antelme writes (219–220): "there are not several human races, there is only one human race. It's because we're men like them that the SS will finally prove powerless before us. It's because they shall have sought to call the unity of this human race into question that they'll finally be crushed. . . . And we have to say that everything in the world that masks this unity, everything that places beings in situations of exploitation and subjugation and thereby implies the existence of various species of mankind, is false and mad."

62. Arendt, "A Reply to Eric Voegelin," in *Essays in Understanding*, 408.

63. Here the discussion would need to consider the writings of Georges Bataille on the one hand and Emmanuel Levinas on the other. There is not space here for such a discussion but, for a start, see Samuel Moyn, "Judaism Against Paganism: Emmanuel Levinas's Response to Heidegger and Nazism in the 1930s," *History & Memory* 10, no. 1 (1998): 25–58.

64. For the text of 1950 and 1952 UNESCO statements on race see Ashley Montagu, *Race, Science and Humanity* (Princeton, 1963), 172–183. Also Claude Lévi-Strauss, *Race and History: The Race Question in Modern Science* (Paris, 1958).

65. Arendt to Jaspers 17 August 1946, in *Arendt / Jaspers Correspondence*, 54. Later Arendt noted that "men are unable to forgive what they cannot punish and that they are unable to punish what has turned out to be unforgivable." See *The Human Condition*, 241.

66. I am indebted here to Richard H. King, *Race, Culture, and the Intellectuals, 1940–1970* (Washington, D.C. / Baltimore, 2004), 313–316. See also Gilroy, *Between Camps*, and Jean-Luc Nancy, *The Experience of Freedom* (Stanford, 1993), for the idea of evil as one facet of human freedom.

67. Françoise Dastur, "Three Questions to Jacques Derrida," in *Ethics and Danger: Essays on Heidegger and Continental Thought*, ed. Arleen B. Dallery and Charles E. Scott (Albany, 1992), 34.

68. Ibid.

69. Ibid.

70. Ibid., 34–35.

71. Jaspers to Arendt, 19 October 1946, in *Arendt / Jaspers Correspondence*, 62: "I'm not altogether comfortable with your view, because a guilt that goes beyond all criminal guilt inevitably takes on a streak of 'greatness'—of satanic greatness— which is, for me, as inappropriate for the Nazis as all the talk about the 'demonic' element in Hitler and so forth. It seems to me that we have to see these things in their total banality, in their prosaic triviality, because that's what truly characterises them."

72. Hannah Arendt, "Fernsehgespräch mit Thilo Koch," in *Ich will verstehen: Selbstauskünfte zu Leben und Werk*, ed. Ursula Ludz (Munich, 1996), 40.

73. Dastur, "Three Questions," 35.

74. I have discussed this in my "Ontology or Bureaucracy?"

75. Léon Poliakov, *Harvest of Hate* (London, 1956 [orig. French ed. 1953]), 286.

76. Giorgio Agamben, *The Open: Man and Animal* (Stanford, 2004), 25–26.

77. Arendt, *Origins*, 459. Or, as the German émigré scholar Sebastian Haffner wrote about the second generation of Nazis: "the question arises in all seriousness as to whether these beings are still to be called men. Physically, to all appearance, they are still men; spiritually, no more." *Germany Jekyll and Hyde: An Eyewitness Analysis of Nazi Germany* (London, 2005 [orig. 1940]), 63. For examples of Nazi theorizing about the exclusion of the Jews from the definition of "human," see Uriel Tal, *Religion, Politics and Ideology in the Third Reich: Selected Essays* (London, 2004), 70–71.

Conclusion

ARENDT BETWEEN PAST AND FUTURE

Richard H. King

> *The Origins of Totalitarianism* still offers not only a model of how to look backwards without worshipping "the ideal of origins," but also how to look forward, even in the face of desolation, crossing boundaries usually not traversed.
> —Ira Katznelson[1]

Ironically for a thinker who has been accused—with some justification—of Euro-centrism, the issues Hannah Arendt addressed in *The Origins of Totalitarianism* (1951) and her work up to the early 1960s are as relevant to the "globalized" world of today as they were to the events of her own time. Already during World War II, Arendt had realized that the West was entering an era that demanded a fundamen-tal rethinking of its basic concepts and traditions. In particular, she contended that "the idea of humanity" entailed the moral necessity of assuming "the obligation of global responsibility . . . for all crimes committed by men."[2] One of the most important implications of this vast expansion of global awareness was the realiza-tion that she must look *outside* of Europe for one of the essential elements—the experience of imperialism—that helped create totalitarianism in Europe.

   If this is the case, then the essays in this collection that address broad philo-sophical questions having to do with "the human" and "evil" are just as relevant to our historical condition as those which take up the concrete cultural and historical issues of imperialism and colonialism, nation and race, slavery and genocide. This is another way of suggesting that, whether intentionally or not, Arendt was search-ing in *Origins* for the basis of a new sort of humanism. Ultimately, it was not to be a humanism that celebrated the glories of modern reason or which explicitly held up the West as the normative standard for other cultures to emulate; nor was it even a humanism that looked back nostalgically to classical antiquity, especially the Greeks, for the source of guidance in the present. It by no means privileged human subjectivity; nor was it even hostile to religion as such. At a minimum it was founded on one of the few moral injunctions that Arendt proposed in her work, particularly in light of the Eichmann trial: the obligation "to think what we are doing."

In what follows, I want to take up two issues raised by Arendt's search for a new basis for understanding human action and being. Though Richard Shorten has touched on the matter of Arendt's method, I want to return to that topic as it re-lated to her own relationship to, and thinking about, history. This is of particular importance, since, as already mentioned, Arendt was often at her most impressive when she was thinking about historical phenomena. Since many of the essays col-lected here have to do with her engagement with history in its various manifesta-tions, it follows that we need to know what the "rules" of that engagement were. The second issue has to do with what it is in her early thought—regarding the non-Western as well as Western world—that speaks most to our contemporary and future situation. Overall, then, not just the past but the present and future are at issue in Arendt's most historically oriented writings.

Arendt and History

It is a mistake to attribute to Hannah Arendt a systematic philosophy of history (i.e., History with a capital H); nor was she particularly interested in working out an explicit methodology for approaching historical phenomena. Yet, a set of rough principles and priorities can be extracted from her writings, particularly from the period around the publication of *Origins*, the period most relevant to us. First, Arendt assumed that human subjects were agents who were generally responsible for their actions, except under the most extreme circumstances. Most of her his-torical attention was engaged by those thoughts which were enunciated and those actions which were undertaken in public, though she could be a sensitive analyst of an individual subject, whether thinker or poet or religious figure, as her unfairly neglected collection *Men in Dark Times* (1968) indicates. But her emphasis upon freedom and responsibility (*not* guilt or empathy) led her old friend, Gershom Scholem, to claim in the wake of *Eichmann in Jerusalem* (1963) that she lacked basic compassion for those of "her people" who had been consumed in the Holocaust. If Arendt's expectation of extraordinary things from ordinary people could seem heartless, she also never patronized or sentimentalized those who had been vic-timized.[3] She was not interested in writing history as a form of apologetics for either the victors or the victims as such. At the same time, she contended that to "describe the camps *sine ira* [without anger] is not to be 'objective' but to condone them."[4] She came from a continental tradition that was decidedly hostile to the notion that there were discoverable laws of history, in relation to which an "objec-tive" attitude was the proper response, if by "objective" one refers to an attitude of moral detachment.

Nor surprisingly, then, Arendt rejected the view that history had a fixed goal or *telos*, which privileged a particular single force or factor and which assumed that historical predictions were possible or desirable. A variation on this was Arendt's fear that understanding historical phenomena in their own setting and in the terms set by those involved in them could lead to justification of the past as somehow inevitable, that it could not have been otherwise. In particular she was afraid of this happening with the Holocaust itself, since, as she wrote in response to Eric Voegelin's review of *Origins*, "all historiography is necessarily salvation and frequently justification."[5] To provide a theodicy of the Holocaust, as it were, would be the worst thing imaginable. Moreover, her distaste was directed not only against Hegelian philosophers of history but also historians in the Rankean tradition who constructed seamless narratives that made it seem as though "the way it was" was "the *only* way it could have been." Put another way, she took strong except to "historicism" in the Popperian sense.[6]

Despite her own commitment to the life of the mind, to the *vita contemplativa* even as it sought to understand the *vita activa*, Arendt did not think that ideas were the motor force of history. As we have seen, her claims about the crucial contribution of imperialism to totalitarianism in Europe emphasized material factors as much or more than ideologies. For instance, racism—both as an unthinking reaction and a worked-out ideology—was one, but by no means the only, factor that needed considering. As has been noted, her sense was that "race-thinking," thinking in terms of race, would have faded from the historical scene had the imperial adventures of the European powers not both given it added life and transformed it into the ideology of racism. She nails this down firmly in her rejoinder to Voegelin when she writes: "I proceed from facts and events instead of intellectual affinities and influence,"[7] a way of contrasting her approach with Voegelin, who saw totalitarianism as the "climax of secular evolution" of ideas originating in the "immanent sectarianism since the high Middle Ages."[8] For Arendt, as opposed to those she referred to as "the historian of ideas" such as Voegelin (and one must add, Leo Strauss), it was "events" rather than ideas or social forces that most attracted her attention as an historical thinker.[9]

But "event" has a complex set of meanings and associations in Arendt's work and is not as straightforward as it may sound. First, an event can clearly be the result of an "action," another privileged term in Arendt's thinking about politics and history. According to her own narrative of Western thought, the modern period, which had been dominated first by political philosophy, especially that of Hobbes and Locke, was superseded in the nineteenth century by the philosophy of history. Thinking about *political action* gave way to thinking about impersonal *social forces*, especially "the social question"—i.e., poverty, and its political implications. History was itself politicized.[10] Second, an event for Arendt is an "interruption" in what Walter Benjamin referred to as the "continuum of history." It is an intervention, which produces unforeseen consequences and leads in unexpected directions. For that reason alone, historical predictions are useless. What is necessary according to Benjamin, to whose "Theses on the Philosophy of History" she was clearly indebted, is to "blast a specific era out of the homogeneous course of history."[11] This helps explain why, for Arendt, the reality of history can hardly be captured by a seamless narrative that implies that there is nothing more to explain. Indeed, it helps explain why *Origins* itself is not a normal work of history, according to professional standards.

Finally, something like the phenomenon of totalitarianism itself can also be an historical *individuum* or "monad" and thus an event as well. As Arendt confessed, it was "not primarily the ideological content, but the event of totalitarian domination itself" that was historically unique, that is an interruption, and thus of interest.[12] It was not that the Nazis came up with any new versions of anti-Semitism; rather, it was the logicality with which they implemented those threadbare ideas that was so startling, even radical. But it should be underlined that an "event" is itself a morally neutral category. Disrupting the historical continuum is neither a positive nor a negative thing as such. Action that creates something new in a positive sense, such as the effort to create "lasting institutions" to protect freedom, was a privileged event for Arendt; but, then, so was the Holocaust. What is hard to imagine is how Arendt could have incorporated *Alltagsgeschichte*, the history of everyday life, or social history into her own doing of history.

Arendt's grounding in phenomenology helps explain her suspicion of causal-genetic or developmental explanations for historical phenomena, including events. Her favorite explanatory trope for the appearance of totalitarianism—that it was a "crystallization" of historical factors[13]—was shrewdly chosen, since the process of crystallization can hardly be perceived as taking place *over* time, as opposed to happening, in the shortest historical duration, *within* a moment of time. Seen in this light, "crystallization" happens in and because of the "interruption" of the historical continuum. The strong influence of Benjamin's attack on historicism in "Theses on the Philosophy of History" is underlined by his own prior use of the term "crystallize" to describe the way thinking drastically reconfigures the "mass of data" that makes up universal history.[14] Not surprisingly, Arendt's emphasis upon events and historical discontinuities went together with her general intention of drawing distinctions rather than looking for continuity between historical phenomena or reducing one historical event to another.[15] Although Arendt spoke of totalitarianism and related historical phenomena such as the "camps" as having an "essence," such an essence was historical rather than ontological or metaphysical: it "did not exist until it [totalitarianism] had come into being. I therefore talk only of 'elements' which crystallize into totalitarianism."[16] From this point of view, Nazism as an ideology was not just the latest in the long decline of the West, as it was for Voegelin; nor was it a continuation of the religious anti-Semitism that was synonymous with the history of Christendom. Because totalitarian ideologies such as Nazism may have functioned *like* a religious ideology, did not mean that it was one. Functional similarity did not equal essential identity.

Arendt would also have agreed with Leo Strauss that ideas and traditions could retain their truth value over long stretches of history and even across cultural boundaries.[17] But she did not restrict the transhistorical validity of ideas to classical natural right thinking or the political thought of the American founders. Nor did she believe that criticizing classical Greek political thought or the founders

of the American republic from the (modern) present was a metaphysical imper-
tinence or a self-canceling paradox. We can, and must, she contended, also roam
backward in time to pick out those events, examples, and ideas that seem particularly worth remembering, i.e., "blasting out of the continuum." Bringing them back
to the present is no easy matter; but it is necessary to make the attempt at times.
Arendt severely criticized the classical and the Christian traditions for failing to
nurture a strong sense of the "political," by which she meant the central importance of public speech and action as opposed to philosophical or religious thought
and meditation. Thus, for her, separation in time was no hindrance to critical
judgment. Put more generally, ideas for Arendt might be transhistorical, but they
were not superhistorical, somehow existing outside of time. Perhaps because she
used the ideas of others primarily as an aid to her own thinking—in other words
because she was not a pure textualist, ideas seem more historically mobile in her
hands and influences can work at a distance as well as close up. Some classical texts
may be authoritative, but they are not sacred.

Most of all, Arendt's self-appointed task as an historically oriented thinker
was to understand the implications of what was (to her) the crisis or "break" in
Western thought and culture. For this task, she assumed no standpoint outside
of history, no God's eye view, from which to judge it. In this sense, she was an
historicist. Paradoxically, her thinking about history and her thinking from within
history fell into the modernist critique of the historicization of modern life and
thought and belonged to the tradition of Nietzsche's *Use and Abuse of History*. She
sought to undermine the idea that the ideal work of history should exemplify
the homogeneity of time or was structured by a dialectical unfolding of history.
Returning to the question of the way she structured *Origins*, we must realize that
she wanted to disabuse the reader of the idea that the narrative of this latest/last
chapter in the story of modernity could be delivered in finished form and with
"closure" having been achieved. Originally, her rejection of historical inevitability
was a way of refusing, at least for a time, to be reconciled to the Holocaust, since
to claim to have understood it *historically* seemed to make it essential to God's,
History's, or Humanity's essential purpose: i.e., it was a way of justifying it. Yet,
one cannot help feeling that for Arendt the only thing worse than the thought
that the Holocaust was meaningless was the idea that it did have a meaning in the
overall historical schema.

There is much more to say about Arendt's conception of history and historiography, particularly, as Robert Eaglestone reminds us in his essay, having to do with
the function of the poet and historian in telling stories and constructing narratives
that help reconcile the present with the past, a work that is never finished but must
be repeated again and again.[18] But specific to the concerns in this volume, one
might wonder how we can square Arendt's desire to make distinctions among historical events and phenomena with her wish to link the European experience of colonial rule and imperial conquest with the emergence of totalitarianism in Europe.
The geographical and even moral gap can seem too great. Yet, one of her basic
assumptions, as already mentioned, was that there was nothing inevitable about

such a connection, no developmental schema or dialectic that would guarantee such a historical "locking together," no essence that was realized by the emergence of the former from the latter. Nor did she ever claim that totalitarianism or the Holocaust could be reduced to the European experience in South Africa or South West Africa or the Congo. As already mentioned, her point was not that these were totalitarian societies nor that they were run by totalitarian governments. Rather, the ideas and practices that emerged there, including bureaucratic rule, racialized thought and behavior, certain sorts of brutality and violence, become essential to what emerged in Europe later on.

Finally, there is also the question of how her work, or at least *Origins*, should be categorized. Until late in her life, Arendt refused to describe what she did as "philosophy." As Stephen Maloney has emphasized, Arendt seemed to prefer the work of precursors such as Montesquieu or Tocqueville or the political thinking found in, say, *The Federalist Papers* over pure, systematic political philosophy. As far as I know, she never referred to herself as an historian; and in her reply to Voegelin, she claimed that *Origins* was not "a history of totalitarianism but an analysis in terms of history."[19] On the evidence presented in this volume, she might also be considered an "historical thinker." Such a label would emphasize that she thought *as* a historical being and thus had to think *about* and *through* history. To that immersion in history, she brought the best philosophical education of her time and an ability to see the way philosophical and ethical concerns arose from historical actions and events. This is certainly not to claim that she thought that history was philosophy teaching by example. But neither was philosophy an activity elevated above, set over and against, history; rather, it was itself saturated with history. It derived from historical experience, but it was also a way of reflecting upon that experience. Finally, Arendt was very much a woman of her historical moment. Though she didn't much care for her contemporary, Jean-Paul Sartre, she implicitly shared his assumption that the writer or intellectual should be engaged and was herself, rarely, if ever, without thoughts about the events of her time. She could be maddeningly opinionated about matters she knew relatively little about (such as the desegregation crisis in Little Rock, Arkansas in 1957) and also just dead wrong in her historical or political judgments. But, not only did she live in history; history lived in and through her. For her, it was a precondition for being human.

The Present/Future

Finally, there are two large areas where Arendt's work is still (or once more) pertinent to former colonial societies and polities today. As Seyla Benhabib has observed, Arendt is the "theorist of the post-totalitarian moment . . . of minority rights and statelessness, of refugees and deported people.[20] In an ironic variation on Europe's alleged advanced historical status, we might now say: "Where Europe was, there the former European colonies ('Third World,' 'underdeveloped' or 'developing' nations) will be." The first area is illustrated most immediately in the massive problem of literal and political "homelessness" (e.g., refugees from war, famine, hunger, and political persecution), which has assumed epidemic proportions particularly in Africa; but it remains, or has become once more, a nagging issue in Europe and North America. Arendt's basic contention in *Origins* was that neither public nor private international organizations could be relied upon to protect the human rights of individuals or groups. The answer lay in the ability of nation-states to implement and guarantee what she designated as a kind of meta-right ("the right to have rights") that would guarantee a place in the world and indeed constitute a world of significance and protection. At the time of the publication of *Origins*, her contention was that all the traditional foundations of human status up to then—a transcendent power, tradition, nature, or, broadly speaking, history—had lost their power to compel, while the grounding of human status in race/biology had proven to be a warrant for genocide. Only a kind of self-imposed political guarantee seemed to promise any sort of answer.

Yet there were and are problems with assuming the nation-state will be any more reliable as a guarantor of human rights than any other entity, such as the UN. For instance, the conflicts that threaten to remain without resolution—from the Jews in Germany to Rwanda and the Tutsis, Yugoslavia and the Bosnians, Israel and the Palestinians, the Sudanese government and the people of Darfur—seem to involve the persecution and cleansing of internal minorities, when another minority or a majority turns the state apparatus to its own purposes. But she was correct that, in such situations, genocide always seems about to happen or actually does happen.[21] Still "the right to have rights" offers at least a kind of normative standard that might provide guidance in a world of collapsing international boundaries and ineffectual regional and international organizations. It seems to be the only enduring justification for the nation-state itself.

This condition of literal and political homelessness is closely linked, and in fact overlaps, with what Arendt named "superfluousness" in *Origins*. As Achille Mbembe has recently pointed out in an essay on the African city, the connotations of superfluity run in two opposing directions. On the one hand, it connotes excess and luxury, what remains after having more than enough.[22] On the other hand, Arendt more often speaks of it in the context of overpopulation, famine, the existence of a surplus labor force, and social and economic uselessness. The central function of the camp system—and a crucial part of what she meant by radical evil—entailed making whole groups of people superfluous, thus making them prime candidates for genocide (as "vermin" or "cockroaches").[23] As André Duarte has noted in this volume, the political and social theorist, Giorgio Agamben, has made powerful use of Arendt's work in developing the idea of "bare life" as "life unworthy of life." However, Agamben overlooks her crucial concept of superfluousness, which is the idea in her own work that we can most closely associate with "bare life." In fact, for Arendt, superflousness refers not just to "bare life" but to *unnecessary* life.[24] Something of the impression it makes can be experienced when viewing the pictures of the German concentration and death camps or endless streams of refugees in the last years of the war in Europe.

Moreover, as Susan Sontag noted in her *Regarding the Pain of Others* (2004), the photographs, videos, and films taken of non-European people have historically been almost eager to show the naked body "full frontally" and, in particular, to show it in conditions of extreme suffering or even death. As she writes: "The more remote or exotic the place, the more likely we are to have full frontal views of the dead and dying."[25] In recent years the vast camps occupied by Hutus and Tutsis fleeing Rwanda and the displaced populations underway on foot—without literal or political homes—in the Democratic Republic of Congo or in the Darfur region of Sudan testify to the relevance of Arendt's work to the contemporary world. Overall, her early work in particular explored, or at least suggested, the way that historical experiences of social and political homelessness were of philosophical and ontological status, and thereby brought home their centrality not only to her time but to ours, not just to Europe but to Africa and Asia. Political thought which consistently fails to address such issues has missed the point of what is among the most important moral facts about the contemporary world.

On a more hopeful level, Arendt's work remains powerfully suggestive for what has been, or should be, involved in the truth and reconciliation projects over the last decade and a half in around 120 different countries.[26] Arendt and her one-time mentor Karl Jaspers are powerful examples to political philosophers and legal theorists as thinkers who attempted to think through the transition from totalitarian or authoritarian states to liberal and democratic regimes. Their work contrasts markedly with the post-World War II silence among political philosophers about, for instance, the Nuremberg Trials. Why Arendt and Jaspers were largely alone in their concerns after World War II is a puzzle.[27] Perhaps it is because political philosophy has been concerned with normative concepts such as equality, liberty, and justice (as they intersect with the realities of power, domination, and interests) rather than with "action" concepts such as acknowledging, apologizing, and forgiving, or internal states of mind such as guilt and responsibility. If, as conventional wisdom has it, politics is concerned with power and violence, then conventional political thought would have trouble dealing with these actions and/or states of mind, since they concern moments when someone or some institution gives up power or abjures violence, and apologizes for having exercised power in certain ways. The hope that such processes can be institutionalized seems hopelessly unrealistic, even apolitical, to those committed to politics as the pursuit of power and the exercise of interests and that alone.

Arendt's (all too brief) discussion of forgiveness in *The Human Condition* (1958) makes clear why she remains so contemporary. There she proposes that forgiving and promising are the two framing "actions" of political life. Making and keeping promises, as exemplified by entering into covenants and contracts, stabilizes the polity by dealing with "unpredictability," while forgiveness, Arendt claims, helps keep open the possibility for "redemption from the predicament of irreversibility."[28] Potentially, political forgiveness breaks the cycle of violence and revenge that seems endemic to political life.[29] Surprisingly, Arendt, an admirer of the Greek polis and by birth a Jew, suggests that the public importance of "freedom from vengeance"[30] was first made manifest in the life and teachings of Jesus, though she doubts the political relevance or wisdom of love as such. She confuses *eros* and *agape*, but her important point is that politics needs the concept of forgiveness in order to break the cycle of vengeance and, more positively, to begin things anew. It is one way to create a future and reconfigure a new past for a polity.

Beyond that, it has been suggested that one way to look at the Truth and Reconciliation hearings in South Africa and elsewhere is as installments of a kind of movable constitutional convention.[31] In those sessions, what Arendt refers to in various places as being political through speaking and acting in public about matters having to do with the maintenance (or in the case of South Africa, the re-creation) of the republic, clearly was at issue. Or to evoke what has just been mentioned: in the TRC sessions what took place was the establishment of a public covenant and public form of amnesty (or political forgiveness).

This emphasis upon the way political forgiveness enables a fresh start comports quite well with Archbishop Desmond Tutu's assertion that his Christian faith is "the faith of ever new beginnings."[32] Arendt, however, places two qualifications on the way forgiveness might work. First, not only does forgiveness not preclude punishment; it may in fact presuppose it. She thus assumes that punishment is fundamentally different from vengeance, which is counterviolence without legitimacy or limits. But truth and reconciliation hearings explicitly, and wisely, sought not to see themselves as revolutionary tribunals, exacting revenge in the name of the "people" or the "proletariat." Second, in a formulation that echoes her discussion in *Origins*, she notes that, "men are unable to punish what has turned out to be unforgivable," the latter being the "true hallmark" of "radical evil." [33] But the assumption of truth and reconciliation processes generally has been that a form of forgiveness is possible or at least the idea can be entertained.

One weakness in Arendt's discussion of forgiveness is that she neglects the issue of apology, the necessary "move" from the Other that aims to elicit forgiveness, and thus she neglects the public element of forgiveness. According to Nicholas Tavuchis, an apology between one individual and another differs importantly from that between two groups. In contrast with an interpersonal apology, where indications of sincerity and remorse are looked for, the crucial point of a collective apology is "to put things on record"[34] as part of a public event. In our time, political apology raises the question of who should apologize for things like crimes against humanity or systematic violations of human rights by one group or nation against another. Those who knowingly perpetrate such actions or formulate such policies are rarely willing, or present, to apologize for them. If this is the case, should a leader of a nation be held responsible for the evil actions his or her nation committed under different leadership at an earlier time? In other words, should the relatively "innocent" be left to apologize for someone else's dirty work and does a later apology for, say, slavery count for much, if anything? Members of one's own polity or descendants of the former victims may see such an apology as inappropriate or too cheaply arrived at. In the case of slavery in the United States, several generations of descendants of perpetrators and victims have profited and suffered respectively, but no one who was directly responsible for the crime or to whom an apology can be directly addressed remains. "Is there," as Elazar Barkan has wondered: "a statute of limitations on national injustice?"[35] In addition, it must be asked to what degree the language of guilt, apology, and forgiveness has resonance in cultures that have not been dominated historically by the three Abrahamic religions. These vital aspects of reconciliation may not have strong counterparts in other religions and cultures.

Within the cultural range of those religious faiths, one conceptual "solution" might be to follow Arendt by distinguishing guilt and responsibility. For her, legal and moral guilt involves the concrete actions of individuals; it is neither collective nor connected with thoughts or attitudes. Whereas one would be *guilty* if he or she directly ordered the enslavement of other human beings or actually participated in crimes against humanity or genocidal actions, citizens who belong to nations which have committed genocide, enslaved people, or deprived groups of their human rights could be said to be *responsible* for trying to rectify the effects of these crimes and violations. Taking responsibility cannot undo a deed literally; but it can, through apology and/or through restitution, address the effects of those earlier violations by acknowledging and responding to them. Whereas guilt has to do with the past, responsibility is also directed toward the future. Overall, then, guilt is individual, but responsibility is collective, and most of all, for Arendt, guilt is a moral issue, while responsibility is also a political one.[36]

Clearly, this is a huge topic and Arendt's work by no means provides a final word on the whole question of guilt and responsibility, innocence, and complicity in situations where massive violations of human rights, crimes against humanity, and genocide have been perpetrated. But she does provide a particularly powerful example of a thinker who, in a time of political, moral, and spiritual confusion, took it upon herself to "think without banisters." It is this example of intellectual courage, even daring, that is perhaps the final lesson she has to teach us when we confront the burden of our time as well as assume responsibility for the past.

Notes

1. Ira Katznelson, *Desolation and Enlightenment: Political Knowledge after Total War, Totalitarianism, and the Holocaust* (New York, 2003), 175.
2. Hannah Arendt, "Organized Guilt and Universal Responsibility"(1945), in *Essays in Understanding* (New York, 1994), 131.
3. Arendt, "*Eichmann in Jerusalem*: Exchange of Letters between Gershom Scholem and Arendt," in *The Jew as Pariah*, ed. Ron H. Feldman (New York, 1978), 240–251.
4. Arendt, "A Reply to Eric Voegelin"(1953), in *Essays in Understanding* (New York, 1994), 402; 403. This short response to Voegelin's critique of *Origins* is perhaps the best single source of her own thinking about what she was doing in that book. See Voegelin, "*The Origins of Totalitarian-*

ism," Review of Politics 15 (January 1953): 68–76. Note: Arendt is alluding here to Tacitus' phrase: "sine ira et studio" meaning "without anger or bias."

5. Arendt, "Reply," 402.

6. Karl R. Popper, *The Poverty of Historicism* (London, 1957). For the perennial question of historicism, see George G. Iggers, "Historicism: The History and Meaning of the Term," *Journal of the History of Ideas* 56 (1996): 129–52. Iggers understands the term to have two very broad referents: (1) a modern relativistic worldview, and (2) an "historiographical outlook"(129).

7. Arendt, "Reply," 403.

8. Voegelin, "Origins," 69, 74. See also, Eric Voegelin, *The New Science of Politics* (Chicago, 1952).

9. Arendt, "The Concept of History," *Between Past and Future: Six Exercises in Political Thought* (Cleveland and New York, 1961), 69, 78. Arendt does not mention Strauss in this essay, but her rejection of the approach of "the historian of ideas" would clearly apply to him as well. By that description, she did not mean scholars who worked within that discipline as such, which neither Voegelin nor Strauss did. Rather, she referred to those who saw ideas and ideologies as the moving force in history.

10. See "The Concept of History," 77–8, and also *On Revolution* (New York, 1963) where she focuses specifically on the politicization of history. Interestingly, in *Natural Right and History* (Chicago, 1953) Strauss also tracks something like a shift but in terms of the move from natural right(s) thinking to historicism.

11. Arendt, "The Concept of History," 43; Walter Benjamin, "Theses on the Philosophy of History," *Illuminations*, Hannah Arendt, ed. (New York, 1969), 263. Benjamin gave Arendt a copy of "Theses" to take with her to New York and hand over to Theodor Adorno, in case he (Benjamin) did not make it to America. He of course did not. See Stephen J. Whitfield, *Into the Dark: Hannah Arendt and Totalitarianism* (Philadelphia, 1980), 136.

12. See David N. Myers, *Resisting History: Historicism and Its Discontents in German-Jewish Thought* (Princeton, 2003), 2. There he notes that in historicism "each event [is] understood as individual unit, assessed on its own terms and according to its own unique development"; Benjamin, "Theses," 263; Arendt, "Reply," 405.

13. Arendt, "Introduction," *Illuminations*, 51. She also uses the term in her Introduction to *Origins* and in her "Reply," 405.

14. Benjamin, "Theses," 262–3.

15. Arendt, "Reply," 407.

16. ibid.

17. See Leo Strauss, *Natural Right and History* (Chicago, 1953).

18. See Arendt, "On Humanity in Dark Times," *Men in Dark Times* (New York, 1968), 20–22; also Richard H. King, "Endings and Beginnings: Politics in Arendt's Early Thought," *Political Theory* 12, no. 2 (1984): 235–51. As Paul Ricoeur has emphasized in *Time and Narrative*, vol. I (Chicago, 1984), the temporal structure of narrative is not just a characteristic of narrative histories. Narrative describes a way of thinking about events in time rather than the name of a genre or method.

19. Arendt, "Reply," 403.

20. Seyla Benhabib, "Political Geographies in a Global World: Arendtian Reflections," *Social Research* 69, no.2 (2002): 542–3.

21. See Arendt, *Origins* (Cleveland, 1958), chapter 9 and Seyla Benhabib, *The Rights of Others: Aliens, Residents and Citizens* (Cambridge, U.K., 2004).

22. See Achille Mbembe, "Aesthetics of Superfluity," *Public Culture* 16, no. 3 (2004): 373–405. Mbembe draws upon Arendt at several points in his discussion. The Sartrean notion of *de trop* refers to a personal sense of worthlessness, as for instance in his novel, *Nausea*.

23. Arendt, *Origins*, chapter 10.

24. Giorgio Agamben, *Homo Sacer: Sovereign Power and Bare Life* (Stanford, 1998).

25. Susan Sontag, *Regarding the Pain of Others* (London, 2004), 63.

26. There is a large literature on the "truth and reconciliation" idea as well as the various examples of it in practice, most notably in South Africa. For an example of the way Arendt and Karl Jaspers have been used to illuminate central issues involved in the process, see Andrew Schaap, "Guilty Subjects and Political Responsibility: Arendt, Jaspers and the Resonance of the 'German Question' in Politics of Reconciliation," *Political Studies* 49 (2001): 749–66.

27. Karl Jaspers, *The Question of German Guilt* (New York, 1946; 1961). For a contemporary use of Jaspers' work in South Africa, see John W. de Gruchy, "Guilt, Amnesty and National Reconciliation," *Journal of Theology for Southern Africa* 83, no. 1 (1993): 3–14.

28. Hannah Arendt, *The Human Condition* (Garden City, N.Y., 1958), 212–213.

29. Though it is not her example, the question of revenge versus forgiveness is also the central theme in Aeschylus's *Eumenides*, a play where the central conflict is the "terror of unending vengeance" by the Furies against Orestes as countered by Pallas Athena's attempt to inhibit its repetition. See Donald Shriver, *An Ethic for Enemies: Forgiveness in Politics* (New York, 1995).

30. Arendt, *The Human Condition*, 216.

31. See Emmanuel Chukwudi Eze, "Transitions and Reasons of Memory," *South Atlantic Quarterly* 103, no. 4 (2004): 768, note 16.

32. Archbishop Desmond Tutu, Address at Vanderbilt University, Nashville, Tennessee, April 16, 2003.

33. Ibid., 217. See also Jacques Derrida, "On Forgiveness," *Cosmopolitanism and Forgiveness*, trans. by Mark Dooley and Michael Hughes (London and New York, 1999), 36, for the idea that there are two kinds of forgiveness, one limited and one "unconditional" (32).

34. Nicholas Tavuchis, *Mea Culpa: A Sociology of Apology and Reconciliation* (Stanford, 1991). Though published before the establishment of the Truth and Reconciliation Commission in South Africa, Tavuchis's book is of great relevance to the whole topic of truth and reconciliation among nations and peoples.

35. See Elazar Barkan, *The Guilt of Nations: Restitution and Negotiating Historical Injustices* (New York and London, 2000), 288.

36. Responsibility closely resembles what Jaspers referred to as "political guilt." See also Hannah Arendt, "Organized Guilt and Universal Responsibility"(1945), in *Essays in Understanding*, 121–132; and, more recently, the essays in her *Responsibility and Judgment*, ed. and intro. Jerome Kohn (New York, 2003).

SELECT BIBLIOGRAPHY

Achebe, Chinua. "An Image of Africa," *The Massachusetts Review* 18, no. 4 (1977), 782–794.

Adorno, Theodor W. *Negative Dialectics.* Translated by E. B. Ashton. London: Routledge, 1973.

———. *Metaphysics: Concepts and Problems.* Edited by Rolf Tiedemann. Translated by Edmund Jephcott. Cambridge: Polity, 2000.

Adorno, Theodor, and Max Horkheimer. *Dialectic of Enlightenment.* Translated by John Cumming. London: Verso, 1997.

Agamben, Giorgio. *Homo Sacer: Sovereign Power and Bare Life.* Translated by Daniel Heller-Roazen. Stanford: Stanford University Press, 1998.

———. *The Open: Man and Animal.* Translated by Kevin Attell. Stanford: Stanford University Press, 2004.

———. *State of Exception.* Translated by Kevin Attell. Chicago: University of Chicago Press, 2005.

Amis, Martin. *Koba the Dread: Laughter and the Twenty Million.* London: Jonathan Cape, 2002.

Anderson, David. *Histories of the Hanged: The Dirty War in Kenya and the End of Empire.* London: Phoenix Press, 2006.

Anghie, Antony. "Finding the Peripheries: Sovereignty and Colonialism in Nineteenth Century Colonial Law," *Harvard International Law Journal* 40 (1999).

Anzulovi, Branimir. *Heavenly Serbia. From Myth to Genocide.* London: C. Hurst, 1999.

Appiah, K. Anthony, and Amy Gutmann. *Color Conscious.* New York: Princeton University Press, 1996.

Arendt, Hannah. *The Human Condition.* Chicago: University of Chicago Press, 1958.

———. *Men in Dark Times.* San Diego: Harcourt Brace Jovanovich, 1968.

———. *Crises of the Republic.* New York: Harcourt Brace Jovanovich, 1972.

———. *Eichmann in Jerusalem: A Report on the Banality of Evil,* rev. ed. New York: Penguin Books, 1977.

———. *Between Past and Future: Eight Exercises in Political Thought.* New York: Penguin, 1977.

———. *The Jew as Pariah,* ed. Ron H. Feldman. New York: Grove Press, 1978.

———. *The Life of the Mind.* San Diego: Harcourt, 1978.

———. *The Origins of Totalitarianism,* rev. ed. San Diego: Harcourt Brace, 1979.

———. *Essays in Understanding 1930–1954.* Edited by Jerome Kohn. New York: Schocken Books, 1994.

———. *Ich will verstehen: Selbstauskünfte zu Leben und Werk.* Edited by Ursula Ludz. Munich: Piper, 1996.

———. *Responsibility and Judgment.* Edited by Jerome Kohn. New York: Schocken Books, 2003.

———. *The Promise of Politics.* Edited by Jerome Kohn. New York: Schocken Books, 2005.

———. *The Jewish Writings.* Edited by Ron H. Feldman and Jerome Kohn. New York: Schocken Books, 2007.

———. *Reflections on Literature and Culture.* Edited by Susannah Young-ah Gottlieb. Stanford: Stanford University Press, 2007.

Arendt, Hannah and Karl Jaspers. *Correspondence 1926–1969*. Edited by Lotte Kohler and Hans Saner. San Diego: Harcourt Brace, 1992.

Aron, Raymond, *Democracy and Totalitarianism*. Translated by Valence Ionescu. London: Weidenfeld and Nicolson, 1968.

Aronson, Ronald, *Camus and Sartre: The Story of a Friendship and the Quarrel that Ended It*. Chicago: University of Chicago Press, 2004.

Aschheim, Steven E., ed. *Hannah Arendt in Jerusalem*. Berkeley: University of California Press, 2001.

Ashforth, Adam. *The Politics of Official Discourse in Twentieth-Century South Africa*. Oxford: Clarendon Press, 1990.

Balibar, Etienne, and Immanuel Wallerstein. *Race, Nation, Class: Ambiguous Identities*. Translated by Chris Turner. London: Verso, 1991.

Barkan, Elazar. *The Guilt of Nations: Restitution and Negotiating Historical Injustices*. Baltimore: Johns Hopkins University Press, 2000.

Barta, Tony. "Relations of Genocide: Land and Lives in the Colonization of Australia." In Isidor Wallimann and Michael N. Dobkowski, eds., *Genocide and the Modern Age: Etiology and Case Studies of Mass Death*. Westport: Greenwood Press, 1987, 237–251.

———. "Discourses of Genocide in Germany and Australia: a Linked History," *Aboriginal History* 25 (2001): 37–56.

———. "Mr. Darwin's Shooters: On Natural Selection and the Naturalizing of Genocide," *Patterns of Prejudice* 39, no. 2 (2005): 116–137.

Bartov, Omer. "Defining Enemies, Making Victims: Germans, Jews, and the Holocaust," *American Historical Review* 103, no. 3 (1998): 771–816.

Bauman, Zygmunt. *Modernity and the Holocaust*. Cambridge: Polity Press, 1989.

Benhabib, Seyla. *The Reluctant Modernism of Hannah Arendt*. London: Sage, 1996.

———. "Political Geographies in a Global World: Arendtian Reflections," *Social Research* 69, no. 2 (2002), 539–66.

———. *The Rights of Others: Aliens, Residents and Citizens*. Cambridge: Cambridge University Press, 2004.

Benjamin, Walter. "Theses on the Philosophy of History." In *Illuminations*, edited by Hannah Arendt. New York: Schocken Books, 1969, 244–255.

Bergen, Bernard. *The Banality of Evil: Hannah Arendt and "The Final Solution."* New York: Rowman and Littlefield Publishers, 1998.

Berman, Russel A. *Enlightenment or Empire: Colonial Discourse in German Culture*. Lincoln: University of Nebraska Press, 1998.

Bermingham, Peg. *Hannah Arendt and Human Rights: The Predicament of Common Responsibility*. Bloomington: Indiana University Press, 2006.

Bernasconi, Robert. "The Double Face of the Political and the Social: Hannah Arendt and America's Racial Divisions," *Research in Phenomenology* 26 (1996), 3–24.

Bernasconi, Robert, and Tommy Lott, eds., *The Idea of Race*. Indianapolis: Hackett Publishing Company, 2000.

Bernstein, Richard J. *Hannah Arendt and the Jewish Question*. Cambridge: Polity Press, 1996.

Berry, John A., and Carol Pott Berry. *Genocide in Rwanda: A Collective Memory*. Washington, D.C.: Howard University Press, 1999

Bjelić, Dušan I., and Obrad Savić, eds., *Balkan as Metaphor: Between Globalization and Fragmentation*. Cambridge: MIT Press, 2002.

Bley, Helmut. *Namibia under German Rule*. Hamburg: LIT, 1996.

Bogoeva, Julija, and Caroline Fetcher. *Srebrenica. Ein Prozess: Dokumente und Materialien aus dem UN-Kriegsverbrechertribunal in Den Haag*. Frankfurt-am-Main: Suhrkamp, 2002.

Bourdieu, Pierre. *Algeria 1960, The Disenchantment of the World, The Kabyle House or the World Reversed*. Translated by Richard Nice. Cambridge: Cambridge University Press, 1979.

———. *The Algerians*. Translated by Alan C.M. Ross. Boston: Beacon Press, 1961.

Bourke, Joanna. *An Intimate History of Killing. Face-to-face Killing in Twentieth-Century Warfare*. London: Granta Books, 1999.

Boynton, Robert S. "F for Effort," *Bookforum* (October/November 2004).

Brantlinger, Patrick. *Dark Vanishings: Discourse on the Extinction of Primitive Races, 1800–1930.* Ithaca: Cornell University Press, 2003

Bridgman, Jon, and Leslie J. Worley. "Genocide of the Hereros." In *Century of Genocide: Eyewitness Accounts and Critical Views*, ed. Samuel Totten, William S. Parsons, and Israel W. Charny. New York: Garland Publishing, 1997, 3–40.

Browning, Christopher R. *Ordinary Men: Reserve Police Battalion 101 and the Final Solution in Poland.* London: Harper Collins, 1992.

———. *Nazi Policy, Jewish Workers, German Killers.* Cambridge: Cambridge University Press, 2000.

Burton, Antoinette, ed. *After the Imperial Turn: Thinking With and Through the Nation.* Durham; Duke University Press, 2003.

Butler, Elizabeth. *The Tyranny of Greece over Germany.* Boston: Beacon Press, 1958.

Calhoun, Craig, and John McGowan, eds., *Hannah Arendt and the Meaning of Politics.* Minneapolis: University of Minnesota Press, 1997.

Camus, Albert, *Actuelles III: Chronique Algérienne: 1939–58.* Paris: Gallimard, 1958.

———. *Réflexions sur le terrorisme.* Paris: Nicolas Philippe, 2002.

Canovan, Margaret. *The Political Thought of Hannah Arendt.* New York: Harcourt Brace and Jovanovich, 1974.

———. *Hannah Arendt: A Reinterpretation of Her Political Thought.* Cambridge: Cambridge University Press, 1992.

Ceaser, James W. *Reconstructing America: The Symbol of America in Modern Thought.* New Haven: Yale University Press, 1997.

Césaire, Aimé. *Discourse on Colonialism.* New York: Monthly Review Press, 1972.

Chickering, Roger. *We Men Who Feel Most German: A Cultural Study of the Pan-German League, 1886–1914.* Boston: Allen & Unwin, 1984.

Cooper, Frederick, and Ann Laura Stoler, eds. *Tensions of Empire: Colonial Cultures in a Bourgeois World.* Berkeley: University of California Press, 1997.

Courtois, Stéphane, Nicolas Werth, et al. *The Black Book of Communism: Crimes, Terror, Repression.* Translated by Jonathan Murphy and Mark Kramer. Cambridge: Harvard University Press, 1999.

Dallin, Alexander. *German Rule in Russia, 1941–1945.* London: Octagon Books, 1980.

Darwin, Charles. *The Origin of Species by Means of Natural Selection.* Harmondsworth: Penguin, 1968.

———. *The Descent of Man.* London: Penguin, 2004.

Dedering, Tilman. "The German-Herero War of 1904: Revisionism of Genocide or Imaginary Historiography?" *Journal of Southern African Studies* 19, no. 1 (1993): 80–88.

de Gruchy, John W. "Guilt, Amnesty and National Reconciliation," *Journal of Theology for Southern Africa* 83, no. 1 (1993): 3–14.

Derrida, Jacques. "On Forgiveness." In *On Cosmopolitanism and Forgiveness.* Translated by Mark Dooley and Michael Hughes. London: Routledge, 2001.

———. *Rogues: Two Essays on Reason.* Stanford: Stanford University Press, 2003.

Des Forges, Alison. *Leave None to Tell the Story: Genocide in Rwanda.* New York: Human Rights Watch, 1999.

De Tocqueville, Alexis. *Democracy in America.* Translated by Harvey C. Mansfield and Delba Winthrop. Chicago: University of Chicago Press, 2002.

Đorđević, Mirko, ed. *Srpska konzervativna misao [Serbian Conservative Thought].* Belgrade: Helsinški odbor za ljudska prava, 2003.

Dossa, Shiraz. "Human Status and Politics: Hannah Arendt on the Holocaust," *Canadian Journal of Political Science* 13, no. 2 (1980): 309–323.

Douglass, Frederick. "What to the Slave is the Forth of July." In *The Frederick Douglass Papers*, ed. John W. Blassingame. Series I, Vol. 2, 1847–54. New Haven: Yale University Press, 1982, 359–388.

Drakulić, Slavenka. *They Would Never Hurt a Fly: War Criminals on Trial in The Hague.* London: Abacus, 2004.

Drechsler, Horst. *"Let Us Die Fighting": The Struggle of the Herero and the Nama against German Imperialism, 1884–1915.* Berlin [East]: Akademie-Verlag, 1986.

Dubiel, Helmut and Gabriel Motzkin, eds. *The Lesser Evil: Moral Approaches to Genocide Practices.* London: Routledge, 2004.

Dubow, Saul. *Racial Segregation and the Origins of Apartheid in South Africa.* Basingstoke: Macmillan in association with St. Antony's College, Oxford, 1989.

Eaglestone, Robert. *The Holocaust and the Postmodern.* Oxford: Oxford University Press, 2004.

Elkins, Caroline. *Britain's Gulag: The Brutal End of Empire in Kenya.* London: Jonathan Cape, 2005.

Eltringham, Nigel. *Accounting for Horror: Post Genocide Debates in Rwanda.* London: Pluto Press, 2004.

Eze, Immanuel Chukwudi. "Transitions and Reasons of Memory," *South Atlantic Quarterly* 103, no. 4 (2004): 755–68.

Fackenheim, Emil. *To Mend the World: Foundations of Jewish Thought.* New York: Schocken Books, 1982.

Fanon, Frantz. *The Wretched of the Earth.* Translated by Constance Farrington. London: Penguin Books, 1973.

———. *Towards The African Revolution.* Translated by Haakon Chevalier. London: Pelican Books, 1970.

Fearon, James D., and David D. Laitin. "Violence and the Social Construction of Ethnic Identity," *International Organization* 54, no. 4 (2000): 845–878.

Feraoun, Mouloud. *Journal: 1955–62.* Paris: Éditions Du Seuil, 1962.

Finaldi, Giuseppe. "European Empire and the Making of the Modern World: Recent Books and Old Arguments," *Contemporary European History* 14, no. 2 (2005): 245–258.

Fleischer, Helmut. *Marxism and History.* New York, Harper Torchbooks, 1973

Foucault, Michel. *History of Sexuality, vol. 1: An Introduction.* Translated by Robert Hurley. New York: Vintage Books, 1990.

———. *Society Must Be Defended.* Translated by David Macey. New York: St Martin's Press, 2003.

Fredrickson, George M. *Racism: A Short History.* Princeton: Princeton University Press, 2002.

Gann, L. H. and Peter Duignan. *The Rulers of German Africa, 1884–1914.* Stanford: Stanford University Press, 1977.

Garcés, Marina. "Possibilidad y Subversión," *Archipiélago: Cuadernos de Crítica de la Cultura* 53 (2002): 11–17.

———. *En las prisiones de lo posible.* Barcelona: Ediciones Bellaterra, 2003.

Gewald, Jan-Bart. *Herero Heroes: A Socio-Political History of the Herero of Namibia, 1890–1923.* Oxford: James Currey, 1999.

Gilroy, Paul. *Against Race: Imagining Political Culture Beyond the Color Line.* Cambridge: Harvard University Press, 2001.

Gong, Gerrit. *The Standard of Civilization in International Society.* Oxford: Clarendon Press, 1984.

Gourevitch, Philip. *We wish to inform you that tomorrow we will be killed with our families: stories from Rwanda.* London: Picador, 1999.

Grosse, Pascal. *Kolonialismus, Eugenik und bürgerliche Gesellschaft in Deutschland, 1850–1918.* Frankfurt: Campus Verlag, 2001.

———. "From Colonialism to National Socialism to Postcolonialism: Hannah Arendt's *The Origins of Totalitarianism*," *Postcolonial Studies* 9, no. 1 (2006): 35–52.

Hadžić, Miroslav. *The Violent Dissolution of Yugoslavia: Causes, Dynamics and Effects.* Belgrade: Centre for Civil-Military Relations, 2004.

Hall, Catherine, ed. *Cultures of Empire: Colonizers in Britain and the Empire in the Nineteenth and Twentieth Centuries.* Manchester: Manchester University Press, 2000.

Hatzfeld, Jean. *Machete Season: The Killers in Rwanda Speak.* Translated by Linda Coverdale. New York: Farrar, Straus and Giroux, 2005.

Heidegger, Martin. *Being and Time.* Translated by John Macquarrie and Edward Robinson. Oxford: Blackwell, 1962.

———. "Overcoming Metaphysics." Translated by Joan Stambaugh. In *The Heidegger Controversy*, ed. Richard Wolin. Cambridge: MIT Press, 1993, pp. 67–90.

———. *Bremer und Freiburger Vorträge.* Gesamtausgabe 79, Frankfurt am Main: Vittorio Klostermann, 1994.

Hertzberg, Arthur, *The French Enlightenment and the Jews.* New York: Columbia University Press, 1968.

Hill, Melvyn A., ed. *Hannah Arendt: The Recovery of the Public World.* New York: St. Martin's Press, 1979.

Hinton, Alexander L., ed. *Annihilating Difference: The Anthropology of Genocide.* Berkeley: University of California Press, 2002.

Hobson, J. A. *Imperialism: A Study.* Ann Arbor: University of Michigan Press, 1965.

Hochschild, Adam. *King Leopold's Ghost: A Story of Greed, Terror, and Heroism in Colonial Africa.* Boston: Houghton Mifflin, 1998.

Horton, James, and Lois Horton. *Slavery in the Making of America.* Oxford: Oxford University Press, 2005.

Hull, Isabel V. Military Culture and the Production of 'Final Solutions' in the Colonies: The Example of Wilhelminian Germany." In *The Specter of Genocide: Mass Murder in Historical Perspective,* ed. Robert Gellately and Ben Kiernan. Cambridge: Cambridge University Press, 2003, 141–62.

————. *Absolute Destruction: Military Culture and the Practices of War in Imperial Germany.* Ithaca: Cornell University Press, 2005.

Iggers, George C. "Historicism: The History and Meaning of the Term," *Journal of the History of Ideas* 56 (1996), 129–152.

Isaac, Jeffrey. *Arendt, Camus, and Modern Rebellion.* New Haven: Yale University Press, 1992.

Jaspers, Karl. *The Question of German Guilt.* New York: Capricorn Books, 1961.

Jefferson, Thomas. *Writings.* New York: Literary Classics of the U.S., Viking Press, c.1984.

Joy, James. "'All Power to the People': Hannah Arendt's Theory of Communicative Power in a Racialized Democracy." In *Race and Racism in Continental Philosophy,* ed. Robert Bernasconi with Sybol Cook. Bloomington: Indiana University Press, 2003, 249–267.

Kaplan, Gisela T. and Clive S. Kessler, ed. *Hannah Arendt: Thinking, Judging, Freedom.* Sydney: Allen and Unwin, 1989.

Kateb, George. *Hannah Arendt: Politics, Conscience, Evil.* Oxford: Oxford University Press, 1983.

Katznelson, Ira. *Desolation and Enlightenment: Political Knowledge after Total War, Totalitarianism, and the Holocaust.* New York: Columbia University Press, 2003.

King, Richard H. "Endings and Beginnings: Politics in Arendt's Early Thought," *Political Theory* 12, no. 2 (1984): 235–251.

————. *Race, Culture, and the Intellectuals, 1940–1970.* Baltimore: Johns Hopkins University Press, 2004.

Koehl, Robert Lewis. "A Prelude to Hitler's Greater Germany," *American Historical Review* 59, no. 1 (1953): 43–65.

————. "Colonialism Inside Germany: 1886–1918," *Journal of Modern History* 25, no. 3 (1953): 255–272.

Kohn, Jerome. "Arendt's Concept and Description of Totalitarianism," *Social Research* 69, no. 2 (2002): 621–56.

Krüger, Gesine. *Kriegsbewältigung und Geschichtsbewußtsein: Realität, Deutung und Verarbeitung des deutschen Kolonialkriegs in Namibia 1904 bis 1907.* Göttingen: Vandenhoeck & Ruprecht, 1999.

Lenin, V. I. *Imperialism: The Highest Stage of Capitalism.* London: Pluto Press, 1996.

Le Sueur, James D. *Uncivil War: Intellectuals and Identity Politics During the Decolonization of Algeria.* Philadelphia: University of Pennsylvania Press, 2001.

Levinas, Emmanuel. *Otherwise than Being: or, Beyond Essence.* Translated by Alphonso Lingis. The Hague: Martinus Nijhoff, 1981.

————. *Totality and Infinity.* Translated by Alphonso Lingis. London: Kluwer Academic Publishers, 1991.

Levins, Richard and Richard Lewontin. *The Dialectical Biologist.* Cambridge: Harvard University Press, 1985.

Lindqvist, Sven. *"Exterminate All the Brutes."* Translated by Joan Tate. New York: The New Press, 1996.

Lozowick, Yaacov. *Hitler's Bureaucrats. The Nazi Security and the Banality of Evil.* Translated by Haim Watzman. London: Continuum, 2002.

MacDonald, David Bruce. *Balkan Holocausts? Serbian and Croatian Victim-Centred Propaganda and the War in Yugoslavia.* Manchester: Manchester University Press, 2002.

Mamdani, Mahmood. *When Victims Become Killers. Colonialism, Nativism, and the Genocide in Rwanda.* Princeton: Princeton University Press, 2001.

Marchand, Suzanne L. *Down from Olympus: Archaeology and Philhellenism in Germany, 1750–1970.* Princeton: Princeton University Press, 1996.

Marx, Anthony W. *Making Race and Nation: A Comparison of the United States, South Africa and Brazil.* Cambridge: Cambridge University Press, 1998.

Marx, K, and Engels, F. *Basic Writings on Politics and Philosophy.* Edited by Lewis S. Feuer. London: Fontana, 1969.

———. "The German Ideology." In *Writings of the Young Marx on Philosophy and Society,* ed. Lloyd D. Easton and Kurt H. Guddat. New York: Anchor, 1967, 403–23.

———. *Selected Correspondence.* Moscow: Progress Publishers, 1955.

Mbembe, Achille. "Aesthetics of Superfluity," *Public Culture* 16, no. 3 (2004): 373–405.

Memmi, Albert. *The Colonizer and the Colonized.* Translated by Howard Greenfeld. London: Earthscan Publications Ltd., 2003.

Mertus, Julie. *Kosovo: How Myths and Truths Started a War.* Berkeley: University of California Press, 1999.

———. "The Role of Racism as a Cause or Factor in Wars and Civil Conflict." In *International Council on Human Rights Policy: Consultation on Racism and Human Rights.* Geneva, 3–4 December 1999. (http://www.ichrp.org/ac/excerpts/50.pdf).

Montesquieu, Baron de. *The Spirit of the Laws.* Translated by Anne M Cohler, Basia Carolyn Miller, and Harold Samuel Stone. Edited by Raymond Geuss and Quentin Skinner. Cambridge: Cambridge University Press, 1989.

Morgan, Edmund. *American Slavery, American Freedom.* New York: W.W. Norton and Company, 2003 [1975].

Moruzzi, Norma. *Speaking Through the Mask: Hannah Arendt and the Politics of Social Identity.* Ithaca: Cornell University Press, 2000.

Moses, A. Dirk. "An Antipodean Genocide? The Origins of the Genocidal Moment in the Colonization of Australia," *Journal of Genocide Research* 2, no. 1 (2000): 89–106.

———. "Coming to Terms with Genocidal Pasts in Comparative Perspective: Germany and Australia," *Aboriginal History* 25 (2001): 91–115.

———. ed. *Genocide and Settler Society: Frontier Violence and Stolen Indigenous Children in Australian History.* New York: Berghahn, 2004.

———. ed. *Empire, Colony, Genocide: Conquest, Occupation, and Subaltern Resistance in World History.* New York: Berghahn. 2008.

Moses, A. Dirk, and Dan Stone, eds. *Colonialism and Genocide.* New York: Routledge, 2007.

Mosse, George. *The Fascist Revolution: Toward a General Theory of Fascism.* London: Howard Fertig, 1999.

Myers, David N. *Resisting History: Historicism and Its Discontents in German-Jewish Thought.* Princeton: Princeton University Press, 2003.

Negri, Antonio, and Michael Hardt. *Empire.* Cambridge: Harvard University Press, 2000.

Norris, Andrew. "'The Exemplary Exception': Philosophical and Political Decisions in Giorgio Agamben's *Homo Sacer*," *Radical Philosophy* 119 (May–June 2003): 6–16.

Norton, Ann. "Heart of Darkness: Africa and African Americans in the Writings of Hannah Arendt." In *Feminist Interpretations of Hannah Arendt,* ed. Bonnie Honig. University Park, PA: Pennsylvania State University Press, 1995, 247–262.

Nozick, Robert. *Anarchy, State, and Utopia.* New York: Basic Books, 1974.

Palmer, Colin, "Rethinking American Slavery." In *The African Diaspora,* ed. Alusine Jalloh and Stephen E. Maizlish. College Station: Texas A&M University Press, 1996, 73–99.

Penny, H. Glenn, *Objects of Culture: Ethnology and Ethnographic Museums in Imperial Germany.* Chapel Hill: University of North Carolina Press, 2002.

Petit, Santiago Lopez. *El infinito y la nada. El querer vivir como desafío.* Barcelona: Ediciones Bellaterra, 2003.

————. *El Estado guerra.* Hiru: Hondarribia, 2003.

Petritsch, Wolfgang, Karl Kaser, and Robert Pichler. *Kosovo, Kosova: Mythen, Daten, Fakten.* Klagenfurt: Wieser Verlag, 1999.

Pitkin, Hannah F. *The Attack of the Blob: Hannah Arendt's Concept of the Social.* Chicago: University of Chicago Press, 1993.

Pocock, J. G. A. *The Machiavellian Moment.* Princeton: Princeton University Press, 1973.

Poiger, Uta G. "Imperialism and Empire in Twentieth-Century Germany," *History & Memory* 17, nos. 1 and 2 (2005): 117–43.

Poliakov, Léon. *The History of Anti-Semitism,* vol. III. Philadelphia: University of Pennsylvania Press, 1968.

————. *The Aryan Myth: A History of Racist and Nationalistic Ideas in Europe.* London: Chatto Heinemann for Sussex University Press, 1974.

Popov, Nebojša, ed. *The Road to War in Serbia: Trauma and Catharsis.* Budapest: Central European University Press, 2000.

Popper, Karl R. *The Poverty of Historicism.* New York: Harper Torchbooks, 1964.

Posel, Deborah. *The Making of Apartheid, 1948–1961: Conflict and Compromise.* Oxford: Clarendon Press, 1991.

Power, Samantha. *"A Problem from Hell": America and the Age of Genocide.* New York: Perennial, 2002.

Presbey, Gail, "Critic of Boers or Africans: Arendt's Treatment of South Africa in *The Origins of Totalitarianism.*" In *Postcolonial African Philosophy,* ed. Emmanuel Chukwudi Eze. Oxford: Blackwell, 1997, 162–180.

Rawls, John, *Justice as Fairness: A Restatement.* Cambridge: The Belknap Press of Harvard University Press, 2001.

Ricoeur, Paul. *Time and Narrative,* vol. I. Translated by Kathleen McLaughlin and David Pellauer. Chicago: University of Chicago Press, 1984.

Ridley, Hugh. "Colonial Society and European Totalitarianism," *Journal of European Studies* 3, no. 2 (1973): 147–159.

Roth, John K., ed. *Genocide and Human Rights.* New York: Macmillan, 2005.

Rousso, Henry, ed. *Stalinism and Nazism: History and Memory Compared.* Lincoln: University of Nebraska Press, 2004.

Rubenstein, Richard L. *The Age of Triage: Fear and Hope in an Overcrowded World.* Boston: Beacon Press, 1982.

Said, Edward W. *Culture and Imperialism.* London: Vintage, 1994.

Sartre, Jean-Paul. *Colonialism and Neocolonialism.* London: Routledge, 2001.

————. *On Genocide.* Boston: Beacon Press, 1968

Schaap, Andrew. "Guilty Subjects and Political Responsibility: Arendt, Jaspers and the Resonance of the 'German Question' in Politics of Reconciliation," *Political Studies* 49 (2001): 749–766.

Scott, David. *Conscripts of Modernity: The Tragedy of Colonial Enlightenment.* Durham: Duke University Press, 2004.

Sell, Michael A. *The Bridge Betrayed: Religion and Genocide in Bosnia.* Berkeley: University of California Press, 1998.

Sewell, William H, Jr. *A Rhetoric of Bourgeois Revolution, The Abbé Sieyes and WHAT IS THE THIRD ESTATE?* Durham: Duke University Press, 1994.

Shriver, Donald. *An Ethic for Enemies: Forgiveness in Politics.* New York, Oxford University Press, 1995.

Sippel, Harald. "Die Klassifizierung 'des Afrikaners' und 'des Europäers' im Rahmen der dualen kolonialen Rechtsordnung am Beispiel von Deutsch-Südwestafrika." In *Transformationen der europäischen Expansion vom 16. bis zum 20. Jahrhundert,* ed. Andreas Eckert and Jürgen Müller Rehburg-Loccum: Evangelische Akademie Loccum, 1997.

Smith, Helmut Walser. "The Talk of Genocide, the Rhetoric of Miscegenation: Notes on Debates in the German Reichstag Concerning Southwest Africa, 1904–14." In *The Imperialist Imagination: German Colonialism and Its Legacy,* ed. Sara Friedrichsmeyer, Sara Lennox, and Susanne Zantop. Ann Arbor: University of Michigan Press, 1998, 107–23.

Smith, Woodruff D. *The Ideological Origins of Nazi Imperialism.* New York: Oxford University Press, 1986.

———. *Politics and the Sciences of Culture in Germany, 1840–1920.* New York: Oxford University Press, 1991.

Sontag, Susan. *Regarding the Pain of Others.* London: Picador, 2004.

Springborg, Patricia. "Hannah Arendt and the Classical Republican Tradition." In *Hannah Arendt, Thinking, Judging, Freedom.* ed. Gisela T. Kaplan and Clive S. Kessler. Sydney: Allen and Unwin, 1989, 9–17.

Stanley, John. "Is Totalitarianism a New Phenomenon?" In *Hannah Arendt: Critical Essays,* ed. Lewis P. Hinchman and Sandra K. Hinchman. Albany: SUNY Press, 1994, pp. 1–40.

Sternhell, Ze'ev. *The Birth of Fascist Ideology: From Cultural Rebellion to Political Revolution.* Princeton: Princeton University Press, 1995.

Stoecker, Helmuth. "The German Empire in Africa before 1914: General Questions." In *German Imperialism in Africa: From the Beginnings until the Second World War,* ed. Helmuth Stoecker. London: Hurst, 1986.

Stone, Dan. "Raphael Lemkin on the Holocaust," *Journal of Genocide Research* 7, no. 4 (2005): 539–550.

———. *History, Memory and Mass Atrocity: Essays on the Holocaust and Genocide.* London: Vallentine Mitchell, 2006.

———. ed. *The Historiography of the Holocaust.* New York: Palgrave Macmillan, 2004.

———. ed. *The Historiography of Genocide.* New York: Palgrave Macmillan, 2008.

Strauss, Leo. *Natural Right and History.* Chicago: University of Chicago Press, 1953.

Taylor, Christopher C. *Sacrifice as Terror: The Rwandan Genocide of 1994.* Oxford: Berg, 1999.

Todorov, Tzvetan. *Hope and Memory: Reflections on the Twentieth Century.* Translated by David Bellos. London: Atlantic Books, 2003.

Traverso, Enzo. *The Origins of Nazi Violence.* Translated by Janet Lloyd. London: New York Press, 2003.

von Trotha, Trutz. "'One for the Kaiser': Beobachtungen zur politischen Soziologie der Prügelstrafe am Beispiel des 'Schutzgebietes Togo.'" In *Studien zur Geschichte des deutschen Kolonialismus in Afrika,* ed. Peter Heine and Ulrich van der Heyden. Pfaffenweiler: Centaurus, 1995.

Tuvachis, Nicholas. *Mea Culpa: A Sociology of Apology and Reconciliation.* Stanford: Stanford University Press, 1991.

Uya, Okon Edet. "Prelude to Disaster: An Analysis of the Racial Policies of Boer and British Settlers in Africa Before 1910." In *Africa and the Afro American Experience,* ed. Loraine Williams. Washington, D.C.: Howard University Press, 1977, 97–136.

Vetlesen, Arne J. "Genocide: A Case for the Responsibility of the Bystander," *Journal of Peace Research* 37, no. 4 (2000), 519–532.

Villa, Dana. *Politics, Philosophy, Terror: Essays on the Thought of Hannah Arendt.* Princeton: Princeton University Press, 1999.

———, ed. *The Cambridge Companion to Hannah Arendt.* Cambridge: Cambridge University Press, 2000.

Voegelin, Eric, *The New Science of Politics.* Chicago: University of Chicago Press, 1952.

———. "The Origins of Totalitarianism," *The Review of Politics* 15, no. 1 (1953): 68–76.

Vollrath Ernst, "Hannah Arendt and the Method of Political Thinking," *Social Research* 44, no. 1 (1977): 161–181.

Walicki, Andrzej. *Marxism and the Leap to the Kingdom of Freedom: The Rise and Fall of the Communist Utopia.* Stanford: Stanford University Press, 1995.

Weindling, Paul. *Health, Race and German Politics Between National Unification and Nazism, 1870–1945.* Cambridge: Cambridge University Press, 1989.

Weitz, Eric. *A Century of Genocide: Utopias of Race and Nation.* Princeton: Princeton University Press, 2003.

Whitfield, Stephen J. *Into the Dark: Hannah Arendt and Totalitarianism.* Philadelphia: Temple University Press, 1980.

Wildenthal, Lora. *German Women for Empire, 1884–1945.* Durham: Duke University Press, 2001.

Williams, Patrick and Laura Chrisman, eds. "Colonial Discourse and Post-Colonial Theory: An Introduction." In *Colonial Discourse and Post-Colonial Theory*. Hemel Hempstead, U.K.: Longman, 1993, 1–20.

Wilmer, Franke. *The Social Construction of Man, the State and War: Identity, Conflict and Violence in Former Yugoslavia*. New York: Routledge, 2002.

Wilson, Kathleen, ed. *A New Imperial History: Culture, Identity and Modernity in Britain and the Empire, 1660–1840*. Cambridge: Cambridge University Press, 2004.

Wolin, Richard. *Heidegger's Children: Hannah Arendt, Karl Löwith, Hans Jonas, and Herbert Marcuse*. Princeton: Princeton University Press, 2001.

Young, Robert. *White Mythologies: Writing History and the West*. London: Routledge, 1990.

Young-Bruehl, Elisabeth. "From the Pariah's Point of View: Reflections on Hannah Arendt's Life and Work." In *Hannah Arendt: The Recovery of the Public World*, ed. Melvyn A. Hill. New York: St. Martin's Press, 1979, 3–26.

———. *Hannah Arendt: For Love of the World*. New Haven: Yale University Press, 1982.

Zimmerer, Jürgen. "The Birth of the *Ostland* Out of the Spirit of Colonialism: a Postcolonial Perspective on the Nazi Policy of Conquest and Extermination," *Patterns of Prejudice* 39, no. 2 (2005): 197–219.

Zimmerman, Andrew. *Anthropology and Antihumanism in Imperial Germany*. Chicago: University of Chicago Press, 2001.

Žižek, Slavoj. *Did Somebody Say Totalitarianism? Four Interventions in the (Mis)use of a Notion*. London: Verso, 2001.

CONTRIBUTORS

Tony Barta is a Research Associate at La Trobe University, where he taught European and Australian history and founded the History and Film program in 1985. In addition to his work on genocide in Australia, he has written on twentieth-century Germany, and on historiography, media, and historical understanding. He is the editor of *Screening the Past: Film and the Representation of History* (1998).

Robert Bernasconi is Moss Professor of Philosophy at the University of Memphis. He has published two books on Heidegger and numerous essays in twentieth-century continental philosophy and in social and political philosophy. He has edited a number of books, including *Race* (2001) and, with Tommy Lott, *The Idea of Race* (2000). His most recent book is *How to Read Sartre* (2007).

Ned Curthoys completed his Ph.D. in the English Department at the University of Sydney in 2002. His doctorate focused on the dissemination of the humanist tradition of classical rhetoric into twentieth-century literary theory, philosophy, and political theory. He is currently a postdoctoral fellow at the Centre for Cross-Cultural Research at the Australian National University, investigating the influence of Goethe's visionary ideal of a *Weltliteratur* on twentieth-century-philology and comparative literature.

André Duarte is Professor of Philosophy at Universidade Federal do Paraná, Curitiba, Brazil. He has translated Arendt's *Lectures on Kant's Political Philosophy* and *On Violence* into Portuguese and has also published a book on her political and philosophical thinking, *O Pensamento à sombra da ruptura: política e filosofia no pensamento de Hannah Arendt* (2000) [*Thinking in the shadow of the rupture: politics and philosophy in Hannah Arendt*].

Robert Eaglestone works on contemporary and twentieth-century literature, literary theory, and philosophy at Royal Holloway, University of London. His publications include *Ethical Criticism: Reading after Levinas* (1997), *Doing English* (1999, 2nd ed. 2002), *Postmodernism and Holocaust Denial* (2001), *The Holocaust and the Postmodern*

(2004). He is a Literary Advisor to the British Council and Deputy Director of Royal Holloway's Research Centre for the Holocaust and Twentieth Century History. He is the editor also of *Routledge Critical Thinkers.*

Kathryn T. Gines received a Ph.D. in Philosophy from the University of Memphis in 2003. She holds a current appointment in the Philosophy Department and the Program in African American and Diaspora Studies at Vanderbilt University. Her research and teaching interests include Continental Philosophy, Social and Political Philosophy, African American Philosophy, and Race and Gender Theory.

Vlasta Jalušič is a Senior Research Fellow at the Peace Institute (Institute for Contemporary Social and Political Studies), Ljubljana (Slovenia) and an Associate Professor of Political Theory and Gender Studies at Ljubljana University. She has written articles and chapters on gender, Eastern European politics and transition, war, violence, and Hannah Arendt. Her recent books include *How We Attended Feminist Gymnasium . . .* (2002); she co-authored *Women–Politics–Opportunities* (2001) and *Erased: Organized Innocence and the Politics of Exclusion* (2003), and coedited the volume *Women's Human Rights* (2004). She has also translated and introduced Hannah Arendt's *The Human Condition* (1996) and *Between Past and Future* (2006) into Slovenian.

Elisa von Joeden-Forgey received her Ph.D. in history from the University of Pennsylvania. Her dissertation, "Nobody's People: Colonial Subjects, Race Power and the German State, 1884–1945," examines the impact of colonialism on German political culture through the stories of Africans in Germany.

Richard H. King is Professor of American Intellectual History in the School of American and Canadian Studies, University of Nottingham, U.K. He is the author most recently of *Race, Culture and the Intellectuals, 1940–1970* (2004), and earlier, *The Party of Eros* (1972), *A Southern Renaissance* (1980), and *Civil Rights and the Idea of Freedom* (1992). He also coedited *Dixie Debates* (1994) with Helen Taylor.

Christopher J. Lee is Assistant Professor of African History at the University of North Carolina at Chapel Hill where he teaches in the African History and Global History programs. His research focus is on British central and southern Africa, and his work has appeared in the *Journal of African History* and *Radical History Review.* He is currently completing a manuscript on multiracial identities in British central Africa from World War I to the early postcolonial period.

Steven Douglas Maloney is a Political Theory Ph.D. candidate at the University of Maryland and an Adjunct Professor of Political Science at Middle Tennessee State University. One of his current projects includes guest editing a symposium on "Rhetoric and Terror: Learning from Arendt's Attack on Cliché" for *The Good Society.* He is currently finishing his dissertation "Abortion Escorts and Participatory Behavior."

Richard Shorten is Lecturer in Political Theory at the University of Birmingham, U.K. He has written articles on totalitarianism, the idea of political religion, and François Furet.

Marcel Stoetzler is Simon Fellow at Manchester University (U.K.), Department of History, Arts and Cultures, and currently does research on relationships between modern anti-Semitism and modern social theory, especially the emergence of sociological theory. Previous publications are mainly in the areas of critical theory and feminist theory.

Dan Stone is Professor of Modern History at Royal Holloway, University of London. He is the author of *Breeding Superman: Nietzsche, Race and Eugenics in Edwardian and Interwar Britain* (2002), *Constructing the Holocaust: A Study in Historiography* (2003), *Responses to Nazism in Britain, 1933–1939: Before War and Holocaust* (2003) and *History, Memory and Mass Atrocity: Essays on the Holocaust and Genocide* (2006); editor of *Theoretical Interpretations of the Holocaust* (2001), *The Historiography of the Holocaust* (2004), and *The Historiography of Genocide* (2008); and coeditor (with A. Dirk Moses) of *Colonialism and Genocide* (2007).

INDEX

Shaka (Zulu King), 10
Shakespeare, William, 232, 233
Shoah (Lanzmann), 238
Shorten, Richard, 1, 251
Sierakowiak, Dawid, 238
Sieyes, Abbé, 138
slavery, 13, 14, 23, 38, 39, 40, 42, 43, 44, 45,
    46, 47, 49, 50, 51, 53 n58, 54, 59, 89, 91,
    185, 224, 258
Slavs, 29, 32
Slovenia, 155, 157
Smith, Helmut W., 7
Smith, Woodruff D., 5
Social Darwinism, 59, 60, 97
Social Research, 9, 11
Sontag, Susan, 257
Soustelle, Jacques, 122
South Africa, 31, 47–49, 60, 61, 68, 70–78, 80,
    81, 142, 143, 255, 258
    apartheid in, 73–78, 81
    "exceptionalism", 77
    historiography of, 74–75
    Truth and Reconciliation Committee,
        258, 261 n26
South African War (1899–1902), 76
South America, 31, 89
    genocide in, 91
Soviet Union, 1, 14, 34, 55, 70, 81, 175, 178,
    184, 192, 198, 234.
    collapse of, 6
    See also Gulag
Spengler, Oswald, 61
Springborg, Patricia, 134
Srebrenica, 147, 159, 160, 162, 164, 165
Sri Lanka, 160
SS, 96, 242
Stalin, Joseph, 72, 95, 98, 175, 198
Stalinism, 11, 57, 89, 93, 139, 173, 177, 181,
    234, 235
    compared with Nazism, 174–186
Stanley, John, 10
Stead, W. T., 58
Sternhell, Ze'ev, 7
Stoetzler, Marcel, 14
Stone, Dan, 2, 14
Strauss, Leo, 252, 253, 260 n9, 260 n10
Struwwelpeter (Hoffmann), 213
student movement (1968), 109–110, 112
Sudan, 160, 229, 256, 257
Szwajger, Adina Blady, 239

T

Talmon, Jacob, 178, 232
Tancred (Disraeli), 58
Tanganyika, 68
Tanzania, 70, 79
Tasmania, 9
Tavuchis, Nicholas, 258, 261 n34

Tennyson, Alfred, 102 n17
The Algerians (Bourdieu), 120
The Black Book of Communism (Courtois et
    al), 176, 177, 183, 184
The Colonizer and the Colonized (Memmi), 109, 114
The Descent of Man (Darwin), 90, 91, 92
"The Eggs Speak Up" (Arendt), 132–133
The German Ideology (Marx and Engels), 92
The History of the Race Idea from Ray to Carus
    (Voegelin), 59
The Human Condition (Arendt), 5, 41, 103 n22,
    111, 191, 192, 198, 222, 257
The Life of the Mind (Arendt), 152
The Passing of an Illusion (Furet), 176
The Wretched of the Earth (Fanon), 117
theodicy, 252
Third Reich. *See* Nazi Germany
Third World, 200
Timm, Uwe, 213
Tito, Josip Broz, 146 n61, 148, 154, 155
Tocqueville, Alexis de, 2, 6, 218, 219, 221, 226,
    227, 228, 229, 255
Todorov, Tzvetan, 176
Totality and Infinity (Levinas), 210
Traverso, Enzo, 7, 178
Treblinka, 237, 238
Treitschke, Heinrich von, 29
Trotha, Lothar von, 68
Tudjman, Franjo, 157, 158, 161, 169 n58
Turgot, A. R. J., 131, 132
Turkey, 233
Tutsis, 79, 80, 81
Tutu, Desmond, 258

U

Uganda, 79
Ukrainian famine, 176, 184
UN, 159, 160, 163, 164, 256
UNAMIR, 241
UNESCO, 242
UN Genocide Convention, 8
United Party (South Africa), 75
United States, 3, 4, 12, 13, 23, 31, 42, 44, 45,
    46, 56, 110, 112, 113, 139, 192, 198, 209,
    225, 235, 239, 258.
    Constitution, 223
    See also America, colonial
USSR. *See* Soviet Union
Ustaša, 157
Uya, Okon Edet, 47, 48

V

Vergès, Jacques, 188 n22
Verwoerd, H. F., 76
Vetlesen, Arne J., 169 n64
Villa, Dana, 50
Voegelin, Eric, 58, 59, 180, 246 n18, 252, 253
Voltaire, 61

Printed in the United States
204963BV00002B/1-102/P